ADJUSTMENT WITH A HUMAN FACE

Volume II

Adjustment with a Human Face

Volume II

Country Case Studies

Edited by

Giovanni Andrea Cornia, Richard Jolly, and Frances Stewart

CLARENDON PRESS · OXFORD

1988

Oxford University Press, Walton Street, Oxford OX2 6DP

Oxford   New York   Toronto
Delhi   Bombay   Calcutta   Madras   Karachi
Petaling Jaya   Singapore   Hong Kong   Tokyo
Nairobi   Dar es Salaam   Cape Town
Melbourne   Auckland

and associated companies in
Beirut   Berlin   Ibadan   Nicosia

Oxford is a trade mark of Oxford University Press

Published in the United States
by Oxford University Press, New York

British Library Cataloguing in Publication Data
Adjustment with a human face.
Vol. 2: Ten country case studies
1.—Developing countries—Social conditions
2. Developing countries—Economic policy
I. Cornia, Giovanni Andrea II. Jolly, Richard
III. Stewart, Francis
909'.097240828   HN980
ISBN 0–19–828611–2

Library of Congress Cataloging in Publication Data
(Revised for vol. 2)
Adjustment with human face.
Bibliograpy: p. Includes index.
Contents: v. 1. Protecting the vulnerable and promoting
growth—v. 2. Ten country case studies.
1. Child welfare.   2. Child welfare—Cross-cultural
studies.   3. Children—Economic conditions.   4. Economic
policy.   5. Depressions.   I. Cornia, Giovanni Andrea.
II. Jolly, Richard.   III. Stewart, Francis.
HV713.A37 1988   362.7'042   87-11137
ISBN 0–19–828610–4 (v. 1) ISBN 0–828609–0 (pbk.: v.1)
ISBN 0–19–828611–2

Set by Butler & Tanner Ltd, Frome, Somerset
Printed in Great Britain
at the University Printing House, Oxford
by David Stanford
Printer to the University

To the memory of Nicholas Kaldor

Contents

Notes on Editors and Contributors

Editors

GIOVANNI ANDREA CORNIA is Senior Planning Officer at UNICEF. He previously worked at UNCTAD, and the Economic Studies Centre of Fiat. His writings include work on savings in developing countries, on land reform, and the impact of world recession on children.

RICHARD JOLLY is Deputy Executive Director of UNICEF responsible for programmes. He was formerly Director of the Institute of Development Studies at the University of Sussex. He has written widely on developing issues, focusing on education, employment, and basic needs.

FRANCES STEWART is a Fellow of Somerville College, and Senior Research Officer at Queen Elizabeth House, Oxford. She worked at UNICEF as Special Adviser on Adjustment. She is a development economist, and has published on technology and development, basic needs, and international issues.

Contributors

DERICK BOYD is a Lecturer in economics at the University of the West Indies, Jamaica. Mr Boyd has written a number of articles on economic affairs in Jamaica and on stabilization.

MARK S. COHEN is a graduate student at the Department of Agricultural Economics at Cornell University and has served as a research support specialist for the Cornell Nutrition Surveillance Programme (CNSP) in Botswana.

ROB DAVIES is with the Department of Economics, University of Zimbabwe.

LEONEL FIGUEROA is the Governor of the Central Bank of Peru. He was formerly with the UN Economic Commission for Latin America.

B. N. KGOSIDINTSI is a Nutritionist, with the Family Health Division, Ministry of Health, Gaborone.

ROBERTO MACEDO is Professor of Economics at the University of São Paulo and has published widely on the labour market, income distribution, and social policy in Brazil. Mr Macedo also contributed to *The Impact of World Recession on Children* (1984).

JOHN MASON has a Ph.D in nutrition and is currently the Secretary of the ACC/SCN at the Food Policy and Nutrition Department, FAO, Rome. Previously Mr Mason served as director for the CNSP.

VICTORIA QUINN is a Nutritionist who graduated from Cornell University and is currently the Regional Co-ordinator of the joint UNICEF–CNSP in East Africa (Nairobi).

DAGMAR RACZYNSKI is a Researcher at CIEPLAN (Corporacion de Investigaciones Economicas para Latino America) and a Professor at the Institute of Sociology, the Catholic University of Chile. Ms. Raczynski also contributed to the *Impact of World Recession on Children* (1984).

DAVID SANDERS is with the Department of Community Medicine, University of Zimbabwe.

SANG-MOK SUH, Vice-President for the Korean Development Institute, Seoul, has been writing extensively on poverty-related issues and economic development in South Korea.

DAVID WILLIAMSON is a Researcher at the Korean Development Institute, Seoul, Korea.

List of Figures

List of Tables

Abbreviations*

CBR	Crude Birth Rate
CPI	Consumer Price Index
FAO	Food and Agriculture Organization
GDP	Gross Domestic Product
GNP	Gross National Product
IMF	International Monetary Fund
LBW	Low Birth Weight
ORS	Oral Rehydration Salts
ORT	Oral Rehydration Therapy
PHC	Primary Health Care
SDR	Special Drawing Rights
WHO	World Health Organization

* Includes only those abbreviations which appear in several chapters.

Currencies and Units

Currencies

The national currency equivalents of one US dollar are as follows:[1]

	1980	1985
Botswana, pulas	0.72	2.10
Brazil, cruzeiros	65.5	10,490
Chile, pesos	39.0	183.9
Ghana, cedis	2.75	59.88
Jamaica, J dollars	1.78	5.48
Peru, intis	0.34	13.94
Philippines, pesos	7.6	19.0
South Korea, won	659.9	890.2
Sri Lanka, rupees	18.0	27.4
Zimbabwe, Z dollars	0.63	1.64

All references in the text to dollars are US dollars unless specified otherwise.

Units

The term 'ton' refers to a metric ton unless specified otherwise.

[1] *International Financial Statistics*, March 1986. All figures relate to end of period.

Introduction

Giovanni Andrea Cornia, Richard Jolly, and Frances Stewart

During the first half of the 1980s many countries faced severe recession, and rising imbalances, especially on their external accounts, and were forced to adopt stringent stabilization and adjustment policies. The major origin of these problems was worsening in the external environment experienced by most countries, with stagnant world output and world trade, falling commodity prices, and high interest rates. In some countries, especially in Africa, the problems were compounded by severe drought. An earlier UNICEF study— *The Impact of World Recession on Children*—had shown deteriorating conditions among children resulting from the world recession of 1980–82. This study had concluded that 'the worst was yet to come'.

With the prolonged economic problems during the 1980s, it seemed probable that the conditions of the vulnerable had worsened further, while in many cases it appeared that stabilization and adjustment policies were themselves neglecting the nutrition and health of the most vulnerable. UNICEF therefore initiated a new study to provide detailed evidence of this situation, in order to develop alternative policies which would protect the vulnerable during recession, stabilization, and adjustment.

This is the second volume of the study of how the adverse economic developments and consequent stabilization and adjustment policies, experienced by the majority of developing countries in the 1980s, have affected vulnerable groups, and especially children. The first volume—*Adjustment with a Human Face: Protecting the Vulnerable and Promoting Growth*—contains a general analysis of the causes of deteriorating conditions for children during the 1980s, and of the effects of economic and other factors on their health and welfare. In the light of evidence of widespread deterioration in health and nutrition, it presents alternative policies, both domestic and international, designed to protect the conditions of the vulnerable during periods of economic decline and adjustment, as well as to accelerate growth over the medium and long term.

In order to arrive at these proposals it was essential to understand what had been happening at a country level—in particular, how vulnerable groups had been affected and the nature and effectiveness of different policies towards the vulnerable during the economic difficulties. UNICEF therefore commissioned 10 country studies on the effects of events in the 1980s on vulnerable groups.

This volume contains the 10 country studies. The studies include countries from all over the world—three from Africa (Botswana, Ghana, and Zimbabwe), three from Asia (the Philippines, South Korea, and Sri Lanka), three from Latin America (São Paulo State in Brazil, Chile, and Peru) and one Caribbean country (Jamaica). For each country a common approach has been adopted: the initial conditions are described, the nature of the economic shocks and changes in policies analysed, and the country's performance in terms of economic growth and key child welfare indicators assessed in a critical fashion.

Despite the common origin of major external problems—world recession, deteriorating commodity prices, high interest rates, and mounting debt problems—these studies encompass a wide range of experience: the precise causes and extent of economic problems vary, as do the policies adopted towards stabilization and adjustment, and the protection (or neglect) of vulnerable groups. The studies do not include either India or China, both of which managed largely to escape the effects of the deteriorating world environment, nor major oil producers, whose problems have been different (although also severe in recent years), nor fully socialist countries. With these exceptions, the wide range of experience covered means that these studies include developments and policies experienced by most Third World countries in the 1980s. For a summary and analysis of the studies, and the development of alternative approaches at macro, meso, sectoral, and micro levels, the reader should turn to Volume I.

The editors would like to thank all the authors of this volume for the hard work and creativity they have contributed to this whole endeavour. In many cases, the range and depth of the original analysis have had to be limited in order to fit within the limits of the book. The ideas contained in this volume reflect the views of the authors—and, to an extent, of the editors—and should not be taken as representing those of their respective organizations, or of UNICEF. In the case of those chapters published under UNICEF's name, final responsibility for the views expressed rests with the editors.

1

Crisis-proofing the Economy: The Response of Botswana to Economic Recession and Drought*

Victoria Quinn, Mark Cohen, John Mason, and B. N. Kgosidintsi

I Introduction

The case of Botswana is particularly important for two reasons. First, extensive measures were undertaken to combat the effects of recession, and especially of drought. Secondly, because Botswana has a comprehensive surveillance system, some conclusions can be reached on the effects of these measures. Although drought is not the main factor considered in the overall context of economic recession and indebtedness, the effects of drought are comparable to those of recession, and much can be learned from the compensatory programmes for drought. To a considerable extent, the experience in Botswana is relevant to measures that could be taken in other countries.

After briefly reviewing development issues in Botswana since independence (Part II), the economic shocks that Botswana suffered during the 1980s are described (Part III). The substantial loss of revenue from the sale of diamonds affected the economy in 1981/82, and measures were taken to protect foreign exchange reserves, and to cushion the effect on the poor. More serious and longer lasting, the severe drought from 1981/82 to 1985/86 both reduced domestic food supplies and exacerbated the poverty of much of the rural population. The food distribution and income generating public works programmes, whose implementation increased in scope and effectiveness during the course of the 1980s, are described in some detail in Part IV. There is reason to believe that these measures contained the crisis. Widespread famine did not

* This study was an activity of the Joint UNICEF/Cornell Nutritional Surveillance Programme in Eastern and Southern Africa. The views expressed are those of the authors and do not necessarily represent the policy of the government of Botswana or UNICEF.

The data quoted in the text are those available to the authors in May 1986. They do not represent final government statistics and are subject to revisions.

Acknowledgements. The authors are grateful for the co-operation of the government of Botswana in preparing this study, in particular to B. Gaolathe, K. Matambo, T. C. Moremi, J. Wilson, and D. Callear (Ministry of Finance); G. Motsemme and K. Garebamono (Ministry of Agriculture); and Derek Hudson (Bank of Botswana). We should also like to thank Charles Harvey of the Institute of Development Studies at the University of Sussex, and S. Kimaryo, the UNICEF Country Programme Officer, who greatly facilitated this paper through her guidance and support.

occur. The prevalence of child malnutrition increased, but very probably less than it would otherwise have done and appeared to fall to around pre-drought levels in 1985. Finally, the attention to surveillance in Botswana (described in Part V) meant that the Botswana government knew a considerable amount of what was happening, and was able to modify its programmes accordingly.

II Development policies

The population of Botswana was estimated as 1.13 million in 1986. Over 80 per cent of the population are rural, and the majority of these are dependent on agriculture for their livelihood, although the agricultural sector accounts for only 8.5 per cent of GDP (1982/83). The vast majority of the population lives in the eastern area of the country, where arable agriculture is feasible. Much of the country is arid, with the sparse population largely dependent on raising livestock. Some 60–70,000 households own land, more or less suitable for growing crops (Table 1.1). Crop yields are not only low, but extremely variable. In two out of every five years, on average, the amount of rainfall has been inadequate for crop production.

A fundamental feature of Botswana is that overall food production, and the availability of land suitable for rainfed crops, is far less than adequate for the population it must support. Even in drought-free years, some 60 per cent of the overall staple food supply must be imported. The present population of Botswana can only survive because of other sources of foreign exchange which finance cereal imports.

Botswana became independent in 1966, and was then among the least developed countries in Africa. Per capita income was around $50 per year, and the economy was highly dependent on the production and sale of cattle. At this time, over 20 per cent of the population were dependent on food aid. During the first years of independence (around 1966–73) government activities centred around four objectives. First, achieving budgetary independence from the United Kingdom; second, constructing infrastructure, schools and health facilities, and administrative facilities; third, developing the agricultural sector; and fourth (as it turned out, crucial) encouraging the development of industry and mining. These policies were successful in generating economic growth: GDP grew at 10.5 per cent per year in real terms from 1974/75 to 1980/81, and was over $900 per capita in 1982.

1 Agricultural sector

Within the agricultural sector, livestock was the main source of growth. Given the relatively abundant grazing areas and the existence of a large state-owned abbatoir with established marketing channels, considerable potential existed for the expansion of the national herd. Partly due to the generally favourable rainfall patterns of the late 1960s and 1970s, and the negotiation of an import

TABLE 1.1   *Estimates related to agricultural production, 1980–1984*

		1980	1981	1982	1983	1984
1.	Households with land	70,240	70.800	71,000	60,900	59,180
2.	Households planting	65,735	68,650	57,000	48,200	51,220
3.	Households harvesting	54,630	57,545	23,400	11,230	19,040
	As % of households planting	83	84	41	23	37
4.	Basic crop production (t)	44,800	54,287	17,220	14,425	6,925
5.	Area planted (000 ha)	268	274	193	229	202
6.	Area harvested (000 ha)	205	210	69	64	67
7.	Average production (kg/ha)	167	198	89	63	34
8.	Estimated value of crops produced (P million)	14.95	18.85	8.02	4.08	2.01
9.	Estimated income from crops per planting household (P)	227	275	141	85	39
10.	Number of cattle (000)	2,911	2,967	2,979	2,818	2,685
11.	Number of smallstock (000)	787	761	776	948	1,057
12.	Cattle birth rate (%)	58.7	57.0	59.6	52.3	53.6
13.	Cattle death rate (%)	12.2	12.1	15.2	16.3	18.0
14.	Cattle offtake (%)	7.8	8.0	8.1	10.4	13.5
15.	Average cattle liveweight per head at BMC[a] abbatoir (kg)	406	434	400	390	n.a.
16.	Freehold farm employment	4,300	4,800	4,200	4,500	5,400
17.	Family labour in agriculture	186,700	188,400	163,000	139,000	139,500
18.	Labour hired in agriculture	60,200	74,700	52,100	47,550	46,650
19.	Total labour engaged	251,200	267,900	219,300	191,050	191,550
20.	Cereal food aid per beneficiary (kg)	37	26	11	45	52

Source: Rural Development Council (1985*a*, *b*).
[a] Botswana Meat Corporation.

quota with the EEC, both the size of the herd and revenue from sales grew rapidly throughout the first 15 years of independence. However, the benefits of growth accrued mainly to a few large cattle owners. By 1974/75, 50 per cent of the national herd was owned by 5 per cent of the rural population.

Due to the poor soils and the limited and erratic rainfall patterns, the potential growth from dry-land agriculture is limited. Even during relatively 'wet' years, the average yield per hectare from dry-land agriculture is less than 200 kilograms, and in drought years the average yield per hectare planted is often below 30 kilograms per hectare. While there exists some potential for arable agriculture in both the northern and eastern border areas, until recently the cost was prohibitive given the government's financial resources. The potential for increasing total yield by expanding the hectarage under dry-land cultivation was limited by the lack of surface water and the skewed distribution of cattle. Otherwise fertile land could not be utilized because it lacked adequate water for livestock and domestic use. Despite the extremely low population density in Botswana (1.8 persons per square kilometre), fewer than half of the rural households felt they had sufficient land, while over 50 per cent were constrained by their lack of oxen for ploughing.

The contribution of the agricultural sector to GDP declined very substantially in relative terms, and less but still significantly in absolute terms (although this is difficult to evaluate due to the effects of drought). It is very clear that without the rapid increase in revenue from mining, both overall food supplies and the availability of income that could be redistributed into rural areas would have suffered very badly.

2 Mining

The discovery of three rich sources of diamonds led to rapid growth of the mining sector in the 1970s and early 1980s. This succeeded the development of copper/nickel mining and smelting, which started in the late 1960s and brought considerable revenue before the fall of copper and nickel prices.

The high rate of overall economic growth was primarily the result of the rapid expansion of the mining industry in Botswana, particularly the diamond mines. Mining currently accounts for a third of GDP, two-thirds of export earnings, and almost one-half of government revenue. In addition, the development of the mining industry in Botswana has provided a major stimulus to other sectors within the economy by creating a demand for transport, electricity and water, retail trade, hotels, business services and banking. The economy thus depends heavily on the diamond industry, and growth slowed during 1981/82 because of the collapse of demand for diamonds on the world market. By 1982/83 this problem was overcome. The opening of the new diamond mine at Jwaneng increased Botswana's quota of diamond sales. This led to sharp increases in the value of production in 1982/83 (221 per cent) and 1983/84 (311 per cent).

3 Manufacturing

The manufacturing sector of the economy is dominated by the Botswana Meat Corporation, which accounts for a third of the value-added in the sector. Growth in this sector has therefore been closely tied to livestock. With the exception of 1979/80, the industrial sector has grown at a slightly faster rate than the overall economy, increasing its share of GDP from 5.5 per cent in 1973/74 to 6.7 per cent of a substantially larger GDP 10 years later. However, because of the strong link with livestock, the rate of growth has been erratic. For example, value added increased by 75 per cent in the 1978/79 fiscal year because of the increased marketing of cattle as a result of the drought, but then decreased sharply in 1979/80 as cattle owners rebuilt their herds.

4 Employment

Botswana has relied primarily on mining and cattle-raising to achieve rapid rates of economic growth. However, given that few jobs are created, the direct benefits of mining to individual Batswana are small. Despite the fact that mining currently accounts for nearly half of GDP and two-thirds of export revenue, the sector employs less than 7,500 workers—less than 7 per cent of those employed in the formal sector, and 1.5 per cent of the entire potential work force. Similarly, the raising of livestock is land- and capital-intensive, and besides the hiring of a few herd boys at very low wages creates little employment.

The Employment Policy Unit of the Ministry of Finance estimated that in 1981, of a total potential labour force of 460,000, approximately 97,000 were employed in the formal sector, an additional 35,000 were employed in the informal sector in domestic service, periodic piecework, and small informal businesses, and 42,000 were employed abroad, mostly in South Africa. Of the 144,000 estimated to be engaged in traditional agriculture, it was estimated that 45,000 were 'redundant' in that their labour made little if any contribution to total output. In addition, 32,000 were unemployed and 110,000 were economically inactive. In other words, over 40 per cent of the potential labour force was either out of work, economically inactive, or redundant.

5 Rural poverty

According to the 1981 census, 47 and 36 per cent of the total population was, respectively, on agricultural (arable) and cattle-raising land. Most families obtain their income from multiple sources. About 55 per cent of rural households derive at least some income from arable agriculture, 45 per cent from owning and/or trading cattle, and 30 per cent from informal employment in rural areas. Crops provide only 6 per cent of total rural income, so income loss during times of drought is probably due more to related changes in employment opportunities and the impact on livestock rearing than to the decline in arable agriculture. Bearing in mind that in non-drought years more than half the food consumed is imported, the vulnerability to loss of crops is nowhere near as great as in many other African countries, where most income for rural families derives from crop production.

Households with below average income earn only about 15 per cent of their income from the production of crops and livestock, on average. Among the poorest 10 per cent of households, 70 per cent of their income was in kind and only 30 per cent in cash, with the most important sources of income being transfers from other households or family members living apart from the household (25 per cent), hunting and gathering (22 per cent), and employment (18 per cent). Agriculture contributed only 13 per cent of the total household income. Only among the higher income groups does agriculture, and in particular livestock, make a substantial contribution to household income levels.

6   *Economic vulnerability*

Botswana has enjoyed the highest rate of growth of all non-oil exporting countries throughout the 1970s and early 1980s. However, like the oil exporting countries, its growth is highly dependent on the export of one commodity and is therefore extremely vulnerable to changes in the demand and supply for that commodity (diamonds). In addition, the rural economy is continuously exposed to the risk of drought, large-scale bush-fires, livestock epidemics, crop diseases, and the closure of foreign markets for livestock or removal by the EEC of preferential import quotas.

Botswana is particularly vulnerable to events in the Republic of South Africa. Economically, Botswana is highly dependent on South Africa, and the rapid rates of growth would not have been possible in the absence of strong trade links with South Africa. These links have enabled Botswana to embark on massive investment projects without causing rapid rates of inflation. For example, in developing the mineral sector, Botswana was able quickly to expand the construction industry by drawing on resources available in South Africa. From 1979 to 1984, between 78 and 87 per cent of Botswana's imports came from South African suppliers, while 6 to 19 per cent of its exports were sold to South Africa. Moreover, a high proportion of Botswana's foreign trade with other countries uses South African rail and port facilities.

Beyond the direct economic impact which a breakdown in trade with South Africa would have on the economy of Botswana, political instability in South Africa has a tendency to spill over the border in the form of refugees and cross-border strikes. The increased political instability in the region has forced the government of Botswana to increase its expenditures on defence, internal security, and care of refugees, while diminishing potential revenue from additional external investments in Botswana.

III   Economic shocks and macro-economic responses

1   *The loss of diamond sales, mid-1981 to mid-1982*

(a) **The crisis**   In mid-1981 De Beers was forced to impose sale quotas on diamond producers in order to maintain the pricing structure of the diamond market in the face of declining demand, particularly for the higher priced gem diamonds, but also for lower value industrial grade diamonds. Botswana chose not to cut production and therefore had to stockpile diamonds. At one stage in late 1981 and early 1982, Botswana was unable to market any diamonds for a period of three months. This led to a sharp decrease in government revenue and foreign exchange earnings. Exports fell by 20 per cent in 1981, while imports continued to rise, following the economic boom in the private sector brought on by construction of the new Jwaneng diamond mine. A large trade deficit developed, and foreign reserves were rapidly depleted, falling 261 million pulas in mid-1981 to 198 million pulas in March 1982.

While the remaining foreign reserves would have sufficed until the end of the year, the government took action in March 1982—in the belief that if it delayed making adjustments, then the required adjustment would be larger and more disruptive to the economy, with a more detrimental impact on the welfare of the population. Given the high import content of basic consumer goods and medical supplies, the government was concerned about the effects of increasing foreign debt and foreign exchange scarcity on its ability to protect vulnerable groups. If foreign reserves and government revenue had been depleted, the government would have been forced into sharp cut-backs in relief and development programmes.

To protect the level of foreign reserves, the government drew down a previously negotiated Eurodollar loan and adopted several measures aimed at reducing the drain on foreign reserves by either reducing the short-term demand for imports or inducing importers and exporters to borrow abroad instead of locally. In order to hold down consumer demand, wages were frozen, the local currency was devalued by 10 per cent, and a sales tax was imposed on a number of non-essential goods. At the same time, the government announced its intention to cut both capital and current expenditure. To reduce commercial demand and encourage short-term capital inflows, interest rates and the required rate of liquidity of commercial banks were increased.

The government chose not to attempt to protect foreign reserves by massive overseas borrowing as it feared that the accumulation of a large foreign debt would lead to serious problems in the future if the diamond market did not recover. Similarly, the government decided not to tighten exchange controls, nor did it adopt import licensing procedures, or credit rationing, as it was felt that these would discourage future investments in Botswana. While interest rates were raised, credit was not rationed to ensure that small borrowers would still have access to borrowed capital.

(b) Response of the economy to the government adjustment policies

The adjustment policies were very successful in increasing foreign exchange reserves, which rose from 198 million pulas in March to an all time high of 310 million pulas in May 1982, mostly as a result of short-term capital movements: as a result of the increase in interest rates, it was less expensive to borrow in South Africa than in Botswana. The reserves remained above 300 million pulas for the rest of the year, partly because of additional capital inflows, but also because of the reduction in the demand for imports due to the devaluation of the pula, the wage freeze, and the slower rate of increase of government spending. While exports increased sharply in the second half of 1982 due to the opening of the Jwaneng diamond mine, imports were kept to their 1981 level in money terms, and therefore fell in real terms. By 1983 the trade deficit was eliminated, and in 1984 there was a large surplus.

The diamond-demand crisis was short lived. While the value of diamonds exported during the second half of 1981 decreased by almost two-thirds in comparison with the previous year, the export value increased during the second half of 1982 due to increased production—and a substantially higher sales quota—as a result of the opening of the Jwaneng mine. At current prices, revenue from the mining sector increased from 130 million pulas in 1980/81 to 286 million in 1982/83 and 403 million in 1983/84.

The measures adopted delayed the emergence of an economic boom in response to the development of the new diamond mine. It is difficult to know whether or not the delay resulted in less growth in the long run. In any case, with the end of the crisis, the economy grew at an exceptionally high rate: 23.6 per cent during 1982/83 and 19.4 per cent during 1983/84. Most of the burden of the stabilization measures fell on the better-off urban groups who had their wages frozen and found it more expensive and difficult to obtain credit.

In retrospect, it appears that with the Jwaneng mine scheduled to open in less than a year and the still sizeable financial reserves, Botswana could have chosen to delay the adoption of its adjustment measures or could have adopted less stringent measures. However, in the early months of 1982 there was no guarantee that (*a*) the Jwaneng mine would open on schedule, (*b*) that the speculative demand for the large gem diamonds would recover, and/or (*c*) that individual producers would not try to sell outside of the Central Sales Organization, bringing about a collapse of the market. By adopting stringent adjustment measures while the economy was still healthy, the government minimized the potential consequences of any of these events.

2 Drought, mid-1982 to the present

Drought is a fact of life in Botswana. In the best of times the country receives only marginal rainfall and experiences a crop failure in two out of every five years. The country is now entering its fifth year of drought, first declared in July 1982 only nine months after the 1979/80 drought had officially ended. The present drought ranks as one of the most severe in history, being only the second drought in 65 years which has lasted for 5 consecutive years. Given the growth in both human and livestock population and the scarcity of unused grazing land, the socio-economic consequences are particularly severe.

The endemic drought situation is by far the most critical development issue facing Botswana today. Drought has seriously eroded the structure of the rural economy and as a result a significant number of rural households, particularly the small and resource-poor, have lost sizeable portions of their incomes and production assets. This places them and the nation as a whole in an extremely precarious position.

According to the Ministry of Agriculture, in 1983 of the 82,000 traditional household farms, 70,250 (85.7 per cent) produced no crops while an additional 7,840 households (9.6 per cent) harvested less than 250 kilograms in total. Only 1 per cent of the traditional farms harvested an amount equal or greater than 1,500 kilograms, which is considered to be the minimal amount sufficient to cover a typical household's food needs. The estimated income per traditional farm from arable agriculture in 1983 was only 29 pulas, equivalent to the income earned by working on labour-based relief projects for $14\frac{1}{2}$ days. Production levels in 1984 were roughly the same. The production levels were slightly higher in 1985, with 4.6 per cent of the traditional farms harvesting over 1,500 kilograms, while 83.3 per cent harvested less than 250 kilograms or nothing at all.

In addition to the substantial decrease in income from crop production, labour opportunities in the rural districts have also declined substantially, with hiring falling by 36 per cent from 1981 to 1982 and the numbers involved in family labour decreasing by 26 per cent. Poorer households who out of necessity are forced to rely on casual and informal employment have been particularly hard hit by the reduction in rural employment opportunities.

Livestock producers, especially the smaller ones, have also suffered greatly from the effects of the current drought. Among owners with less than 10 head of cattle, the livestock mortality rate is estimated to have increased from 30 per cent in 1982 to 54 per cent in 1983, against an average for all herds of 17 per cent. Sales and home slaughter also tend to be greater in the smallest herds, which indicate off-take due to distress.

The effects of the drought on overall food availability is shown in Table 1.2

TABLE 1.2   *Food availability, 1980–1985*

	1980	1981	1982	1983	1984	1985
Domestic food production (000 t)[a]	40,300	48,860	15,500	12,980	6,030	20,000
Cereal imports (000 t)	109,288	79,423	111,020	175,000[b]	158,000[b]	120,000[b]
Of which food aid (000 t)	13,462	9,248	4,906	24,278	31,237[b]	53,000[b]
Total available (000 t)	149,588	128,283	126,520	165,980[b]	164,030	193,200[b]
Total available (kg/head)	164	136	130	165	158	186
Food aid (kg/head)	15	10	5	24	30	40
Food aid as % total supply	9	7	4	15	19	27

Source: Adapted from Ministry of Finance and Development Planning (1985*a*).
[a] Assumes 10% allowance for losses.
[b] Estimates.

and Fig. 1.1. In the 1979/80 and 1980/81 cropping seasons, near-normal production of food crops was obtained, around 40–50,000 metric tonnes after

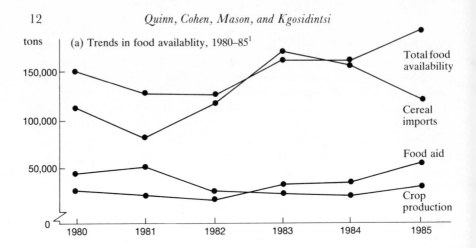

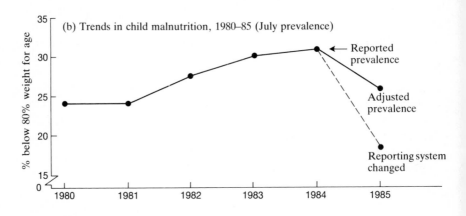

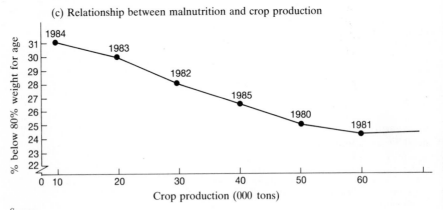

Sources
(*a*) and (*b*): compiled from Ministry of Finance and Development Planning (1985*a*); (*b*): Ministry of Health.

Fig. 1.1 Botswana: changes in (*a*) food availability, (*b*) nutritional status, and (*c*) relationship between crop production and malnutrition, 1980–1985

allowing for seed waste, etc. Production dropped very substantially in 1982, further in 1983, and reached its lowest point in 1984, when only around 10–15 per cent of normal cereal production was harvested. Current estimates for 1985 were of around 20,000 tons, and about the same was expected for 1986. Food availability declined with lowered imports in 1981 (presumably due to foreign exchange constraints), and although imports rose to 1980 levels in 1982, total food availability reached its lowest point during this year. Food aid was also particularly low in 1982, but built up rapidly in 1983 to 1985. By 1983, due to greatly increased imports (including food aid), food availability had been restored to 1980 levels on average, and rose further by 1985. There was thus a lag period from 1981 to 1983, as first commercial imports and then food aid built up in response to the drought.

These overall figures give little indication of the distribution of access to food, particularly in rural areas. It is notable (Table 1.1) that the number of households harvesting dropped to as low as 23 per cent of those planting by 1983. Among the poorest, losses of livestock may have had a more important impact on income loss than crop failure. No data on this are available, but bearing in mind that the contribution of livestock to income even in non-drought years is much greater than that of crops, it is arguable that the contribution of relief programmes to replacing income should be judged in relation to the sum of livestock, crop, and employment effects.

Fig. 1.1*c* indicates that there is some relationship between the drought and the extent of the malnutrition. The decline in crop production itself is not necessarily the direct cause of malnutrition but it can be used as a convenient indicator of the severity of the drought.

IV Compensatory programmes in response to the drought

1 Institutional framework

The government's ability to respond financially contributed to the success of Botswana's response during the current drought, but a major factor was the permanent institutional set-up which was established in response to problems that developed in earlier drought relief activities. One of the key actors involved in the Drought Relief Programme is the Early Warning Technical Committee (EWTC), which is responsible for monitoring drought and its effects on the human population within the country. The EWTC report their findings on drought conditions to the Inter-Ministerial Drought Committee (IMDC) which co-ordinates all drought relief activities in the country, including the allocation of funds. Another key body is the Food Resources Department, which is in charge of the acquisition, processing, and distribution of food relief to the districts.

The IMDC meets on a regular basis during drought periods and less regularly during non-drought years. Both the EWTC and the IMDC are chaired by members of the Rural Development Unit of the Ministry of Finance and Development Planning, and this helps to facilitate the communication and co-ordination of relief efforts. The IMDC reports directly to the Rural Development Council which is chaired by the Vice President and oversees all rural development activities. District and village development committees which were established in order to facilitate local input into the determination of development strategies at the local level are also used to help plan and implement drought relief efforts.

2   Identifying the vulnerable groups

The Botswana government has used the data inputs of the early warning information system to identify who and where the most severely affected population groups are. These include:

1. Batswana, and in particular children under five, who live in remote areas, on cattle-posts, or in small villages, tend to be the most heavily stressed nutritionally by drought, due to the reduction in the availability of wild nuts, fruits, and vegetables, and reductions in the supply of milk and crop production.

2. Small-scale arable farmers, who even in good years depend heavily on non-agricultural sources of income to meet their basic needs, become even more dependent on other sources of income during droughts, while at the same time the availability of such alternative sources of income is reduced.

3. During prolonged droughts, households with cattle herds of less than 40 head tend to experience high rates of mortality in their herds. In addition to reducing the capital assets of the household, the loss of cattle diminishes the household's ability successfully to engage in arable agriculture.

Given these considerations, the IMDC plans and co-ordinates a broad based Drought Relief Programme aimed at alleviating the loss of earnings, the loss of access to food, and the loss of assets, among the most vulnerable. Botswana's Drought Relief Programme has been designed to encompass the following six objectives:

1. *Supplementation of food supplies* as a preventive measure to reduce the incidence of, and forestall rises in, malnutrition among those groups considered at high risk.

2. *Rehabilitation of severely malnourished children* through direct on-site feeding at health facilities.

3. *Creation of rural employment opportunities* in order to compensate in part for the loss of agricultural income due to drought.

4. *Provision of water supplies* for human consumption and financial assistance for farmers' groups interested in developing communal water sources for cattle.

5. *Special assistance to arable farmers* to increase their ability to regain productivity.

6. *Improvement of the condition of livestock.*

The activities of the Drought Relief Programme are in three major categories, defined as 'human relief', 'human water relief', and 'agricultural relief'. These programmes are described in detail below.

3 Human relief programmes

(a) Supplementary feeding programmes Since independence, the Botswana government has provided food supplements to population groups deemed to be especially vulnerable to periods of nutritional stress: these include primary school children, medically selected children under five years of age, all pregnant and lactating women, and tuberculosis patients. In addition to protecting vulnerable groups in non-drought years, the ongoing programme provides the government with a food distribution system which can be quickly expanded to include additional categories when necessary.

In response to the current drought, the government expanded the supplementary feeding programme by introducing blanket coverage of all vulnerable groups in the rural areas. This resulted in the following changes being made in the food distribution programme:

1. Medical selection was dropped in rural and peri-urban areas, thereby extending eligibility for supplementary feeding to all under-5s living outside the urban areas and attending health facilities.

2. The School Feeding Programme was extended to provide take-home rations at weekends and holidays, in rural and peri-rural areas.

3. Two additional groups were selected for supplementary feeding: children between the ages of 5 and 10 who are not attending school, and individuals identified by their communities as having no means of support as a result of the drought (subsequently classified as group B destitutes).

4. Inclusion of (group A) destitutes whose needs in non-drought years were the responsibility of District Councils.

5. Extension of the Supplementary Feeding Programme to Remote Area Dwellers (RADs) who are particularly susceptible to the adverse effects of drought.

6. The supplementary food rations were increased for all vulnerable groups. The RADs ration has been set so as to fulfil the daily energy and protein requirement of an adult. In contrast, both the school ration and the supplementary ration provide approximately a third of adult nutritional needs.

To discourage rural families from migrating to urban areas during the drought, medical selection was maintained at health facilities in urban areas,

TABLE 1.3   *Numbers of beneficiaries per vulnerable group, 1982–1986*

	1982	1983	1984	1985	1986
School attenders	189,498	198,819	209,570	257,916	236,758
Pre-school children					
Under 5	133,000	209,000	179,000	180,000	170,000
6–10	n.a.	n.a.	64,000	85,000	81,000
Lactating mothers	40,000	59,000	49,000	54,000	50,000
Pregnant women	n.a.	n.a.	23,000	22,000	19,000
Tuberculosis patients	6,000	8,000	10,000	13,000	11,000
Destitutes	n.a.	26,665			
Group A			10,204	8,582	7,000
Group B			25,227	27,956	34,000
Remote area dwellers (RADs)	n.a.	n.a.	20,000	20,000	19,000
Direct feeding	—	—	4,000	9,000	14,000

Sources: Food Resources Department and Rural Development Unit.

while urban school attenders and those in recovery zones were fed only on school days.

With the exception of the School Feeding Programme, which is the responsibility of the Ministry of Education, and food distribution to RADs, which is carried out by the Remote Area Development Unit, the drought relief food is distributed through the Food Resources Department of the Ministry of Local Government and Lands, using the 600 public schools and 575 primary health care facilities in addition to 175 mobile health stops as food distribution points. The existence of an extensive network of distribution sites provides Botswana with an invaluable base for the expansion of the regular feeding programmes in response to drought. Despite the ruggedness, vastness, and inaccessibility of a large part of the country, the Food Resource Department has been successful in solving most of the logistical problems encountered during the early stages of the drought in the transportation, storage, and distribution of food to clinics and schools.

As Table 1.3 shows, the numbers of beneficiaries receiving food rations has increased sharply since the drought feeding programme began in 1982. The number of infants and children under 10 covered rose by 200,000 from 1982 to 1985, or over 60 per cent. The increase is partly a reflection of the increasing impoverishment of the rural population as the drought continues. In addition, it reflects the increasing ability of the Food Resources Unit to distribute large quantities of food to vulnerable groups throughout the country.

One of the unintended benefits of the drought feeding programme has been the dramatic increase in attendance of vulnerable groups at health facilities because of the free food being distributed. Attendance of under-5s at health facilities has nearly quadrupled since the start of the drought, rising from a monthly average of 40,000 in 1980 to about 140,000 in 1985, thus permitting improvement of immunization coverage and nutritional assessment. This has not only improved the health care given to individual children but has also increased the coverage and effectiveness of the nutritional surveillance system in monitoring the effects of drought and the efficacy of the Drought Relief Programme. In addition, more mothers than ever before are attending maternal and child health clinics and gaining exposure to health education activities.

(b) Direct feeding The primary objective of direct feeding is the nutritional rehabilitation of malnourished children by on-site feeding of specially prepared foods at health facilities and other designated sites in remote areas. If a rehabilitation programme is to be effective, it is important that children are fed small, frequent meals throughout the day. Therefore, the feeding of malnourished children was intended to be a daily activity in which several small meals providing a day's nutritional requirements were given to the participants at the feeding site.

The children selected for direct feeding are divided into two groups: the DISCO milk group and the regular feeding group. The DISCO milk group are those children with weights for age of 60 per cent or less of the Gomez Standard (Harvard reference population), who are therefore considered to be severely malnourished. Less than 1 per cent of children in Botswana fall into this category. The regular feeding group which currently serves an average of 13,700 children daily, consists of those children with weights for age of 80 per cent or less of the Harvard standard, as well as children failing to show adequate growth for three consecutive months.

Unfortunately, the effectiveness of the Direct Feeding Programme has been limited by problems of screening. Many of the children in the direct feeding group are not currently malnourished, rather they are stunted children who are otherwise healthy. Second, mothers, particularly in households in which the father is absent, do not have the time to bring their children in daily. This problem is particularly serious for mothers who participate in the Labour-based Relief Programme or depend on casual employment opportunities. There is therefore reason to be concerned that the programme may not be reaching many of the most vulnerable children, and that for these reasons it may have achieved only moderate success.

(c) Labour-based relief The Labour-based Relief Programme (LBRP) has two objectives. First, to compensate for the reduction in rural incomes due to drought, by providing employment opportunities for the able-bodied. Second, by constructing socially useful and productive infrastructure, the programme aims to increase the income earning potential of the village.

All LBRP projects are selected initially by Village Development Committees. An appraisal committee of the IMDC then helps to screen and approve the projects chosen by villagers. Projects are required to be labour intensive and

TABLE 1.4   *Percentage of income from crop failure replaced by Labour-based Relief Programme, 1981–1985*

	1981	1982	1983	1984	1985[a]
Crop production (t million)	54,287	17,220	14,425	6,925	20,000
Shortfall from normal	5,713	42,780	45,575	53,075	40,000
Income lost (P)	2.55	9.37	11.48	15.13	14.40
Income replaced (P)	0.12	1.87	3.45	4.99	5.43
LBRP wages as % of income lost	10.90	19.90	30.50	32.90	33.70

Source: Rural Development Unit, Ministry of Finance.
[a] Estimate.

utilize simple hand tools. Once approved, the responsibility for carrying out a project falls on the Food Resources Department. In order not to detract from essential agricultural activities, the LBRP is suspended for several weeks during the planting season to allow workers to work in their own fields. For a variety of reasons, LBRP workers are paid in cash (instead of in kind).

In 1985/86, the LBRP provided approximately 70,000 temporary work-places. According to the government, the number of workplaces created was almost equivalent to the number of workplaces lost in the rural economy as a result of the drought. During the 1985/86 drought year, workers on the LBRP were paid 2 pulas a day, which, while only two-thirds of the national minimum wage, was roughly equivalent to the salary earned by maids and security guards in urban areas and considerably more than cattle herders earned on the cattle-posts. For the 1986/87 drought programme, the wage was raised to 2.25 pulas. Because the wage was considerably higher than the opportunity cost of labour in a drought year, the supply of able-bodied workers desiring employment has consistently exceeded the number of available LBRP jobs. The available workplaces were therefore supposed to be rotated among those desiring employment.

The contribution that the LBRP has made to replacing rural income lost from crop failure due to drought has grown from an estimated 10.9 per cent in 1981 to 37.7 per cent of income lost in 1985 (Table 1.4). The government objective is to replace 50 per cent of income loss due to crop failure through the LBRP.

Many of the LBRP's beneficiaries are women. This factor plays an important role in helping to protect child health and nutrition during the drought since it is recognized that women are more likely than men to spend their income on meeting their family's food requirements. The 'Hand-Stamping' programme is particularly noteworthy in this respect, as it involves about 6,000 to 7,000 women per year on a rotating basis to mill sorghum for the School Feeding Programme. The only non-labour inputs in the project are the traditional pestles and mortars. Since these are produced locally, the project also helps to support local artisans.

The contribution of LBRPs to investing in socially useful and productive infrastructure is also significant. For example, in 1984 projects were accepted to build and upgrade 15,200 kilometres of roads, 12 airstrips, 220 dams for livestock water, 112 village meeting houses, and 452 pit latrines. Other activities included clearing land and planting community gardens. While not all of the projects have been successfully completed, the government has improved the level of productivity on the projects over the past year by introducing technical officers.

(d) Coverage of the human relief programmes During 1985/86, about 62 per cent of Botswana's population was receiving some type of food relief ration. The government's contribution to the food relief programme was roughly 12 pulas per beneficiary per year. If the donor's food aid contribution of US$21.1 million (36.9 million pulas) is added, then the average cost per beneficiary in 1985/86 was 66 pulas.

TABLE 1.5 *Estimated coverage of eligible vulnerable groups in Drought Feeding Programme, 1985/86*

	Numbers attending	Estimated eligible	Total estimated coverage (%)
Pre-school (0–5 years)	180,000	218,000	83
Pregnant and/or lactating women	76,000	119–158,000[a]	48–64
Children 6–10 years not in school	85,000	n.a.	n.a.
Primary school children	258,000	223,000[b]	100
Direct feeding of severely malnourished (DISCO)	2,500[c]	2,180	100

[a] Total eligible estimated from 1984 population projections plus assumption one half to two-thirds of women 15–49 years are pregnant and/or lactating.
[b] From school enrollment figures for early 1985 (from CSO. Dec. 1985).
[c] From Ministry of Finance and Development Planning (1986e) (Request for Emergency Assistance with Food Supplies). Assumes less than 1 per cent of pre-school children severely malnourished and therefore eligible.

The coverage of specific vulnerable groups is very high. Table 1.5 shows that over 80 per cent of the under-5s eligible for food relief were actually receiving it. Approximately 48 to 64 per cent of pregnant and lactating women eligible are also benefiting from the programme. The coverage is even greater for primary school children enrolled in the School Feeding Programme, which appears to be reaching nearly all of this group. There has been concern, however, that children 5 to 10 years of age who are not in school may not be benefiting from the take-home food rations distributed at health facilities. Although the figures for coverage of severely malnourished children receiving DISCO milk at health facilities indicate high coverage of this particularly vulnerable group, problems with screening and implementation would suggest caution in interpreting these figures.

Of the 188,000 individuals estimated to be involved in agriculture as family labour during non-drought years, approximately 40 per cent have participated in LBRP activities and received wages during 1985/86. During that period, the sum of 6.12 million pulas was dispensed as wages, which averages about 83 pula per participant. Judged by the socially useful infrastructures which have been built through the LBRP, the majority of rural Batswana have benefited indirectly from this programme.

While the distribution of food is very extensive, the amount of food which an individual household receives is only adequate if the household has additional sources of income. The LBRP provides some households with employment opportunities, and the two programmes are complementary.

4   Human Water Relief Programme

The Human Water Relief Programme makes special funds available to District Council Water Units to improve their capacity to repair water systems, to transport emergency water supplies, and to cover the cost of emergency drilling programmes. This is in addition to the normal non-drought Village Water Supply Programme.

5   Arable Agricultural Relief and Recovery Programme

The Agricultural Relief Programme is designed to complement on-going agricultural development programmes (such as the Arable Land Development Programme and the Accelerated Rainfed Arable Programme) during periods of drought to provide a viable safety net for livestock owners and arable farmers. The various components of the Agricultural Relief Programme are aimed at assisting both small producers and commercial farmers and consist in the free distribution of seeds, provision of grants for land clearance, and equipping watering facilities for livestock.

In 1985/86, 121,000 farmers, or 64 per cent of the population engaged in family agriculture, each received 20 kilograms of seed with which to plant three hectares, while 13,000 farmers participated in destumping, which provided wages averaging approximately 92 pulas to each participant. The programme has increased the supply of potential arable land, but in some areas of the country land has been destumped with no intention of bringing it into arable production, thereby contributing to the problem of desertification.

6   Agricultural relief and recovery programmes for livestock

During the current drought, the population of the national herd has dropped by one-sixth, from over 3 million head four years ago to roughly 2.5 million.

In response to this, the government has intensified its botulism vaccination programme for cattle, and provided subsidized stockfeed, while a cattle purchase scheme was initiated in 1983 to provide livestock producers with a guaranteed market for culled cattle and a source of emergency income. The programme guarantees livestock producers a fixed minimum price for their animals, irrespective of their condition. Cattle purchased under the scheme are used to supplement the School Feeding Programme.

7   Summary of the drought relief programme

Botswana's Drought Relief Programme, as summarized in Table 1.6, appears to have been effective at safeguarding the welfare of the most vulnerable groups within the population. Part of the success of the current relief programme is a result of the experiences gained in dealing with earlier drought situations, as the government modified its drought relief programmes as unforeseen problems developed and the situation changed.

Other factors which have contributed to the success of the programme

TABLE 1.6   *Beneficiaries and costs of 1985/86 Drought Relief Programme*

	Beneficiaries	Cost of programme (P000) To government	Other	Cost per beneficiary (P)	Estimated coverage (%)
Drought Feeding Programme	678,000 people	7.8[a]	36.9[b]	12	62
Labour-based Relief	74,000 workers	11.0[a,c]	—	149[d]	40[e]
Human Water Relief	n.a.	5.7[f]	—	n.a.	n.a.
Funds for agricultural groups	545 farmers	0.6[g]	—	1,123	Less than 1
Arable Agricultural Relief					
Seed distribution	121,000 farmers	1.8[g]	—	15	64[e]
Destumping	13,000 farmers	2.1[a]	—	162	7[e]
Stock watering	500 farmers	1.5[a]	—	n.a.	Less than 1[e]
Livestock Agricultural Relief					
Cattle purchase	n.a.	0.3[h]	—	n.a.	n.a.
Draught power hire	11,000 farmers[i]	1.4[g,h]	—	127	6[e]
Botulism vaccine	2,200,000 cattle	n.a.	—	n.a.	80[j]
Subsidized feed	n.a.	n.a.	—	n.a.	n.a.
ALL PROGRAMMES	n.a.	36.2[k]	36.9	67[l]	n.a.

[a] Estimated expenditure (MFDP 1985c).
[b] Donors' contribution of 53,000 tons of food aid.
[c] P 6.12m disbursed as wages (actuals, MFDP 1986a).
[d] P 83 per beneficiary, on average, received as wages per annum.
[e] Based on estimated family labour in agriculture in 1981/82 (non-drought year) of 188,000 persons.
[f] Actual expenditure (personal communication from official).
[g] Actual expenditure (MFDP 1986a).
[h] Approximate, actual (MFDP 1986a).
[i] 1984/85.
[j] Proportion of national herd.
[k] Includes P 6.7m allocated by Botswana government for human and livestock relief.
[l] Equivalent to $38 at July 1985 exchange rate.

include the ability to divert significant amounts of national resources to relief activities, a relatively small population, improved infrastructures in most areas compared with previous droughts, and the ability to attract donor support, especially food aid and technical assistance. The participation of the private sector in transportation, milling, and ploughing is also noteworthy.

(a) Protecting nutritional status The 1982–86 Drought Relief Programme appears to have been successful in containing a rise in hunger and malnutrition despite severe losses in incomes and output. Malnutrition rates (Fig. 1.1) began to increase fairly steadily in 1982, a time of lowest overall food availability since compensatory measures of food imports and donor aid had not yet picked up enough to fill the food gap. By 1983 the levels of cereal imports and food aid donations were high enough to offset the production shortfall and raise overall food availability to pre-drought levels. By 1983/84 the prevalence of child malnutrition appears to have been contained and may have even declined in 1985.

Fig. 1.1c shows the association between cereal production and malnutrition, with each data point being one year. It should be emphasized that production here is a convenient measure of the severity of the drought, and not necessarily the only—or even major—determinant of nutritional status. However, it appears that malnutrition rates did respond to the drought. Although this requires further analysis, it is highly probable that malnutrition rates would have risen more without (*a*) the food imports (commercial and food aid) maintaining overall supplies, and (*b*) income support, through the public works programmes (LBRP) and food distribution system.

There is concern, however, that even with the support of the present Drought Relief Programme, rural households are still short of income to invest in productive assets after consumption needs have been met. The Rural Development Unit estimates that a typical rural household has little surplus cash left over after food requirements are satisfied in spite of the household's full participation in the Drought Feeding and Labour-based Relief Programmes.

(b) Cost of the Drought Relief Programme To date, an economic analysis of the total contribution that the Drought Relief Programme is making to replenishing drought losses incurred by rural households has not yet been done. It is not only difficult to quantify the many types of drought relief inputs given in the form of human, labour, agricultural, and water relief, but it is also difficult to measure the various effects that these may have on households in the short and long term. In addition, little is known about how well the benefits are distributed across small and large farming households in different areas of the country.

The actual and estimated costs of the 1985/86 Drought Relief Programme for the government are shown in Table 1.6 separately for each activity. A total amount of 36.2 million pulas ($21 million) was allocated by government towards drought relief, which is approximately equivalent to 17 per cent of government development expenditure or 2 per cent of GDP. The largest percentage of this budget went towards food relief (22 per cent) and labour-based relief (30 per cent). When the donor's food contribution is included, the total cost of the 1985/86 Drought Relief Programme nearly doubles, to 73.1 million pulas ($42 million), or roughly 67 pulas per capita, of the total population.

V Nutritional surveillance and early warning systems

Drought monitoring activities in Botswana depend on a comprehensive system of data collection, analysis, and interpretation conducted on a regular basis by participating departments. These departments, which comprise the Early Warning Technical Committee (EWTC), meet on a regular basis to review rainfall and agro-meteorological data, reports from the Nutrition Surveillance System, and the agricultural situation reports issued by the Agricultural Statistics Unit. The EWTC also monitors the availability and prices of food supplies, for both the relief programmes and the Strategic Grain Reserve held on behalf of the government by the Botswana Agricultural Marketing Board. Most of the sources of data are from regular administrative sources.

The function of the EWTC is, first, to use the various sources of available data to assess the incidence and severity of drought conditions throughout the country, the effects of such conditions on the human population, and the supply of basic foodstuffs. Secondly, the EWTC formulates and reports recommendations to the Inter-Ministerial Drought Committee on the types and amount of drought recovery assistance needed in each administrative district.

While there are no set minimum levels of any indicator used to determine drought, emphasis is placed on the direction of change in the prevalence of underweight children, condition of livestock, and forecasts of cereal grain production. It is recognized that the indicators exhibit a ripple effect: low rainfall adversely affects both crop production and livestock, which in turn reduces the supply of food produced by the household and the amount of income which can be earned from the sale of livestock and field crops. The resulting reduction in farm incomes and household-produced consumption items has detrimental effects on the nutritional status of household members.

1 The National Nutrition Surveillance system

The National Nutrition Surveillance (NNS) system reports on the nutritional status of all under-5s throughout the country attending health facilities. In Botswana, young children are appropriate for monitoring nutritional status for two reasons. First, the Ministry of Health had already instituted a system for monitoring the incidence of common illnesses in all health facilities. It was therefore relatively simple to institute a nutritional surveillance system of children attending the child welfare clinics. Second, young children are particularly vulnerable to acute and chronic malnutrition as a result of short and long-term food shortages. Changes in their nutritional status thus provides an early indication of likely changes in the nutritional status of the overall population. In addition, the risks of mortality and morbidity as a result of malnutrition are higher among children under five than any other vulnerable group. In any given month, an average of 136,000 of the approximately 200,000 under-5s visit one of the more than 750 health points in the country, although these are not necessarily the same children every month.

The Nutrition Surveillance System collects data on the monthly prevalence of underweight children (below 80 per cent of the Harvard standard) by health facility, clusters of facilities, and region. Assessment of changes in prevalence figures at these levels can be compared to changes in the other early warning indicators and when appropriate, interventions can be mounted by district and national authorities. There are 15 health regions, stratified into urban areas, villages, lands, cattle-posts, farms and ranches, and various remote areas such as swamps and settlements, which can be aggregated in economically and ecologically similar zones.

In addition to data collected for nutrition surveillance purposes, growth monitoring of individual children is done at the health facilities using the preschool child growth card, which provides a continuous record of the child's health and growth status. The Child Growth Monitoring Programme helps to detect children who are likely to become malnourished, in order that corrective action can be taken by mothers and health workers. These are the children who are recorded as failing to grow but are not currently underweight, as well as those who are underweight and continue to show signs of growth failure.

2   *The agricultural situation reports*

Extension agents in each of the 120 extension districts submit monthly reports on the status of field crops, grazing conditions, and livestock in their area of the country. In order to estimate aggregate production levels in their districts, the agents provide reports on the area ploughed, area planted by crop, and the estimated yields by crop. The crop reports are then aggregated for each of the 16 agricultural districts by the Agriculture Statistics Unit.

Similarly, assessments are made of overall livestock, grazing, and water conditions for cattle, using a scale of one to five. These reports are then used to draw national maps depicting livestock, water, and grazing conditions by district. Finally, the agents also report on the amount of food in store at the household level.

3   The agro-meteorology reports

Weekly rainfall data are collected by radio from 250 recording points around the country. The resulting data are analysed on a weekly basis in terms of percentage departure from the long-term mean (i.e. normal rainfall), both for the particular month and cumulatively for the season. The Agro-Meteorology Unit uses the rainfall data to calculate a water satisfaction index. The information derived from the water satisfaction index enables the unit to make timely predictions on the probability of harvest reductions or failures for the country's two main crops, sorghum and maize.

4   Food supply monitoring

The Botswana Agricultural Marketing Board monitors the stock levels of the National Strategic Grain Reserve, while the Food Resources Department (FRD) monitors the supply of supplementary food rations. In addition, the FRD is also responsible for insuring that the supply of rations is adequate for current and future needs. To this end, it secures donor commitments of food aid, and when necessary, purchases additional stocks out of government funds. In addition, the FRD co-ordinates the distribution of food rations to all feeding points throughout the country.

5   Additional data sources

In addition to the established avenues of data collection for the early warning information system, there are other sources which may corroborate the data collected or highlight deficit areas. These include District Drought Committee reports, survey findings, and Drought Assessment Tours.

The District Drought Committees submit regular reports to the IMDC on water, agricultural, and nutritional conditions in their area, and the status of drought relief and recovery activities. In addition, the District Drought Committees meet with members of the Drought Assessment Tours which occur twice a year: in February, midway through the cropping season, and in April–May as the harvest is being completed.

6   Mechanisms for data use and links with policy formulation

The data collected by the participating departments of the EWTC, together with the reports of the District Drought Committees and research findings, form the basis of recommendations by the IMDC to the Rural Development Council, which approves and finalizes them for presentation to the Botswana cabinet. The recommendations concern the requirements for drought relief or post-drought recovery measures, funding needs of the drought programmes, and any changes recommended in the programmes. Initial drought relief recovery programme recommendations are made at the beginning of March in order to ensure ample time for their implementation in June, which is when the consequences of reduced harvest or dwindling resources begin to be felt by both the human and animal populations.

Furthermore, the severity of drought as measured by prevalence of underweight is the basis for setting ration levels and establishing beneficiary groups and target areas for supplementary feeding programmes. For example, in 1984 when underweight prevalence rates appeared to be escalating, this prompted a stepping-up of relief measures, especially supplementary feeding, by establishing more feeding points, hiring feeding clerks, and introducing a fund for direct feeding. The result was increased coverage of the supplementary feeding programmes and increased food imports.

VI Conclusion

Botswana's comprehensive system of drought relief indicates that malnutrition can be controlled, even with severe drought, at fairly low cost. The success of the programme contains many lessons of potential use for other countries seeking to protect vulnerable groups against severe fluctuations, whether these are due to weather or to changing economic circumstances.

Documents consulted

Official Botswana documents:

Central Statistics Office (1976), *The Rural Income Distribution Survey in Botswana, 1974/75* (1976).
—— (1983), *Employment Survey, August 1981.*
—— (1984), *National Accounts of Botswana, 1982/1984.*
—— (1985a), *National Accounts of Botswana, 1983/84; Preliminary Figures.*
—— (1985b), *Statistical Bulletin 10/4.*
—— (1986), *Botswana Country Profile.*
Ministry of Agriculture (1974). *A Study of Constraints on Agricultural Development in the Republic of Botswana.*
—— (1978–85) *Botswana Agricultural Statistics.*
Ministry of Finance and Development Planning (MFDP) (1973). *National Development Plan, 1973–78.*
—— (1977), *National Development Plan, 1976–80.*
—— (1980), *National Development Plan, 1979–85.*
—— (1981), *Evaluation of 1979/80 Drought Relief Programme* (by Toby Gooch and John MacDonald).
—— (1985a), *An Overview of Food Relief Operations in Botswana During the 1982–1986 Drought* (by Richard Morgan, National Food Strategy Co-ordinator).
—— (1985b), *Possible Measures for Post-drought Recovery During National Development Plan 6: Discussion Paper* (by R. Morgan).

——— (1985c), *The Drought Situation in Botswana, March 1985, and Estimated Requirements for Relief and Recovery Measures: Aide Memoire.*

——— (1986a), *The Drought Situation in Botswana, March 1986, and Estimated Requirements for Relief and Recovery Measures: Aide Memoire.*

——— (1986b), *Contribution of Labour-based Projects to Drought Relief and Post-drought Recovery: Discussion Paper* (by R. Morgan).

——— (1986c), *National Development Plan, 1985–1991.*

——— (1986d), *Request to Donors for Emergency Assistance with Food Supplies During the 1986/87 Drought Relief Programme.*

——— (1986e), *Lessons From Drought Operations in Botswana During the 1982/87 Drought.*

National Institute of Research, University of Botswana (1983), *Report on the Botswana Brigades, 1975–1983* (by Q. N. Parsons).

Nutrition Unit, Ministry of Health (1986), *Supplementing Food and Incomes During Drought* (by Bill Clay).

Republic of Botswana (1966), *Transitional Plan for Social and Economic Development.*

——— (1968), *National Development Plan, 1968–1973.*

——— (1970), *National Development Plan, 1970–1975.*

Rural Development Council (1985a), *Report on the National Food Strategy.*

——— (1985b), *National Food Strategy.*

——— (1986), *Post-drought Recovery Strategy Guidelines.*

Other documents and publications

Barclays Bank (1985), *Botswana: an Economic Survey and Businessman's Guide.* Gaborone.

Borton, J. (1984), *Disaster Preparedness and Response in Botswana.* London: Relief and Development Institute.

Colclough, C., and S. McCarthy (1980), *The Political Economy of Botswana: A Study of Growth and Distribution.* London: Oxford University Press.

Devitt, P. (1979), 'Drought and Poverty', in *Symposium on Drought in Botswana.* The Botswana Society, University Press of New England.

Harvey, C. (1985), *The Use of Monetary Policy in Botswana in Good Times and Bad,* Institute of Development Studies, University of Sussex.

Hay, R., S. Burke, and D. Y. Dako (1985), *A Socio-economic Assessment of Drought in Botswana.* Gaborone: UNICEF/UNDP/WHO.

Jolly, R., and G. A. Cornia, eds. (1984), *The Impact of World Recession on Children.* Oxford: Pergamon Press.

Salkin, J. (1985), 'Research on Employment and Unemployment in Botswana'. Mimeographed. Botswana Society, Symposium on Research for Development, Aug. 1985, Gaborone.

UNICEF – Botswana (1986), *Situation of Children and Women in Botswana.* Gaborone.

Brazilian Children and the Economic Crisis: The Evidence from the State of Saõ Paulo

Roberto Macedo

I Introduction

This study reviews the evidence on the impact of the crisis and recovery on the welfare of Brazilian children over the 1980–85 period, drawing mostly on data for the State of Saõ Paulo. It also examines the nature and performance of economic and social policies adopted by the government authorities in response to the recession which were intended to sustain the living conditions of the population and children in particular.

As will become clear, in São Paulo during the first part of the 1980s all the usual economic indicators, as well as several indicators of child welfare (infant mortality rate, incidence of low birth weight, primary school achievement, etc.), portrayed growing deterioration. Preliminary data for 1985, however, suggest that with a vigorous recovery underway, employment, household incomes, and income distribution have started to improve, but data on child welfare do not yet show the hoped for improvements.

This study is organized as follows. Part II presents a review of recent economic performance and a discussion of the policies adopted by the government. Part III examines the effects of economic performance and government policies on the economic conditions of households, and discusses the social policies adopted by the government in response to the crisis. Part IV reviews recent trends in indicators of child welfare, while Part V draws some lessons from the experience of the State of São Paulo.

II Economic conditions: recent developments and government policies

In order to understand the difficulties faced by the Brazilian economy in the early 1980s it is necessary to turn back to 1973 when, at the end of a period of high economic growth rates, the economy was affected by the first 'oil shock'. The initial government reaction was to avoid taking measures to eliminate the external imbalance caused by the shock. Instead, external indebtedness expanded. As a result, throughout the period 1974 to 1979 the economy was able to maintain acceptable rates of economic growth. However, more serious difficulties appeared towards the end of the 1970s when a new 'oil shock' occurred, along with a sharp increase in international interest rates.

The problems which emerged at the end of 1979 and during 1980 were aggravated by the economic policy followed by the government. Although the external accounts and inflation showed signs of deterioration, the government chose to expand aggregate demand through expansionary fiscal and monetary policies, more rapid indexation of wages—which was changed from yearly to half-yearly—negative real interest rates domestically, and exchange rate overvaluation.

With these policies, the growth rate again reached a high level in 1980, but at the same time internal and external imbalances increased substantially. The country tried the course of growing indebtedness again, but this time there was resistance among the international bankers, who imposed stricter ceilings on the availability of additional funds. As a result, Brazil began to introduce adjustment measures at the end of 1980.

The year 1981 was particularly disastrous for the economy, but by mid-1982 further deterioration seemed to be contained. However, the crisis which then affected Mexico and other indebted countries also forced Brazil to declare its incapacity to meet external debt servicing commitments. That happened in September, on the eve of elections for the state governors, congress, state legislative assemblies, municipal councils, and city halls. Fearing unfavourable political repercussions, the government postponed arrangements with the IMF and international bankers until the end of that year.

At the very beginning of 1983, an adjustment programme was negotiated which caused renewed and substantial decline of GDP. Although Brazil did not follow the programme's prescriptions strictly, its most important goal, the creation of large surpluses in the trade balance, was consistently achieved. In 1983 this occurred mainly through import restraints, which had a serious recessionary impact. Yet in 1984, there was substantial growth of exports in the wake of the economic recovery of the United States, while the economy started benefiting from the import substitution programmes carried out in the preceding years. As a result, after three years of serious declines, per capita GDP increased again in 1984.

National accounting identities help to understand the nature of the economic policy from 1981 to 1984 that emerged in response to pressures from international banks and, since early 1983, the IMF. GNP, which determines aggregate demand in the economy, is given by

$$Y = C + I + G + (X - M) \tag{1}$$

where C represents private consumption, I investment, G government expenditure, X exports, and M imports of goods and services. The total expenditure of a country's residents is given by

$$Y^E = C + I + G \tag{2}$$

Substituting (2) into (1) yields

$$Y - Y^E = (X - M) \tag{3}$$

that is, the difference between GNP and residents' expenditure reflects the current account balance. The economic policy focused on eliminating the negative difference illustrated by (3). One can decompose the current account balance into its three components, that is,

$$X - M = (X^g - M^g) + (X^s - M^s) + (X^{fs} - M^{fs}) \tag{4}$$

where superscripts g, s, and fs refer to merchandise, services (e.g. tourism, shipments) and foreign factor incomes (wages, interest, and profits), respectively.

The first term on the right-hand side of (4) represents the merchandise or trade balance, the second represents the balance in invisibles, other than factor payments, and the third represents the net income from factors of production involved in external transactions.

Between 1978 and 1980, the merchandise balance became negative, mainly as a result of the oil shock, while invisibles and factor income balances remained negative. In addition the factor income balance worsened rapidly, especially after 1979, due to increased indebtedness and the 'interest rate shock'. If 'sfs' designates the services balance as a whole, then bringing the current account balance to zero requires that

$$(X^g - M^g) = (M^{sfs} - X^{sfs}) \tag{5}$$

that is, the trade balance surplus must cover the service balance, including the net income of foreign factors, composed essentially of interest payments on the external debt.

Equation (3) can be rewritten as:

$$Y - Y^E = (X - M) = (S - I) + (T - G) \tag{6}$$

where S represents private savings and T taxes. With the goal of eliminating the negative balance described by (6), the government designed a package of adjustment policies including:

1. *Fiscal policy directed to increase taxes* and to reduce the government's expenditure and therefore to make $T - G$ positive or less negative.

2. *Monetary policy maintaining high interest rates* in order to make $(S - I)$ positive, with negative effects on investment exceeding the positive impact on savings. The growth of the latter was negatively influenced by the decline in the level of income which resulted from the adjustment process.

3. *A 30 per cent maxi-devaluation of the cruzeiro* adopted in the beginning of 1983, followed by shortening intervals between successive mini-devaluations, together with the elimination of the external inflation's discount imbedded in

the purchasing power parity previously observed. The overall result was a sharp real devaluation of the cruzeiro.

4. *Trade policy of new incentives to exports and additional restrictions on imports.*

5. *Industrial policy giving new impulse to import substitution* in, among other areas, oil, non-ferrous metals, and chemical products.

6. *Nominal wage readjustments below inflation*, which restrained consumption (including imports) and reduced the wage/exchange rate ratio, as a further export incentive.

Given the slow growth of world trade, the impact of such policies on exports was initially limited, although they were prevented from falling below the 1980 level. During the 1981–83 period, the largest domestic effect of this policy package was therefore on levels of consumption, investment, and government expenditure. This led to recession with the fall in aggregate demand, which in turn reduced imports. In this way, the major goal of government policy, i.e. eliminating the negative current account balance, was achieved. As expected, however, the impact on domestic production and income was negative, further worsening the negative effects of the recession.

Only in 1984 did the economic recovery of the United States permit a substantial increase in exports, which grew 23 per cent in just one year. The expansion in exports and advances in import substitution partially reversed the recessionary character of the adjustment process. GDP grew by 4.5 per cent in 1984 and by 7.4 per cent in 1985.

During 1981–84 there was a sharp increase in inflation, partly due to mismanagement of monetary and fiscal policies and partly to the effects of the widespread indexation system which absorbed shocks, like those of oil and international interest rates, by means of increases in inflation which have been shown to be irreversible.

These developments are shown in Table 2.1, which presents data on economic growth, inflation rates, and the performance of the external sector from 1973 until 1985. Table 2.1 shows the recessionary phase of 1981–83 together with the recovery that started in 1984; the worsening of the inflation rates is also evident, along with the substantial achievement in containing the external deficit. This achievement is reflected mainly in the enormous trade surplus of 1982–85, and the improvement in the current account, which went into surplus in 1984.

As noted, the combination of advances in import substitution and export expansion contributed to the recovery of 1984. The same factors continued to work in 1985, but the recovery accelerated for other reasons. The increase in domestic income which followed the recovery stimulated increase in the production of consumer goods, which received additional impulse from wage increases above inflation rates, due to growing demand for labour, union activity, and relaxation of the earlier wage policy. At the end of 1985, sales of consumer goods were increasing so sharply that many businessmen

TABLE 2.1 Growth, inflation, foreign trade, and external debt, 1978–1985

	GDP: annual rate of change (%)		Annual inflation[a] rate (%)	Balance of payments ($m)		Gross debt[c]
	Total	Per capita		Trade	Current account	
1973	14.0	11.2	23.4	7	-1,088	12,572
1974	9.5	6.3	33.5	-4,690	-7,122	17,166
1975	5.6	3.0	35.3	-3,540	-6,700	21,171
1976	9.7	7.0	46.7	-2,255	-6,017	25,985
1977	5.4	2.8	44.7	97	-4,037	32,037
1978	4.8	2.3	44.1	-1,024	-6,090	43,511
1979	6.7	4.2	57.6	-2,840	-10,742	49,904
1980	7.9	5.3	94.6	-2,823	-12,007	53,847
1981	-1.9	-4.3	97.8	1,202	-11,734	61,411
1982	1.4	-1.1	96.4	780	-14,755	70,198
1983	-3.3	-5.7	144.4	6,470	-6,171	81,319
1984	4.5	2.1	207.9	13,068	34	88,261
1985[b]	7.4	5.0	225.5	12,450	650	87,700

	Dept service ratio	Exports	Imports	Debt service	Interest	Amortization	Reserves
1973	0.42	99	6,192	2,577	514	2,063	6,416
1974	0.33	7,951	12,641	2,595	652	1,943	5,269
1975	0.42	8,670	12,210	3,666	1,498	2,168	4,040
1976	0.48	10,128	12,383	4,814	1,810	3,004	6,544
1977	0.51	12,120	12,023	6,226	2,103	4,123	7,256
1978	0.64	12,639	13,683	8,122	2,696	5,426	11,895
1979	0.70	15,244	18,084	10,713	4,186	6,527	9,689
1980	0.65	20,132	22,955	13,000	6,311	6,689	6,913
1981	0.72	23,293	22,091	16,657	9,161	7,496	7,507
1982	0.96	20,175	19,395	19,451	11,353	8,098	3,994
1983	0.89	21,899	15,429	19,485	9,555	9,930	4,563
1984	0.68	27,005	13,937	18,267	10,076	8,191	7,950
1985[b]	0.78	25,739	13,189	20,118	10,400	9,718	...

Source: Central Bank of Brazil, Getulio Vargas Foundation.
[a] Measured by national accounts implicit deflator (new series).
[b] Preliminary.
[c] Refers only to debt registered at the Central Bank (unregistered debt as estimated by central bank at the end of 1984: $8,920m).

started saying that the good old days of the 'miracle years' (1968–73) were back.

Inflation, however, became an increasing concern as monthly rates indicated that it could move to around 400 per cent a year if countermeasures were not taken.

Disappointed with the 'gradual approach' to curb inflation, which had been tried without success for over a decade, the government resorted to the so-called 'heterodox shock' of 28 February 1986—also known as the Cruzado Plan. Its major features were:

1 The cruzado (Cz$) was substituted for the cruzeiro (Cr$) at the rate of Cr$1,000 to Cz$1.

2 Non-indexed future payments in cruzeiros were discounted at 14.36 per cent a month when converted into cruzados.

3 Most indexation mechanisms were abolished or sharply reduced in their coverage and frequency.

4 Wages and salaries were converted into cruzados by their average pur-chasing power in the previous six months and their automatic indexation was limited to 60 per cent of the inflation rate in the annual negotiations, together with a trigger mechanism imposing automatic readjustments only if the inflation rate exceeded 20 per cent after the 'shock'.

5 A price freeze went into effect.

In the first few months the measures gained strong support from the popu-lation, which was an important force behind their initial success. In March 1986, the nation-wide cost of living index showed a negative rate of 0.11 per cent.

However, the policy was subject to considerable strains, including continued monetary expansion and fiscal deficit as well as pressure from unions for wage increases. The government began to give way to wage demands, and to relax the price freeze, from November 1986. Indexation was partially reintroduced. In 1987 inflation began to accelerate towards its pre-plan level. The Cruzado Plan thus offered a temporary respite, but turned out to be unsustainable in the prevailing environment.

Government policy-makers, economists, and businessmen are also concerned with the very substantial transfers abroad, particularly for interest payments, which are reducing resources available for resuming badly needed investments. A temporary suspension of interest payments was introduced in April 1987.

Data on the proportion of GDP absorbed by income payments to foreign factors and on consumption and investment are presented in Table 2.2. Net factor income sent abroad has increased substantially, both in absolute terms and as a share of GNP. As a result the difference between GDP and GNP has increased. Total consumption decreased less sharply than either GDP or GNP. Savings and investment have been sacrificed, as the figures for gross fixed capital formation reveal. The drop in investment was then greater than the decrease in the other economic aggregates, as is evident from the data on the ratio between GCF and GNP (Table 2.2). In per capita terms, the reduction of these aggretates is more dramatic. The fall in gross capital formation is particularly sharp because of the interruption in the flow of foreign savings.

The improvement in the growth rate of the Brazilian economy from 1984 was to a large extent based on increased utilization of existing productive capacity. As its full utilization is approached, the need for resuming a higher investment ratio becomes evident.

This is, then, a major obstacle that must be passed if the spurt in the growth rate is not to be interrupted. The task would be much less difficult if the outflow of interest payments on the external debt were to be curtailed by partial capitalization of these payments and/or obtaining new loans. The recent fall in the price of oil and international interest rates is, of course, of help for alleviating the external constraint on economic growth. However, it is not enough to allow the attainment of the high rates of growth required by the Brazilian economy, given the increased population and the enormous social problems that remain to be tackled.

1   Social impact and government social policies

(a)   The social impact of economic adjustment: an overview   The labour market was seriously affected by the adjustment process of 1981. In view of the peculiar characteristics of the Brazilian economy, where the modern sector coexists with traditional forms of production organization, the effects of adjustment must be measured not only in terms of open unemployment but also in the growth of the non-organized or informal sector activities which absorb those who, while not finding employment in the modern sectors, cannot remain openly unemployed.

Table 2.3 shows a worsening in open unemployment for the six major metropolitan areas of the country throughout the period 1981–84. The situation was more serious in 1981 and 1983, the years in which the recession was stronger. In 1982, the picture was mixed, while in 1984, the worsening of unemployment was minimal in the first four regions, the most important in terms of labour absorption, possibly because of the improvement in production levels which began in early 1984. Unemployment started falling unambiguously only in 1985.

Employment in the non-organized activities, to a great extent, reflects the expansion of underemployment: estimates made by the Ministry of Labour for the period 1981–83 reveal that out of an increase of 2.4 million units in the urban labour force, 1.8 million were in the non-organized labour market (Ministerio de Trabalho 1984, p. 66, Table 6). The expansion in the urban informal market, which was substantial, worked as a buffer mechanism in mediating impact of the crisis on the population.

Another buffering mechanism adopted by households during crisis is

TABLE 2.2 *GDP, net income to foreign factors (NIFF), GNP, consumption, gross capital formation (GCF), and population, 1980–1984*

	GDP		NIFF		GNP		Consumption[a]		GCF	
	Cr$m	Index	Cr$m	Index	Cr$m	Index	Cr$m	Index	Cr$m	Index
1980	445,520.7	100.0	13,683.3	100.0	431,837.4	100.0	357,999.1	100.0	96,940.5	100.0
1981	438,585.3	98.4	17,374.5	127.0	421,210.8	97.5	347,068.9	96.9	93,107.7	96.1
1982	442,661.3	99.4	22,565.5	164.9	420,095.8	97.3	351,522.3	98.2	94,059.8	97.0
1983	428,657.2	96.2	24,378.7	178.2	404,278.5	93.6	345,811.3	96.6	72,758.5	75.1
1984	447,955.1	100.5	n.a.		n.a.		n.a.		n.a.	

Year	NIFF/GNP (%)	GCF/GNP (%)	Population (000)	Per capita indices (1980 = 100)			
				GDP	GNP	Consumption[a]	GCF
1980	3.1	23.2	119,056	100.0	100.0	100.0	100.0
1981	4.0	22.1	122,020	96.1	95.2	94.6	93.7
1982	5.1	22.4	125,059	94.6	92.6	93.5	92.4
1983	5.7	18.0	128,173	89.4	87.0	89.7	69.7
1984	n.a.	n.a.	131,365	91.1	n.a.	n.a.	n.a.

Source: National accounts, Getulio Vargas Foundation.
Note: Cr$ million at 1970 prices   Index: 1980 = 100.
[a] Includes changes in inventories

TABLE 2.3 *Rates of unemployment in the six major metropolitan areas, 1980–1986* (*percentages*)

	São Paulo	Rio de Janeiro	Belo Horizonte	Porto Alegre	Salvador	Recife	Average
1980a	5.7	7.5	7.6	4.5	7.1	6.8	n.a.
1981a	7.2	8.6	8.7	5.7	8.5	8.5	
1981b	7.4	8.3	9.9	5.9	8.7	8.3	n.a.
1982b	8.3	9.3	8.9	6.3	8.4	9.1	
1982c	5.2	5.6	6.3	4.9	5.6	7.0	5.8
1983e	6.8	6.2	7.5	7.2	5.7	8.1	6.8
1983d	6.8	6.2	7.5	6.9	5.6	7.9	6.7
1984d	6.8	6.8	7.5	7.7	8.2	8.5	7.1
1984d	6.8	6.8	7.5	7.7	8.2	8.5	7.1
1985d	5.0	4.6	5.7	5.4	6.0	7.2	5.2
1985b	6.0	6.0	5.8	7.5	7.8	6.9	6.3
1986b	4.2	4.0	4.9	4.7	4.8	4.9	4.3

Source: IBGE.
Note:
a Annual averages for Rio and São Paulo, Apr.–Dec. averages for Belo Horizonte and Porto Alegre, and June–Dec. averages for Salvador and Recife.
b First-quarter averages, c Apr.–Dec. averages.
d Annual averages.

revealed by the results of a survey recently undertaken in the city of Campinas (1984 population 800,000), examining changes in household budgets from 1982 to 1984. It showed that families were following advice and belt-tightening during the crisis. Price rather than brand names gained growing importance and sometimes became predominant in consumers' choices; the consumption of imported beverages fell throughout the period, cheaper types of transportation were utilized, the use of own car decreased; purchases of clothing were not made so often, and credit applications were more frequent; the use of free public health services increased rapidly; and finally, visits to beauty shops became less frequent (Economistas de São Paulo 1985).

Together with the increase in the average propensity to consume and the search for employment opportunities in the non-organized sector of the economy, this adjustment of household budgets was a buffer mechanism for reducing the effects of the crisis. These mechanisms are likely to have reduced or delayed some of the more serious consequences of the adjustment process.

The crisis was accompanied by negative changes in mean income and income distribution from 1979 to 1984 (Table 2.4). There was an overall deterioration of mean income, and income loss for most income groups for the

TABLE 2.4   *Changes in average real personal income by percentile group, 1979–1984*
(*percentages*)

	1979–81	1981–83	1983–84
Lowest decile	0.65	−4.55	− 4.27
2nd decile	−2.31	−8.61	−13.63
3rd decile	−1.53	−7.86	− 3.59
4th decile	1.55	−9.99	− 3.20
5th decile	0.47	−8.18	4.09
6th decile	1.36	−9.04	− 6.97
7th decile	1.92	−7.50	0.54
8th decile	0.51	−6.17	0.74
9th decile	−0.70	−3.86	− 1.93
Highest decile	−3.19	−3.63	− 2.29
Top 5%	−3.73	−3.70	− 2.76
Top 1%	−5.84	−1.96	− 4.88
OVERALL MEAN	−1.34	−5.21	− 1.33

Source: Federal Government Census Bureau.
Note: Nominal values deflated by the National Consumer Price Index.

TABLE 2.5   *Personal income distribution, 1979–1984 (percentages)*

	1979a		1981b		1983b		1984b	
	By decile	Cumulative	By decile	Cumulative	By decile	Cumulative	By decile	Cumulative
Lowest decile	0.9	0.9	1.0	1.0	1.0	1.0	1.0	1.0
2nd decile	1.9	2.8	1.9	2.9	1.8	2.8	2.0	3.0
3rd decile	2.9	5.7	2.9	5.8	2.7	5.5	2.6	5.6
4th decile	3.7	9.4	3.9	9.7	3.5	9.0	3.6	9.2
5th decile	4.3	13.7	4.5	14.2	4.2	13.2	4.4	13.6
6th decile	5.6	19.3	5.9	20.1	5.4	18.6	5.2	18.8
7th decile	7.4	26.7	7.8	27.9	7.5	26.1	7.6	26.4
8th decile	10.1	36.8	10.5	38.4	10.3	36.4	10.5	36.9
9th decile	15.9	52.7	16.1	54.5	16.5	52.9	16.5	53.4
Highest	47.3	100.0	45.5	100.0	47.1	100.0	46.6	100.0
Top 5%	34.4	—	32.7	—	33.8	—	33.3	—
Top 1%	14.2	—	13.0	—	13.9	—	13.4	—
Gini coefficientc								
Lower limit	0.578		0.565		0.584		0.576	
Upper limit	0.589		0.576		0.595		0.533	

Source: Federal government Census Bureau, *National Household Surveys.*
a Does not include rural population of northern region and states of Mato Grosso do Sul, Mato Grosso and Goias.
b Does not include rural population of northern region.
c In 1984 the Gina coefficient was measured by taking 8 income groups.
  In 1979, 1981, and 1983 11 groups were used.

period as a whole. In general, the pattern of changes over time of the mean income of the various groups was irregular—except in the period 1981–83 when the recession deepened, at which time the losses suffered by the poorer groups were larger than those faced by richer groups. This resulted in an increase in income concentration, as shown by the values of the Gini coefficients in Table 2.5. This worsening of the income distribution was largely the result of the higher incidence of income losses and growing unemployment and under-employment among poorer groups.

Available evidence shows that the production of basic food staples was stagnant or decreasing in the years 1975–85, while the production of other agricultural products for export was increasing, reflecting misguided priorities for agriculture, with an undesirable social impact.

Table 2.6 shows that the production of food for domestic consumption fell, while exportables and sugar cane increased. The last item has been singled out because its expansion is linked to the increase in production of alcohol as an oil substitute. This expansion took place in fertile lands previously used for the production of food staples. Credit and price incentives, and agricultural research by government institutes, tended to be biased in favour of exportables and crops that lend themselves to industrial exploitation.

It is clear from Table 2.7 that on average the price of food increased over 1981–85 more rapidly than other prices and that this occurred both at the wholesale and retail levels. Since food expenditure absorbs a larger share of the budget of poor families than of the rich, the effect is clearly regressive.

2   Federal government social policies in response to the crisis

The wage policy had particularly important social implications. A liberal wage policy had been adopted late in 1979 (see Macedo 1983), but that approach was modified in the wake of the agreements with the IMF and the international banks in early 1983. The new policy was more restrictive, and together with the changes in labour market conditions noted above, this caused a continuous reduction in real wages until the second part of 1985. Following the economic recovery and increased non-compliance with the restrictive wage policy, wage adjustments began to be more freely negotiated between unions and businessmen.

In developed economies, the effects of falls in employment following an economic crisis are partially offset by payments to the unemployed. In contrast, an unemployment insurance programme was only established by the Brazilian government in 1986 as part of the same policy package that introduced the monetary reform. This programme gave every worker fired from the organized sector of the economy the right to an indemnity proportional to the duration of employment. Nevertheless, since labour turnover is very high, laid-off workers generally receive a very low indemnity. In other words, this system functions as an unemployment insurance only for limited periods of time, and

T ABLE 2.6 *Agricultural products: indices of per capita production, 1977–1984 (1977 = 100)*

	Exportables	Sugar cane	Food staples					
			total	Rice	Beans	Corn	Cassava	Potatoes
1978	88.0	105.1	86.0	78.9	93.4	68.8	95.2	110.9
1979	94.0	110.5	87.3	80.4	90.9/	80.6	91.7	108.2
1980	112.8	115.6	90.8	100.9	79.9	98.3	84.0	95.0
1981	110.6	118.3	90.2	83.0	92.7	99.6	85.9	91.6
1982	104.2	137.9	96.5	96.1	112.5	100.8	82.4	101.0
1983	107.2	156.4	73.6	74.7	60.0	84.5	72.1	83.2
1984	113.3	174.8	84.9	84.8	98.4	93.7	67.6	96.8

Source: Compiled from data obtained from the Federal Government Census Bureau by Dr Fernando Homem de Mello.
Note: Indices of per capita production are Laspeyres indices at 1977 prices. Population growth is assumed at 2.5% a year from 1977 to 1980 and 2.3% from 1980 to 1984. Exportables are cotton, peanuts, tobacco, soybeans, oranges, and cocoa.

T ABLE 2.7 *Percentage change in various price indices, 1981–1985*

	1981	1982	1983	1984	1985	1980–85
General price index	120.6	91.3	117.4	228.9	231.7	9,821
Wholesale price index	128.7	90.4	119.0	250.9	233.4	11,063
Food (staples)	138.3	82.1	138.8	310.9	196.2	13,416
Agricultural products	129.1	71.8	138.6	349.5	184.7	12,512
Food (manufactured)	110.8	95.0	138.6	223.6	263.1	11,927
Cost of living, Rio	105.0	94.8	118.3	192.1	220.0	8,051
Food	120.0	84.8	133.3	228.6	219.1	9,853
Cost of living, São Paulo	99.1	85.6	114.9	175.1	188.9	6,211
Food	102.8	75.4	128.9	215.4	170.7	6,852

Source: Conjuntura Economica and Fundacao Instituto de Pesquisas Economicas
Note: Annual rates except for the final column; years end in April.

on the whole does not provide the workers with a level of support comparable with that in other countries (see Macedo and Chahad 1985).

During the crisis, an unemployment insurance scheme was often proposed. The government reacted strongly against the idea, because of lack of resources and preference for an 'employment policy', but no progress was made in developing the latter.

On the whole, the federal government only exceptionally did something concrete during the crisis to alleviate the social impact of the recession. These exceptions essentially consisted of three cases briefly presented below. The first was the creation of FINSOCIAL (Fund for Social Investment), in May 1982. Following the tradition of Brazil's tax system, this fund is mostly provided by an indirect tax of 0.5 per cent on sales, together with a surcharge of 5 per cent on corporate income tax. Like most other indirect taxes, that feeding FINSOCIAL is likely to be regressive. The fund is designed for programmes in the areas of food and nutrition, housing for the poor, health, education, and support to small farming. Within these broad categories, the government can spend it as it wishes or even avoid expenses, keeping the money as a liquid asset in an attempt to curb monetary expansion. In the first year of the programme (1982), a total of approximately $300 million was collected but not immediately spent. In 1984 the funds came to almost $1 billion, of which the government allocated only $500 million, retaining the rest in its cash flow (National Bank of Economic and Social Development (BNDES) 1985, p. 26). Of the amount allocated in 1984, 41 per cent went to small farmers, 29 per cent to food and nutrition, 13 per cent to health, and 3 per cent to education. No analysis of the impact of these expenditures has yet been made, though the size of the overall expenditure appears modest in a country with a GNP of roughly $200 billion, while part of the money allocated substituted for other funds which were reduced by the recession or by budget cuts.

The second measure was a subsidy given for mortgage payments on home acquisitions made in accordance with the National Housing Plan administered by the federal government. The monthly instalments of these mortgages are indexed to inflation, but because of wages lagging behind inflation and widespread unemployment, many families found themselves unable to pay their debts. Under pressure to solve the problem, the government resorted to subsidies, taking the form of a reduction in the rate of indexation and an explicit discount during 1984.

A basic problem with these subsidies is that they are given to all mortgage debtors without specific provisions for low-income workers. Apartments and homes bought for weekend use and vacations also receive subsidies. In addition, the subsidy was not given to those who had acquired their homes without using the official system. Since the subsidy is a fixed percentage of monthly installments, it is regressive in its distributive impact. Moreover, since it is given only to a specific group, it also fails the horizontal equity test.

A third measure with an alleged social content has been the introduction of rent control for residential contracts. It was limited to the rate of indexation of rental agreements already signed, this limit being 80 per cent of the rate of inflation occurring between two successive adjustments of the rental price. The length of time between these adjustments cannot be less than six months. Preliminary evidence shows that the scheme backfired, at least in part. Home owners and builders were discouraged from offering houses for rent; moreover, since this rent control applies only to property already rented and not to the initial price of a new contract, it has induced landlords to seek a rapid turnover of tenants in order to charge higher prices. Recent reports in the press indicate that rent control has reduced the supply, and that in some cities rental prices are rising well above inflation.

The measures taken were not part of an integrated and well-designed plan for alleviating the impact of the crisis. In general, they were taken under pressure of events and of specific interest groups, such as tenants and home buyers. As such they are open to criticism in terms of their administration, scope, efficacy, and distributive impact. On the whole, evaluation of them is negative, not in the sense that they should not have been taken but that more attention should have been paid to their distributional implications: far greater emphasis was placed on the achievement of macro-economic goals than on the social impact of adjustment policies. When the government reacted to the pressure of the events, the response was ill-suited to a genuine concern for the impact on the poor and their families.

3 Responses at the state and local levels

It is at the state and city levels of government that the major concern for the plight of those affected by the crisis are found. In part, this is because these two levels of government develop their activities closer to the communities where the effects are felt. Moreover, for the first time since 1966, in 1982, the Governor of the State of São Paulo was elected by direct vote and chose as Mayor of São Paulo a politician who had also shown responsiveness to the community needs.

Both the state and the city of São Paulo adopted various measures to mitigate the negative impact of the crisis. However, state and local governments in Brazil faced a chronic scarcity of resources which was made much worse by the crisis. Although they tried to do something, the scope of their action was limited in comparison with the needs created by the crisis. Among the initiatives taken by the state, those for reducing the cost of food deserve particular mention. They include:

1. *Incentives to vegetable gardening.* This programme seeks to use land available in public and private institutions to grow vegetables for collective consumption. It is estimated that 135 gardens have been established, benefiting 8,000 people. The programme also provides technical assistance to schools, public and private institutions, and community organizations which want to develop their own projects. Moreover, the state government has signed agreements with 320 cities and towns for the provision of seeds for local projects.

2. *Varejoes ('large retail' sales).* The *varejoes* or wholesale markets of vegetables, fruits, eggs, poultry, fish amd meat sell directly to the public on selected days of the week at prices close to wholesale. This successful programme started in 1982 at the São Paulo central wholesale market. Due to increased demand, the government established 24 other *varejoes* in the same area, and 16 in the interior of the state. Government estimates indicate that the prices in the *varejoes* are as much as 40 per cent lower than in street markets and supermarkets, and that the programme reaches 10 per cent of the population in the areas where they have been established. While being located closer to lower middle class

areas, the *varejoes* do not necessarily reach the poorest who live in shanty towns and slums scattered all over the urban area.

3. *Sacoloes* ('*large bags*'). Large bag (supermarket size) of fruits and vegetables are sold at a single price close to the wholesale price. The government, in collaboration with cities and towns, also organizes *sacoloes* schemes in poor communities, by helping them to buy produce at wholesale prices and to resell it in *sacaloes*.

4. *Comboio de alimentos* ('*food convoys*'). In this system a community organizes the purchase of around 12 basic household needs at wholesale prices and brings them for sale in their neighbourhood. The government helps in the organization. Sometimes private businessmen participate in the scheme, but their mark-up is subject to control. In mid-1985, the monthly convoys operating in the Greater São Paulo area and in the interior of the state reached, respectively, an estimated 168,000 and 250,000 people.

5. *Central de alimentos* ('*Food Network*'). This scheme, similar to the previous one, is especially targeted at low-income families. Groups of around 20 families are organized to buy a basic list of products—rice, beans, soybean oil, wheat flour, cassava, potatoes, onions, garlic, eggs, and pasta. Each group presents a monthly order to the Food network office, stating the quantities desired. The Food Network buys the products at wholesale prices and resells them to the families without a mark-up. It is estimated that this saves 30 per cent of usual retail prices. This project began in May 1984 and in mid-1985 it reached approximately 500 groups of families.

6. *Soup kitchens.* This programme, targeted at poor families with an income lower than two minimum wages per month (roughly $100), seeks to provide one meal of soup daily per person. The soup is prepared and distributed by the women of the poor communities, while ingredients and kitchen equipment are provided free of charge by the government. In mid-1985 there were 29 soup kitchens in the Greater São Paulo area, providing 40,000 bowls of soup a day. The target is to provide 500,000 bowls of soup daily.

IV What the indicators of the impact on children show

This section assesses the effects of the crisis on child welfare, assessing outcome, process, behaviour, and input indicators separately.

1 *Outcome indicators*

(a) Infant mortality rates The infant mortality rate (IMR) is defined as the yearly number of deaths of children younger than one year per 1,000 live births. For the purpose of analysis, data for the state as a whole, the capital, and the interior of the state are considered separately. The seasonally adjusted IMR from 1980 to 1984 illustrated in Fig. 2.1 shows a declining trend until

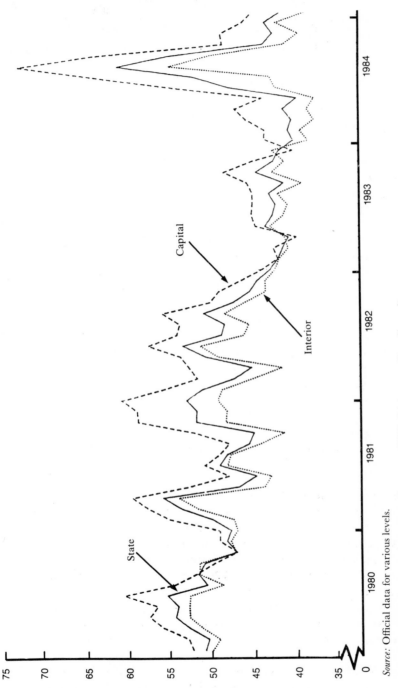

Source: Official data for various levels.

Fig. 2.1. São Paulo: infant mortality rates, 1980–84 (seasonally adjusted)

the beginning of 1984, when it increases sharply, ultimately decreasing but remaining higher than the lowest points reached in 1983.

The increase in IMR resulted mainly from an outbreak of measles in mid-1984. Two reasons are believed to explain this increase, but it is not possible to distinguish which was the most important: on the one hand there was a delay in the annual immunization against measles (due to administrative problems rather than to a shortage of resources); but there are those who claim, among them the State's secretary of health (*Gaseta Mercantil*, 1 Feb. 1985), that the outbreak would not have been so serious, nor would its impact on mortality have been so evident, were it not for the fact that the children were physically weak as a consequence of the economic difficulties faced by their families during the crisis.

After falling from 1980 to 1983, the proportion of infant deaths due to infectious and parasitic diseases clearly increased in 1984, thus confirming that the outbreak of measles played an important role in the increase of IMR in 1984. Respiratory diseases also made an important contribution to the increase in IMR in 1984, and the percentage of infant deaths related to malnutrition has increased persistently since 1982.

One can therefore conclude that even if the outbreak of measles were linked to the delay of vaccination caused by administrative problems, there were increases in other diseases affecting IMR which cannot be explained by problems of this nature. The IMR data also reflects weakened health conditions, malnutrition, and other difficulties faced by the infants and their families because of the economic decline. This view is supported by studies showing that, after several years of decline, IMR for Brazil as a whole increased between 1982 and 1984 from 65 to 73 per 1,000. Such studies point to the sharp decline in wages and earnings, particularly among low-income families, as a main determinant of this change in trend (Becker and Lechtig 1986).

(b) Low birth weight Tables 2.8 and 2.9 present data on low birth weights (LBW). In the case of data suppled by hospitals (Table 2.8), the indicator shows deterioration from 1980 to 1982 in the São Paulo Maternity and from 1980 to 1983 in the São Paulo Hospital. The latter shows a minor improvement in 1984, but the rate observed then is still close to the 1983 rate and well above those of the previous years. The same deterioration is shown until 1983 in Table 2.9, which has a wider coverage. The data on LBW indicate a deteriorating situation, and are consistent with the hypothesis that the increasing economic difficulties faced by families has had harmful effects on their children.

(c) Morbidity: the FAISA data FAISA (Foundation for the Assistance of the Children of São Paulo) is an institution supported by public funds which gives medical assistance to children in the city of Santo André (1981 population

TABLE 2.8   *City of São Paulo: low birth weight data from two hospitals, 1980–1984*

	1980	1981	1982	1983	1984
São Paulo Hospital	14.5	15.0	15.4	16.3	16.1
São Paulo Maternity	14.8	16.1	15.4	n.a.	n.a.

Sources: São Paulo Hospital and São Paulo Maternity.
Note: Low birth weight = less than 2.5 kilograms.

TABLE 2.9   *State, Capital, and Greater São Paulo Region: Percentage of children with low birth weight who died before first birthday, 1979–1983*

	State of São Paulo	Greater São Paulo	City of São Paulo
1979	17.1	19.3	19.7
1980	18.2	21.6	22.2
1981	19.9	22.0	23.1
1982	20.3	22.7	25.8
1983	21.6	25.5	26.4

Source: Foundation SEADE (Statistical Agency of the State of São Paulo).

550,000), one of the most important cities of the state, which was particularly affected by the crisis because its productive structure is industrial and urban. The FAISA figures attract special attention not only for this reason but also because they are disaggregated, up-to-date, and contain a large amount of information regarding the services of an institution which covers 85 per cent of local children. FAISA is highly regarded for its good management and for the quality of its service.

FAISA is supported mainly by the resources of Santo André's municipal budget. As Table 2.10 shows, the city's revenues were severely hit by the crisis, but it sought to avoid a fall in FAISA's resources by increasing the percentage of the revenues allocated to the institution. FAISA's budget, which includes funds from other sources, is also presented in Table 2.10: it began to drop only in 1983, although at a very sharp rate. The increase in the budget of 1985, following the economic recovery, shows how closely the budget follows the economic cycle.

Details as to how FAISA felt the impact of the crisis were obtained through interviews with some of the institution's officers. According to them, it was necessary to reduce some of the services offered since the costs increased while the revenues fell. In particular, it was necessary to cut staff, including in medical and paramedical areas, and 14 of the 21 health care centres began to operate at reduced hours due to fewer doctors and employees on the staff, although an attempt was made to increase the efficiency of the persons remaining on duty. It became difficult to maintain the quantity and quality of services

TABLE 2.10   *City of Santo André and FAISA: annual budgets, 1979–1985*

	Municipal revenue			FAISA budget	
	Amount[a]	Annual change (%)	% allocated to FAISA	Amount[a]	Annual change (%)
1979	2,031	—	n.a.	44.8	—
1980	1,712	− 15.7	1.6	52.7	17.5
1981	1,293	− 24.4	2.0	53.0	0.6
1982	1,146	− 11.4	2.5	57.8	9.1
1983	1,005	− 12.3	2.7	44.5	− 23.0
1984	995	− 0.3	2.4	39.4	− 11.4
1985	n.a.	—	n.a.	48.3	12.3

Sources: City of Santo André and FAISA.
[a] 1979 Cr$million (figures deflated by General Price Index).

rendered to the children and their mothers. The reduction of attendance hours at the health care centres caused long waiting lines, making attendance more difficult and discouraging mothers from bringing their children for routine and preventive examinations, with negative effects on their health. According to FAISA officers, the condition of children arriving at FAISA was deteriorating.

The data collected from FAISA confirms that the situation worsened as a result of the combined effects of the difficulties encountered in the functioning of the health care centres and of the aggravation of household conditions. For the period 1981–84, the data show a 24 per cent increase in the number of children attending emergency services and a 12 per cent increase in children treated for the same reasons at FAISA's hospital, while at the same time there was a reduction in total numbers attending the health care centres (from 8,612 monthly cases in 1980 to 7,630 in 1984).

To emphasize the importance of this finding, additional information for 1980–84, taken from FAISA's health care centres only, show that the proportion of appointments for sick children increased relative to that for routine examinations. This finding again reflects a worsening picture.

There was an increase in the incidence of measles in 1984 following the outbreak which occurred in that year, as discussed earlier. There was also a steady decrease in the percentage of cases of gastro-enterocolitis. New methods of preventing this disease have been put into practice by FAISA, including the dissemination of information to families. At the same time, cases of anaemia increased, possibly another indication of the children's worsening health and nutritional conditions.

Figures concerning the economic conditions of families who registered their children at the health care centres are presented in Table 2.11. These data confirm that family conditions became more severe during the crisis, with the

TABLE 2.11 *City of Santo André, FAISA health centres: evaluation of economic conditions of families registering children at the centres, 1980–1985 (monthly averages)*

	1980	1981	1982	1983	1984	1985
Cases of income shortage	164	188	172	143	157	110
Cases of income surplus	55	44	50	31	26	25
Ratio	0.34	0.24	0.26	0.22	0.16	0.23

Source: Faisa.
Note: Shortage and surplus are defined in comparison to a standard family budget, adjusted for family size.

proportion of families with insufficient incomes rising steadily throughout the period 1981–84.

Thus far the analysis has focused on the period 1981–84. The 1985 data provide important indications of the cyclical nature of some of the indicators presented. In 1985, there was a fall in the number of out-patients, hospital diagnoses, and anaemia rates, and an improvement in the economic conditions of the families and in the FAISA budget.

These signs of a cyclical association between health and economic conditions suggest the need for continued analysis of this association and for improvement of short-run time-series indicators covering both the availability of services and the economic conditions of the families, which strongly influence the extent and nature of their use of health facilities. As far as policy is concerned, these signs are also indictive of the importance of avoiding delays when taking corrective action, because the time-lags between causes and effects are apparently very short.

2 Process indicators

(a) School attendance Figures for children's drop out rates and lack of achievement are presented in Table 2.12. These rates refer to the state's school system up to the eighth grade. They cover the Greater São Paulo area, the interior, and the state as a whole. In all three cases, the total rate of failure continues to show a persistent deterioration, which comes mainly from a sharp increase in the drop-out rates. The increase in the lack of achievement rates is less conspicuous but it is also widespread, with only rare exceptions. These results are also consistent with what would be expected from the crisis. They reflect demand-side as much as supply-side conditions. On the demand side, the economic difficulties led to lower income and changes in employment, which caused movements to other residential areas. This affects children's performance at school. On the other hand, conditions on the supply side have also worsened. The public education system offers an education which is

TABLE 2.12 *Greater São Paulo, Interior, and State of São Paulo: first-grade schools supported by the state, rates of failure by dropping out, and lack of achievement, 1981–1983*

Grade	Drop-out rate						Lack of achievement rate					
	1978	1979	1980	1981	1982	1983	1978	1979	1980	1981	1982	1983
Greater São Paulo												
1st	4.7	4.6	5.2	5.5	8.9	13.4	33.3	34.1	35.1	35.2	31.7	27.8
2nd	3.5	3.3	3.6	3.5	6.6	9.2	21.1	21.7	21.8	22.3	21.0	18.6
3rd	3.5	3.4	3.7	3.4	6.7	7.8	16.7	16.9	16.0	18.3	17.0	17.2
4th	3.3	3.4	3.6	3.2	6.3	6.7	9.0	9.9	9.0	11.6	11.8	13.4
5th	11.4	11.4	11.9	11.1	16.0	17.1	20.8	22.0	22.4	29.6	27.6	26.3
6th	11.2	11.6	11.5	10.9	15.0	16.3	19.2	18.3	17.9	26.2	23.9	24.9
7th	10.7	11.7	11.5	10.4	15.2	16.4	17.0	15.3	14.3	22.6	19.6	19.3
8th	7.5	8.0	8.5	7.8	11.2	12.3	9.1	9.4	8.1	14.9	11.5	9.6
Interior of São Paulo												
1st	5.8	6.5	7.1	6.9	11.7	13.2	28.6	29.8	30.6	32.3	31.2	30.1
2nd	3.9	4.1	4.3	4.1	7.4	8.1	19.3	18.7	19.4	21.1	20.9	20.9
3rd	3.9	4.0	4.4	3.9	6.4	7.1	14.0	14.1	13.8	16.3	15.9	15.5
4th	3.7	4.0	4.5	3.7	7.2	7.8	8.4	8.9	8.0	11.1	11.1	12.3
5th	12.3	13.2	13.8	13.6	18.9	20.2	20.5	21.2	21.5	28.8	27.2	28.0
6th	10.4	11.5	11.3	11.6	16.6	17.5	19.9	17.8	17.9	26.0	23.7	24.6
7th	9.6	11.0	11.2	10.8	15.8	16.8	16.4	15.6	14.7	22.1	20.0	20.2
8th	7.2	8.2	8.2	8.2	12.4	12.6	9.8	8.9	8.7	14.9	12.5	12.1
State of São Paulo												
1st	5.3	5.6	6.2	6.2	10.1	13.3	30.8	31.9	32.8	33.7	31.5	28.9
2nd	3.7	3.7	4.0	3.8	7.0	8.6	20.2	20.2	20.5	21.7	20.9	19.8
3rd	3.7	3.7	4.1	3.7	7.0	7.4	15.3	15.4	14.8	17.2	16.6	16.3
4th	3.5	3.7	4.1	3.5	6.7	7.2	8.7	9.4	8.4	11.3	11.5	12.9
5th	11.9	12.4	13.0	12.4	17.4	18.6	20.6	21.7	21.3	29.2	27.4	27.2
6th	10.8	11.6	11.4	11.3	15.7	16.9	19.5	18.0	17.9	26.1	23.8	24.7
7th	10.1	11.3	11.3	10.6	15.5	16.6	16.7	15.5	14.5	22.4	19.7	19.7
8th	7.4	8.1	8.3	8.0	11.7	12.4	9.4	9.1	8.5	14.9	11.9	10.9

Source: Compiled from raw data from the São Paulo, Department of Education.
Note: Rates are percentages of enrolment.

considered to be in general inferior to that offered by the private system. The public system suffers from many problems, excessive size being one of them, along with a poorly paid administration, teachers and administration officers lacking adequate training and motivation, and a shortage of resources for school supplies. These supply-side problems are associated with the economic crisis since some of them are caused by loss of revenue and lack of resources in the state's budget.

(b) immunization coverage This is an area where significant improvements have been accomplished since the late 1970s. These improvements played an important role in the declining trend of infant and child mortality rates. Data on coverage of immunization in the State of São Paulo are presented in Table 2.13 for the period 1975–84. There is no evidence that the progress of the late 1970s was interrupted, although the events of 1984, related to the outbreak of measles, indicate that the coverage of immunization is a complex issue that cannot be evaluated only by the number of vaccines administered.

TABLE 2.13   *State of São Paulo: number of doses of various vaccines administered, 1975–1984*

	Sabin[a]	Measles	Diphtheria, pertussis tetanus	Diptheria toxoid	Smallpox	Tetanus	BCG[b]
1975	3,966,329	420,725	1,744,591	447,622	1,619,838	1,284,729	—
1976	4,296,003	738,114	1,773,290	679,206	1,220,738	802,242	907,234
1977	4,615,139	659,961	2,279,745	472,445	1,190,748	880,448	2,528,644
1978	4,739,294	727,446	2,444,167	364,642	1,106,931	782,128	1,919,888
1979	4,783,700	901,316	2,572,494	329,951	808,828	758,101	1,658,907
1980	13,228,018	1,530,257	2,951,394	418,750	189,685	770,391	1,502,943
1981	11,858,922	1,641,405	3,145,097	1,057,346	3,195	783,418	1,386,168
1982	11,502,374	1,578,520	3,191,532	303,705	n.a.	797,030	1,099,641
1983	12,226,365	1,475,724	3,259,396	284,304	n.a.	969,583	1,000,932
1984	11,520,654	1,610,966	3,214,210	253,949	n.a.	1,057,488	973,826

Source: Health Information Centre, State of São Paulo, Department of Health.
[a] Polio vaccine.
[b] Tuberculosis vaccine.

3   Behaviour indicators

FEBEM (the state's Foundation for the Welfare of Minors) receives children abandoned on the streets or given up by their parents because of lack of resources. FEBEM also takes into custody children involved in crimes and other violations. It provides services such as housing, education, and health care. Table 2.14 shows the number of children receiving assistance from FEBEM during 1979–85. The sharp rise from 1982 to 1984 can be associated with the economic crisis, as interviews with FEBEM office's revealed that the growth in admissions was due to an increase in demand. Consistently with the cyclical behaviour of the economy, the rate of growth declined in 1985. A distinctive characteristic of the figures in Table 2.14 is the sharp increase of the cases classified as violation of law since 1982. Child delinquency has been a subject of extensive press coverage, where it is considered one of the most important consequences of the economic crisis. Nevertheless, a large proportion of the violations committed by children remain unreported, since many victims do not take the trouble of going to the police to sign a complaint. Crime statistics provided by the police and by the Special Courts of Minors are consequently deficient. Perhaps the most distinctive feature of Table 2.14 is

TABLE 2.14   *Greater São Paulo: children received by FEBEM, 1979–1985*

	1979	1980	1981	1982	1983	1984	1985
Number assisted	26,851	31,384	29,503	28,433	30,487	37,353	38,394
Percentage of cases of:							
Abandonment	51.7	50.4	44.6	41.4	43.2 ⎫	66.9	61.3
Given up by parents	20.8	18.8	25.0	30.8	27.0 ⎭		
Violation of law	25.4	30.8	30.4	27.9	29.8	33.1	38.7

Source: FEBEM.

thus that it supports the hypothesis of increased child delinquency which other official stastics do not necessarily reveal. Since the school drop-out rates presented above can also be viewed as a behaviour indicator, taken together the data in tables 2.12 and 2.14 provide consistent evidence of the worsening of indicators of this type.

4   Input indicators

The data examined in this section concern the availability of services and government expenditures in sectors with a direct impact on children, such as education and health. Previous studies (as reviewed in Macedo 1984) have shown trends in living conditions (housing, water and sanitation services). Conditions in the city of São Paulo substantially improved in the 1970s, as a result of housing programmes organized by the Federal government and of the State's expenditures on water and sanitation services. Although it was not possible to obtain the same specific data for the 1980s, it is well known that these advances have been cut short. Families are coping with increased difficulties in paying for housing, while the government has further reduced investments in this area due to decline in revenue. House starts fell sharply, and investment expenditures were reduced at various levels of government.

The negative impact in this case falls on the expansion of the public services, including water and sanitation facilities, with the noticeable exception of the electricity sector which continued to expand.

The total government expenditure of the State of São Paulo and of its Department of Health and Education in the years 1980–84 is illustrated in Table 2.15. The drop in total expenditure is evident, especially in the case of capital expenditure of the Department of Education. The Department of Health was able to maintain its slice of the reduced total budget, and to recover the absolute value of its capital expenditures. It also faced better prospects in 1985 since the state obtained a loan of $55.5 million from the World Bank to improve the services provided in this area. In the Greater São Paulo area, the loan will be used to build five hospitals and to rehabilitate three others and to establish 99 new health posts in areas where there was the most serious gap between health service provision and population growth (interview with Dr Joao Yunes 1985). The municipal budget data for the period 1980–85 are presented in Table 2.16. It can be seen that until 1984 the share of the Health and Education departments increased so sharply that even with a falling total budget their expenditure actually increased in absolute values. However, when classified by function (lower half of Table 2.16), both shares and absolute expenditure on health and education fell.

It should be noted that the expenditures by departments largely reflect personnel expenditures. The fall observed in the state's case is mainly a result of a wage freeze to which the salaries of the state's public servants have long been subjected, particularly during the crisis. Sooner or later, this affects the quality of the services provided: the strikes of public servants common in the health and education areas during the crisis are an example. In the case of the city of São Paulo, rising expenditure was also due to an expansion of the educational services, particularly day care centres, kindergartens, and other pre-school facilities. But since the state is the most important provider of educational and health services to children, the expansion of the city budget was insufficient to cover needs.

It was not possible to obtain a consistent set of figures for social expenditures by the federal government. Moreover, in the State of São Paulo the federal government plays only a marginal role with respect to expenses in the area of education. As far as health expenditures are concerned, the major programme supported by the federal government is the health care programme, under the umbrella of the social security system, which also covers the State of São Paulo. Table 2.17 shows how this programme suffered cuts from 1981 to 1984. The fall was particularly severe in 1983, since in 1982 the social security tax was increased and the system was able to count on larger funds. Since part of the health care is provided through private hospitals, the reduced funds are causing some of them to refuse in-patients and/or to send them home before completing treatment. There are, however, no estimates of how these developments have affected the health care provided to the population.

TABLE 2.15   *State of São Paulo: total expenditures by the State Departments of Health and Education, 1980–1984 (1982 Cr$ billion)*

		Department of Education				Department of Health			
	Total state budget	Current	Capital	Total	% State budget	Current	Capital	Total	% State budget
1980	1,323.2	202.7	24.0	226.8	17.1	40.8	3.2	44.0	3.3
1981	1,283.3	199.3	15.3	214.7	16.7	42.7	3.5	46.3	3.6
1982	1,331.2	202.7	20.9	223.6	16.8	42.2	1.1	43.3	3.3
1983	1,118.8	165.4	9.5	174.9	15.6	36.0	2.4	38.4	3.4
1984	1,097.9	153.0	14.7	167.7	15.3	34.9	3.4	38.3	3.5

Source: State of São Paulo, Department of Finance.

TABLE 2.16   *City of São Paulo: government expenditures on health and education by department and function, 1980–1985*

		Education		Health	
	Total expenditure[a]	Amount[a]	Share (%)	Amount[a]	Share (%)
		By department			
1980	250.5	23.5	9.4	12.8	5.1
1981	244.9	24.1	9.8	15.1	6.1
1982	246.1	24.7	10.0	13.5	5.5
1983	216.6	22.6	10.4	13.7	6.3
1984	208.6	27.8	13.3	17.0	8.2
1985	241.7	31.4	13.0	17.8	7.4
		By function			
1980	250.5	32.4	12.9	25.5	10.2
1981	244.9	32.7	13.3	29.6	12.1
1982	246.1	33.9	13.8	27.6	11.2
1983	216.6	28.1	13.0	21.1	9.7
1984	208.6	23.4	11.2	13.2	6.3
1985	241.7	36.7	15.2	27.8	11.5

Source: City of São Paulo, Department of Finance.
Note: The education function figures includes expenses on culture, sports, and welfare and the health figures include expenses on sanitation, which are not the responsibility of the Education or Health Departments.
[a] In 1982 Cr$ billion (figures deflated by General Price Index).

V   Conclusions and policy implications

If one wants to understand an economic crisis beyond a simple analysis of the statistics of GDP or GNP, unemployment, inflation, and external balance, the human or social dimension must be brought into the picture. The evidence presented in this study shows that the effects of the crisis came with lags of

TOTAL 2.17   *Expenditures by the social security system and the share of health care,*
1980–1984

	Total real expenditures (1982 Cr$m)	Real expenditures on healthcare	
		(1982 Cr$m)	(%)
1980	2,800,713	766,091	27.3
1981	2,907,138	704,909	24.2
1982	3,102,981	772,678	24.9
1983	2,653,225	581,237	21.9
1984	2,702,536	570,618	21.1

Source: Social Security, Welfare, and Health Care System.

various sorts, as the individuals and families sought to adjust to the crisis. Buffer mechanisms emerged, such as the reduction in the propensity to save, the expansion of the non-organized economy, and the reallocation of family budgets.

As the crisis continued, however, these mechanisms became weaker. Under the pressures of events, the federal government responded with policies which were very limited in scope, ineffective and often misguided. As shown in Part III, the social effects of the crisis, which continued after the end of the recession, are more evident at the state and local level, where governments are less well-equipped both in terms of the small size of their budgets and their limited experience, to deal with the effects of the costs. Their response was also lagged and limited, but at least showed more concern for the plight of those affected by the crisis than did that of the federal government. In some cases, their attempts to preserve or increase expenditure in the social sectors were partially successful.

On balance, however, government policies—particularly those of a macro-economic nature—aggravated the social effects of the crisis, and have had a stronger impact than those improvised to mitigate this negative impact.

The macro-economic adjustment policies adopted at the federal level from 1981 to 1984 were implemented without any concern for their social impact. In addition, while the adjustment of the external accounts has been successful from the point of view of the IMF and foreign banks, the Brazilian economy is still suffering from the adjustment as enormous amounts of badly needed resources are being transferred abroad in the form of interest payments. If this transfer is not sharply reduced, the country's medium and long-term growth will be jeopardized.

It would be unrealistic to say that Brazil should seek ways to avoid any payment of interest on its foreign debt, but it is obvious that a substantial reduction is necessary and that the remaining transfer of resources abroad must be made keeping in mind the social cost of this continuing drain of resources. The amount of interest that Brazil paid abroad in 1985 is roughly equivalent to the entire budget of the federal social security, welfare, and medicare system, a comparison that gives an idea of the importance of the continuing cost of the debt.

Drawing on the lessons of the recent recession, it is important that the country re-examines its apparatus of social support so that the next recession will not find Brazil again ill prepared to cope with the impact of the crisis on the more vulnerable social groups in general, and on children in particular.

Since the new government took office early in 1985, there have been encouraging signs of concern for social problems, and some actions have already been taken. Some of these actions have been ill planned or mismanaged, like the Milk Programme which sought to distribute milk to needy families on the basis of 'milk stamps' but failed to a large extent because of insufficient milk supply. Others, such as the unemployment insurance programme established together with the Cruzado Plan, have restricted coverage, while the operating modalities and expected results are not yet clearly defined. It is still too early, however, to make a fair evaluation of these and other programmes, such as land distribution, because they are at their initial stages. It is well known how difficult it is to establish a new social programme in Brazil because of bureaucratic problems, lack of experience, and the size of the country.

In any case, this new concern with social problems will help in tackling problems such as those discussed in this study. The concrete lessons of this analysis would facilitate the formulation of such an approach:

1. Programmes for the provision of food or for reducing its cost such as food stamps and also those listed on pp. 41–42, should be extended. Moreover, in the light of the recent discouraging trends in the production of food crops and of the price of food in Brazil, food and agricultural policies should be directed at reversing these trends, given their serious impact on the budgets of the poor families.

2. Government social expenditures, particularly at the state and local levels, should be protected or increased in accordance with the emerging needs. In Brazil, this involves a redefinition of the allocation of tax resources among different levels of government, since the federal government takes the lion's share.

3. Given the difficulties of transferring resources within or between levels of government, international lending institutions should, particularly during periods of recession, give priority to loans directed to expand or complement social expenditures. The recent World Bank loan to the State of São Paulo for the expansion of the health centres network, as mentioned in Part IV, is illustrative of what can be done in this respect.

4. All policies directed at mitigating the impact of the crisis, whether focusing on the poor or specifically on the welfare of children, should be means-tested since many measures taken by the government have been in-

effective or have had harmful distributive effects because their clientele was not well defined.

5. There are many specific policies which have a bearing on the welfare of the children. Some areas emerge from the analysis of Part IV—among others, improved administration and coverage of immunization campaigns, support of organizations such as FAISA or FEBEM, improvements in the school system (including day care centres and nutrition programmes at the school level), and a concentrated attack on specific causes of mortality and morbidity.

If the government were to enlarge the scope of its action in this area, identifying key problems would not constitute an impediment. There is relevant experience in Brazil, and additional guidance can be provided by international agencies. What is still lacking is political will to consider the welfare of the children a priority and to redirect government actions and resources accordingly.

6. Concerned persons and institutions should undertake a strong effort to make public opinion and government authorities aware of the damaging effects of economic conditions on the welfare of the Brazilian children, whose standards are already low because of widespread poverty, particularly during recessionary periods.

The relation between economic conditions and the welfare of children should be monitored in a systematic way and the results of this monitoring activity should be given wide publicity in the hope of reaching those who have the political power, arousing their concern with the bad and deteriorating conditions and inducing them to act. Writing this chapter entailed assembling scattered data and organizing and analysing them. Although most of the sources contacted were willing to provide information, some did not have the necessary data readily accessible. Others could not provide updated information, the major reason apparently being that priority for this task was not established at higher levels of the hierarchy.

Efforts aimed at arousing the government's concern must be combined with proposals for policies with respect to children's welfare. These efforts, however, should not depend only on isolated initiatives. It is time for Brazilian institutions, with outside support, to organize this effort of monitoring and advocacy in a systematic fashion; to assemble the information in a way that is easy to understand; and to produce monthly or quarterly reports to be sent to public authorities, to the media, congressmen and other influential individuals and organizations.

References

Becker, R., and A. Lechtig (1986), *Brasil: Evolucâs da mortalidade infantil no periodo 1977–1984*. Brasilia; Centro de Documentacâo do Ministerio da Sañde.

Economistas de São Paulo (1985), 'Pesquisa de orcamentos familiares da classe media, na cidade de Campinas e mundancas recentes no Padroa de Vida'. Research report prepared by the economists of São Paulo and the State of São Paulo.

Macedo, R. (1983), 'Wage Indexation and Inflation: The Recent Brazilian Experience', in Dornbusch R., and M. Simonsen, eds., *Inflation, Debt, and Indexation*, pp. 133–59. Cambridge, Mass.: MIT Press.

— (1984), 'Brazilian Children and Economic Crisis: Evidence from the State of São Paulo', in Jolly, R., and G. A. Cornia, eds., *The Impact of the World Recession on Children*. Oxford: Pergamon Press.

Macedo, R., and J. P. Chahad (1985), *FGTS e a rotatividade*. São Paulo: Nobel.

Ministerio de Trabalho (1984), 'Brasil: Recomendações para a formulação de políticas de emprego e renda'. Mimeographed. Brasilia: Office of Employment and Wages.

National Bank of Economic and Social Development (1985), *BNDES Report 1984*, Rio de Janeiro: BNDES.

3

Social Policy, Poverty, and Vulnerable Groups: Children in Chile

Dagmar Raczynski

I Introduction

This study examines the impact of economic conditions and social policies on poor households, and especially on the age-group that is particularly vulnerable, i.e. children less than 14 years of age.

The period under examination is 1974–85, a period during which the Chilean economy and social structure experienced profound modifications. Over more than 12 years, a politically authoritarian and economically neo-liberal model has been implemented, representing a departure from development strategies that characterized the country from the 1930s until September 1973. Between 1930 and 1973 the socio-economic development of the country was defined by an import substitution industrial strategy with strong government support. Under this strategy the state played an increasingly important role in the social sphere—education, health, housing, and social security—benefiting middle- as well as low-income sectors. Poor households, particularly the urban ones, benefited through stable employment and public programmes in housing, health, and education. Living conditions improved, including education standards and the health situation. To differing extents, households had access to services and urban consumption, i.e. water, electricity, sewerage, gas, and durable goods. Some experienced upward social mobility.

During the first years of the 1970s the country faced severe economic dislocations as well as socio-political conflicts and contradictions which the system was unable to resolve. The military government that took power at the end of 1973 implemented a monetarist policy package which has been defined as 'the main case of modern application of monetarist orthodoxy due to its "purity", depth and coverage' (Ffrench-Davis 1983), and which led to a contraction of demand as well as an abrupt opening of the economy. A set of reforms were also introduced to increase privatization and reduce the role of the state. These reforms were accompanied by a severe weakening and increased control over popular organizations, particularly those of a unionist or political nature, as well as over other groups putting forward demands and pressuring the state.

From the beginning these policies involved great social costs which were born particularly heavily by the lower segments of the population. They lost their jobs, wages and incomes, organization and social participation, and much more. There have been some highly selective remedial policies to aid the extremely poor sectors, although they were frequently introduced after substantial delays. Some were only a weak remedy for major needs. Others did not reach the neediest. But others—those related to mother and child care and nutritional intervention for pregnant women and the under-6s—were on the whole successful.

This study is divided into five parts. Parts II and III examine the nature of the economic policies implemented in Chile in 1974–85, their effects on income distribution and on the material living conditions of poor households. Part IV looks in more detail into the social policies, government expenditure, and the main programmes directed towards poor households and children, as well as at the significant changes in child welfare which followed. Part IV is based on several in-depth studies of small samples of households in the Santiago metropolitan area during the years 1982–85. It describes the daily experiences of poor households regarding deteriorating economic conditions and social policies, and deals with the behaviour adopted in order to increase scarce resources to satisfy basic needs. The impact of the economic deterioration is also assessed in terms of household organization and social relationships. Finally, Part V attempts to draw some lessons from the Chilean case.

II   The Chilean economy: the neo-liberal model and some results

The performance of the Chilean economy over the 1974–85 period showed stagnation or even a downward trend. According to official figures GDP per capita in 1985 was only 1.8 per cent higher than in 1974, and 2.7 per cent lower than in 1970. Yearly figures show two periods of recession, first in 1975–76 and then in 1982–83. Between the recessions there was a recovery period characterized by high growth of GDP. The years 1984–85 have shown a slow and unstable recovery (Table 3.1). The stagnation of the economy between 1974 and 1985 was accompanied by a weakening of the productive base and a fall in domestic investment (which had been low historically). This caused a downward trend in industrial production and employment and (as will be shown in Part III) a deterioration in income distribution and in the standards of living of both urban and rural low-income groups.

Several factors contributed to this performance. On the one hand, there were external factors: the 1975 and 1981 recessions in the world economy, and increased international liquidity and foreign loans towards the end of the 1970s. On the other hand, there were internal factors: macro-economic dislocations and the socio-political crisis that Chile experienced in 1972/3 and the neo-liberal monetarist policy packages implemented by the military

TABLE 3.1 Growth, inflation, investment, foreign trade, and external debt, 1970–1985

	GDP Total		GDP From manufacturing		Inflation rate (%)	Gross fixed investment as % age of GDP	Exports (fob)	Imports (fob)	Trade balance	Balance of payment[a]	Total external debt
	Per capita 1977 $000	Annual rate of change (%)	Per capita 1977 $000	Annual rate of change (%)			($m at current prices)				
1970	30.31		7.48		36.1	20.2[a]	1,036	1,074	−38	108	—
1971	32.31	6.7	8.33	11.4	26.5	18.3	998	1,140	−142	−241	—
1972	31.42	−2.9	8.37	0.5	254.5	14.8	849	1,239	−390	−124	—
1973	29.18	−7.1	7.60	−9.2	606.1	14.7	1,309	1,288	21	−21	—
1974	28.98	−0.7	7.28	−4.2	369.2	17.4	2,151	1,794	357	−55	
1975	24.82	−14.4	5.34	−26.6	343.3	15.4	1,590	1,520	70	−344	5,453
1976	25.26	1.8	5.56	4.1	197.9	12.7	2,116	1,473	643	414	5,392
1977	27.27	8.0	5.93	6.6	84.2	13.3	2,185	2,151	34	113	5,763
1978	29.02	6.4	6.40	7.9	37.2	14.4	2,460	2,886	−426	712	7,153
1979	30.89	6.5	6.76	5.6	38.9	15.6	3,835	4,190	−355	1,047	8,790
1980	32.73	6.0	7.05	4.3	31.2	17.6	4,705	5,469	−764	1,244	11,331
1981	33.96	3.9	7.11	0.8	9.5	19.5	3,836	6,513	−2,677	67	15,700
1982	28.69	−15.5	5.52	−22.4	20.7	15.0	3,706	3,643	63	−1,165	17,263
1983	28.01	−2.4	5.60	1.4	23.1	12.9	3,827	2,818	1,009	−541	18,133
1984[b]	29.29	4.6	6.05	8.0	23.0	13.2	3,650	3,357	293	17	19,746
1985[b]	29.50	0.7	6.02	−0.5	26.4	14.8	3,722	2,963	759	−99	20,929

Source: Central Bank, Official National Accounts; Cortazar and Marshall (1980); Ffrench-Davis (1983).
[a] Average for the period 1960–70.
[b] Provisional.

government that took power in 1973 (see Foxley 1980, 1982; Ffrench-Davis 1983; Vergara 1981; Arellano and Cortázar 1982; Muñoz 1985).

The world recession of 1975 led to a substantial deterioration—about 40 per cent—in the country's terms of trade. This occurred at a time when an orthodox stabilization programme was being introduced domestically to deal with the two severe dislocations that prevailed in 1973—a high inflation rate and a large deficit in the balance of payments. Monetarist policies were adopted, aiming at contracting aggregate demand by reducing public expenditure and freezing wages, as well as at activating institutional reforms to liberalize trade, open the economy, and reduce the role of the state by transferring to the private sector many functions that were previously in the government domain. This programme had a strong negative impact on the economy which was accentuated by the world economic crisis of 1975: in that year, industrial production dropped 26.6 per cent; per capita product fell 14.4 per cent; the unemployment rate, including the population covered by the emergency employment programme (PEM), increased to 17.6 per cent; and real wages were less than 35 per cent those of 1970. Inflation fell, but remained above 300 per cent.

In 1977, at a time when the world economy was improving, the Chilean economy began a recovery which lasted until 1981. Between 1977 and 1981 'the Chilean economic model' crystallized. There was a sharp opening of the economy, tariffs went down to 10 per cent, and other restrictions on imports were eliminated. Capital markets were liberalized and public enterprises including nationalized banks and land holdings were sold to the private sector on favourable conditions. All this resulted in a strong concentration of wealth.

The foremost goal of the economic team until 1981 was the struggle against inflation, and the main tool selected for its regulation was the exchange rate. Inflation dropped, but other economic objectives, such as equilibrium in the foreign sector and domestic production, were sacrificed. Between 1977 and 1981, the economy showed high growth rates and decreasing yearly rates of inflation. In 1981, inflation was below 10 per cent and there was talk about the 'Chilean miracle'. However, the unemployment rate was 16 per cent, wage recovery was slow, and the investment rate was low and directed mainly to financial and real-estate markets, particularly in luxury buildings, and not to investments that would strengthen the productive structure. The investment which took place increased the private sector's indebtedness abroad and domestically.

The 'Chilean miracle' was based on the abundance of international resources and foreign loans. In 1979 a fixed exchange rate along with significant domestic inflation led to over valuation of the Chilean peso. That, together with the extreme reduction of tariffs, stimulated imports. In spite of an increase in exports, the deficit on the trade balance in 1981 was five times that of 1978. The excessive domestic expenditure of the private sector, which was stimulated by the unrestricted opening of the economy, led to an unmanageable external deficit. The international recession that began in 1981, associated with reductions in foreign credit and a large fall in the price of copper (which represented one-half of Chilean exports), deepened the problems. It was necessary, somehow, to adjust. The government then sponsored an automatic adjustment, similar to that of 1975, in order to keep inflation and the exchange rate under control. The negative consequences of this policy on unemployment rates and on the growth of productive sectors oriented to the domestic market were soon to appear. Domestic recession reached higher levels than in 1975–76. Per capita product dropped by 15.5 per cent in 1982 and 2.4 per cent in 1983. The unemployment rate increased to one-fifth of the labour force in 1982 and one-third in 1983. Wages fell slightly in 1982, but in 1985 they were still falling. Business failure was frequent and the delays in payment of domestic debt put the national banking system in a difficult situation. The latter was supported by the government in order to avoid panic. There were several attempts to gain control over the economy which represented partial departures from the original policy: greater protectionist measures regarding imports, successive devaluations of the peso and modification of the exchange policy, significant subsidies to businesses and to the private financial system, negotiations over foreign debt, etc. At the same time, however, there were additional attempts to privatize, including selling banks which had been taken into public ownership to avoid collapse and shares in some public enterprises.

In summary, GDP per capita in 1985 was lower not only than in 1981 but also than in 1974 and 1970. The country's productive base, particularly its industrial base, had been weakened. The burden of a heavy foreign debt hangs over the economic future of the country. Control over inflation (which was bordering 26 per cent in December 1985) and an increase in exports were positive signs within a generally negative economic situation.

III Effects on employment, incomes and household consumption

The aggregate indicators of real wages, pensions, and unemployment rates showed a substantial downward trend in 1975–76 (Table 3.2). Between 1977 and 1981 along with economic recovery there was a slow improvement in these indicators. However, in 1981 they were still at a level below that of 1970. Pensions and real wages were 18 per cent and 3 per cent lower, respectively, and unemployment was never below 16 per cent during the 1960s. The absence of jobs particularly affected poorer households. For example, in Greater Santiago, inhabited by more than one-third of the country's population, unemployment among blue-collar workers was double the rate among white-collar workers, and the layoff rate among heads of households of the lowest quintile was triple that for heads of households in a relatively better position. Moreover, low-income households typically have a lower number of income-earning members per household. Several surveys in low-income sectors of Greater

TABLE 3.2 *Unemployment, wages, average pension, and family allowance, 1970–1985*

			Real wages (1970 = 100)	Average pension[b] (1970) = 100)	Family allowance[c]	Real value of PEM + POJH subsidy[a] (1983 pesos)	
	Unemployment rates (%)					PEM	POJH[d]
	Open	With PEM + POJH[a]					
1970	5.9		100.0	100.0	100.0		
1971	5.2		..	..	..		
1972	4.1		..	..	..		
1973	4.8		..	..	..		
1974	9.1		65.0	51.3	104.8		
1975	15.6	17.6	62.9	50.4	110.8	5,01!	
1976	16.7	21.9	64.7	52.3	93.6	4,571	
1977	13.3	18.9	71.4	57.0	87.2	3,260	
1978	13.8	18.0	76.0	62.1	84.8	2,577	
1979	13.5	17.3	82.2	72.1	82.0	2,244	
1980	11.7	16.9	89.3	74.3	82.2	2,134	
1981	10.4	15.1	97.3	78.0	81.5	1,819	
1982	19.6	26.1	97.6	83.5	80.0	2,099	4,359
1983	18.7	31.4	86.9	83.2	64.1	2,000	4,000
1984	16.3	24.0	87.1	89.7	62.8	1,668	3,336
1985	13.8		83.2		54.8	1,915	3,191

Sources: Jadresic (1985), Cortázar (1983), Arellano (1985), CIEPLAN (1986).
[a] Employment emergency programme: PEM = minimum employment programme; POJH = occupational programme for heads of household.
[b] Excludes social assistance pensions; includes all other civilian pensions.
[c] The reference in 1970 is the blue-collar (orberro) allowance.
[d] The majority of the labour force in POJH receives a monthly subsidy of this amount. A minority receives more.
.. Not available.

Santiago showed that less than half of the labour force residing there had stable employment (Morales 1982).

Data on income distribution reveals increasing concentration. Throughout 1974–83 there was a systematic drop in the percentage of total income earned by the poorest segments of the population in Greater Santiago, and a persistent increase in that of the richest segment (Riveros 1984).

Information for 1969 and 1978 on household consumption confirms the increasing concentration of income. Only the wealthiest 20 per cent of households increased their consumption; for the poorest 60 per cent there was a drop. In spite of the reorientation of consumption towards food, there was a significant deterioration in the absolute expenditure level on food items in the poorest households, which translated into a greater consumption of starch and flour and a lower consumption of meat, oils, eggs, and vegetables. Estimates of calorie and protein intake per person show that during this period there was a significant increase in the deficit in 40 per cent of the poorest households (Tables 3.3 and 3.4), as measured by the minimum requirements per person defined by FAO/WHO.

The fall in family consumption was a result of the lower purchasing power of poor households due to higher relative prices for goods and services consumed

TABLE 3.3 *Greater Santiago: total and food consumption by income quintile, 1969 and 1978*

Quintile	Consumption (Dec. 1979 $)		Food consumption (Dec. 1979 $)		Average daily per capita calorie consumption			
					Calories		Distance from FAO/OMS norm[a]	
	1969	1978	1969	1978	1969	1978	1969	1978
Lowest	5,953	4,112	3,108	2,438	1,925	1,626	−393	−692
2nd	9,243	7,354	4,150	4,118	2,113	1,875	−205	−443
3rd	12,219	10,754	5,389	5,721	2,422	2,176	+104	−142
4th	16,058	16,527	7,797	7,867	2,830	2,504	+512	+186
Highest	34,857	40,328	10,004	12,945	3,160	3,186	+842	+868
TOTAL/MEAN	15,666	15,815	6,454	7,851	2,587	2,328	+269	+10

Sources: Cortázar (1980), Filgueira (1981), Garcia (1983).
[a] The FAO/WHO norm establishes a minimum of 2,318 daily calories per person.

TABLE 3.4 *Greater Santiago: composition of expenditures by income quintile, 1969 and 1978 (percentages)*

	Lowest		2nd		3rd		4th		Highest	
	1969	1978	1969	1978	1969	1978	1969	1978	1969	1978
Food	52.2	59.3	44.9	56.0	44.1	53.2	36.1	47.6	28.7	32.1
Clothing, shoes	8.5	5.6	10.4	7.2	11.4	7.9	13.1	8.0	13.3	7.7
Housing	25.4	17.9	26.3	14.7	27.5	15.9	30.9	18.1	35.9	20.1
Transport	3.7	5.6	3.1	6.5	3.4	6.9	3.8	8.5	4.8	15.9
Durable goods[a]	2.5	4.1	5.9	6.6	6.1	6.7	6.0	7.4	7.0	8.8
Personal hygiene	1.8	1.8	2.3	2.0	2.4	2.0	2.5	2.8	2.6	1.9
Health	1.2	1.8	1.3	2.0	1.3	2.2	1.3	2.8	1.5	4.1
Education	0.4	0.7	0.4	0.9	0.7	1.4	0.9	2.1	1.5	4.0
Other	4.2	4.4	5.4	4.3	3.6	3.8	5.4	3.7	4.7	5.5
TOTAL	100.0	100.0	100.0	100.0	100.0	100.0	100.0	100.0	100.0	100.0

Source: Filgueira (1981).
[a] Includes recreation and housing, furniture, and appliances

by the poor (Table 3.5) as well as increasing unemployment and the fall in wages. Between 1978 and 1981 there was a slow recovery in employment and wages. As a result, the situation of poor households probably slightly improved.

With the recession at the end of 1981, wages, income, and employment conditions of households experienced a new and more significant deterioration. The unemployment rate increased to almost one-third of the labour force in 1983. The index of wages and salaries dropped 10 per cent in 1983 relative to 1981. Different income concentration indices show increasing inequality (Riveros 1984, Altimir 1984).

The nature of unemployment in 1982–83, relative to previous years, shows that the increase in the unemployment rate was accompanied by an increase in the length of time for which workers remained laid off. This was even more significant for the population aged 25 or older, which suggests that a large percentage of the laid-off were heads of households. Among these households family income in 1982–83 was 23 per cent lower than that of 1979–80 (Riveros 1984). In 1984–85 the employment situation showed signs of recovery. However, part of this recovery took place in low-productivity jobs in the informal urban sector (Jadresic 1985 and 1986). Simultaneously, the active population covered by social security fell from 79 per cent in 1974 to 63 per cent in 1980, and was probably lower for 1985 (Arellano 1985).

These developments all point to a further deterioration of the welfare of poor households in 1982–85, with negative repercussions on their ability to meet basic needs. The evolution of the price index of a basic basket of goods of the poor headed in the same direction. Between September 1981 and September 1984 the consumer price index for the poor increased 105 per cent, while the official index increased only 67 per cent (Table 3.5).

There are no data available on family budgets similar to that of 1969 and 1978 for more rigorous analysis of consumption patterns. Studies based on small samples in poor sectors of greater Santiago during 1983/84 and 1985 agree that there was a drop in family expenditures, an increasing proportion of expenditure devoted to food, and a reorientation of food expenditures towards bread, starches, flour, and cereals, away from products richer in proteins, minerals, and vitamins. Schkolnik (1985) shows that by mid-1985, in two communities of Greater Santiago, more than two-thirds of the households consumed less calories per capita than the amount recommended by FAO/WHO. Cereceda and Cifuentes (1987) conclude for a representative sample of poor households during the second half of 1984 located in La Florida in the metropolitan area of Santiago, 63 per cent of households had income below the cost of a basic basket of goods. A study at the national level in 1983 concludes that 32 per cent of the population did not have enough income to purchase the minimum food basket defined by CEPAL (Rodriguez 1985a). In 1969, acording to CEPAL data, no more than 10 per cent of the population faced such a situation.

In summary, the distributive dimension of economic policy translated into a greater income concentration, i.e. the gap between the incomes of poor and rich households increased. Poor and middle-class households experienced an absolute drop in income to the extent that in 1983/85 a significantly higher proportion of households did not have enough income to purchase the minimum basket of goods.

In contrast, in 1977–81, access to durable goods, in particular televisions, radios, and appliances had increased, a trend that started in the 1960s. Between 1969 and 1978, household expenditures on leisure and durable goods increased in absolute terms and as a percentage of total expenditure for all income quintiles (Table 3.4). Data from the housing and population national census of 1970 and 1982 show that there was a significant increase in the percentage of households that owned a television set (from 19 to 78 per cent), a radio (74–

TABLE 3.5   *Indices of consumer prices, 1974–1984 (Sept. 1974 = 100)*

	Official CPI[a]	Yearly changes (%)	CPI for poor households[b]	Yearly changes (%)
Sept. 1975	487	387	668	568
Sept. 1976	1,442	196	1,841	176
Sept. 1977	2,500	73	3,913	113
Sept. 1978	3,415	37	5,561	42
Sept. 1979	4,646	36	8,215	48
Sept. 1980	6,057	30	10,438	27
Sept. 1981	7,072	17	11,336	9
Sept. 1982	7,876	11	13,558	20
Sept. 1983	10.197	30	18,493	37
Sept. 1984	11,816	16	23,267	26
Sept. 1985	15,864	34	30,456	31

Source: Ruiz-Tagle (1984).
[a] Official consumer price index based on basket of goods consumed by a household with average income.
[b] CPI for poor households based on basket of goods consumed by poor households.

84 per cent), a gas stove (50–74 per cent) a refrigerator (29–48 per cent), and other similar goods. Rodriguez (1985a) also confirmed that the ownership of these goods spread to lower income groups. Some 83 per cent of the households in the lower quintile owned a radio, 68 per cent owned a black-and-white television, and 7 per cent a colour one.

This situation seems to be paradoxical, with a fall in total expenditures and food consumption of poor households at the same time as increases in the ownership of domestic appliances. The factors that led to this situation are related to the economic model that was implemented, i.e. the opening of the economy and drastic reduction of tariffs on imports, as well as technological developments internationally which reduced the relative prices of durable goods for Chileans. The emphasis of the model on competition, the market, and the individual consumer accelerated publicity and advertisements for all types of goods, especially for modern durable goods. Competition for marketing these products increased tremendously, not only in terms of advertising campaigns (Filgueira 1981), but also credit; the combined effect was to persuade the population to purchase goods, which diminished the resources available for food and other basic needs. To the extent that expenditures on food and other essentials were insufficient in quality and quantity, it is difficult to interpret the ownership of durable goods as an advancement in social development or an increase in family welfare of lower segments of the population.

With the 1982–83 recession and unemployment rates that bordered on 30 per cent of the labour force, the situation of the poor became so acute that many households stopped using goods purchased in the past because they could not continue paying their debts or because they had to be sold in order to satisfy more urgent needs, or even because they could not afford repairs or maintenance.

IV   Public expenditure and social policies in the neo-liberal model

1   *Social policies and public expenditure under the military regime*

Public expenditure and policies in social sectors in Chile developed gradually from the 1920s. By the end of the 1960s, public expenditure on education, health, housing, social security, and labour represented 20 per cent of GDP. Registration in primary education covered 95 per cent of the population 6–14 years old, 81 per cent of births were delivered by professionals, and 76 per cent of the economically active population were covered by social security. One study (Foxley *et al.* 1979) showed that for 1969 the distribution of public expenditure in the social sector was progressive as compared to income distribution. The poorest 30 per cent of households received 8 per cent of the national income, but received 18 per cent of the benefits of social public expenditure. However, within these sectors important inequalities remained. Except for health sector benefits, richer households benefited more in absolute terms than poor ones. In each of the social sectors there was significant potential for more progressive social expenditure that would contribute to reducing the gap between higher and lower income groups.

When the military government came to power in 1973, five decades of almost continuous expansion of the welfare state came to an end. The government reduced public expenditure, including social expenditure, in accordance with a neo-liberal approach in which the state plays only a subsidiary role, and under pressure from the economic restrictions and budgetary adjustments required by the economic policy. Social expenditure per capita in 1975–76 was 27 per cent lower than in 1970. There has been a recovery since 1977, but over the whole period expenditure per capita remained below the 1970 level. With the 1982–83 recession, per capita social expenditure was only slightly reduced (Table 3.6). As will be shown later, this is a consequence of developments in two sectors: social security and labour. In housing, health, and education, per capita expenditure in 1983 was lower than in 1981 by 45 per cent, 12 per cent, and 11 per cent, respectively. Official figures of fiscal social expenditure show an increase from 1974, in contrast to the data in Table 3.6. This is due to the increasing fiscal component of social expenditure and differences in indices used for deflating to constant prices (Marshall 1981, Marcel 1984*b*).

The advocates of the monetarist approach have argued that the negative effects of some of the macro-economic variables on the income levels of the poor have been compensated by an increase in social expenditure and a more efficient use of it. They say there is an efficient social network for those who

TABLE 3.6 *Per capita public social expenditures, 1970–1983 (thousand pesos 1978 prices)*

	Education	Health	Social security	Labour	Housing	Other	Total
1970	1,877	1,389	4,463	18	1,385	63	9,195
1974	2,129	1,348	3,084	15	1,815	39	8,429
1975	1,640	1,060	2,887	179	1,085	41	6,892
1976	1,636	933	2,661	456	777	83	6,546
1977	1,747	1,066	2,924	405	971	128	7,241
1978	1,837	1,209	3,058	312	739	108	7,264
1979	1,876	1,194	3,364	280	753	145	7,612
1980	1,706	1,170	3,441	296	835	231	7,679
1981	1,874	1,241	3,497	129	730	286	7,758
1982	1,937	1,280	3,763	257	509	240	7,987
1983	1,672	1,093	3,726	590	404	157	7,641

Sources: Marshall (1981), Marcel (1984*b*).

have suffered a deterioration in their incomes and have a standard of living that is below the minimum.

The government's social policy was aimed at eliminating extreme poverty through the direct provision of monetary and non-monetary subsidies to poorer households. As the social costs of the economic model became more evident, the government developed a system of identification of those in extreme poverty and started to implement several types of subsidies. However, the tool that was designed for this purpose—the Social Stratification Card or CAS card— has had design as well as application problems which have affected the validity and reliability of the information collected. (Raczynski 1983*a*).

The social support network, consisting of subsidies designed to counteract the social costs of the economic policy, relies heavily on social programmes that existed prior to the military government. However, there are several new programmes. Some are aimed at poor households in general, or at some of their adult members. Others are geared specifically towards children. The government has also implemented institutional reforms aimed at broadening the role of the market as a resource allocating mechanism, supporting private participation in the management of services in education, health, social security, and housing. These reforms, which have been actively implemented since 1981, have constituted a direct cost to the state at a time when it was coping with budgetary restrictions. It is not possible to give an appraisal of these reforms in this chapter. Arellano (1985) has estimated that the social security reform implied an increase in the public sector deficit equivalent to 3 per cent of GNP in 1985, while the reforms in the health sector reduced revenues for public health by 11–13 per cent.

2   *Social programmes directed to increasing the welfare of poor households*

(a)   Emergency unemployment policies In 1975, in the face of growing
unemployment, the government channelled increasing amounts of money to
fighting unemployment or its effects. Initiatives included indirect subsidies for
hiring workers and direct subsidies to partially compensate for the effects of
unemployment on family income. Subsidies for hiring additional labour were
implemented in 1976, and from 1977 there was a reduction in the employers'
contribution to social security which almost disappeared in 1984. These policies
have not had a significant impact on the creation of jobs, but they have led to
a reduction of costs for enterprises (Solimano 1983).

The direct subsidy policy had a more immediate effect. The most important
programmes were the minimum employment programme (PEM), which
began in 1975, and the occupation programme for heads of households
(POJH), which was implemented at the end of 1982. In both cases the
unemployed worker receives a monetary subsidy in exchange for a day of
labour that would benefit the community, organized and managed by the
municipalities. The participants in the programmes are not eligible for social
security. The monetary compensation received is below minimum salary and
with time has decreased both relatively and absolutely. In real terms the value
of the PEM subsidy per work-day in 1985 was less than one-half that of 1975
(Table 3.2).

The programmes were intensified during the 1982–83 recession, when POJH
was initiated. In 1983, almost 13 per cent of the labour force participated in
one or other of the programmes. In 1984–85, there was a reduction of participation in PEM. This coincided with the creation of new unemployment
programmes—the Intensive Employment Programme, the Local Development
Programme and others—on which there is not much information. The
reduction in PEM did not result in a greater open unemployment but in
increasing hidden unemployment, with a greater number of people participating in informal activities of unstable income and low productivity, in
sectors such as trade and services (Jadresic 1986).

Studies show that the income generated from PEM and POJH has played
an important role in family survival. In spite of the low value of the subsidy
it represented a stable source of income in a context of high income instability
(Raczynski and Serrano 1985, Ruiz-Tagle and Urmeneta 1984, Cereceda and
Cifuentes 1987). Other studies have stressed that these programmes have led
to a new category of labour, which gives few satisfactions to the participants
and is socially less valued, does not give access to social security, and does not
promote the advancement of the worker (Ruiz-Tagle and Urmeneta 1984,
Martinez and Leon 1984). At the same time these programmes have led to
savings for the state and municipalities. The PEM and POJH workers have
frequently replaced permanent personnel to whom municipalities would have
had to pay at least the legal minimum salary.

Coverage of social security, pensions, and layoff subsidies The coverage of social security, which historically has been high in Chile, was reduced by the military government. In 1970 the system covered 76 per cent of the labour force, while in 1980 it covered only 63 per cent (Arellano 1985). This situation is a result both of high and prolonged lay-offs and a modification of the labour legislation, which resulted in a weakening of the unions and less control and higher flexibility of labour contracts.

Social security is the social sector that absorbs the highest percentage of resources. Expenditures on social security dropped in 1975 and 1976 and recovered later; in 1983, expenditure was higher than in 1981.

The bulk of the sector's expenditure is accounted for by pension payments, the real value of which fell more than 40 per cent in 1975–76 and recovered between 1977–81, to fall back again later. The minimum pension that goes to poorer households moved more favourably. In 1978 it rose above the 1970 level and has remained there. Since 1975, there has been an increase in the number of pensions for the elderly and handicapped who lack resources and are not covered by social security. These pensions that benefit the poorest people rose from 33,000 in December 1975 to 295,000 in December 1984. Two studies (Foxley *et al.* 1979, Rodriguez 1985*b*) indicate that pensions were progressive for poorer households (lower 20–30 per cent of households). Pensions for the armed forces have always been above the average, and the difference has increased in recent years—from between 2.0 and 2.5 times the average at the end of the 1960s to between 3.5 and 3.7 times the average between 1977 and 1980 (Arellano 1985). A press report shows that in May 1985, 61.2 per cent of the armed forces' pensions were over 50,000 pesos per month, compared with only 3.5 per cent of pensions in the civil sector. At the other extreme, 68.1 per cent of pensions of the civil sector were lower than 8,000 pesos, while this was true for only 1.6 per cent of the armed forces' pensions (*El Mercurio*, 15 May 1986).

Coverage of the lay-off subsidies has increased since 1974, but in 1983 the benefits reached barely 20 per cent of the laid-off, excluding participants in the emergency employment programmes.

In 1974 the government raised family allowances for blue-collar workers to the same level as white-collar workers. However, from then on there was chronic deterioration of the real value of this benefit, to the extent that in 1985 the amount was 45 per cent lower than the allowance of blue-collar workers in 1970. As a consequence of the reductions in coverage of social security since 1973, the benefit has reached fewer people. Social security expenditure on family allowances was reduced by 47 per cent between 1974 and 1981 (Arellano 1985). In August 1981, a new family subsidy was distributed for children below eight years old in households with scarce resources (see p. 71).

(c) Housing programmes and policies Housing suffered a permanent cut during 1974–83. Yearly average construction of dwellings was reduced from 4.6 units per 1,000 inhabitants in 1970–72 to 2.8 in 1974–83, falling to 1.8 by the end of the period. Poor households were particularly affected by the reductions. Public programmes subsidizing housing favoured the middle class (Arellano 1985) while programmes of variable subsidies and social dwellings were more favourable to poor households, but their effective coverage was low (Arellano 1985, Rodriguez 1985*b*). In 1981 there were 210,000 applicants for the variable subsidies. Twelve per cent of them received subsidies and of those less than 20 per cent were cashed (Ministry of Housing 1985).

Since 1982 a new policy has acquired significance: the *radications* and *eradications* (see Rojas 1984, Morales and Rojas 1986, Labbe and Llevenes 1986). *Radications* (urbanization, electrification, water supply, sewerage) in settled populations, and has covered an average of 6,000 families per year since 1979. *Eradications* consist in moving deteriorating *campamentos* and *poblaciones* (the population of shanty towns) to plots equipped with 'social dwellings', i.e. 25 square metres of construction with sanitary cubicles. The programme covered nearly 23,000 families between 1977 and 1984. This has led to a deepening of social segregation in Santiago's metropolitan area. The *eradications* have eliminated *campamentos* and *poblaciones* from higher level communities in the centre and the east of the city, recovering plots with a high market value for the state and the private sector, and moving their inhabitants to plots further from the centre of the city, in poorer communities and often with scarce social infrastructure. The *eradications* entail a social cost for the family that is moved that extend from losing job opportunities and access to health and education services to increasing expenditures and time on transport, and most importantly, to alienation from their network of social relations, which in times of economic crisis provides support that facilitates survival (Raczynski and Serrano 1985).

The limited coverage of low-income public housing programmes has led to an increase in the population density of poor areas, which absorb the low-income households not included in the public housing programmes. However, the numbers and proportion of inhabitants with access to sewerage and potable water have increased. The percentage of private dwellings connected to a water system increased from 57 per cent in 1970 to 81 per cent in 1982, and the percentage of dwelling with some sewerage system increased from 47 to 66 per cent over the same period. Some evidence for 1970 and 1982 (Rodriguez 1985*a*) showed that in urban areas there were almost no inequalities in access to potable water according to income level, but there were important differences in the consumption of water between richer and poorer households.

Since the recession of 1982, however, the poor segments of the population in Santiago's metropolitan area have had difficulty in getting effective access to potable water. Declining income prevented them from paying their bills on time, and their access to the network was cut. During the first months of 1983, around 26 per cent of the customers of the Empresa Metropolitana de Obras Sanitarias were one or two months behind in their payment, and it is estimated that around 130,000 inhabitants were cut off from the service (Avec 1983). A similar situation also prevailed with regard to electricity. By the end of 1983, the government recognized the situation and a legal department was set up in order to provide support for payment of debts to the public services.

3   Subsidies and programmes directed to children

In relative terms, mothers and children have been favoured by social policies from 1974–85. There have been repeated official statements regarding the importance of investment in human capital at an early age, and specific programmes have been designed for children.

(a) Family subsidies for poor children In August 1981 the municipalities began to distribute a family subsidy for under-8s in extreme poverty and not covered by the social security system. Under-6s must attend check-ups at health clinics, and 6–8 year olds must be registered at school. In July 1982, a benefit to pregnant women was added, and in April 1985, children of 8–14 years were also included. The amount of the subsidy is equivalent to that given as social security family allowances. During 1982, a monthly average of 227,000 subsidies were given, and in 1983 the figure increased to 527,000 (ODEPLAN 1984). During the latter year the monthly number of subsidies paid represented 24 per cent of the total population of under-8s.

(b) Health programmes and nutritional interventions aimed at mothers infants and pre-schoolers Chile has had a long history of social medicine, and when the military government took power the public health sector had wide social and geographical coverage (see de Kadt *et al.* 1976, Arellano 1976, and *Revista Medica de Chile* (1977), 105/10). During the 1975–76 recession, there was a drastic reduction in public expenditure on health. Between 1977 and 1982 a partial recovery took place and in 1983 there was another drop. The reductions in public expenditure mainly affected capital investment and hospital equipment (Table 3.7). There were also cuts in personnel expenditures due to the fall in wages and the partial replacement of medical personnel by para-medical personnel (see Raczynski and Oyzara 1981, Castañeda 1984, Romero 1985). The deterioration in the level of hospital care has been repeatedly denounced by doctors. The situation became critical in 1984–85. For example, in October of 1984, the Professional Association of Doctors from the Regional Council of Concepcion in a public statement denounced the increasing decapitalization of hospitals, the deterioration of the

TABLE 3.7 *Public expenditure on health, resources, and services provided to the mother–child population, 1970–1985.*

	Public expenditure on health (1978 $ million)		Check-ups:		Midwife per live birth	Professional deliveries as % of total	Hospital beds	
	Total	Investment	Obstetrics per live birth[a]	Pediatric per under-15[b]			Obstetric	Pediatric
1970	13,016	1,193	2.1	1.0	4.7	81	3,682	6,163
1974	13,511	1,490	2.0	1.1	8.4	86	4,296	7,038
1975	10,805	661	2.2	1.0	10.1	87	4,368	7,038
1976	9,674	445	2.5	1.1	11.5	87	4,367	7,120
1977	11,250	215	2.9	1.1	12.7	89	4,451	6,762
1978	12,979	276	3.2	1.1	13.3	89	4,320	6,934
1979	13,032	362	3.4	1.2	13.8	90	4,923	7,354
1980	12,388	268	3.5	1.2	13.5	91	4,933	7,419
1981	14,016	411	3.4	1.3	13.1	92	4,923	7,294
1982	14,708	385	3.8	1.5	13.8	94	5,054	7,380
1983	12,774	129	4.3	1.6	14.6	95	5,101	7,211
1984			3.1	1.7	14.6	97	5,452	7,740
1985			4.5	1.7	15.4	97	5,147	9,198

Source: Marshall (1981) and Marcel (1984a); INE-Ministerio de Salud, *Anuario de recursos y atenciones*; *Anuario de nacimientos*; INE-CELADE, *Proyecciones de Poblacion*, July 1979.
[a] Excludes emergency and 'responsible fatherhood' check-ups.
[b] Excludes emergency check-ups.

infrastructure and technological level, the shortage of medicines, personnel, physical space and working materials.

It is important to recall here that the incidence of typhoid fever and hepatitis showed a significant increase. The number of notified cases of typhoid went from 48 per 10,000 in 1970–73 to 86 in 1974–81 and to 103 in 1982–84; and hepatitis cases from 20 to 55 and to 90 per 10,000 in the same period (INE— Health Ministry, various issues). These figures refer to all the population regardless of age. However, the incidence of typhoid fever has been greater for the population of 5–14 years than for younger or older people (Ferreiro *et al.* 1983).

The market and the private sector were brought into the health sector (Raczynski 1983*b*, Giaconi 1985), most significantly by the creation of the Institutos de Salud Previsional (ISAPRE), by which workers could give their health contributions, initially 4 per cent and today 7 per cent of taxable income, to a private profit-seeking organization. The legislation provided easier access to health to high income groups by reducing their direct expenditure on health. Approximately 5 per cent of the population benefited from this legislation—the high-income, low-risk population. The shift of this segment of the population to the ISAPRE system undermined resources for public health by 11–13 per cent (Arellano 1985).

The regime's health policy concentrated almost exclusively on the provision of care for women and children. Health and nutrition programmes for women and children have a long history in the country. They include periodic pre-natal and post-natal attention until the child reaches 6 years of age; pathological diagnosis; prevention, vaccination, and immunization of the population; health and nutritional education for the mother; the promotion of breast-feeding; actions towards responsible fatherhood and birth-control; and most important, a diversity of nutritional intervention programmes. These programmes were improved and targeted towards the most vulnerable groups, on the basis of studies diagnosing problem areas in infant health and nutrition and evaluating alternative interventions. (See, for example, the many studies done by the Nutrition National Council, the Institute of Food Technology, and the Universidad de Chile.)

In 1975 a system was instituted at the health clinic level for the identification and treatment of under-6s showing signs of nutritional deficiency. Programmes include:

1. *Supplementary Feeding Programme (PNAC)* A universal programme (for all children that attend the well-baby check-up at public sector health clinics) and one with high coverage (over 90 per cent in poverty areas) which includes the provision of milk and protein supplements for pregnant and breast-feeding women and pre-schoolers (2–5 years old). The scale of the programme is indicated in Table 3.8, and many studies have emphasized its importance for

T A B L E 3.8 *Tons of milk and milk substitutes distributed by the Supplementary Feeding Programme (PNAC), 1974–1984*

	Basic programme				Targeted programme[b]
	Pregnant women	Under-2s and lactating mothers	Children 2–5 years	Total	
1974	1,784	8,722	10,233	20,739	
1975	1,805	10,364	11,415	23,504	
1976	1,881	10,504	12,106	24,480	
1977	2,294	12,485	13,872	28,651	
1978	2,360	11,946	12,874	27,180	2,646
1979	2,462	12,040	11,206	25,707	3,012
1980	2,542	12,256	10,397	25,195	4,020
1981	3,386	12,183	9,067	24,636	5,146
1982	4,074	12,286	8,402	24,762	5,525
1983	1,277	9,853	5,924	17,053	4,993
1984	823[a]	5,381[a]	5,513[a]	11,718[a]	16,132[c]
1985	810[a]	5,557[a]	6,274[a]	12,641[a]	17,630[c]

Source: National Institute of Statistics (INE)–Ministry of Health, *Anuario de Recursos y Atenciones.*
[a] Milk and milk substitutes distributed to beneficiaries not at risk.
[b] Targeted programmes include OFASA (1979–81), targeted PNAC (1982–83), and compulsory programmes for children at risk (1984–5).
[c] In 1984, two-thirds of the beneficiaries were subject to biomedical risks and one-third to socio-economic risks.

children from poor households (Gonzalez *et al.* 1980, Gonzalez and Infante 1980, Instituto de Economia 1980, and Garcia 1983).

2. Another programme for *nutritionally deficient* children provides supplementary foods to children suffering from or at high risk of malnutrition, or refers them to *Jardines Infantiles* or to Open Centres. In the first, children get psychological, medical, and nutritional care. The latter provide three daily meals that cover 80 per cent of their calorie requirements. Malnourished children receive an additional food supplement. In the selection of children for these programmes priority is given to malnourished children, those with fathers who are unemployed, those with working mothers, and those in families from lower levels of the social strata. The Open Centres, which are run by voluntary workers and personnel from the emergency employment schemes, provide free care for children of 2 to 5 from extremely poor households, especially those showing signs of malnutrition. At the centres children receive food, entertainment, and habit-forming education. However, the personnel have often not received the training necessary for fulfilling their educational role (ODEPLAN 1984). Pre-school care has risen from 8 per cent of the population of 5 and below in 1974 to 15 per cent in 1983, including those in Open Centres and Jardines Infantiles. There are also some municipal centres for nutritional education for pre-school children from poor families.

Women participating in the emergency employment programmes work at these centres.

Evaluation of the medical and economic efficiency of the two alternatives for the treatment of malnourished children—at home or in Jardines Infantiles—has shown mixed results, varying according to the age and degree of malnutrition when the child joins the programme (Gomez *et al.* 1983). In both programmes the probability of complete recovery during the period covered by the study (18 months for at-home care and 10 for Jardines Infantiles) is relatively low, and is directly related to the degree of nutritional deficiency.

3. *Recovery centres* Over-2s who are malnourished or at high-risk are admitted to a network of recovery centres run by the Infant Nutritional Corporation. Table 3.9 shows some characteristics of these programmes. Those malnourished or at high risk are identified through the primary health care establishments, at which attendance is very high in order to get access to PNAC which is available for all children. This ensures the detection of malnourished children and their referral to the 'recovery programmes'. The combination of health surveillance and nutritional interventions with a system that picks up children at high risk showed efficient performance until 1982. In spite of the fall in income of poor households, the indicators of birth weight, nutrition, and infant and child mortality improved significantly.

In 1983, for the first time since 1975, there was a deterioration in some of the survival indices and in the nutritional status of children (Tables 3.9 and 3.10), the decline in infant mortality slowed down, while the child (1–4) death rate increased markedly. This happened at a time when the economic crisis was deepening, but instead of the nutritional programmes being intensified they faced restrictions. The amount of milk distributed by PNAC was 31 per cent lower in 1983 than in 1982, and the additional food distribution to malnourished children was reduced by 10 per cent. The results of this showed almost immediately. Malnutrition figures for the months of February, March, and April of 1983 show a stagnation in the nutritional status of children younger than 5 months and a deterioration in that of children 6–23 months old (ODEPLAN and Superintendency of Education n.d.). The yearly figures confirm this negative trend. The percentage of mothers underweight also increased from 17 per cent (end 1982) to 19 per cent (first nine months of 1983) (ODEPLAN n.d.).

During 1984, the malnutrition and mortality indices showed an improvement. This coincided with intensification of remedial actions—even though PNAC remained restricted, the delivery of several types of food to beneficiaries at high socio-economic and biomedical risk was extended (Table 3.8). The improvement shows the extent to which the nutritional status of children from poor households depends on public programmes. In July 1985, due to budgetary restrictions, the government put forward further limits on PNAC,

TABLE 3.9 *Nutritional state of under-6s under surveillance in Ministry of Health establishments, 1975–1985*

	% of undernourished children[a]					No. of children examined (000)	% of total under-5s
	0–5 months	6–11 months	12–23 months	2–5 years	Total		
1975	12.3	18.0	19.0	14.5	15.5	1,015.0	72
1976	11.2	18.5	19.4	15.2	15.9	1,047.8	74
1977	9.6	16.9	18.5	14.3	14.9	1,070.8	75
1978	6.5	13.5	16.0	13.0	13.0	1,047.6	72
1979	5.4	11.9	15.6	12.3	12.2	1,022.8	69
1980	5.0	11.5	14.3	11.7	11.5	1,055.2	70
1981	3.9	9.8	12.3	10.1	9.9	1,062.9	70
1982	3.3	9.4	11.9	8.6	8.8	1,160.9	75
1983	3.4	10.3	13.4	9.4	9.8	1,194.4	76
1984	2.9	8.9	10.8	8.4	8.4	1,226.6	77
1985	2.8	8.8	11.9	8.6	8.7	1,258.2	78

Source: INE-Ministerio de Salud, Anuario de *Recursos y atenciones de salud.*

[a] Measured by the Sempé weight-for-age criterion.

TABLE 3.10 *Mortality rates, crude birth rate, and low-weight live birth, 1970–1985*

	Infant mortality[a]		Mortality at age[b]				Crude death rate[c]	Crude birth rate[c]	Low-weight live births[d] (%)
	Neonatal	Post-neonatal	Total	1–4 years	5–9 years	10–14 years			
1970	31.7	50.5	82.2	3.78	0.96	0.77	8.9	26.8	
1971	28.9	45.0	73.9	3.23	0.92	0.74	8.8	27.4	
1972	29.4	43.3	72.7	3.08	0.92	0.78	9.0	27.8	
1973	27.4	38.4	65.8	2.49	0.80	0.72	8.2	27.2	
1974	26.1	39.1	65.2	2.78	0.76	0.68	7.8	26.3	
1975	25.4	32.2	57.6	2.35	0.74	0.62	7.3	24.6	11.6
1976	24.1	32.5	56.6	2.27	0.75	0.65	7.8	23.3	11.4
1977	21.4	28.7	50.1	1.83	0.70	0.65	7.0	21.6	10.9
1978	18.7	21.4	40.1	1.60	0.64	0.56	6.7	21.4	9.8
1979	18.7	19.2	37.9	1.49	0.60	0.57	6.8	21.5	8.8
1980	16.7	16.3	33.0	1.24	0.58	0.53	6.7	22.2	8.2
1981	13.1	13.9	27.0	1.13	0.50	0.54	6.2	23.4	7.6
1982	11.8	11.8	23.6	1.09	0.43	0.52	6.1	23.9	6.8
1983	10.7	11.2	21.9	1.22	0.44	0.52	6.4	22.3	6.0
1984	9.2	10.4	19.6	1.03	0.39	0.45	6.3	22.3	6.0
1985	9.9	9.6	19.5	0.88	0.37	0.40	6.1	21.7	6.3

Source: INE, *Anuario de demografia.*

[a] Per 1,000 live births.
[b] Per 1,000 in each age group.
[c] Per 1,000 inhabitants.
[d] Less than 2.5 kg.

and replaced milk by rice. Fortunately, under pressure from expert opinion and mothers, the measures were reversed. But there have been reductions in the delivery of milk and other food products. Official data have yet to be published, but interviews with personnel from health clinics indicate a deterioration in nutritional indices for mothers and children. Data for June 1984 and

June of 1985 show stagnation or even slight increases of malnutrition indices for under-2s which is not reflected in the overall malnutrition rate for under-6s (Tables 3.9 and 3.11).[1]

In summary, nutritional intervention programmes for infants and young children were clearly successful until 1982. After that the evidence is ambiguous, showing fluctuating indices.

TABLE 3.11   *Percentage of under-6s malnourished, June 1984 and June 1985*

	0–11 months	12–23 months	2–5 years	Total
Weight/age (Sempé)				
June 1984	9.2	15.0	13.7	13.2
June 1985	9.5	15.1	12.1	12.2
Weight/age (WHO)				
June 1984	11.8	23.0	19.9	19.1
June 1985	10.8	23.1	17.7	17.7
Height/age (WHO)				
June 1984	34.8	48.2	51.1	48.4
June 1985	36.0	47.9	48.4	46.1

Source: Ministerio de Salud, SISVAN.

The success of the nutritional intervention programmes until 1982 was largely built on the previous coverage and structures of the health sector in Chile (Monckeberg *et al.* 1984). The experience of Chilean mothers with primary health care, their relatively high level of schooling, and their belief in their entitlement to well-baby check-ups and supplementary feeding also contributed to the success of these programmes. The fall in infant mortality and birth rates and the concentration of births in low-risk socio-demographic segments were further factors (Raczynski and Oyarzo 1981, Taucher 1982).

(c) Programmes for school children Since 1974 there. has been a reduction in government resources directed to education, and there were also changes in the composition of expenditure. An increasing proportion of public expenditure on education was redirected from universities, to pre-school, primary, and intermediate levels. Resources for primary education increased substantially both in absolute and relative terms. The amount almost doubled between 1974 and 1983, when it absorbed more than one-half of public expenditure in education. Paradoxically, the statistics regarding primary registration and drop-out rates do not show improvement (Table 3.12). Both primary education registration as well as the schooling rate of the population 6–14 years of age fell, while the drop-out rates tended to increase (see Briones 1984 and Bralic *et al.* 1984). Both tendencies are stronger for Santiago's metropolitan area. The schooling rate in this region goes from 106 in 1977 to barely 88 in 1982, while the national figures change from 105 to 100 (Raczynski 1986). A report dealing with 1984 by The Intendencia of the Metropolitan region shows that at least 12 per cent of children from poor households of the metropolitan area of Santiago are not attending school. This percentage— high by Chilean standards—coincides with the visual perception of increasing infant vagrancy and begging in the cities.

TABLE 3.12   *Public expenditure in education, pre-school and primary school enrolment, and primary school drop-out rate, 1970 and 1974–1985*

	Public expenditure (1978 $ million)			Enrolment (%)		Drop-out rate[c]	
	Total	Pre-school	Primary school (8 years)	Pre-school in population 0–5 years old[a]	Primary in population 6–14 years of age[b]	Public schools	Private schools
1970	17,587		5,927		96.8	5.9	
1974	21,344	194	7,147	7.8	107.5	6.9	
1975	16,772	191	5,967	8.8	106.0	6.2	
1976	16,972	225	6,414	9.4	103.8	7.7	
1977	18,434	334	6,568	10.3	104.9	7.1	3.5
1978	19,721	441	7,443	10.8	105.2	6.4	3.6
1979	20,479	526	7,768	11.0	104.0	6.5	2.5
1980	18,940	427[d]	7,568[d]	11.7	104.5	4.8	1.7
1981	21,169	593	10,210	11.5	102.2	9.3	6.2
1982	22,252	816	11,470	11.9	99.7	2.8	2.5
1983	19,522	783	10,327	12.2	98.8	5.1	3.0
1984				14.9	96.2	5.1	
1985				12.5	95.1		

Sources: Marshal (1981), Marcel (1984*b*), Castañeda (1985), JUNJI (National Kindergarten Board); Superintendencia, Ministerio de Educación Pública; INE–CELADE.
[a] Ministry of Education and JUNJI establishments.
[b] Excludes adult enrolment.
[c] Enrolment in March of each year less enrolment in December of the same year divided by the March enrolment. Abnormally high fluctuations between 1980 and 1983 throw doubts on the figures.
[d] From 1980 onwards the total public expenditure registered by Marcel (1984*b*) were assigned to each level according to the proportions given in Castañeda (1984*b*).

It is hard to determine the relative importance of different factors leading to deterioration in school registration and attendance. The trends in public expenditure in primary education show that monetary restrictions were not the central problem. Probably the economic deterioration of households and nutritional status of children played an important role. Although primary education is free for poor households, some of the materials required are not—equipment, clothing, shoes, and so on. These factors weigh in the poor households' daily struggle (see part V).

Aid programmes within the educational system have been cut back. The School Feeding Programme, aimed at helping to reduce drop-out and repetition problems among children 6–14 years old and to improve school activity and maintain nutritional status of these children, was reduced in 1975–76

(Table 3.13). Compared with the past (1975), there were improvements in protein and calorie content, preparation, and distribution of meals, but the number of total (snacks and meals) rations distributed is less. However, during 1983 to 1985 there was some increase in the meals distributed by this programme.

TABLE 3.13 *School Feeding Programme: meals distributed, 1970–1985 (daily average in thousands)*

	Snacks[a]	Lunches/dinners
1970	1,301	619
1971	1,408	654
1972	1,537	716
1973	1,446	674
1974	1,339	663
1975	746	594
1976	770	361
1977	1,055	296
1978	1,055	308
1979	759	295
1980	760	295
1981	759	295
1982	759	295
1983	674	323
1984	665	418
1985	680	541

Source: Junta Nacional de Auxilio Escolar y Becas.
[a] The term *onces* literally means 'elevenses'.

The programme includes the distribution of snacks (*onces*) and lunches, covering 33 per cent of daily calorie requirements. A child receiving the full ration would be given 800 calories and 15–20 grammes of protein daily. The child receiving a 'snack' (half a ration) would get 300 calories a day. Until 1984 the programme covered five days a week but by the end of 1984, because of the scarcity of resources of poor households, the government extended the programme to include Saturdays, and Sundays, and school vacations. In 1985, this was interrupted.

It is the responsiblity of teachers or school directors to distribute the rations provided. They consider three criteria: the household socio-economic situation, the results of the health check-ups, and personal assessment of the teacher. According to conversations with teachers in poverty areas, food needs are so widespread their available rations are frequently distributed among all children, and the caloric intake per child is reduced. For many, the school meals are a substitute for meals at home, so that they do not supplement the child's home feedings as much as intended.

A report on the second half of the 1970s shows that children of school age in marginal communities of Santiago's metropolitan area present higher malnutrition indices (36 per cent) than pre-school children of similar social characteristics (29 per cent) (Chateau 1981). A study on poverty areas of San Miguel in Santiago's metropolitan area shows that malnutrition in school age children increased from 4.6 per cent in 1980 to 15.8 per cent in 1983 (ODEPLAN and Superintendency of Education n.d.). Data covering 10 of the 12 regions in the country (excluding the metropolitan region) indicate some increases in malnutrition for school children benefiting from school feeding programmes between 1984 (when the proportion below 90 per cent of the FAO/WHO criteria fluctuated between 8 and 18.2 per cent) and 1985 (19.2 to 19.6 per cent). Teachers have observed a deterioration in the quality of daily school activities of children in poverty areas with regard to concentration, disposition, sociability, clarity, etc.

V The urban poor family: unemployment and survival strategies

Different studies on the poverty areas of Greater Santiago during recent years have described the human dimensions of the rising unemployment and the prolonged and drastic drop in family income. Drawing on these, this part aims to describe unemployment from 'within'—that is, the impact of unemployment at the household level, the mechanisms and behaviour to which households resort in order to survive, and the significance of these survival mechanisms for the family and in particular for the woman who is responsible for the management of the household. In order to do this, it is necessary to analyse briefly some characteristics of family organization of the urban poor (for more details see Raczynski and Serrano 1985).

1 The urban poor family: composition and organization

In poor, urban Chile, a woman and a man are rarely consciously united by common projects regarding the future. The couple's union has many aspects of a contract with important economic considerations. Emotional ties are rather secondary. The man goes out to work and gives the woman an income which she manages and stretches in order to ensure the subsistence of the family members. The household's material subsistence is ensured by these two indispensable elements: the income provided by the husband and the domestic work of the wife. It is up to her to maximize consumption, and in doing so she relies on social relationships as well as on household resources. Assistance from public programmes—education, maternity subsidies and others from social system, health benefits, supplementary feeding programmes, housing programmes, etc.—also regularly contribute to household subsistence.

The home is mainly devoted to material survival, and often lacks intimacy, mutual understanding, and real emotional links. The man and the woman tend to lead separate lives (see Bastias 1984 and Cifuentes 1983). This is reflected in the organization of their time. The woman spends most of the day at home, going out only to take the children to school, to health check-ups, i.e. to fulfil her role. Daily life is monotonous and lonely. The husband, on the other hand, spends most of his day away from home, whether he has a job or not, going out early and coming back late. The woman faces problems alone (economic, child-rearing, health, social, and sexual problems). Opportunities for discussing them with others are rare. Under these circumstances, the emotional links are stronger between the women and her children, especially when they are young. They are her reason for living and struggling and her only possession. At the same time, she perceives them as a burden and a source of tension. They demand time and energy, clothes, and money.

The nature of the couple's relationship, its contractual character, and the absence of strong emotional links, intimacy, and mutual understanding is evident in the expression used by many women assessing their relationship with their mate: 'He has given me a bad life.' There seem to be three elements to this 'bad life' given by the husband. The first and foremost is that he does not provide the household with money and wastes resources that would otherwise be available for the family's feeding and dressing. The other two are related to the couple's relationship and the treatment received by the woman. He 'does not give her a bad life' when he does not use physical violence or does so only occasionally, and when he is 'calm', meaning that he does not constantly force the woman to have sexual relationships, especially when drunk. Alcoholism and adultery are not necessarily rejected, only when they affect his role as a provider.

With such a family organization—income provided by the male, domestic resources, an informal social network, and the benefits provided by social public programmes—a good portion of poor families in the past moved upward socially. Others have had a stable social situation with expectations of upward mobility for their children through education, and others have always lived in extreme poverty.

2   *Survival strategies*

How does a poor family manage when facing a drastic and prolonged fall in income? A study of households facing unemployment during 1983 (Raczynski and Serrano 1985) shows that as a result of the macro-economic situation, the resources that are secured by the male and other members of the household, with great effort and through all sorts of labour arrangements, are unstable and insufficient in contrast with the past when labour participation provided the most important survival strategy (Duque and Pastrana 1973, Fries 1977). Labour arrangements last only short periods of time; neither formal qualification nor work experience ensure access to employment. It seems that it is much more important to have contacts through a social network. The women, many of whom stopped working outside the home when they got married, intensify their efforts to obtain some sort of supplementary income, generally through part-time activities which are unstable (sewing, knitting, washing laundry, or selling cigarettes or ice cream, etc.). The income obtained is low.

These circumstances require the maximum use of domestic resources and activation of solidarity networks. They extend woman's responsibility for material survival, and increase dependence on social public programmes.

(a) Domestic arrangements Numerous patterns of behaviour and social relationships develop in reaction to these circumstances. These include changes in consumption patterns, increased debt, sale of goods, and change in household composition. Each relate to an informal social network, to be discussed below.

Most of the income that comes into the household is used for food consumption; other expenditures (transport, cleaning products, shoes, electricity, water, debt payments, etc.) are eliminated. In spite of this, for many households there is not enough food. Family income is not enough for three or four meals a day, even when the ingredients are reduced to a minimum. In such circumstances, talking about 'food' becomes a key preoccupation of the woman, reflecting her desperation when unable to feed her family. Items such as meat, fruit, vegetables, and drinks, are reduced or eliminated. The household attempts to reduce expenditures on several fronts. However, there seems to be a certain order. In the first place, leisure activities are cut; the purchase of certain food items is reduced; investment in the maintenance of the dwelling is stopped; shoes and dresses are not bought, electricity bills not paid, savings are made in the use of gas; and finally, public transport is not used anymore. As a consequence of lower and irregular flows of income, households are forced to purchase small quantities at a local grocery at higher prices. This eliminates expenditure on transport, and the customer may be able to buy on credit. When the reduction in such expenditures is not enough, food consumption is restricted almost exclusively to *masas* (starch and flour), and occasionally vegetables. Debt is increased, and goods such as clothes, stoves, refrigerators, irons, TV sets, china, furniture, and so on, are sold or pawned. The last resort is stopping payments of the water bill (further increasing debt), and further sales of goods.

The main preoccupation of the woman becomes feeding and educating the children. They know the consequences of malnourishment for small children so, after the husband, it is the children who are given priority in the distribution of food (Cereceda and Cifuentes 1987). The mother hopes for upward social mobility for her children through education, and therefore regards this as a priority. One frequently hears expressions such as 'the main thing is the food issue and sending the little ones to school', or 'education is all we can give them'.

(b) Solidarity and co-operation among households Households are not isolated, they are rooted in social networks and have links of support and solidarity. The support network includes exchange of goods and services, information, moral support, loans, and child-care, as well as the extended family. In each home both the woman and the man have built at least one support network. In the woman's case this is formed mainly by neighbours. For the man it is mainly friends, relatives, and working colleagues, and the support is related to the search for a job or for the means to get *pololo* (self-employment) as well as loans. The woman's network deals with daily domestic chores: loans of food and small amounts of money, utensils, child care, washing laundry, information, advice, etc. These spontaneous forms of co-operation include modifications in the household's composition which take place in two directions: the arrival of new members who then share the housing and food expenses, and the outward movement of children to other households. Although the family's desire is to live on their own, they take in individuals as well as families that have no place to stay. In the face of precarious economic conditions, children are sometimes sent to relatives who will look after them and give them an education.

Parallel to this, there are initiatives for action and association, aimed at collectively facing the survival problem and the satisfaction of basic needs (Razetto *et al.* 1983). They are called *organicaciones economicas populares* (OEPs). The OEPs are heterogeneous and dynamic. Some are based on territorial considerations, others on having worked in the same firm or belonging to the same religious community, or even sharing similar political beliefs. The more common associations are: (*a*) basic consumption organizations, such as community kitchens, purchase and supply associations, and self-help groups; (*b*) productive workshops—small units with 3–15 people producing and selling goods and services such as bread, clothing, knitting, laundry, carpentry, etc. (Klenner and Zuñiga 1984); (*c*) organizations for the unemployed, (*d*) organizations related to housing problems, such as housing committees, water, electricity, and mortgage committees and committees for the homeless; and (*e*) diverse organizations aimed at health, education, and entertainment needs.

None of these organizations are quantitatively very significant. There are approximately 1.2 million people living in shanty towns in Santiago's metropolitan area (Chateau and Pozo 1985), while a register of OEP for 1982 shows only 18,200 beneficiaries, or 3 per cent of the poor, assuming the register covered one-half of the actual OEP beneficiaries. Nevertheless, these new forms of social organization have great potential for assisting the poor in crisis.

(c) The official social network The social public programmes are another mechanism to which poor and unemployed households have access. Some are regarded as a right (i.e. health, supplementary feeding, and education). But those introduced in recent years are often partially rejected or used only as a last resort. Several factors affect family use of these programmes, including information, compliance with a minimum of requirements, the ability to go through the necessary paperwork, and the acceptability of the benefit offered.

Households have a general knowledge of assistance programmes, but such knowledge is not always complete; and in any case, knowledge is only part of the problem. Eligibility requirements are hard to meet. Applicants have to prove to officials that the household qualifies as poor, requiring them to 'publicize' a status that they often try to hide. They also have to show personal documents, such as IDs, certificates of residence, etc., which they often lack. Getting such documents requires more paperwork, which is always regarded as difficult as well as expenses which are significant in the context of the family budget. In spite of these difficulties, households make use of these government relief resources, and even though the benefits are small, they are still relevant for their material survival.

The Emergency Employment Programmes—PEM and POJH—are resources used when all other alternatives have failed. These programmes have negative connotations, related to the low remuneration and to the perception that the type of work is humiliating. However, once registered in the programmes, the incomes offered by PEM or POJH become an important resource for the family.

3   *Family organization and social relationships: the 'jitters of unemployment'*

Unemployment and the fall in family income are not only material problems but also have repercussions on family organization and on the psychological and emotional aspects of family life. (On the connection between material problems and the stability of the family in Chile see Lira and Weinstein 1981, Acuña and Reyes 1982, and Vives 1983).

A woman's reaction to her husband's being laid off and to extreme material shortages depends on several psycho-social factors, which in turn influence her ability to recognize and cope with the material crisis affecting her household. These factors are related to the personalities of both the woman and the man, their past relationship, and communication between them and their children. Some women who have always tried to be in charge of their lives, have greater initiative and dynamism. They confront the crisis situation better and 'buffer' its impact on their families. They have also had 'social experience' outside their homes during their married lives, which has given them the opportunity of sharing, helping, and expressing themselves with others as well as of earning income. They are more secure and in command when confronting the crisis.

Another decisive factor when dealing with the crisis and its impact on the family is the quality of the couple's relationship. There are couples—the minority—who communicate and share. Others have always had conflictive and violent relationships. The majority arrive at an intermediate situation by leading 'separate lives'. For these, the husband's unemployment and resulting fall in family income remove the basis for the family organization. The husband, who used to go out to 'work', frequently finds himself with no place to go. He loses his identity and his position as the working man whom the woman has to serve and look after when he returns from work. According to women, this results in male aggression, sleeplessness, bad temper, isolation, anguish, and evasion through alcohol.

The woman's domestic role is based on the economic support provided by the man. If this precondition fails, his being out of work means no money for her, which in turn translates into no food, no clothing, no shoes, and, therefore, hunger and cold for her children who are her reason for living. The impossibility of feeding and rearing her children and keeping her house as she used to has psychological repercussions for the woman. She is dissatisfied and feels incapable, guilty: 'In the past, during other crises, I have managed, now I think and think and I don't know how to get out of it.' She wants to escape and forget about everything. The majority of women recognize that they are undergoing an important change, the 'unemployment jitters'. She becomes worn out emotionally and psychologically, ends up seeking professional help at a health clinic, and in extreme cases thinking about suicide. The psychological and emotional impact of unemployment and material shortages creates more tensions among couples with an unsatisfactory relationship. The husband's being laid off makes the tensions more explicit and acute. The impact of the crisis is less evident where the relationship between the husband has been satisfactory and there has been communication and sharing.

VI Conclusions and policy implications

1   Summary of main findings

The main conclusions from the analysis of the Chilean case can be summarized as follows:

1. Chile has been strongly affected by the world recessions of 1975 and 1981. The adjustment policies inspired by the monetarist neo-liberal model contributed to the economic recessions experienced in 1975–76 and from 1982 onwards. The international recession of 1975 was felt domestically through a 'shock policy', i.e. monetary contraction and abrupt reduction of fiscal expenditure, including capital expenditures and investment programmes. The world recession that began in 1981 found Chile much more open and vulnerable to the international situation. It multiplied the problems arising from domestic economic policy which had been accumulating. The adjustment policy implemented was similar to that of 1975 and increased the domestic effects of the international recession.

Between the two recessions there was a recovery period with high growth rates. However, the intensity of the 1975 recession and the nature of the neo-liberal economic model resulted in a downward trend in industrial production and a shortage of new jobs, which led to high rates of unemployment and low real wages, which had not recovered pre-recession levels by 1981. At the end of 1981, poor households had to face the recession in a worse situation than 1974 or 1970. During 1983, the unemployment rate grew to around one-third of the labour force, affecting heads of households more and for a longer period of time, with an immediate impact on families' welfare and on their children. For those who did have a job, wages fell. In 1985, wages were 14 per cent lower than in 1981 and 17 per cent lower than in 1970.

2. As a reaction to high and permanent unemployment levels and to the fall in the family income of poor households, the government implemented social programmes to benefit the unemployed and poor families. Almost all of these programmes were targeted towards the poor and partially compensated for the fall in their standard of living. In 1982–85 there was a big increase in the numbers of the poor and their needs became more severe. However, the benefits from the public programmes were reduced as a result of budgetary restrictions and of the redirection of public resources to other ends. Relief programmes were also affected by institutional reforms aimed at increasing the participation of the private sector and broadening the role of the market. These reforms led to reduced government revenues and an increased public deficit. Reform of the social security system is a clear example of this phenomenon, which also took place in the health sector.

3. Some of the programmes for the poor were successful until 1982 i.e. mother–infant health care and supplementary feeding. In 1983–85, the combination of increased household needs and reduced programme resources made them quite inadequate. The figures for child malnutrition (and even those of child mortality, which had been gradually declining since 1975), stagnated and became unstable. Other programmes were unsuccessful. The emergency employment programmes PEM and POJH reached the unemployed poor and were of a countercyclical nature, but the benefits for the unemployed during the recession that began in 1982 were less than those received in 1975–76 or in 1977–81. Initially, housing programmes did not benefit the poor. During recent years the situation has improved, but in Santiago's metropolitan area it has resulted in a rupture in the social habitat of those affected, alienating them from their social networks, their job opportunities, and their social infrastructure of education, health, etc. Relief programmes for the school population have been insufficient. There was no significant expansion in the distribution of food, and since household needs were increasing there was an increase in malnutrition among school-age children. Expenditure related to primary education, such as shoes and clothing, etc., became a significant burden for poor households, in extreme cases leading to school drop-outs. From 1982, the school attendance rate has declined, particularly in Santiago's metropolitan area.

4. As falling income and unemployment persist, the repercussions on the

household go beyond material ones, damaging the family psychologically and undermining its stability. For the households of the unemployed, the benefits of public programmes are of great importance but none the less insufficient, and a variety of buffer mechanisms are used by households facing the crisis—in particular, solidarity and co-operation networks with and among families. Households have human resources that, with minimum support, moderate adverse effects on their standards of living at both material and socio-psychological levels.

2 *The implication of the Chilean experience*

The Chilean experience shows the enormous social cost when neo-liberal economic policies are applied with extreme orthodoxy. It confirms the strong links between economic policies and the standard of living of vulnerable groups. In particular, it appears that:

1. The cuts in social expenditure in Chile were selective, as recommended by experts in social development. However, macro-economic development meant that policies that were initially selective have in time had to be aimed at broader sectors of the population, which in a situation of economic contraction may not be possible. Selective social policies, regardless of how effective they are, will always eventually be insufficient when implemented in a context of economic policies that create poverty.

2. Pregnant mothers and under-6s have been favoured by Chile's social policies in an explicit and efficient effort to benefit these groups directly. Until 1983–85, interrelated programmes of nutrition and health were successful. Their success was due to the political will of the authorities to fight malnutrition and infant mortality directly, as well as the consequence of favourable historical circumstances. The Chilean experience shows that under such circumstances nutritional intervention and health programmes for pregnant mothers and small children can be effective in spite of very significant falls in the standard of living of the population. However, there appears to have been some increase in the prevalence of illnesses. The fluctuation in the indices of nutrition and mortality in 1983 and 1985 reflects the high dependency of the population on social programmes.

3. The magnitude of the needs of poor households in Chile today requires that social programmes of relief be maintained and intensified. But the deepest problem that the country faces is unemployment and underemployment. It has been estimated that if the country grows at 5 per cent a year, which is above the average of 4.2 per cent in the 1960s, unemployment will be reduced to its historical level of 6 per cent only after 10 years (Meller and Solimano 1983).

4. In this perspective, the various household and social buffer mechanisms that allow households to maintain the quality of life gain increased relevance.

Supporting such mechanisms would promote initiative, participation, and control of the adult members of the household over their own destiny. It also offers a possibility of implementing social policies at a lower cost, for example, by the participation of mothers in primary health care and also in pre-school care. Such strategies are difficult to implement at a national and centralized level since these income-generating and resource-saving type of activities and those geared towards health and pre-school care require adaptability to the circumstances, resources, and problems of specific households and communities. In this respect, the shift of responsibilities and economic resources to the local level is potentially favourable. However, since local authorities confront very unequal situations in terms of human resources, social infrastructures, and financial resources, it is important to develop effective compensatory mechanisms among them.

Note

1. Comparison of Table 3.11 with the bottom lines of Table 3.9 indicates that (a) measurement with the Sempé criteria weight/age by the SISVAN system gives malnutrition indices that are 2 and 3 points higher than the regular and universal system used by the Health Ministry (Table 3.8); (b) if the standard WHO weight/age is applied rather than the standard Sempé weight/age, almost 20 per cent of the under-2s will show slight or moderate malnutrition, and if the WHO standard height/age is considered, almost 50 per cent of the under-6s will register some degree of malnutrition. Recent anthropometric studies show that the WHO standard is more appropriate for the Chilean population than the Sempé standard. The latter tends to significantly undervalue the malnutrition of Chilean children.

References

Acuña, E., and O. Reyes (1982), 'El desempleo y sus efectos psicosociales'. IDERTO, Universidad de Chile.

Altimir, O. (1984), 'Poverty, Income Distribution and Child Welfare in Latin America: A Comparison of Pre- and Post-recession data', in Jolly, R., and G. A. Cornia, eds., *The Impact of World Recession on Children*. London: Pergamon Press.

Arellano, J. P. (1976), 'Gasto público en salud y distribución del ingreso', in Livingstone, M., and D. Raczynski, eds., *Salud pública y bienestar social*. Santiago: CEIPLAN–Universidad Católica de Chile.

—— (1985), *Politicas sociales y desarrollo: Chile 1924–1984*. Santiago: CIEPLAN.

Arellano, J. P., and R. Cortázar (1982), 'Del milagro a la crisis: Algunas reflexiones sobre el momento económico', *Colección estudios CIEPLAN* (Santiago), no. 8.

Avec 1983), *Codo a codo* (Arzobispado de Santiago), 2/14.

Bastias, M. (1984), 'Projecto Nos Junta mos' y?: Una experiencia de educación

3 Chile 89

comunitaria de la sexualidad con pasejas de sectores populares (Chile)' in *La mujer en el sector popular urbano, America Latina y el Caribe*. Santiago: LC/G, Naciones Unidas.

Briones, G. (1984), 'La distribución de la educación en el modelo de economía neo-liberal (1974–82)', in Briones, G. *et al.*, *Desigualdad educativa en Chile*. Santiago: Programa Interdisciplinario de Investigaciones en Educación (PIIE).

Bralic *et al.* (1984) (Prevalencia de trastornes psignicos en la pobleción de Santiego', Documento de Trabajo, Centro de Estudios de Desarollo y Estimulanión Psilosocial and UNICEF, Santiago.

Castañeda, T. (1984), 'Contexto socioeconómico del descenso de la mortalidad infantil en Chile', *Estudios públicos* (Santiago), no. 16.

—— (1985), 'El impacto de las inversiones en educación en Chile, 1960–1983', *Revista de economía*, no. 80. Santiago: Universidad de Chile.

Cereceda, L. E., and M. Cifuentes (1987), *Que comen los pobres? Habitos, alimenticios, estrategics de compra y mecanismors de sobrevirencia* Cuardemos del Instituto de Sociología, Pontificia Universidad Católica de Chile, Santiago.

Chateau, J. (1981), 'Algunos antecedentes sobre la situación de los pobladores en el Gran Santiago', *Documento de trabajo*, no. 115, FLACSO Santiago.

——, and H. Pozo (1985), 'Los pobladores en el area metropolitana: situación y características', *Notas técnicas*, no. 71, Santiago: CIEPLAN.

CIEPLAN (1982), Various authors, *Modelo económico chileno: Trayectoria de una crítica*. Santiago: Editorial Aconcagua—CIEPLAN.

—— (1983), *Reconstrucción económica para la democracia*. Santiago: Editorial Aconcagua—CIEPLAN.

—— (1986), *Set de estadísticas económicas* (Santiago), no. 28.

Cifuentes, M. (1983), 'Mujer: pareja y familia' in Covarrubias, P. *et al.* (eds.), *Crisis en la familia*. Santiago: Cuadernos del Instituto de Sociología, Universidad Católica.

Colegio Medico de Chile (1983), *La salud publica en Chile, hoy*. Santiago.

Cortázar, R. (1977), 'Necesidades básicas y extrema pobreza', *Colección estudios CIEPLAN* (Santiago), no. 17.

—— (1980), 'Distribucion del ingreso, empleo y remuneraciones reales en Chile, 1970–78', *Colección estudios CIEPLAN* (Santiago), no. 3.

—— (1983), 'Chile: Resultados distributivos, 1973–1982', *Notas técnicas* (Santiago: CIEPLAN), no. 57.

——, and J. Marshall (1980), 'Indice de precios al consumidor en Chile: 1970–78', *Colección estudios CIEPLAN* (Santiago), no. 4.

de Kadt, E., M. Livingstone, and D. Raczynski (1976), 'Políticas y programs de salud, 1964–73', in Livingstone, M., and D. Raczynski, eds., *Salud pública y bienestar social*. Santiago: CIEPLAN, Universidad Católica de Chile.

Department of Economics University of Chile (various years), *Ocupación y desocupación*. Facultad de Ciencias Económicas y Administrativas, Santiago.

Duque, J., and E. Pastrana (1973), 'Las estrategias de supervivencia económica de las unidades familiares del sector popular urbano', in *Documento de Trabajo*. Santiago: CELADE-PROELCE.

Ferreiro, C. *et al.* (1983), 'Bacteremia por salmonela typhi y paratyphi en el menor de dos años', *Jornada chilena de salud* (Santiago), 9.

Ffrench-Davis, R. (1983), 'The Monetarist Experiment in Chile: A critical Survey', *World Development*, 11/11.

Filgueira, C. (1981), 'Acerca del consumo en los nuevos modelos latinoamericanos', *Revista de la CEPAL* (Santiago: ECLA), no. 15.

Foxley, A. (1980), 'Hacia una economía de libre mercado: Chile 1970–78', *Colección estudios CIEPLAN* (Santiago), no. 4.

——(1982), 'Latin American Experiments in Neo-conservative economics', *Colección estudios CIEPLAN* (Santiago), no. 7; and in University California Press, California 1983.

Foxley, A., E. Aniat, and J. P. Arellano (1979), *Redistributive Effects of Government Programmes*. Oxford: Pergamon Press.

Frias (1977), 'Cesantía y estrategia de supervivencia', *Documento de Trabajo*. Santiago: FLASCO.

Garcia, A. (1983), 'El problema alimentario y nutricional en Chile: diagnóstico y evaluación de políticas', in *Monografía sobre empleo*, 33 (PREALC/ISS 5387). Santiago: Programa Regional del Empleo para América Latina y el Caribe, OTT.

Giaconi, J. (1985), 'Organización y estructura del sector salud en Chile, 1974–84: Análisis preliminar', in Jimenez, J., ed., *Políticas y sistemas de salud: Análisis Preliminar de la década 74–83*. Santiago: CPU.

Gomez, E., B. Salinas, and E. Alalah (1983), 'Metodología de análisis de costo-efecto social, aplicada a sistemas de atención de desnutridos', *Cuadernos médico-sociales*, 24/3.

Gonzalez, N., and A. Infante (1980), 'Programas de alimentación complementaria del sector salud en Chile', *Boletín de la oficia sanitaria panamericana*, Washington, DC: OPS.

Gonzalez, N., A. Infante, and F. Mardones (1980), 'Análisis del impacto de la atención primaria de salud sobre los indicadores de salud y nutrición. Chile 1969–78', *Revista pediatría* Hospital Roberto del Río), 23.

Jadresic, E. (1985), 'Evolución del empleo sectorial: Chile, 1970–83', *Notas técnicas* (Santiago: CIEPLAN), no. 79.

——(1986), 'Por qué disminuye la tasa de desempleo?', *Mensaje* (Santiago), 35/348.

Jimenez, J. (1985), 'La salud pública en Chile 1985', *Vida médica* (Santiago: Colegio Médico de Chile), 36/1.

Klenner, A., and L. Zuñiga (1984), 'Generación de ingresos y vinculación a los mercados en la economía de la pobreza', *Documento*, UNICEF—Santiago.

Labbe, F., and M. Llevenes (1986), 'Efectos distributivos denivado del proceso de erradicoción de poblaciones en el Gran Santiago', *Documento de Trabajo*, no. 70, Centro de Estudios Publicos (CEP), Santiago.

Lira, E., and L. Weinstein (1981), 'Desempleo y daño psicológico', *Revista chilena de psicología* (Santiago), 4/2.

Marcel, M. (1984a), 'La juventud chilena: Del régimen militar a la democratización', *Notas téchnicas* (Santiago: CIEPLAN), no. 64.

——(1984b), 'Gasto social en Chile: 1979–83', *Notas técnicas* (Santiago: CIEPLAN), no. 66.

Marshall, J. (1981), 'Gasto público en Chile 1969–79: Metodología y resultados', *Notas técnicas* (Santiago: CIEPLAN), no. 33.

Martinez, J., and A. Leon (1984), 'La involución del proceso de desarrollo y la estructura social', *Materiales para discusión* (Santiago: Centro de Estudios del Desarrollo), no. 53.

Meller, P., and A. Solimano (1983), 'Desempleo en Chile: interpretacíon y polítics económicas alternativas' in A. Foxley et al. *Reconstrucción económica para la democracia*. Editorial Aconcagua—Santiago: CIEPLAN.

Ministry of Housing (1985), *Informativo estadístico*, no. 98.

Monckeberg, F., J. Mardones, and S. Valiente (1984), 'Evolución de la desnutrición y mortalidad infantil en Chile en los últimos años', *Creces*, 10, (Santiago).

Morales, E. (1982), 'Integración social, marginalidad y mercados de trabajo', *Material de discusión* (Santiago: FLACSO), no. 32.

——, and S. Rojas (1986), 'Relocalización socio-espacial de la pobreza: Política estatal y presión popular, 1979–85', *Documento de Trabajo*, no. 280. Santiago: FLACSO.

Muñoz, O. (1985), 'Chile: The Collapse of Economic Experiment and its Political Effects', *Apuntes CIEPLAN* No. 57. Santiago: CIEPLAN.

ODEPLAN (1984), *Informe social 1983*. República de Chile, Presidencia de la República.

——, and the Superintendency of Education (n.d.) 'Integrated evolution of the programme aimed at eliminating extreme poverty for children 0–14 years of age'. Mimeographed.

Raczynski, D. (1983*a*), 'Municipalización y políticas sociales'. Mimeographed. Santiago: CIEPLAN.

—— (1983*b*), 'Reformas al sector salud: Diálogos y debates', *Colección estudios CIEPLAN* (Santiago), no. 10.

—— (1986), 'La regionaizacíon y la politica econômico-social del regimen militar: el impacto regional', *Notas tecnicas*, 84. Santiago: CIEPLAN.

——, and C. Oyarzo (1981), 'Por qué cae la tasa de mortalidad infantil en Chile?', *Colección estudios CIEPLAN* (Santiago), no. 6.

——, and C. Serrano (1985), *Vivir en la pobreza: Testimonios de mujeres*. Santiago: CIEPLAN–PISPAL.

Razetto, L. *et al.* (1983), *Las organizaciones económicas populares*. Santiago: Programa de Economía del trabajo, academia de Humanismo Cristiano.

Riveros, L. (1984), 'Distribución del ingreso, empleo y política social en Chile', *Documento de trabajo*, no. 25, Centro de Estudios Públicos, Santiago.

Rodriguez, J. (1985*a*), *La distribución del ingreso y el gasto social en Chile. 1983*, Santiago: ILADES–Editorial Salesiana.

—— (1985*b*), 'School Achievement and Decentralization Policy: The Chilean Case'. Draft paper. Santiago: ILADES.

Rojas, S. (1984), 'Políticas de erradicación y radicación de campamentos 1982–84: Discurso, logros y problemas', *Documento de trabajo* (Santiago: FLASCO), no. 215.

Romero, M. I. (1985), 'Recurso humanos en salud en Chile: Análisis de una decade,' in Jimenez, J., ed., *Politicas y sistemas de salud: Análisis preliminar de la décede 74–83*. Santiago: CPU.

Ruiz-Tagle, J. (1984), 'El poder de compra de las familias populares', *Mensaje* (Santiago), no. 335.

——, and R. Urmeneta (1984), *Los trabajadores del programa de empleo mínimo*. Santiago: PET–PISPAL.

Schkolnik, M. (1985), 'Condiciones de vida y nutrición en dos poblaciones de Santiago', *Documento de trabajo* no. 42, Santiago: PET–AHC.

Solimano, A. (1983), 'Towards an Understanding of Chilean Unemployment: A Short-run Disequilibrium Analysis'. Mimeographed. Santiago: CIEPLAN.

Tacher, E. (1982), 'Effects of Declining Fertility on Infant Mortality Levels: A Study Based on Data from Five Latin American Countries'. Mimeographed report to the Ford Foundation and the Rockefeller Foundation. Santiago: CELADE.

Vargas, N. *et al.* (1984), 'Tendencias del peso de nacimiento y puntaje de APGAR 1979–1983 en el área occidente de Santiago', *Revista Chilena de Pediatría*, 55/3.

Vergara, P. (1981), 'Las transformaciones de las funciones económicas del estado en Chile bajo el régimen miitar', *Colección estudios CIEPLAM* (Santiago), no. 5.

Vives, C. (1983), *Crisis en la familia popular y su visión de futuro*. Centro Bellarmino, Departamento de Investigaciones Sociológicas, Santiago.

4

Adjustment Policies and Programmes to Protect Children and Other Vulnerable Groups in Ghana

UNICEF, Accra

Improving the living standards of the rural populace and the working classes generally is, in the final analysis, the very essence of the Economic Recovery Programme and the ultimate standard by which its success will need to be judged.

The economic difficulties of the late seventies and early eighties have had serious consequences for the living standards of many Ghanaians, especially on their health and nutrition status, and on access to education by lower income groups. The sacrifices involved have been in many cases, crushing. The Economy Recovery Programme will need to address issues related to rehabilitating the country's human capital through programmes targeted at specific vulnerable groups, the upgrading of our local training and retraining capability as well as increased expenditures and improved policies in the health and education sectors.

Dr Kwesi Botchwey, PNDC Secretary for Finance and Economic Planning, 'Overview' to *Progress of the Economic Recovery Programme 1984–86 and Policy Framework 1986–88* (Accra 1985).

I Economic stagnation and human welfare

1 The economic stagnation and drought, 1974–1984

Throughout the latter half of the 1960s and 1970s, the Ghanaian economy was caught in the grip of a downward spiral which Ghanaians thought was almost irreversible. This was due to a combination of economic mismanagement and adverse external developments. GNP per capita declined in every year except one between 1974 and 1982. Between 1974 and 1982, constant price GNP per capita fell by 28 per cent (Table 4.1) amidst major food shortages and greatly increased living costs.

The most serious problems that faced the economy were the declines in production in all sectors of the economy and most particularly exports and food (Table 4.1). Food self-sufficiency ratios in relation to basic consumption requirements declined from 83 per cent in 1964–66 to 71 in 1978–80 and then to only 60 in 1982. With neither commercial imports nor food aid available in adequate volume, by 1982 total food availability was equal to only 68 per cent of estimated minimum basic calorie requirements.

The index of mineral production declined by 46 percentage points between 1975 and 1982, while the index for all manufacturing output declined by 50 per cent between 1975 and 1981. The output of cocoa, which is the major source of foreign exchange and a substantial source of government revenue, fell precipitously from nearly 400,000 tons in 1975 to 179,000 tons in 1982.

The sharp decline in economic activities concentrated especially in tax paying activities, led to a dwindling of government resources. The ratio of government revenue to current GDP fell from 16.2 per cent in 1974–75 to 6 per cent in 1982 (Table 4.2). There was an equally dramatic fall in government expenditure. Total recurrent and capital expenditure fell from over 27 per cent of GDP in 1975 to 10.1 per cent in 1983. The ensuing large budgetary deficits and persistent expansion in money supply, combined with declining production and import capacity, generated high rates of inflation. In 1977, for the first—but not the last—time, Ghana experienced a three-digit inflation, with the inflation rate rising to 117 per cent (Table 4.3).

In the external sector, there was a persistent decline in export volume from the mid-1960s and especially after 1975. By 1981, export volume was less than one-half that of 1975 with a decline in the production of cocoa being the main factor, but production of other major exports (timber and gold) also fell. The fall in production was in large part a consequence of domestic policies. But the effects were greatly magnified by severe adverse developments in Ghana's external circumstances. World prices of major exports fell; combined with the rise in the oil price in 1973–74 and 1978–79, this led to a sharp worsening in Ghana's terms of trade. In 1982 Ghana's terms of trade index was less than half of the 1974 index. Assistance from the international community was also extremely low. For example, in 1982 Ghana received $12.6 aid per capita, which compares with $26.1 received by low-income countries as a whole in Sub-Saharan Africa.

The combined effect of falling export volume, deteriorating terms of trade, and falling capital inflows was a very large reduction in Ghana's import capacity. Import volume in 1982 was 36 per cent of the 1974 level.

In summary, the principal features of the economic crisis from a standard macro-economic perspective can be identified as follows:

1. A fall in the production of food, minerals and manufactured goods.
2. Deterioration in the terms of trade.
3. Critical shortage of foreign exchange.
4. Dislocation of the transport and communications system through lack of maintenance and unavailability of spare parts and other necessary imported inputs.
5. Acute shortages of consumer goods, industrial raw materials, and spare parts.

TABLE 4.1 *Selected economic indicators, 1974–1983*

	Unit	1974	1975	1976	1977	1978	1979	1980	1981	1982	1983	1984
Real GNP (1975 prices)	C million	5,687	4,918	4,718	4,850	5,321	5,173	5,183	5,004	4,670	4,694	5,071
Per capita national income	C million (1975 prices)	587	493	460	459	504	478	467	439	399	391	415
Money supply	C million	697	1,009	1,430	2,386	4,088	4,631	6,058	9,415	11,440	16,861	23,744
Government revenues	C million	805	815	1,075	1,539	2,188	3,026	3,279	4,855	5,253	10,241	22,641
Government expenditure	C million	1,162	1,439	1,945	3,018	4,094	4,672	7,719	9,530	8,846	14,752	22,694
Exports	C million	841	928	961	1,166	1,581	2,737	3,158	2,686	2,402	6,999	21,356
Imports	C million	944	909	992	1,193	1,682	2,344	3,104	3,484	1,939	8,740	28,911
Balance on current account	C million		7	−70	−216	−321	110	−151	−1,397	−435	−4,600	−4,160
External debt (end year)	$ million			744	797	848	924	1,035	1,114	1,121	1,141	1,122
Agricultural production												
Cereals	000 t	890	672	689	639	540	780	674	725	543	308	871
Starchy staples	000 t	7,988	5,462	4,435	5,995	4,105	3,927	4,349	4,114	4,431	3,657	4,083[a]
Cocoa	000 t	382	397	327	277	268	281	254	220	179	159	172
Petrol (net imports)	000 t		777	854	850	857	867	806	883	811	337	884
All manufacturing	1975 = 100	92	100	96	98	95	79	78	63	50	48	52
Electricity generation			3,966	4,226	4,447	3,771	4,683	5,309	5,382	4,973	2,578	1,830
All mineral	1975 = 100		100	97	87	76	65	64	60	54	46	—

Source: Adapted from World Bank (1985*a*), Vol. II.
[a] Cassava only. Excludes cocoyam, yam, plantain, which were 1,928 t in 1983.

TABLE 4.2 *Selected budgetary indicators, 1974–1984*

	1974	1975	1976	1977	1978	1979	1980	1981	1982	1983	1984
GDP (current prices, C million)	4,660	5,283	6,526	11,163	20,986	28,222	42,852	72,626	87,470	191,640	275,035
Government revenue (C million)[a]	805	815	1,075	1,539	2,188	3,026	3,279	4,855	5,253	10,241	22,641
Government revenue/GDP[b]	16.2	13.8	12.1	9.6	8.9	8.5	5.6	6.0	6.0	5.3	8.2
Government expenditure (C million)[a]											
Recurrent	—	997	1,308	2,322	3,335	4,077	6,329	8,603	8,029	13,404	22,710
Capital[c]	—	714	887	971	1,007	7,107	1,657	1,101	1,191	1,774	5,052
Total	—	1,711	2,195	3,293	4,341	4,787	7,986	9,703	9,220	15,178	27,762
Government expenditure/GDP[b]											
Recurrent	—	16.8	14.8	14.4	13.6	11.5	10.6	10.6	9.2	7.05	8.1
Capital	—	10.4	11.1	6.1	4.1	2.0	2.8	1.4	1.4	0.91	1.8
Total	—	27.2	25.9	20.5	17.7	13.5	13.4	12.0	10.6	7.96	9.9
Government financing requirement (C million)[a]	482	897	1,120	1,754	2,154	1,760	4,707	4,848	3,967	4,937	54,844
Government financing requirement/GDP[b]	—	13.4	13.8	10.9	8.8	5.0	8.0	6.0	4.5	2.6	1.8

Source: Adapted from World Bank (1985a) vol. ii.

[a] Fiscal year. From 1982 fiscal and calendar years are the same.

[b] Fiscal year data as per cent of average of GDP of two relevant calendar years, until 1982.

[c] Development expenditure plus net lending.

TABLE 4.3   *Prices, 1975–1985 (1977 = 100)*

	National	Rural	Urban	Food prices	Inflation rate[a]
1975	30	29	31		29.8
1976	46	46	47		56.1
1977	100	100	100	100	116.5
1978	173	175	172	159	73.7
1979	267	279	257	258	53.9
1980	401	448	363	393	50.1
1981	869	939	800	829	116.5
1982	1,062	1,150	978	1,125	22.3
1983	2,367	2,640	2,193	2,755	122.8
1984	3,305	3,654	2,960	3,059	39.4
1985	3,649	3,935[b]	3,230[b]	2,719	10.4

Sources: government statistics
[a] National consumer prices, percentage increase over previous year
[b] First six months.

6. High rates of inflation.
7. An increasingly overvalued exchange rate with resulting increases in the share of external trade accounted for by smuggling.

These factors were self-reinforcing with one accentuating others, while action designed to deal with one factor tended to be counteracted by others.

In 1982 and 1983, the economy was subjected to three further shocks. First, the prolonged drought and the accompanying bush-fires aggravated the already low production of food crops and created the worst food shortages since independence. Secondly, the sudden influx of about one million Ghanaians from Nigeria in January 1983 put a severe strain on the already critical food and unemployment situation. Thirdly, the cocoa price fell markedly.

The drought was the worst in living memory, with effects that extended well into 1984. There was a dramatic escalation in food prices from the beginning of 1982, and they continued to rise until the middle of 1984.

2   *Impact of the recession on Ghanaians*

The impact of the recession on the Ghanaians, viewed from the perspectives of household incomes, government expenditure, service coverage, and health and nutritional status, was every bit as severe as the failures shown by the macro-economic indicators imply. What these indicators do not readily convey is the human cost.

(a) Household incomes Real incomes per head have fallen substantially among most Ghanaians since 1970.

In the *urban* areas, high rates of inflation in relation to money incomes have

TABLE 4.4   *Index of employees' earnings, 1974–1985 (1974 = 100)*

	Minimum wage			Average monthly earnings[a]		
	C/day	Index (nominal)	Index (real)	C/month	Index (nominal)	Index (real)
1974	2.00	67	292	95.0	79	345
1975	2.00	67	225	101.6	84	285
1976	2.00	67	144	114.0	95	204
1977	3.00[b]	100	100	215.0	100	100
1978	4.00	133	77	226.1	188	109
1979	4.00	133	50	285.8	238	89
1980	5.33[c]	178	44	461.0	352	88
1981	12.00	400	46	(575.0)[e]	539	62
1982	12.00	400	38	645	—	11
1983	25.00[f]	833	32	—	—	—
1984	35.00[g]	1,167	39	—	—	—
1985	70.00[h]	2,333	72[d]	—	—	—

Source: World Bank (1985*a*), vol. ii, Tables 9.07, 9.08.
[a] Salaries and wages and other remunerations in establishments with more than 10 employees.
[b] C2 up to June and C4 thereafter.
[c] C4 up to October and C12 thereafter.
[d] Provisional.
[e] Partially interpolated (1981 data incomplete in basic source).
[f] From April 1983.
[g] From April 1984.
[h] From March 1985.

drastically reduced real incomes. Formal sector wage and salaried employees were severely affected. By 1980, the real minimum wage had fallen to 15 per cent of its 1974 value (Table 4.4). Despite subsequent nominal wage increases, the real minimum wage continued to fall until 1983. In 1985 and 1986 there were modest increases in the real value of the minimum wage, but it remained substantially below the 1974 level.

This meant that for many employees, the real remuneration for formal sector work could not support the food requirements of one single adult, let alone those of the family plus their clothing, education, health, and housing requirements.

At the worst point following the drought when food prices were at their peak (June 1984), an estimate of the market cost of a minimum-nutrition diet in the urban areas was 168 cedis per person daily. For a household of five this comes to 25,200 cedis monthly. Assuming 80 per cent of expenditure on food and 20 per cent on all other items, the minimum socially acceptable household budget would have been of the order of 31,500 cedis a month in mid-1984. At that time the minimum wage was 35 cedis a day—or under 1,000 cedis a month—and upper middle-level civil service salaries were 2,000 cedis a month.

It is clear that households of formal sector wage earners must have been receiving additional sources of income—in cash or kind, or both—in order to survive in these circumstances. This is supported by data from a household sample survey in Accra's major low-income area, Nima/Maamobi, which showed monthly expenditure per person of 1,230 cedis on food and 1,450 cedis overall—7,250 cedis for a five-person household. Even using 85 per cent of its expenditure on food and (for a household of five) spending 8 times the minimum wage, the food purchased was only 40.75 cedis per day, or under 30 per cent of the World Bank estimates of the cost of an acceptable diet. With the end of the drought, the situation has improved—food prices have declined by about 30 per cent and minimum wages have doubled. But this still leaves a very large gap between household budget requirements for an acceptable diet (of around 23,800 cedis) and the minimum wage (of 1,750 cedis a month).

A majority of economically active Ghanaians, even in urban areas, are informally employed rather than in recorded wage employment. Open unemployment is not high in Ghana, since most people have to find some employment to survive. In the 1970s, incomes in the informal sector were on average lower than those of formal sector wage earners. There are no adequate data to show the relationship between formal and informal sector earnings in recent years. Imbalances between supply and demand—associated especially with price controls, the import licensing system, and the vastly overvalued exchange rate—gave rise to unofficial markets and to opportunities for remunerative rent-seeking activities which raised informal sector earnings for some households. But other factors acted to depress earnings, including the stagnation of wage employment which swelled the supply of entrants into the increasingly overcrowded informal sector.

Income data have become hard to interpret because no household can survive on one minimum wage and *virtually none maintain even moderately acceptable* living standards on any public or most private sector salaries. Most low-income households who have a member working in formal employment also participate in informal sector activities. Second occupations—ranging from farming and sheep-raising through baking bread and artisanry to a variety of illicit activities—are common and necessary.

Rural dwellers were for the most part at least as severely affected by the economic stagnation as most urban Ghanaians. Their incomes dwindled because of the fall in agricultural cash crop production and a high rate of inflation. Until the drought, food producers' incomes seem to have been less severely affected than most other groups (see Horton 1985).

Cocoa farmers' incomes fell from 1970 onwards as a result of declining agricultural output combined with a sharp drop in the real producer price of cocoa until 1983. In 1982 the producer price of cocoa was about one-third of the 1970 price in real terms. As a result cocoa was not replanted, disease control was minimal, and even relatively healthy, productive farms were not well tended. Cocoa production fell from 413,000 tons in 1970 to 159,000 in 1983. The fall in cocoa output was a major cause of the falls in export earnings and government revenues which have plagued Ghana. While cocoa farmers did shift in part to food production—to some degree limiting falls in their own incomes—this did not lead to a rapid growth of food output; on the contrary food production has risen less rapidly than population over the past quarter century.

Nominal and real wages of agricultural labourers grew more slowly than wages in manufacturing from 1970 to 1979. Their monthly wages fell from about half to under two-fifths of those of manufacturing sector employees.

The trend in the real income of food growing farmers is less certain and more diversified. There has been some increase in real unit prices, but this was generally more than offset by declining per capita production.

Northern and Upper Region farmers fared particularly badly with respect to prices and production. Their main cash crops—yams and ground nuts— showed the lowest real price increases, while they were worst affected by drought. Since the improvement in the weather, food prices have fallen significantly, but the Northern and Upper Regions have not shared fully in the recovery in production.

Over 1984–85 it seems there has been some recovery in rural smallholder real incomes largely because of better food output for self-provisioning and higher real agricultural wages.

Absolute poverty indices have not been constructed for Ghana in recent years. The World Bank estimated an absolute poverty line in Ghana in 1978 of $307 per capita in urban and $130 per capita in rural areas, when GDP per capita was $390. Roughly 30 to 35 per cent of urban households and 60 to 65 per cent of rural households were then in absolute poverty. Despite data deficiencies, there is sufficient information to show the very severe deterioration in incomes among most households in both rural and urban areas that accompanied the prolonged stagnation, while the drought produced a further sharp decline. It is clear that the proportion of households falling below the absolute poverty line is now over 50 per cent. There is a need for improved data to clarify the situation further.

(b) Government expenditure in the social sectors The fall in government revenue and the spiralling inflation have made it impossible to allocate adequate resources to the basic social services—health, education, and water. While the share of education and health in the budget has been fairly constant—declining from 20.7 per cent in 1972 to 20.2 per cent for education in 1982 and from 7.8 per cent to 6.1 per cent for health—this is within a budget which fell over that period from 18.3 per cent to 10.1 per cent of GNP, while GNP per capita was itself declining, falling by nearly one-third over the period. Therefore, real expenditure, both absolutely and per capita, has fallen sharply (Table 4.5). This has led to acute shortages of drugs and equipment, while real salaries of personnel have been reduced substantially.

1. *Health sector.* The foreign exchange constraint considerably reduced the availability of imported inputs for the social services. In the health sector, for

TABLE 4.5 *Index of health and education expenditure per capita, 1969/70–1982 (1975/76 = 100)*

	Education	Health
1969/70	77.3	71.6
1975/76	100.0	100.0
1978/79	94.4	84.9
1979/80	55.2	47.2
1980/81	35.7	35.8
1982	28.7	22.6

Source: World Bank (1985*a*), vol. ii.
Note: All figures are in real terms, deflated by GDP deflator for services.

instance, old equipment in health institutions could neither be repaired for lack of spare parts nor replaced. The supply situation has deteriorated over the past five years. Basic drugs such as nivaquine and aspirin and consumables such as bandages, needles, and syringes are today in desperately short supply, often not available for months on end in many rural clinics. The foreign exchange allocated to the Ministry of Health has been a very low proportion of ministry estimates of needs. The poor road system and the lack of a fleet of vehicles in good running condition has made the distribution of the few supplies extremely difficult in the rural areas, although private hospitals and clinics have been relatively successful in securing supplies. Urban and regional hospital facilities have fallen into disrepair for lack of maintenance.

The exodus of health manpower has worsened an already inequitable distribution of health personnel. The country lost more than 50 per cent of its doctors between 1981 and April 1984, and about 8.5 per cent of nurses in 1982 alone.

These constraints facing the health services led to a contraction of the services in a situation where effective coverage was already poor and health status low: in 1977/78 it was estimated that only 30 per cent of the population had access to formal health care, including public and private facilities. The consequences of the constraints are that those health services which are available have been functioning below capacity and have been incapable of tackling the major health problems of the country. These health problems include communicable diseases, environmental problems, and maternal and child health, including nutrition.

Hospital records show that annual attendances have dropped considerably. For example, in Korle Bu Hospital, the out-patient attendance in 1983 was 117,000, compared with 198,000 in 1979. The situation in the mission hospitals was much better because medical equipment was functioning more efficiently, drugs and medical supplies were more adequate, and the loss in health manpower was less. Annual attendances in Duayaw-Nkwanta (a Catholic hospital), for instance, increased fom 40,000 in 1979 to 49,000 in 1983. Overall, health unit attendances fell from 7,613,624 in 1979 to 4,468,482 in 1984.

2. *Education.* Educational expenditures per capita fell by over 70 per cent from 1975 to 1982. The education sector has also been adversely affected by foreign exchange shortages and by the exodus of trained people. There have been shortages of textbooks, paper and other school materials, teaching aids, and school equipment.

The proportion of trained teachers in elementary schools dropped from 71 per cent in 1976/77 to 54 per cent in 1980/81 because of the exodus to better-paying occupations both in Ghana and abroad. The education sector lost 4,000 trained teachers between 1976/77 and 1980/81.

3. *Water.* In the water sector, coverage increased from 27 per cent in 1960 to around 59 per cent by 1983 (urban coverage in 1983 was 94 per cent and rural 38 per cent). But the average per capita consumption has been low (it is estimated sometimes as low as 19 litres per capita per day in the major urban areas) because of the lack of spares to repair over-aged equipment. In the rural areas, most communities do not have access to good drinking water since many of the boreholes or wells which have been provided have fallen out of use because of inadequate pump maintenance. The situation is particularly bad among small communities. The majority of rural communities therefore depend on polluted sources of water, resulting in a high incidence of water-borne diseases.

Substantial progress was made in the water sector in the late 1970s and early 1980s particularly in the Northern, Upper, and Volta regions and in the forest belt. However, despite continued assistance toward maintenance, sustaining these gains is precariously balanced given present budgetary constraints. Older sets of boreholes have become largely non-functional.

(c) The human impact Information on the human dimensions of the economic stagnation in Ghana is not systematically collected, published, and used in the way that information on economic indicators is routinely made available. Changing trends in welfare indicators have therefore been difficult to measure. However, enough data are available to show that the negative impact of the recession in terms of poverty and human deprivation led to a substantial deterioration in the well-being of Ghanaians (Table 4.6).

1. *Growing morbidity and mortality.* Parasitic and infectious diseases related to poverty and underdevelopment like malaria, intestinal parasites, malnutrition, and scabies, continue to afflict a majority of Ghanaians. In addition diseases virtually eradicated by campaigns in the 1950s and 1960s—notably yaws and yellow fever—began to reappear in the late 1970s as nutrition and health services declined, with major epidemics in the Northern and Upper regions in

TABLE 4.6   *Selected quality of life indicators, 1960—mid 1980s*

		Ghana				Low-income Sub-Saharan Africa 1982
		1960	1970	Late 1970s	1980s	
1.	Average life expectancy at Birth	45	49	55	53	48
2.	Infant mortality rate	132	107	86	107–120	118
3	Child death rate	27	21	15	25–30	24
4.	Access to health facilities	—	—	—	30	45
5.	Public health facility visits per person per year	—	—	0.7	0.4	2
6.	Health budget as % of GDP	—	1.2	—	0.26	0.95
7.	Access to pure water	—	35	35	60	22
	Rural	—	14	14	48	14
	Urban	—	86	86	75	62
8.	Access to excreta disposal	—	55	56	44	32
	Rural	—	40	40	30	25
	Urban	—	92	95	65	69
9.	Average calorie availability as % of requirements	92	97	88	68	91
10.	Child malnutrition[a]	—	—	36	50–55	40
11.	Primary education enrolment ratio[b]	38 (46)	64 (75)	69 (80)	– (80)	69 (–)
12.	Adult literacy	27	30	—	35–45	44
13	Education budget as % of GDP	—	3.9	—	0.85	2.81
14.	% population below absolute poverty line					
	Rural	—	—	60–65	65–75	65
	Urban	—	—	30–35	45–50	35

Sources: World Bank, *World Development Reports*; Ghana government statistics; UNICEF estimates.
[a] Moderate and severe.
[b] Figures in parentheses are for boys only.

1977, 1981, and 1983. The crude death rate is still high, between 19 and 20 per 1,000.

Infant mortality fell from around 130 per 1,000 in the mid-1960s to 107 per 1,000 in 1970 and was perhaps as low as 80 per 1,000 in the mid-1970s. However by 1980, UNICEF estimates based on demographic data suggested it was around 100, and 1983–84 estimates are in the range of 110 to 120. Similarly the child (1–4) death rate, which fell from 27 per 1,000 in 1960 to 21 in 1970 and as low as 15 in the late 1970s, we believe rose as high as 30 per 1,000 in 1983–84. Over half of all deaths in Ghana are of infants and children under 5, and of these over half would be preventable with general availability and application of low-cost health measures.

2. *The nutritional status of under-5s deteriorates.* The decreased production of food, coupled with the declining purchasing power of Ghanaians and the dramatic increase in food prices had a most devastating effect on the nutritional status of Ghanaians, particularly pregnant and lactating mothers and pre-school children. Estimates from the Ministry of Agriculture show that per capita food availability in 1982 was 30 per cent lower than 10 years before. During the recession, most Ghanaian families were reduced to having one meal a day, with a very high dependence on root crops since these were relatively cheaper.

Nutritional studies undertaken between 1982 and 1983 in the Brong Ahafo, Northern, Greater Accra, Central, and Eastern regions indicate that the caloric and protein intake of children was below 69 per cent and 87 per cent of requirements respectively. Pregnant and lactating mothers also satisfied less than 85 per cent of their caloric needs and less than 90 per cent of their protein needs. A small-scale nutrition survey carried out in 1983 in eight southern villages indicated that 5 per cent of under-5s were severely malnourished, and that 50 per cent weighed less than 90 per cent of the standard weight for age. Recent World Bank and UNICEF estimates show 45–50 per cent moderately and 2–7 per cent severely undernourished.

Data collected while administering feeding supplements during the drought (Fig. 4.1) show that the nutritional situation of pre-school children worsened in all regions between 1980 and 1983, with 1983 being the worst year because of the drought, and the Northern and Upper regions having the worst rates. The proportion of children whose weight for age was below the third percentile of the Harvard standard increased from 35 per cent in 1980 to 42 per cent in 1982 and 47 per cent in 1983. In the second half of 1984 the proportion fell following a better harvest, but remained well above that of 1980–81.

The above data are not representative as they are confined to children taken to clinics to participate in feeding programmes. This may bias the data in two opposing directions. On the one hand mainly children who are in need are taken to the clinics. But on the other hand, the most seriously impoverished and deprived normally do not get to the clinics. The precise extent of malnutrition is not known, but available data show that it is a very serious problem and give a realistic indication of changes over time.

The data on food availability, food prices, and nutritional status, taken together with those on incomes, underline the fact that Ghana's nutrition problem is not simply one of food availability. True, unless food supply is restored to, say, 90 per cent of basic calorie requirements, substantial mal-

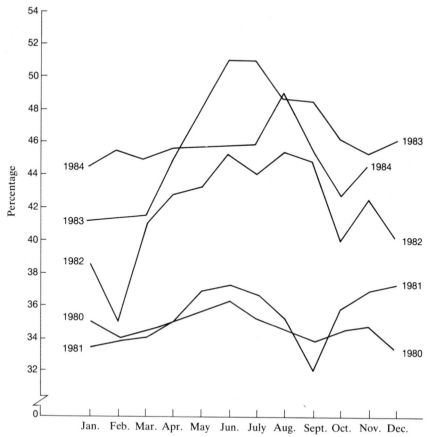

Source: Catholic Relief Services.
Note: The Catholic Relief Services (CRS) data are based on children attending health posts.
Nutritional levels are assessed relative to the Harvard standards of weight for age. The cutoff
point used by CRS is whether or not children are below the third percentile of the Harvard
standard. The measure is almost identical to the more commonly used cutoff (80 per cent of the
median value for weight for age in the Harvard population).

Fig. 4.1   Ghana: malnutrition among under-5s, 1980–1984

nutrition will inevitably remain. But as the urban budget data cited earlier
show, the main problem for many urban households is the low level of their
real incomes. With 1985 levels of the minimum wage, a large cut in food prices
(e.g. of one-quarter below 1985 levels) would still leave many families relying
on wage-employment with insufficient incomes to support adequate food consumption. For rural families too, an increase in incomes is essential for them
to improve household diets.

The Northern and Upper Regions' position is especially precarious. They are usually perceived as food deficit regions. This is certainly true in nutritional terms but is the inverse of reality on a commercial flow basis. They are large net exporters of groundnuts, yams, cattle, and (from large farms) rice to southern Ghana and smaller importers of maize (largely to the regional capitals). They also export groundnuts, and in many years millet and guinea corn, to Burkina Faso. The cause of this apparent paradox is not hard to find. The rural households of the Northern and Upper regions are very poor and their basic cash crops are food crops. As they have non-food needs which can be met only by cash, they must sell food even if this holds household consumption—especially during the notorious pre-harvest 'hungry season'— far below nutritionally acceptable levels. The way to improve the situation is not by encouraging food production at the expense of cash crops. Rather, it can only be found through enabling Northern and Upper Region peasants to grow *more of all types of crop*—including food for own-consumption, food crops for sale, and non-food crops and cattle.

3. *Declining education quality and growing child labour.* There have been chronic shortages of teaching materials and a massive flight of trained teachers. This has resulted in a serious deterioration in the quality of primary education most vividly illustrated by an increase in child labour and high drop-out rates in primary schools. In 1978/79 an estimated 75 per cent of boys and 63 per cent of girls in the age-group were enrolled in the first grade of primary school. There were very large regional differences, with much lower enrolment rates in the Northern Region (50 per cent of boys and 30 per cent of girls) and the Upper Region (39 per cent boys, 26 per cent of girls). Annual drop-out rates were 8 per cent for girls and 5 per cent for boys.

The deteriorating educational system will have adverse effects on the future potential of the Ghanaian labour force. Lower rates of education among girls will further constrain the household's capacity to raise, or even maintain, standards of health and nutrition.

There is evidence of increasing intensity of child labour which illustrates the interconnection between deepening poverty and reduced access to basic services. Child labour—in the sense of domestic household chores and agricultural work, especially at seasonal peaks—is traditional in Ghana. When moderate in amount it need not be inconsistent with child welfare nor—given suitable phasing of school vacations to coincide with regional peak labour requirements in agriculture—with benefiting from primary school. But as households have become poorer, child labour has become more crucial to making ends meet and has therefore been intensified. It has contributed to the high drop-out rates, especially among girls, as well as to irregular attendance and children too tired to benefit from classes. Further, child labour in the informal urban sector, most apparent in hawking—and a modern (and much worse) form, 'child pawning' into domestic service to reduce the living costs of poor households—has reached levels markedly above those which existed 20 or even 10 years ago. These child labourers, virtually without exception, will never attend school. Again, the intense use of child labour is more prevalent in the northern zone, in the rural areas, and in the urban informal sector in the cities.

3 Groups affected by the recession

While almost all Ghanaians have been adversely affected by the recession, some groups were especially acutely affected by the economic crisis. These groups can be identified as low-income households in the urban centres and small rural farmers. In the rural areas, the most severely affected groups are small farmers in northern Ghana. Within the households of these severely affected categories, women and children have been especially vulnerable.

The physical quality of life index (Table 4.7) shows regional disparities which have not altered significantly over the years. The Northern, Upper East, and Upper West regions stand out as the poorest, both in their urban and rural areas.

TABLE 4.7 *Physical quality of life index, 1969–1970 (percentage scores)*

	Urban	Rural
ALL REGIONS	58.6	37.3
Greater Accra	76.6	52.4
Eastern	53.2	46.8
Central	50.5	36.3
Western	62.6	40.8
Volta	53.6	49.3
Ashanti	62.0	45.2
Brong-Ahafo	50.1	35.2
Northern	42.7	13.0
Upper	45.3	13.9

Source: UNICEF—Ghana (1984).

The particularly depressed situation in the northern sector of the country is also confirmed by data on infant mortality rates and the Catholic Relief Services data on nutrition. The southern sector, on the other hand, is better endowed in terms of natural resources and social and physical infrastructure, while data show a better health and nutritional status there. Nonetheless, there were groups in the southern sector who were as severely affected as those in the northern sector, including some small-scale farmers and low-income urban dwellers.

A brief description of the characteristics which made some categories especially susceptible to the effects of the recession is contained in the following paragraphs.

(a) **Women and children** The nutritional status of pregnant and lactating mothers and children is the lowest in the country, and they were severely affected by the inadequate food supply during the stagnation and especially during the drought in 1982 and 1983, as has been shown above. Other health indicators also demonstrate the low health status of women and children.

The maternal mortality rate is estimated at between 5 and 15 per 1,000 live births. The high rate is due to the frequency of births and the high fertility rate, estimated at about 6–7 per woman. These problems are more acute in the rural areas. More than 80 per cent of rural women are delivered at home by traditional birth attendants or relatives because of the poor provision of midwifery services. Such personnel are untrained and their practices are unhygienic, thus increasing maternal mortality.

As indicated earlier, infant and child mortality rates are also very high. It is estimated that although the under-5s account for less than 20 per cent of the total population, they account for 50 per cent of all reported deaths. Forty-five per cent of all infant deaths occur in the neonatal period. The causes of the high neonatal mortality are considered to be high fertility rates, low maternal nutrition leading to low birth weight, and lack of antenatal care.

(b) **The northern sector of the country** The poor health status of people in the northern sector is partly due to the sparse distribution of health personnel and facilities. For the Upper and Northern regions, in 1975, the population per hospital bed was 1:1,209 compared with a ratio of 1:952 for the Greater Accra Region. In 1984 these regions, with about 19 per cent of Ghana's population, accounted for only 5 per cent of public health facility attendance (Table 4.8). There are also big differences in primary school enrolment, with the Northern and Upper regions having much lower enrolment rates than the rest of the country.

Regional differences in resource endowments and imbalances in development between the north and the south have affected agricultural production. The latest data available show that in 1979 the Northern and Upper regions accounted for over 40 per cent of the total area but produced only 14 per cent of the tonnage of agricultural produce. Compared to the rest of the country, shortages of food occur with greater intensity and for longer periods in the year in the north because of the single rainfall regime. In 1982, for instance, as a result of the drought, the percentage of pre-school children below the third percentile of the Harvard standard in the Upper and Northern regions was the highest, at about 60 per cent compared to 42 per cent for the rest of the country.

TABLE 4.8   *Health unit attendance (thousands) by region, 1979–1984*

	1979	1980	1981	1982	1983	1984
Greater Accra	117.2	95.3	69.9	77.2	61.9	75.6
Index	100.0	81.2	59.6	65.8	52.8	64.5
Eastern	151.3	113.4	90.1	111.2	114.9	86.2
Index	100.0	74.9	59.5	73.4	75.9	56.9
Central	57.3	51.4	47.2	49.7	28.1	22.0
Index	100.0	89.7	82.4	86.8	49.0	38.3
Volta	111.6	92.6	79.8	94.4	68.3	95.3
Index	100.0	83.0	71.5	84.6	61.2	85.4
Western	62.3	53.8	34.7	55.4	18.6	21.1
Index	100.0	86.3	55.6	88.9	29.9	33.8
Ashanti	98.0	98.4	90.0	87.9	66.4	69.2
Index	100.0	100.4	91.8	89.6	67.7	70.5
Brong Ahafo	106.1	97.7	91.8	91.0	83.4	58.2
Index	100.0	92.0	86.4	85.5	78.5	54.8
Northern	26.4	17.6	12.3	14.2	09.7	09.6
Index	100.0	66.6	46.4	53.9	36.6	36.3
Upper	31.0	13.5	28.9[a]	43.6[a]	22.3[a]	09.8
Index	100.0	43.4	93.0	140.6	72.0	31.6
TOTAL	7614.0	6240.0	5346.0	6244.0	4736.0	4468.0
Index	100.0	82.0	70.2	82.1	62.2	58.7

Source: Ministry of Health.
Note: Coverage comprises all government health service facilities including CHAG, the Christian hospital group. Level of reporting constant over period.
[a] Includes mass vaccinations against yaws and yellow fever which recurred after near-elimination in 1960s.

(c) **Small-scale farmers** Small-scale farmers form about 80 per cent of farmers in the country, and produce the bulk of the country's food supplies. On average, only about 3.0 per cent of the country's expenditures is spent on capital development in the rural areas. This means that small-scale farmers— and especially farmers off main roads—generally have little access to social infrastructural facilities such as education, health, water, and sanitation. Despite the nominal availability of uncultivated land, the reality is that farmers have decreasing access to agriculturally suitable land with adequate transport and social infrastructure.

With increasing population, average land per person fell 30 per cent from 3.5 hectares in 1970 to 2.4 hectares in 1984. This fall has not been offset by any substantial increase in output per hectare, so that output of food per peasant household has fallen. In some areas—notably, the Upper East Region—this relates directly to the increased number of years of cultivation, reducing the historic fallow period. A second cause is that agricultural research, especially on farm economics and farming systems, has paid very little attention to the food crops produced by small farmers primarily for their own consumption. This is particularly true of yams, groundnuts, millet, and guinea corn, the main crops grown for own-consumption and cash in the northern sector. Input supply has also been biased against this type of farmer.

The seasonality of rainfall is a further problem for the small-scale farmer, especially in times of drought. The most critical period for the small-scale farmer begins just before the rains, when cash and other resources become depleted and body weights fall. The rainy season is often the least healthy time since this is also the time that debilitating diseases like malaria peak, while the immune response is at its lowest.

Among small-scale farmers those, who live in small communities with populations less than 1,000 and cultivating less than two acres of land are the most deprived: they have no access to irrigation facilities and their supply of agricultural inputs is very limited and often untimely. Because of their scattered distribution such communities have benefited little from programmes in the social sectors.

(d) The urban poor The households which have been hardest hit by the economic stagnation are the urban poor. This is hard to prove quantitatively because of the aggregation of available data. However, it is supported by data on incomes and food prices (Table 4.4), as well as casual observation of the urban situation. Greater Accra was found to have the highest proportion of clinics with very high levels of child malnutrition (14 out of 17, or 83 per cent), compared with 73 per cent in the Upper Region, 50 per cent in the Northern Region, and 27 per cent in the rest of the country.

The nature of the human situation in low-income urban households can be illustrated by Nima-Maamobi, Accra's largest slum area, with a current population estimated at over 80,000. These people are crammed into 473 acres, giving a residential density of about 170 per acre. In 1976, when the population was significantly lower, 60 per cent of all families (with a median size of 4.5) occupied only one room.

About 65 per cent of heads of household in 1976 (the latest survey data available) earned less than the average annual wage and salary income, and almost all households required two or more incomes to survive. As shown earlier, family expenditure during the drought period was grossly inadequate to secure enough food.

Nima-Maamobi has only one public health facility (a polyclinic) for its 80,000 people—about twice the national ratio—and 13 primary schools, which suggests an enrolment ratio substantially below the national average.

There are 12 public water points in the area, and 300 houses with piped connections. This means roughly 6,000 per standpipe, compared with a target level of 500. The 12 points would theoretically allow approximately one and a half minutes per person per day if they were in use 12 hours a day—a figure amply demonstrating their total inadequacy. Water can indeed be bought from water carriers and private households with connections, but given typical income levels few households can afford to procure adequate quantities by such means. Public sanitation and refuse disposal are next to non-existent. There are eight aqua privy blocks and 200 drop-holes, one per 400 persons. Greatly overloaded, ill-serviced, and unmaintained, these are grossly insanitary as well as inadequate (at one use per person per day on a 20-hour basis there would theoretically be three minutes per person). As a result much of the area is clogged with excrement.

Nima-Maamobi is an extreme case, but only in degree. Many other low-income urban areas are almost as deprived in their combination of poverty, overcrowding, malnutrition, squalor, lack of access to basic services, and gross environmental pollution.

II Managing the crisis 1983–1985

The prolonged economic decline called for difficult measures in order to reverse the downward spiral. In 1983, the government adopted a comprehensive package of economic reforms.

1 Stabilization policies

Stabilization policies were backed by IMF stand-by arrangements together with concessional finance from multilateral and bilateral sources. They aimed to:

1. Re-align interest rates.
2. Adjust the exchange rate.
3. Reduce the budget deficit.
4. Reform prices and restore production incentives.
5. Rehabilitate run-down infrastructure.
6. Establish improved priorities for the allocation of foreign exchange.
7. Improve the financial position of public enterprises.
8. Encourage private investment.

The overall strategy was one of fiscal and monetary measures to promote productivity, production, and investment.

2 Investment programme

During the 1984–85 period, selective investments in key sectors of the economy were undertaken to improve the foreign exchange earning capacity. The allocation of resources was consequently geared towards sectors that would earn foreign exchange or reduce imports. Greater emphasis was also placed on the rehabilitation of the country's infrastructure, which was necessary in order to revive the export sector.

Programmes geared towards food production aimed at increasing the production of major cereal crops but did not envisage self-sufficiency in Ghana in meeting food requirements in the short-term. They did not cover cocoyams, plantains, yams, millet, guinea corn (sorghum), or groundnuts, and thus excluded the crops grown for own-consumption and for cash by a majority of small-scale farmers and virtually all the small-scale farmers in the Northern and Upper Region.

The major emphasis of the first stage of the recovery programme was on the productive sectors of the economy, both in terms of the monetary and fiscal measures being implemented and of resource allocations under the investment programme. The rationale behind these macro-economic measures is clear, as is the urgent necessity to rehabilitate the export sectors of the economy.

However, there is a parallel and equally urgent need now for the formulation of a more comprehensive programme to rehabilitate the human dimension of the economy. This is fully acknowledged by the Ghana government and forms a central part of its proposals for 1986–88.

3   *Performance of the programme*

Some substantial achievements have been made, although it is early to make a full assessment of the response of the economy to the recovery programme, while the critically important agricultural sector has been substantially affected by favourable weather conditions. The performance of the programme must be viewed against the background of unforeseen difficulties, including the repatriation of about one million Ghanaians from Nigeria and the drought and bush-fires of 1982–84.

The government has secured a remarkable turn-around in policies in areas in which it is often very difficult to secure effective change. Government revenues recovered from the very low level of 5.3 per cent of GDP in 1983 to an estimated 9.0 per cent in 1985. The exchange rate was devalued from 2.75 cedis to the dollar in April 1983 to 90.00 cedis in April 1986. Nominal interest rates have been raised to 18 per cent (deposit rates) and 23 per cent (lending rates), and real interest rates were positive in 1985 for the first time in over two decades. There has been an orderly reduction of arrears by cash payments. Producer prices for cocoa have been increased 17-fold, price subsidies have been cut or eliminated, and price controls relaxed.

Significant mobilization of popular support for economic reform has been achieved, and a belief that the economic problems can be overcome has been recreated in the community. Substantial community and communal action— in time, labour, and cash—has been mobilized in support of sectoral rehabilitation, including health, education, and water.

Significant progress has been recorded in realizing economic objectives. Real gross domestic product rose by 0.7 per cent in 1983, and over 6 per cent p.a. between 1984 and 1986—the first three years of consecutive growth in over two decades. Gross fixed capital formation, which had fallen from 12 per cent of GNP in 1970 to 3 per cent in 1982, rose to 6 per cent in 1984 and 8–9 per cent in 1985. There was also a recovery of development expenditure from a low of 0.5 per cent of GDP in 1983 to an estimated 2.1 per cent in 1985.

The inflation rate decelerated sharply in 1984, largely as a result of a lower rise in food prices following the good harvest. In the second half of 1984 and first half of 1985 food prices fell. For 1985 inflation is estimated around 10 per cent, which is a substantial achievement compared with the three-digit inflation rate earlier in the 1980s. The reduction in inflation was achieved at the same time as the very substantial devaluation of the cedi. However, since mid-1985, inflation appears to have accelerated.

Cocoa production made a small recovery in 1984, but was still below the 1982 level. More substantial recovery occurred in 1985/86 to a production level of 219,000 tons, compared with 157,000 in 1983. Gold production rose by 7 per cent in 1985 compared with 1984. The estimated dollar value of exports in 1985 was 19 per cent above the 1983 value, partly because of some recovery in the world cocoa price. Imports were estimated to be 8 per cent up in 1985 compared with 1983. The current account deficit was 4.6 per cent of GDP in 1985. There was a significant rise in net aid disbursements in 1984 over 1983, but a fall in 1985 as disbursements lagged behind commitments.

External payment arrears were reduced from $601 million in 1983 to $287 million in late 1984, and the trend remains downward. However, debt servicing obligations (including to the IMF) have been rising sharply and will consume over 50 per cent of export earnings in 1987, compared with about 14 per cent in 1982.

These are substantial achievements, obtained in spite of most difficult external circumstances. However, the positive effects of economic recovery have not been reflected fully in improvements in human welfare. The evidence suggests that health care and education remain on declining trends. The water supply situation has not changed materially. The nutritional situation has improved compared with the worst of the drought, but remains precariously balanced. Real incomes of low-income households are still quite inadequate to meet dietary needs. While this in no way refutes the reality or magnitude of what has been achieved, it does point to the urgent need for additional actions if the policy changes and economic progress secured since 1983 are to be sustained and built upon, and the renewed spirit of determination, willingness to sacrifice, and ability to mobilize for reconstruction throughout society is to be kept alive and strengthened by perceived successes.

III   Strengthening people with the economy

The economic recovery programme has been successful in arresting the economic collapse and initiating economic growth. The government, with the
support of the World Bank and other aid donors, is now introducing programmes for rehabilitation of the health and education sectors. It is essential
to build on these to protect and improve the conditions of vulnerable groups—
to help those worst affected until the benefits of the recovery are widely spread,
and to reach those groups that would otherwise be unlikely to benefit from a
general improvement in economic conditions.

This part lays out the main elements of a programme for human recovery
which should become an integral component of an economic and social policy.
Decisions on the precise dimensions of such a programme must clearly depend
on choices within the country in the light of human needs, institutional
capacities, and resource availability. There is an immediate need to launch
this debate and set in process its more detailed evolution. An essential and
immediate priority is to institute a set of human indicators which will permit
improved identification of needs and effective monitoring of the achievements
on the human dimension.

The main elements of the strategy follow from identification of the vulnerable
groups in Ghana in the earlier parts of this study and from the analysis of the
major obstacles these groups face in meeting their basic needs.

Within each category, children as well as pregnant and lactating mothers
are especially badly affected, showing the worst dietary deficiencies and the
greatest vulnerability to disease; and it is for them that the effects of such
deficiencies will be most permanent and damaging. For infants and children,
therefore, specific interventions, particularly in health and nutrition, will be
necessary in addition to those actions aiming at improving the living conditions
of their families.

The fundamental source of the progressive failure to meet the basic needs
of these vulnerable groups in Ghana has been the chronic economic crisis
and economic stagnation. There have, however, been two distinct elements
involved: (*a*) the collapse of food entitlements, and (*b*) the debilitation of social
infrastructure and the social services. Different types of policy are appropriate
for each.

1   *Food security and food entitlements*

The long-run objective must be that real incomes, land yields, and food
availability rise sufficiently among vulnerable groups for households to grow
enough food or earn enough to meet their food needs without special assistance.
While this is the long-run objective of the recovery programme, major attention
has been placed initially on rehabilitating the export sector. Policies should be
strengthened for the promotion of food production, especially among low-

TABLE 4.9   *Characterization of the worst-affected household groups*

	Millions of people affected	
Urban		
Low-income wage earners	0.5	Real wage grossly insufficient for adequate diet
		Deterioration in social services coverage
Informal sector	2.0	Widespread underemployment; low real incomes
		Deterioration in social services coverage
Rural		
Small farmers/agricultural labourers in rural areas (other than North)	3.0	Affected by decline in agricultural production and rise in population
		Sharp decline in social services availability
Northern farmers	1.5	Lower incomes and productivity than elsewhere
		Near total collapse of the few social services previously available

Source: UNICEF estimates.

income farmers and female-headed households. However, these policies, and those intended to raise incomes in the urban areas, are not likely to have a sufficiently big effect in the immediate future.

In the short term, *some* policies to assist nutritional standards of the most vulnerable groups are essential, to offset some of the major nutritional deficiencies until incomes and food availability are more adequate. The approach adopted must depend on the views of the Ghanaian government and community and those of aid donors as well as administrative considerations, and it is recommended that a National Nutrition Action Meeting be convened immediately to consider the options. A recent World Bank report (1985*b*) provides a general intellectual framework for considering nutritional interventions and identifies policy options. Some major policy options for consideration in Ghana in this area are described below.

(a) Special nutritional support for children and women To meet the worst problems of nutrition, interventions need to be targeted towards children and pregnant and lactating mothers. Supplementary feeding programmes for these groups could be provided by supporting and extending voluntary activities mounted during the drought in the urban areas and by supporting community feeding projects at the village level in the rural areas in the hungry season.

In the urban areas feeding could be targeted to the most deprived, using growth monitoring to identify the most malnourished in a systematic manner. The rural community-based scheme should initially start only in the north of the country, which accounts for approximately a quarter of the population. The programme there could be targeted in three ways: first to the most deprived areas within the northern sector; secondly to pre-school children and pregnant and lactating mothers; or thirdly, the scheme could provide extra food only in the hungry season (i.e. about one-third of the year). The target group in the rural areas would be very approximately 1.5 million, of whom about 500,000 would be in the specially deprived areas.

In the rural areas, the programme should buy locally produced foods, purchased at the time of year when they are abundant and prices are low, thereby supporting local incomes. The urban programme could make use of food aid.

(b) Urban area: wage earners In the short run, policies to supplement the diets of very low-income households are needed because incomes are grossly inadequate to meet minimum food needs. For formal sector low-wage employees, food stamps would present an effective and relatively cheap way of achieving this, which would help reduce absenteeism and raise productivity as well as improve dietary standards. The stamps could be administered by employers, and their face value would be reimbursable to food sellers by the government. A balance needs to be struck between what would be desirable to bring food consumption up to more reasonable levels and what is financially feasible. As real incomes of minimum-wage urban employees grow with the recovery, such a programme should be phased out.

For the informal sector, additional employment opportunities would raise the capacity to buy food. In the short run, food-for-work schemes would help raise food consumption while the 'works' could contribute to rehabilitating social infrastructure—drains, sanitation, and roads. Support for small-scale enterprises—through assistance in providing credit, development of appropriate technology centres, and marketing advice—would help create income-earning opportunities in the medium term. The programme would build up gradually. As income earning opportunities grew, the food-for-work programme could be phased out.

(c) Rural areas: small farmers In the rural areas, households of northern farmers represent substantially the most deprived group according to every measure—income, nutrition, health, etc. Not only are their absolute incomes very low, but they are the group that suffer most from seasonal deprivation. The economic recovery programme has had little effect on northern farmers.

The problems of northern farmers (and low-income farmers elsewhere) may be tackled in four different ways. These include (*a*) increasing agricultural productivity, and consequently incomes; and (*b*) promoting other income-earning activities in the area, such as crop processing and construction work. These first two types of policy should be introduced immediately, but are not likely to have substantial effects in the short term. They therefore need to be supplemented by (*c*) food-for-work schemes; and (*d*) the establishment of food reserves and special distribution schemes to meet acute needs due to seasonal shortages.

Raising the agricultural productivity of low-income farmers would assist in improving nutritional standards by increasing food production and incomes. The main policies required are indicated below.

1. Extending priority programmes to basic food crops—yams, cocoyams, millet, guinea corn, groundnut, and oil palm. *Supporting changes are needed in research, extension and the supply of inputs, all of which are biased against smaller farmers and against food crops.*
2. Promoting other agricultural activities in the north, including secondary export crops (e.g. shea nuts) and livestock.
3. Increasing non-farm activities in low-income areas. Financial support should be given to promoting processing activities as well as to the rehabilitation of economic infrastructure.
4. Creating a fund to support income-generating activities in low-income communities. Communities should develop the projects themselves, committing some financial and labour resources. One area of high potential is food processing (e.g. gari production); others include poultry and carpentry.

Food-for-work schemes could contribute to the rehabilitation of infrastructure while helping to raise nutritional standards. Schemes could cover such activities as the construction and maintenance of minor roads and improvement of smaller-scale irrigation (e.g. fadama); and social projects, including the construction and rehabilitation of primary schools, of safe dug wells, and improved pit latrines. The work should be designed to be seasonal, concentrated in periods of low demand for agricultural labour. Works schemes may be financed by food-aid but wherever possible rural programmes should use food purchased locally, with any food-aid being sold in the urban areas to finance the schemes. Operated on this basis such programmes can have a positive effect on incentives to produce food, which is critical to their being part of any overall approach to nutritional self-sufficiency.

Another priority is storage at the village level. Much traditional storage is very poor, involving losses of up to 30 per cent in a season, and it is also deficient in quantity. Lack of adequate storage causes many low-income food producers to sell grain after the harvest when the price is very low. They are then often forced to buy it back at the end of the season when the price is usually substantially higher (sometimes five or six times as great), leading to deficient purchases and malnutrition within the family. Improved village (and household) storage would permit low-income households to raise their nutritional levels during the hungry season, adding to their incomes and to total food availability. Technical improvements can be made to traditional storage methods—for example, the laterite block silo—and technical assistance with implementing improvements, with transferring the technology, and with initial financial requirements are urgently needed.

2   *Rehabilitation of existing social services infrastructure*

Social infrastructure has been eroded during the past decade, leading to a continued deterioration in coverage and quality of service in each of the major social sectors. Not only have physical facilities gradually fallen into total disrepair owing to lack of maintenance and almost no new investment, but also the level of utilization of the facilities still functioning has dropped dramatically because of lack of finance to purchase recurrent inputs and because of a quite dramatic and still continuing outflow of personnel, especially medical, abroad, which has further reduced the effectiveness of use of the limited resources available. Imbalance of resource use—towards the urban areas and the middle classes and regionally—has further eroded the ability to meet the needs of the most vulnerable.

What is needed is action aiming at:

1. *Restoring adequate working conditions* in existing facilities (polyclinics, health centres, schools, water supply systems, etc.), possibly through food-for-work schemes.
2. *Halting and if possible reversing the flight of personnel.* This will be facilitated by improved conditions, but may also require higher real remuneration.
3. *Increasing the availability of recurrent inputs* (essential drugs, exercise books, paper and pencils, basic spare parts, etc) indispensable for the delivery and fruition of social services. Special procurement schemes, like that for the UNICEF/WHO essential drugs programme, can help greatly in increasing the availability of recurrent inputs at moderate cost.

In the social sectors, a hierarchy of actions is appropriate, with the order depending on urgency of need and organizational and financial constraints as well as on costs. Some short-term rehabilitation may produce results quickly and cheaply. Expansion of services will take longer and may be more costly.

(a) Health sector Ghana has adopted the Primary Health Care Programme as its basic strategy for consolidation and expansion of health coverage. At present the programme is being partially implemented in a limited number of districts. Even in these, however, severe financial, manpower, and organizational problems limit the effectiveness of the programme. It is crucial that normal functioning conditions are restored in the districts where the programme has been launched. UNICEF and the World Bank have begun to support programmes for a considerable expansion and improvement in primary health care activities.

In view of the expensive nature of hospital-based care, the government should consider putting a stop to new hospital construction and even to major extensions to existing hospitals. Ideally, increases in expenditures under hospital medical care should be allowed to cover only salary increases, inflation, maintenance, and the costs directly attributable to increases in numbers of patients treated.

All projects which have been planned but not completed should be reviewed, and savings from such projects could be channelled into priority programmes. Additional savings could be obtained from the simplification of the existing administrative structure of health centres, health posts, and so forth.

In view of the acute shortage of basic drugs and medical supplies it is suggested that a basic drug programme be adopted. Over the next few years the basic drugs should be imported under the WHO/UNICEF Drugs Procurement Facility, which can lead to cost savings of 30 to 40 per cent.

This programme should be adequate to boost first-level health care attendance to at least 10 million—well over double the present level. There is strong evidence that present low attendance rates at all levels are closely related to the lack of drugs and supplies, and that whenever these are known to have arrived people flock to health facilities.

(b) Water sector The most urgent need is to consolidate and preserve hard won gains, repairing the many borehole handpumps which are now out of operation and raising the number of urban water points in low income areas.

(c) Sanitation sector The sanitation situation in Ghana—with perhaps 30 per cent rural, 65 per cent urban, and 44 per cent national access to sanitary excreta disposal—is above the low-income Sub-Saharan African average. But the position in low-income urban areas is deteriorating rapidly, while the rural situation is not improving quantitatively and is becoming qualitatively weaker in regions of high population density. Refuse disposal is an almost equally serious problem in urban areas. Collection systems (like those of public sanitary facility cleansing and emptying) have virtually broken down because of inadequate supplies of operational vehicles. Rubbish taken to existing public collection points piles up into festering tips on which children play and in which the very poor scavenge.

In rural areas, an effective campaign approach could restore and extend facilities, with costs mostly born by households and communities. The problem lies in convincing them sanitation is important enough to mobilize the time, labour, and funds. In urban low-income areas, initial costs will have to fall on general budget resources. Until a poor urban area has seen its public sanitation facilities cleansed and brought up to adequate numbers, user charges will generate more resentment than revenue. Once the programme is operational an annual household user charge might be feasible.

(d) Education sector In the area of *primary education* the major problem is not quantitative, except in parts of the Northern and Upper regions and extremely poor slums like Nima-Maamobi. The main immediate challenge is qualitative and organizational, as indicated by the flight or irregular attendance of qualified teachers because of very low salaries, degradation of the infrastructure, the decreasing availability of basic items such as desks, chairs, books, papers, and pencils, and the large number of children dropping out of school. The following actions should be seen as high priority to reverse these negative trends:

1. Support for local communities to restore and re-equip buildings. The essential inputs for this—labour and materials—are generally available locally. Incentives in the form of food-for-work schemes could be provided.
2. Support for a project to increase Ghana's capacity to produce basic reading materials, making use of existing printing and publishing capacity. The capital costs would be relatively modest. Supplies of paper might be secured by commodity aid, while some direct cash recovery would be possible through book sales.
3. Action is needed in the area of early child care and development. This would be of a more exploratory nature and would require lower levels of financial support. The increased necessity for most women to seek work outside their households has made the need to develop early child care and development even more urgent. The extended family network is no longer able to cope, and *de facto* day care services are increasingly common. An entirely state-supported child care centre or nursery school programme for Ghana is clearly not a plausible proposition for the foreseeable future. What can be done is to seek ways of strengthening existing services.

3   Rapid expansion of critical low-cost interventions

A less evident but equally severe consequence of the deterioration in social services has been the slowness with which the social sector has introduced a number of recent technical breakthroughs, particularly in the health sector, which hold great potential for improving human welfare, and child welfare in particular. Rapid expansion of crucial interventions is required, including expanded immunization, oral rehydration therapy, child growth monitoring, improved management of pregnancy, and malaria control.

4   Community action

Ghana has a long tradition of community action, based on the village. This too has been a victim of the recession; lacking financial support, many communal activities have faded away. Revitalization of community action, which is a basic thrust of current government policy, is an essential mechanism for rehabilitating the social services and developing new initiatives to protect vulnerable groups. Properly tapped, there is a huge reservoir of enthusiasm and potential supplies of labour, materials, even food, which villages themselves can supply to meet their own needs. Community action should form an essential part of the strategy to protect vulnerable groups, and may assist in identifying needs, organizing a response, and part-financing priority projects.

It is proposed that a Fund be established, using external funds and Ghana government funds in equal proportions, for villages to finance community action to promote health and nutrition. The scheme should be operated through local institutions. In many villages the Committees for the Defence of the Revolution and the associated National Mobilization Programme provide the structures appropriate for organizing community action; elsewhere, active women's groups, co-operatives, or other institutions may take the initiative. Local institutions should determine priority projects in consultation with traditional and local authorities and with the technical support of relevant governmental and non-governmental agencies. Any project which is likely to improve health and nutrition would be acceptable. These could include, for example:

1.   Feeding programmes for children.
2.   Women's programmes.
3.   Monitoring child health.
4.   Rehabilitating or introducing new latrines.
5.   Processing weaning foods.
6.   Rehabilitating boreholes and drainage.
7.   Improving primary school facilities.

The Fund could be started on a limited basis—say for 3 years. If it proved successful and continued to meet priority needs as recovery proceeded, it could be continued.

The Community Fund could provide financial support to each village of, say, up to 50,000 cedis, if a local institution identified a promising project, and committed village resources—labour, local materials, or food—towards the project. The finance from the Fund would be used for materials from outside the community (e.g. weighing scales and charts for child monitoring, equipment for community kitchens), and for necessary expertise and training.

Successful community action could initiate a new spiral of self-reliant development, with effects far beyond those of the initial projects; the availability of some outside support for village initiatives could have a multiplier effect, harnessing the manifest enthusiasm that has been inspired by recent developments in Ghana.

5   Macro-economic developments and human recovery

Developments in the macro-economy have an important bearing on the welfare of vulnerable groups by affecting incomes, employment, and food prices, as well as influencing the government's budgetary potential to meet needs in the social sectors. Indeed, as shown earlier, it was the prolonged erosion of the Ghana economy at a macro level that led to the present critical situation.

Consequently, sustained economic growth, which is the objective of the economic recovery programme, is essential for long-run progress in raising the living levels of vulnerable groups.

In the short term, the immediate priority in Ghana has been to renew the process of economic growth after the long period of stagnation, and for this an essential requirement was to revitalize the export crop sector. This priority remains, but it is also important to ensure that the foundations are laid for an equitable pattern of growth involving the full participation of vulnerable groups. In the agricultural sector, this will require that the programme is extended to include small-farmers and subsistence crops. Special attention needs to be paid to the crucial role of women in food production. Research and development and extension services need to be designed specifically to meet the needs of women and small-farmers. Renewed industrial expansion should be based on labour-intensive technologies wherever possible, and should produce products appropriate to meet the needs of low-income groups, with provision of improved technologies, credit, and training for small-scale producers, including those in the informal sector. Continued care will be needed to ensure that a large proportion of the extra expenditures, made possible as the economy expands, goes to meet the needs of the lower 40 per cent of the population in primary health care, primary schools, sanitation for low-income areas, and economic infrastructure.

These requirements for participatory growth are not, as experience elsewhere has amply shown, by any means an automatic consequence of economic growth. They will require appropriate macro policies towards prices, wages and credit, policies towards the regional balance of development, and relevant policies within and between sectors. It is not the task of this chapter to explore these policies further, but it is necessary to point out that economic recovery will only remove the need for special programmes to protect vulnerable groups if policies ensuring an equitable pattern of growth in the medium term are consistently followed. *Unfavourable macro developments can undermine any special programmes to protect vulnerable groups.*

6 Monitoring of the human recovery programme

The absence of data has proved to be a serious obstacle to identifying problems among vulnerable groups early enough and to devising appropriate interventions. The importance of improving data collection, publication, and dissemination can hardly be exaggerated. Children are dying in part because of lack of information about their situation. It is impossible to devise effective interventions without a fuller knowledge of their situation.

Monitoring the implementation of human recovery will require improved data collection, particularly in the following areas:

1. Geographically comprehensive data on *child nutrition* through the use of minimum weight-for-age and wherever possible height-for-age indicators, together with information about major diseases associated with malnutrition.

2. Data on *incomes*: better data are needed on the level, distribution and source of real incomes and on real expenditure by income group, with special information on expenditure on food, both in the urban and the rural areas. More regional disaggregation of data is required.

3. Data on *food prices* provide a rapid way of helping to identify the emergency of critical situations. The data should be disaggregated regionally as far as possible.

4. Improved data on *food production* (including subsistence) is needed to identify trends in real incomes among food producers, food availability, and agricultural productivity.

5. *Leading indicators of social stress*. The 1982–83 experience, with too long a period between mounting stress and its identification, and further delay before any action was taken, underlined the need for an early warning system. The initial drought occurred in the first half of 1982. The international community was alerted in February 1983, and emergency food aid started to arrive in July 1983. There is need to develop a set of leading indicators of stress. These should include major indicators of human deprivation which can be quickly and efficiently collected. Possible elements of the indicators would be early warnings of food supply problems (FAO is currently instituting such a system); changes in the proportion of babies with low birth weights recorded at major clinics and hospitals; nutrition data; deaths from measles as a proportion of measles cases; and infant mortality rates. The most important requirement is that the data should be collected regularly and transmitted quickly to a central point. Partial data rapidly collected is preferable to comprehensive data collected irregularly or available only after substantial delay.

IV Costs and funding

The years of stagnation and neglect in Ghana left their mark on sources of funds. There was a collapse in each of the main elements—in community activity, in the domestic tax base, and in foreign aid and capital flows. At this

point, the collapse in each represents a potential opportunity, since reversing
them and restoring normalcy will generate the resources needed for the
rehabilitation programme.

Since the economic recession and drought, rural communities have become
aware that the government alone cannot provide for all their needs. The
success of the various 'Save Our Hospital Committees' demonstrates the ability
of many communities to raise substantial sums of money to support community-
based projects. Communities should make an important contribution to
financing the programme, to be stimulated by the creation of a Fund to help
finance projects initiated and supported at the village level. Further recovery
of the tax base would provide additional finance for human recovery. Some
extra government support for human programmes could mobilize greater
effort by local communities, as well as by the foreign aid community, which
likes to place resources where they see genuine government commitment.

Restructuring within the government budget, and in particular within the
social sectors, from low-priority to high priority items would provide a further
source of resources for priority programmes (as, for example, the earlier
suggestion that all investment in new hospitals or hospital extensions should
be stopped for the time being).

Aid and capital flows from abroad also fell to very low levels during the
years of stagnation. In 1983, the net inflow of public and publicly guaranteed
capital to Ghana was $2.4 per capita compared with $4.2 in Kenya or $13.6
in Tanzania. While some recovery has already occurred much more can be
expected, especially if Ghana provides comprehensive support for protecting
vulnerable groups. But action will be essential to prevent the escalation in debt
servicing that is occurring. Unless debt servicing obligations for the 1980s are
reduced, the positive effects of increasing aid and export earnings on import
capacity will be largely negated.

There are major administrative constraints in Ghana which may prove as
formidable as the financial constraints. Administrative capacity has been
undermined by the prolonged recession: many people of high education and
ability have left the country, while the resources needed by those who remain
are seriously inadequate. Communications are poor and transport links weak.
These factors will constrain the size and rate of expansion of any programme,
and also influence its shape, since administrative and institutional capacities
will help determine which projects are most appropriate.

In many areas, it will be necessary to start rather small and build up, as
organizational constraints are lessened and the value of particular approaches
becomes clearer through the experience of pilot projects. Some of the proposals
could be initiated immediately (e.g. food supplements) but would be phased
out as others involving income creation and improved storage grew in magnitude. Moreover, as economic recovery proceeds, the need for special programmes will diminish.

The international community has already given a positive response to

Ghana's economic recovery programme. A similar strong commitment to human recovery would elicit substantial support—indeed, there is already commitment from donors to elements of such a programme.

Ghana now has the opportunity and challenge of initiating a comprehensive programme to protect vulnerable groups during adjustment, as the human complement to the pioneering Economic Recovery Programme.

References

Horton, S. (1985), 'Agricultural Policies and the protection of vulnerable groups in Ghana'. Mimeo, UNICEF, New York.

UNICEF-Ghana (1984), *Situation Analysis of Women and Children in Ghana*. Accra: UNICEF.

World Bank (1985*a*), *Ghana: Towards Structural Adjustment* 2 vols. Washington, DC: World Bank.

—— (1985*b*), *Ensuring Food Security in the Developing World: Issues and Options*. Washington, DC: World Bank.

5

The Impact of Adjustment Policies on Vulnerable Groups:
The Case of Jamaica, 1973–1985

Derick Boyd

I The macro-economic policies and performance of the Jamaican economy

Jamaica is a small, lower-middle-income Caribbean island economy with a population of approximately 2.3 million people.

Its economic experience over the years 1973–85 has been marked by significant overall decline (Boyd 1986a, Sharpley 1984, Girvan *et al.* 1980). Over the 12-year period 1973–84, real GDP declined in every year except three (1981–83), when small increases were recorded (Table 5.1). This is in marked contrast to the preceding 12-year period (1961–72), which saw an average rate of growth of 4.4 per cent per year.

TABLE 5.1 *Rate of growth of the economy, 1969–1984 (percentages)*

Year	Growth (%)	Year	Growth (%)	Year	Growth (%)
1969	7.5	1975	− 2.6	1981	2.5
1970	10.6	1976	− 6.1	1982	1.0
1971	1.7	1977	− 1.7	1983	2.0
1972	7.5	1978	− 0.1	1984	− 4.0
1973	− 2.6	1979	− 1.5		
1974	− 0.7	1980	− 7.3		

Source: Planning Institute of Jamaica, *Economic and Social Survey of Jamaica,* various years.

It should be noted, however, that although the economy experienced a boom period in the post-war years up to the early 1970s, for the vast majority this was a period of significant hardship, and indeed poverty. This was largely responsible for the high level of migration to the United Kingdom in the 1950s and 1960s by people who were on the whole poorly educated and poorly skilled. Considerable migration also took place to the United States and

Canada, especially after 1962 when Caribbean migration to Britain was severely curtailed by the 1962 British Immigration Act. Substantial evidence exists to support the view that the main reasons for the migration were push rather than pull factors.

Thus, whilst the 1952–72 period of export-led expansion based on foreign investment in the bauxite/alumina industry and in tourism led to growth of the national economy, many Jamaicans continued to be vulnerable to considerable social and economic hardships. Moreover, these hardships increased with economic decline from the latter part of the 1960s into the 1970s.

The unemployment rate, estimated for 1943 at 25 per cent, declined in the post-war years to reach 13.5 per cent of the labour force in 1960 (Table 5.2). During the 1960s, however, the rate began to increase and by the early 1970s it had climbed back to the high levels recorded in the 1940s and early 1950s.

TABLE 5.2   *Selected unemployment and migration statistics*

	Unemployment		Migration (net)	Employed (000)
	Rate %	Numbers (000)		
1943	25.1	139.5	n.a.	416.3
1953	17.5	111.1	4,300	523.8
1957	17.1	112.6	15,000	545.9
1960	13.5	88.5	30,000	567.1
1969	17.0	131.7	n.a.	617.2
1972	23.0	182.9	n.a.	611.3
1980	26.8	270.8	22,770	720.4
1984	25.8	246.7	22,650	724.7

Source: Jefferson (1972), 22, 28; Institute of Statistics, *Statistical Year-book of Jamaica 1982,* and *The Labour Force 1976,* and *1982;* Planning Institute of Jamaica, *Economic and Social Survey of Jamaica,* 1984.

Whilst the overall decline in the unemployment rate coincided with rapid export-led expansion of the economy, it would be incorrect to ascribe the former primarily to the latter. Migration had a major role in reducing the rate of unemployment, especially during the 1960s. Although the economy grew rapidly it did not absorb a significant number of the unemployed into formal employment.

Another salient feature of economic development over this period, and one which was to play an important role in the determination of the disequilibrium of the 1970s, was its unbalanced trade structure. The export sector, established over the 1950s and 1960s, was highly concentrated. From its initial investments in 1952, the bauxite/alumina industry accounted for 49 per cent of merchandise exports by 1968, and this proportion increased in later years. There was, moreover, widespread demand for imports which deepened import dependency in many areas of society.

1 The 1970s: a period of decline

The 1970s was a period of economic decline unprecedented in the post-war period. Analyses of the decline over what are sometimes called 'the Manley years' (1972–80), are to be readily found (Sharpley 1984, Brown 1981, Girvan *et al.* 1980). The differences which emerge from these analyses do not question the existence or indeed the pronounced severity of the decline, but rather whether or not external forces were more or less responsible for the decline than internal factors.

The decline of the economy occurred both on the domestic and the balance of payments front. GDP showed considerable decline in real terms: at constant prices, GDP in 1980 was 77.5 per cent of that in 1972. From 1973 to 1980, eight successive years of negative real growth were recorded. The per capita impact was compounded by a positive population growth. Real per capita income reversed its upward trend from 1972, falling from a peak in that year of J$1,221 to J$842 by 1980 (Table 5.3).

TABLE 5.3   *Selected macro-economic indicators, 1970–1984*

	GDP[a] constant prices (J$m)	Per capita income (J$)	Bauxite/alumina export ratio per cent	Terms of trade (1972 = 100)
1970	2,159	1,155	66.8	115
1971	2,195	1,155	65.1	95
1972	2,360	1,221	64.2	100
1973	2,299	1,164	67.2	82
1974	2,270	1,121	62.4	84
1975	2,212	1,074	64.9	109
1976	2,026	978	69.3	101
1977	1,993	951	70.5	95
1978	1,986	935	71.6	98
1979	1,941	903	71.4	98
1980	1,829	842	78.1	90
1981	1,875	851	78.8	—
1982	1,893	864	71.0	78
1983	1,931	862	61.8	—
1984	1,924	844	42.2	77

Source: Planning Institute of Jamaica, *Economic and Social Survey of Jamaica*, various years; Statistical Institute of Jamaica, *Statistical Yearbook*, various years; World Bank, *World Development Report 1986.*
[a] *1974 prices.*

The election victory of the People's National Party (PNP) led by Michael Manley in 1972 gave rise to the implementation of government programmes focused on increasing employment, maintaining real wages, and reducing poverty, and economic and social inequalities. The evidence suggests, however, that due regard was not taken of the internal and external constraints within which the economy had to perform, and this in large measure led to the difficulties later experienced. As a result of these difficulties, in many respects there was a worsening of social and economic conditions rather than the reverse.

2   Worsening internal and external disequilibria

The government's fiscal policy on both the expenditure and the revenue side had far-reaching implications for the performance of the domestic economy as well as the balance of payments. Growth of government nominal expenditures averaged 32 per cent per year from 1972/73 to 1976/77. Expenditure grew from 25 per cent of GDP in 1972 to 46 per cent in 1976, and the overall budget deficit increased from 5 per cent of GDP to 24 per cent.

Both the rate of expansion and the structure of the expenditure had adverse implications for the economy. As Brown (1981, p. 199) writes: 'There is little doubt that the government was, itself, a contributor to the crisis of the 1970s ... government expenditure reflected consumption rather than investment as transfers through the government budget raised consumption levels and contributed to price increases but did not induce private investment ... a substantial proportion of government's expenditure on capital account represented asset transfer.' Indeed, the government over the 1970s took an increasingly anti-capitalist stance.

Rapid fiscal expansion together with government policy to increase real wages led to wage inflation. Over 1974 and 1975, wage increases averaged 50 to 60 per cent and substantially exceeded the cost of living increases. This not only fuelled inflation but also led to a significant worsening of the balance of payments. This fiscal expansion financed by external borrowing also aggravated the current account imbalance as foreign debt payments increased.

Increasing concentration in the Jamaican export sector was established, with the bauxite/alumina industry accounting for more than 50 per cent of merchandise export earnings before the end of the 1960s, in spite of the industry's recent beginning. By 1980 the bauxite/alumina industry accounted for 78 per cent of the total value of goods exported (Table 5.3).

In May 1974, the government imposed a production levy on the bauxite industry which increased the tax revenue from bauxite from J$25 million to J$200 million in one year. The response of the bauxite companies was to cut back production and curtail investment in Jamaica even at the time when bauxite investment was expanding world-wide. The volume index of bauxite production fell from a high of 111 in 1974 to a low of 77 in 1975, while the alumina volume index fell from a high of 128 in 1974 to a low of 73 in 1976.

Given the export concentration, the cut-backs in bauxite and alumina production significantly affected exports. Export earnings rose by 6.5 per cent over 1975 but fell by 14.6 per cent over 1976, precipitating the crisis which led to the exhaustion of international reserves in 1976. The balance on current account recorded a peak deficit for the decade in 1976 of US\$ 303 million, equivalent to 10 per cent of GDP.

The massive increase in oil and other import prices are often regarded as, of themselves, having a debilitating impact on the economics of non-oil importing countries. In the case of Jamaica, however, the evidence suggests that over the 1970s these price increases were in the main offset by increases in the price of Jamaican exports. Whilst the terms of trade index declined over the two years 1973 and 1974, it recovered to reach 109 in 1975 (1972 = 100). Although it declined again between 1976 and 1980, the decline, as Table 5.8 shows, was slight over these years. Over the years 1975–80, for instance, it averaged 98.5, the really bad period for the terms of trade were mainly 1973 and 1974, with the years following showing a significant recovery.

On the whole, the evidence suggests that structural features of the economy and the policies followed by the Manley government were the main factors in the decline of the economy. The government pursued its objectives without recognizing the importance of the constraints imposed by declining investment and output and persistent balance of payments disequilibria on this small, open economy. The result of this and other exogenous factors was rapid social and economic decline which attracted the attention of the world, especially as the government ascribed a significant part of the blame for the deepening problem to the nature of the relationship it was increasingly forced into with the IMF.

In the latter part of the 1970s, the government was for the most part unwilling to enter into agreements for upper-tranche programmes with the IMF since this would entail stiff conditionality. Consequently, although net foreign reserves fell below zero in March 1976, it was not until 14 months later, in May 1977, that negotiations with the IMF resulted in the abortive August 1977 programme.

The main landmarks in terms of the agreements concluded with the IMF over 1976–80 were the following:

1. *August 1977*. A two year Stand-By Arrangement which was suspended soon afterwards on failing the first quarterly test.

2. *May 1978*. A three-year Extended Programme was pursued for one year, and then re-negotiated.

3. *June 1979*. The 1978 Extended Fund Facility was renegotiated to take advantage of additional drawings under the Supplementary Finance Facility, but this collapsed in December 1979 when the performance tests were failed. There was no further agreement until after the violent 1980 elections.

3 Stagflation in the 1980s

In the October 1980 general election, the Jamaica Labour Party (JLP), led by Edward Seaga, won an overwhelming victory. This election was dubbed the 'IMF election' since the central point of dispute between the opposing parties was whether Jamaica should continue to seek IMF assistance or whether an alternative path should be pursued. In the event, the strongly pro-IMF party won 53 of the 60 seats to the elected House of Representatives. Consequently, there was considerable political pressure on both the government and the Fund to come to some early agreement to ameliorate the severe foreign exchange and social and economic crises for which Jamaica had attracted world attention.

Immediately after the election, a wave of relief and optimism among business and many sections of labour replaced the crisis level of pessimism which had caused net migration of capital and highly skilled labour during the late 1970s. This immediately resulted in foreign capital inflows, and the supply of food and other items improved considerably as empty shop shelves were refilled.

In April 1981, an agreement was concluded with the Fund for an amount of SDR 537 million to cover the three fiscal years 1981/82 to 1983/84. The IMF agreement was an essential part of the need to expand output and investment through relaxing the production constraints imposed by foreign exchange shortages, opening up the economy to imports, freeing prices, and instituting a programme of divestment of certain public enterprises.

4 Foreign sector performance

In this immediate post-election period, the easing of the foreign exchange constraint through renewed official and private inflows and the partial relaxation of quantitative restrictions brought about a deterioration in the merchandise and current accounts. In 1980 the former stood at US$69 million and the latter at US$204 million, and in 1981 these deficits increased to US$323 million and US$337 million respectively. The magnitude of the trade and current account imbalance under the Seaga regime has been considerably greater than during the 1970s under the Manley government.

These massive current account deficits have been financed by equally massive inflows on the capital account. However, it is important to note that net inflows of capital have been dominated by net official movements. The magnitude of net official inflows over the 1980s were considerably greater than anything experienced during the 1970s.

Moreover, there has not been an increase in net private inflows in the 1980s. In fact, levels of net private capital inflows during the 1970s were greater than in the 1980s. Indeed, the official statistics show an all-time record net private capital *outflow* of US$312 million during 1983. It should be noted that following this the official statistics began the curious policy of including the net errors and omissions item with that of net private capital flows.

A disturbing feature of the trading balance in the 1980s was the poor performance of Jamaica's main export of bauxite/alumina, under pressure of declining international demand. Even though the bauxite/alumina companies obviously prefer the JLP administration to that of the PNP which had introduced the bauxite levy, and in spite of the renegotiation of the structure and level of the levy, bauxite production fell to its lowest level in 20 years during 1983.

Bauxite/alumina export value has fallen considerably, as Table 5.4 shows.

TABLE 5.4   *Bauxite/alumina exports, 1978–1984*

	Export value (US$m)	Percentage of exports
1978	430.0	71.6
1979	578.0	71.4
1980	756.5	78.1
1981	760.1	78.8
1982	514.5	71.0
1983	423.8	61.8
1984	501.8	42.2

Source: Planning Institute of Jamaica, *Economic and Social Survey of Jamaica*, various years.

The dollar export value of bauxite/alumina in 1984 was only 66 per cent of that of 1980. This reduction in output has been accompanied by reduction in capacity utilization and closures, resulting in increasing unemployment and economic hardship especially in the areas in which the industry is located.

The structural concentration of Jamaican exports is demonstrated by the fact that in spite of the deteriorating performance of the bauxite sector, it still accounted for a major proportion of total Jamaican exports. An important implication of this is that the structural imbalance of exports makes it difficult for successful external adjustment to take place in the short run in the absence of recovery in the bauxite/alumina sector.

5   *Fiscal performance*

The rapid growth in public expenditure and the budget deficit over the 1970s has been recognized as a factor contributing to the overinflation of aggregate demand, exacerbating the balance of payments disequilibria of the 1970s. An important objective of the 1981 government programme, therefore, was to reduce the relative size of the public sector and produce a fiscal surplus of 1 per cent of GDP by the end of the three-year IMF programme.

The budget deficit showed a significant worsening over the latter years of the 1970s. Total expenditure in the election year of 1980/81 increased by 40 per cent, and this high level of expenditure was further increased in nominal terms in the following years, in spite of some degree of success in holding down the rate of inflation in the early years of the Seaga regime.

The ratio of total expenditure to GDP, estimated as 40 per cent in 1980/81, increased in successive years, and the deficit/GDP ratio only showed a significant fall during 1984/85 (Table 5.5). The decreased deficit of 1984/85 was achieved by a remarkable 58 per cent increase in total revenue in that year, with most of this increase from collection of taxes.

TABLE 5.5   Selected fiscal indicators, 1973/74–1984/85 (J$ million)

	Revenue		Exports		Gross deficit	
	Total	% GDP	Total	% GDP	Total	% GDP
1973/74	352		472		−119	
1974/75	451		728		−276	
1975/76	680		967		−287	
1976/77	756		1,290		−534	
1977/78	796		1,274		−478	
1978/79	1,118		1,656		−538	
1979/80	1,129		1,711		−582	
1980/81	1,375	23.0	2,392	40.0	−1,016	17.0
1981/82	1,555	28.3	2,471	45.0	−917	16.7
1982/83	1,750	29.5	2,707	45.7	−957	16.2
1983/84	1,718	24.2	3,396	47.9	−1,678	23.7
1984/85	2,718	28.0	3,905	40.2	−1,186	12.5

Source: National Planning Agency, Economic and Social Survey of Jamaica, 1980, 1981, 1982, and 1983; Bank of Jamaica, Statistical Digests, July 1980, Oct. 1984.

Largely as a result of the devaluation of the Jamaican dollar since 1983, the budget targets became increasingly difficult to achieve since foreign debt service increased by the rate of the devaluation in domestic currency terms. Over 1983 the rate of devaluation was 84 per cent, and between January 1984 and February 1986 the Jamaican dollar declined by a further 67 per cent, bringing the rate of devaluation between January 1983 and February 1986 to 207 per cent. The result of these adjustments was that in 1983, for example, the external debt service increased by 110 per cent in Jamaican dollar terms, and the government had to borrow the equivalent of 25 per cent of GDP in order to finance the budget deficit.

6   Vigorous stabilization policies from 1984

The poor performance of the economy in 1983 and the failure of two IMF tests led to the introduction of a strong IMF monetarist package in January 1984. This policy package provided the basis for the highly deflationary approach followed over 1985 and 1986.

The measures announced on 24 January 1984 included the following:

1. A ceiling of 12 per cent was imposed on the increase in commercial banks' lending to the private sector for 1984.

2. The liquid asset ratio of commercial banks was increased by 4 percentage points to 40 per cent.

3. The cash reserve ratio of the commercial banks was increased in stages from 5 per cent to 10 per cent, effective 11 April 1984.

4. The liquid assets ratio of non-bank financial intermediaries was increased from 10 per cent to 15 per cent in order to keep their credit expansion low.

5. Bank rate was increased from 11 per cent to 13 per cent.

6. The minimum interest rate on savings deposits was increased from 9 per cent to 11 per cent.

7. The maximum lending rate of building societies was increased from 14 per cent to 16 per cent.

Other measures included the freeing of all prices from direct control and the removal of subsidies. A restructuring of custom duties and tariffs accompanied the opening up of the economy, and the import licensing system was dismantled so that goods might be freely imported subject to the tariffs levied on entry.

During 1985 and 1986, these measures were augmented by further increases in the minimum interest rate on savings accounts to 20 per cent per year, and the bank rate was increased to 21 per cent. These increases were accompanied by several restrictive credit policies which had a severely contractionary impact on industry. The massive devaluations which accompanied these policies have had significant stagflationary effects on the economy. There are signs that the government has lost confidence in the approach. For example the Prime Minister has requested a team from the World Bank, the IMF, and the USAID to have a new look in order to develop a new approach.

II   Impact on households

1   Income distribution and rural inequality in Jamaica

The adverse poverty effects of economic decline are made worse by the extremely unequal distribution of income in Jamaica. Income distribution data for 1958, 1963, and 1971/72 show Jamaica to be among the countries with the most unequal distribution of incomes (Boyd 1986*b*).

Moreover, as Table 5.6 shows, the degree of the inequality increased over the 1958–72 period. The proportion of aggregate income going to the lowest 40 per cent fell from 8.2 per cent in 1958 to 7.0 in 1971/72, and there are good reasons to think that this proportion has declined further over the 1980s.

TABLE 5.6 *Decile distribution of income, 1958, 1971/72*

Decile	By decile		Cumulative	
	1958	1971/72	1958	1971/72
1 and 2	2.2	2.0	2.2	2.0
3	2.5	2.0	4.7	4.0
4	3.5	3.0	8.2	7.0
5	4.7	4.0	12.9	11.0
6	6.1	6.5	19.0	17.3
7	8.3	9.0	27.3	26.5
8	11.2	9.5	38.5	36.0
9	18.0	14.0	56.5	50.0
10 (1st 5%)	13.3	13.0	69.8	63.8
10 (2nd 5%)	30.2	37.0	100.0	100.0

Sources: Ahiram (1964), McLure (1977).

The level of income going to the vast majority of households is very low in absolute terms. In 1971/72, the bottom 58 per cent of households earned less than 16 per cent of aggregate income, while the top 10 per cent earned 50 per cent of aggregate income. If the relative distribution in Jamaica in 1971/72 had been the same as that in the USA, the per capita income of the poorest 60 per cent of Jamaicans would have been 99.4 per cent higher. If the bottom 40 per cent of households had managed to maintain their 1971/72 proportion of aggregate income, in 1984 their aggregate income would still have declined by more than 14 per cent in real terms.

The impact of the increasing inequality in the distribution of the gross incomes of households over 1958–72 could have been mitigated through direct and indirect taxation policies. The incidence of taxation in Jamaica was estimated for 1958 and 1971/72 by McLure (1977). McLure (p. 74) found that the tax system was moderately progressive, due primarily to the individual income tax and the tax on local companies. The indirect taxes he found to be proportional. In all, the distribution of income was not significantly affected by taxation. It should be noted, however, that the income tax reform of 1986 reintroduced an income allowance system with a single rate of tax on personal incomes. This will have the effect of eradicating the progressivity of the taxes on personal incomes and, given the high rates of indirect taxes on cigarettes and alcohol, is likely to make the overall impact of the system regressive.

Data from the 1958, 1963, and 1971/72 surveys show rural inequality to be considerably greater than urban inequality (Ahiram 1974, pp. 347–9; McLure 1977, pp. 23–4). Inequality in both the urban and the rural sectors increased over the 1958–72 period.

The basis of rural inequality resides primarily in the structure of agricultural production and its factor income distribution. Bauxite/alumina production, which takes place in the rural areas, employs such a small proportion of the labour force that, although contributing to rural inequality through the dualism it introduces in rural production, it is unlikely to play a very significant role.

The inequality in the distribution of rural incomes to a considerable degree reflects the very unequal distribution of agricultural land. Table 5.7 shows that farms of less than five acres account for an increasing proportion of farms, rising from roughly 70 per cent in 1954 to 82 per cent in 1978/79 while accounting for only 16 per cent of the total agricultural land. Farms of 25 acres and above were less than 2 per cent of the total number of farms but accounted for roughly 65 per cent of agricultural land in 1978/79, and the figures show this to be increasing on trend.

TABLE 5.7 · *Distribution of agricultural land*

Size (acres)	Farms (%)	Acreage (%)	Farms (%)	Acreage (%)
		1954		*1958*
TOTAL (number)	(198,883)	(1,914,315)	(199,489)	(1,822,743)
0–5	69.91	13.01	70.79	14.86
5–25	26.66	26.27	26.72	29.97
Over 25	3.43	60.72	2.49	55.17
		1968/69		*1978/79*
TOTAL	(193,359)	(1,489,188)	(183,988)	(1,327,045)
0–5	78.55	14.85	81.87	16.01
5–25	19.35	22.13	16.22	19.28
Over 25	2.10	63.12	1.90	64.70

Source: Department of Statistics, *Census of Agriculture 1978–79* (preliminary report).

Agricultural inequality is further increased by the fact that the larger farms concentrated on the generally more lucrative areas of export crops, livestock, and poultry rather than on the poorer, domestic crop production on which the small farms concentrated. Figures for 1978/79 show, for example, that for farms of 100 acres and over, 80 per cent of their acreage went into export crops, livestock, and poultry, and less than 7 per cent went into domestic crop production. Small farms (up to five acres), on the other hand, had only 38 per cent of their acreage in export crops, livestock, and poultry, and 48 per cent in domestic crop production.

2   Incomes and basic consumption requirements

Over the 1970s the income of labour declined significantly. The index of median income declined from 100.0 in 1974 to 75.8 in 1980 (Boyd 1986*b*, p. 15). This decline in the income of labour, which was most pronounced in the latter half of the 1970s, continued in the 1980s with the implementation of deflationary adjustment policies in which holding down labour costs was a primary objective. The extent of the decline in income cannot be calculated as the wage indicators available for the 1970s have not been published for the 1980s, but the minimum wage deflated by a least-cost basket of food (see Table 5.9) declined by 11.8 per cent from September 1983 to July 1985.

Labour force statistics also indicate a clear informalization of the labour force as investment and output declined and people entered the informal sector in order to earn a living. Over 1972–80 the labour force grew by 24.7 per cent, while the self-employed category, which consists mainly of informal sector workers, grew by 37.7 per cent. In all, these indicators suggest a deterioration in the economic position of labour, which was made worse by the stagflationary effects of government policies of the 1980s.

A least-cost basket of goods covering food items for a household of five (two adults and three children), developed by the Caribbean Food and Nutrition Institute (CFNI), is reproduced in Table 5.8. The cost of this basic basket exceeds the income of many households in Jamaica. The total cost of the basket in October 1984 was estimated at J$120.63 per week. The minimum wage at that time was J$40.00 per week, which meant that a household of five with two members earning the minimum wage would be able to buy only 50 per cent of the total basket if they spent 75 per cent of their income on food. This excludes consideration of other basic necessities such as housing, fuel, clothing, water, transportation, and so on, some of which increased in price by over 100 per cent in a single year as the massive devaluations caused prices to soar.

The price of the overall basket of goods is estimated to have increased by 44.9 per cent from October 1984 to March 1986. The price increases are not concentrated in any single item or group of items, but are spread across all items. This means that there is no room for substitution within the basket even if this were nutritionally possible. Further, there is no room for substitution outside the basket since prices of all goods have increased considerably.

The prices of the high-calorie imports which provide the lowest-cost access to nutrition—cornmeal, flour, rice—have increased by an average of 52 per cent, which is greater than the rate of increase for the entire basket, so that access to low-cost nutrition was eroded faster than the general rate.

A 2-lb loaf of bread which sells for J$3.85 is outside the reach of the majority of Jamaicans. Moreover, for the poorer Jamaicans who are unable to afford a whole loaf but who seek to purchase some bread, the price is greater since the small retailers who sell part of a load add a markup. This is true for many grocery items as well as for fuel. The prices of certain items are higher in

TABLE 5.8   *Basket of groceries for five-person household for one week: estimated cost, 1984 and 1986 (Jamaican dollars)*

		Oct. '84	Mar. '86
6 lb.	Green bananas	3.00	3.40
4 lb.	Sweet potato	4.00	5.40
2 lb.	Dried peas (1 quart)	8.00	12.00
2 lb.	Pumpkin/carrot	2.00	2.60
2 lb.	Callaloo (spinach)	1.60	2.00
2 lb.	Cabbage	3.00	5.00
1 doz.	(3 lb.) Oranges	2.50	3.70
1 doz.	Limes (6 oz. juice)	0.40	0.70
1 doz.	Ripe bananas	1.50	2.00
Subtotal		26.00	36.80
6 lb.	Rice	7.80	10.92
6 lb.	Cornmeal	2.70	4.92
6 lb.	Flour	4.50	6.96
4 lb.	Bread	5.32	7.70
1 lb.	Crackers	2.67	3.30
Subtotal		22.99	33.80
2 lb.	Skimmed milk powder	3.50	5.06
2 tins	Sweetened condensed milk	3.20	5.00
Subtotal		6.70	10.06
5 lb.	Chicken necks and backs	7.10	11.80
1 lb.	Salt fish	3.40	3.50
2 lb.	Pork (medium fat)	8.00	16.60
2 lb.	(4 tins) Canned mackerel	5.56	6.20
2 lb.	Tripe	7.00	11.80
1 lb.	Minced beef	6.00	8.47
Subtotal		37.06	58.37
1 quart	Cooking oil	8.00	10.40
2 lb.	Margarine	8.00	9.10
Subtotal		16.00	19.50
6 lb.	Dark brown sugar	5.00	8.10
Miscellaneous: spices, beverages, condiments		6.00	8.20
Subtotal		11.00	16.30
Total		119.75	174.83

Source: 'Caribbean Food and Nutrition', Background paper for Workshop on Household Food Availability and Nutritional Status: The Challenge for the Future, Oct. 1984, University of the West Indies, Mona, Jamaica.
Note: Household composition: female, 35 years; male, 40 years; girl, 15 years; boys, 10 and 6 years.

the rural areas, increasing with the remoteness of the area. This is partly compensated in some cases by lower prices for domestically produced agricultural items. Consequently, there is little scope for any significant cushioning of the price increases on grocery items. The poor are generally discriminated against in the pricing system.

The Nutrition and Dietetics Division of the Ministry of Health (MOH) constructed a least-cost minimum basket of goods for the same five-person household as that of the CFNI, which is slightly cheaper than the CFNI basket (Table 5.9). Between December 1983 and August 1984 the price of their least-cost basket increased by 32 per cent, and over the following year by a further 26 per cent. In all, over the 18-month period between December 1983 and July 1985, the price of the MOH least-cost basket increased by 67 per cent. Over the six-year period June 1979 to July 1985, the MOH least-cost basket increased in price by 429 per cent.

TABLE 5.9   *Ministry of Health least-cost basket of goods* (five-person household)

	Cost (J$)	Change (%)	Minimum wage (J$)	Minimum wage as % of cost of basket
June 1979	24.27	—		—
Sept. 1983	65.31	69.1	30.00	45.9
Dec. 1983	77.00	17.9	30.00	39.0
Aug. 1984	101.60	31.9	40.00	39.4
July 1985	128.40	26.4	52.00	40.5

Source: Ministry of Health, Nutrition and Dietetics Division.

On the whole over these years the minimum wage covered less than 40 per cent of the value of the basket. Moreover, this percentage understates the erosion of purchasing power of the minimum wage, since the minimum wage moves in an *ad hoc* manner in jumps while food prices move continuously.

Table 5.10 compares the nutrient purchase value of the Jamaican dollar for selected items over 1984 and 1985. It shows that the nutrient purchasing value with respect to cornmeal, rice, and condensed milk fell by more than 40 per cent over the 10-month period August 1984–May 1985. Nutrient cost tables prepared by the Nutrition and Dietetics Division of the MOH for August 1984 gave the cheapest sources of calories as cornmeal, flour, brown sugar, and rice.

CFNI estimates show that cornmeal provides 11 times more calories per dollar than yams at October 1984 prices. This margin is very unlikely to be eroded by increases in the relative price of cornmeal to yam. In fact, the available evidence suggests that the nutrient cost of locally produced food has increased relative to imported foods. In terms of nutrients per dollar and also convenience and ease of preparation, imported foods are more attractive to

TABLE 5.10 *Changes in cost/nutrient value of selected food items, August 1984–November 1985* (kilocalories)

	Aug. 1984	May 1985	Nov. 1985	% Change May '84– May '85	% Change May '85– Nov. '85
Flour	2,232	1,522	1,443	− 31.8	− 5.2
Cornmeal	3,669	2,013	2,013	− 45.1	0.0
Rice	1,649	941	905	− 42.9	− 3.8
Chicken	220	188	174	− 14.5	− 7.4
Condensed milk	1,037	546	508	− 47.3	− 7.0
Oil	1,003	823	823	− 17.9	0.0
Margarine	817	653	653	− 20.1	0.0
Dark sugar	1,727	1,726	1,253	0.0	− 27.4

Source: Ministry of Health, Nutrition and Dietetics Division.

the consumer, since cereals—cornmeal, flour, rice—which feature as the best of these goods are almost entirely imported.

3 Food intervention by government

Between 1972 and 1975 the share of national disposable income going to subsidies was constant at 1 per cent. In the early part of the 1970s, the economic welfare of households was protected through increases in money and real wages, with a shift in the relative share of labour. Subsidies were therefore neither an undue burden to the government during this period nor a primary instrument for improving household welfare. During the latter half of the 1970s subsidies were used to cushion the poverty impact of the reduction in real wages which resulted from the IMF and other adjustment programmes implemented. As the government reversed its wages policy from 1977 and permitted real wages to fall, the role of subsidies increased dramatically, their share of national disposable income increasing from 2 per cent in 1976 to 6 per cent in 1977. Due to the pressure on the government's budget the real level of subsidies was not maintained at the high level of 1977 and 1978, but even so the real level of subsidies in 1980 (in constant 1971/72 prices) was 4.2 times that of 1971/72. (Boyd 1986*b*, p. 27) Subsidies and price controls on basic items have been removed in the period since 1980.

(a) The Food Aid Programme The Food Aid Programme (FAP) is a new initiative and by far the most important component of the government's welfare schemes. It was introduced in July 1984 to cushion the most vulnerable and poorest group—school children, pregnant and nursing women and infants, the elderly, and very poor people—from some of the effects of the government's economic policies.

The FAP is administered by the Ministry of Social Security and is targeted to reach one million persons. The magnitude of the poverty problem is indicated by the fact that this target population is half of the total population of Jamaica.

The stated aim of the programme is to maintain existing nutrition levels of persons who are at risk of falling into the category of being malnourished because of changes in their purchasing power.

The benefits involved in the programme are not sufficient to achieve this. Moreover, so far there have been administrative problems preventing people from receiving their full entitlements. The FAP was initially financed by a J$141 million foreign loan and questions must be raised as to the sustainability of this source of finance. Prices are rising too rapidly for the J$2.00 per week received by mothers with infants, for example, to go anywhere near maintaining the nutritional levels of the previous year. In real terms, the value of this sum fell by more than 17 per cent between the introduction of the programme in July 1984 and June the following year, and the rate of increase in the prices of basic items was even greater than the 17 per cent increase in the consumer price index, used here to calculate its real value.

Implementation of the programme has not been smooth. It was suspended from around the end of 1984 and restarted late in 1985 for what were apparently organizational reasons, and there are still reports of difficulties in implementation in some areas. In particular, the feeding of school children from infant to secondary school levels has been reported as falling considerably behind the target set. Under this programme the lunches of some school children are subsidized, but the supplies of these lunches have not always materialized, and during the first six months of the programme only 15 per cent of this target group was reached.

Overall, during the first six months of the FAP, of the one million targeted recipients less than 20 per cent received benefits, and even these not consistently. Less than J$2 million was paid out in total.

Recipients of the FAP will be better off for receiving payments, but the payments received cannot balance the deterioration in the standard of living brought about by the government's economic policies. The removal of subsidies and price controls, along with other measures such as large devaluation of the Jamaican dollar, have resulted in considerable increases in the price of basic food items. Moreover, as prices increase, the quality of the basic items seems to worsen, and there are no measures implemented to keep this in check. Cornmeal and condensed milk, for example, which are staples of the poor, have markedly deteriorated, and provide neither the quantity nor quality of food they previously did.

(b) The vulnerable groups While by no means the only ones vulnerable to the poverty effects of short-run economic policies, three main groups may be identified: children in low-income households, the aged, and the young members of the labour force. Together these three groups account for more than half of the population.

Children in low-income households are especially vulnerable. These households include the unemployed, underemployed, many of those in the informal sector, and those dependent on the minimum wage. In 1982 the under-5s comprised 12.2 per cent of the population, and the 5–9 age-group a further 26.1 per cent. Thus in all, the 0–14 age-group covers 38.3 per cent of the population. Given the very high levels of unemployment, underemployment, and income and wealth inequalities which exist, at least half of these children are among those acutely affected by the economic decline. Suffering is considerable, as will be indicated when we examine the nutritional status of children in a later section.

In 1982, the over-65s comprised nearly 7.0 per cent of the population. This group is highly vulnerable to poverty. The income going to this group is very low, consisting mainly of pensions and non-labour incomes. Many of the aged have to exist on what they can scrape together, on gifts and as dependants of others. A small number receive pensions from private pension schemes, but pensions are typically very small in real terms. Public provision for the aged by way of such facilities as retirement homes or pensions is limited. The public old age homes which exist are very few and all too often of deplorable condition, catering for the destitute. Private charity initiatives offer better facilities—for the few lucky enough to get in—and provision is increasing because of the inadequacy of public facilities.

The national insurance scheme (NIS) covers the entire labour force, but its impact is extremely limited. The level of both contributions and benefits are grossly inadequate, and it covers only a small proportion of the target population. For instance, in 1984 the NIS paid out 29,149 old-age pensions—but in 1982 the over-65s numbered 151,427. This means the NIS pension benefit reached only about 19 per cent of the eligible population. Moreover, the full flat-rate pension is only J\$15.00 per week, which is less than the cost of an average chicken in a Jamaican supermarket. Other benefits are lower—the widows/widowers' pensions is only J\$12.50 a week. Pensioners may receive more than the full flat-rate if they have made income-supplement contributions, but even these are unable to raise pensions to an adequate level because of the statutory cut-off point for these contributions.

The 14–24 age group, i.e. the young members of the labour force, are also considered a vulnerable group. The latest available figures show that in 1982 this age-group comprised 22.1 per cent of the population (495,600) and 31.7 per cent of the labour force (332,300). High underemployment, unemployment, and low income are the characteristic features of this age group. The overall unemployment rate for the group was 50.5 per cent. Females were particularly disadvantaged with an unemployment rate of 68.6 per cent, while the male unemployment rate was 34.5 per cent.

The widespread vulnerability to economic hardship is indicated by the fact already noted that the Food Aid Programme is aimed at a target group of one million people, approximately half the population, and although these overlap with the groups noted above they are not identical.

4   Impact on the nutritional status of children

Relative to other countries, the level of malnutrition in Jamaica is not bad. Although it does not belong to the group of countries which made headline news throughout the world because of mass starvation, there are nevertheless people in Jamaica who suffer from starvation and malnutrition. Notable among the victims are children, the aged, invalids, and the sick. The presence of well-established charity organizations with a long history of activity in Jamaica help to reduce the incidence of malnutrition, but nonetheless evidence persists of high levels of malnutrition.

(a) Data on food and nutrition The main data sources in this area are the Nutrition and Dietetics Division of the Ministry of Health (MOH) and the Caribbean Food and Nutrition Institute (CFNI).

Table 5.11 shows the results of two national nutrition surveys, 1978 and 1985. The 1978 sample of children 0–4 showed 30.4 per cent of children to be mildly malnourished (Gomez 1) 6.8 per cent to be moderately malnourished (Gomez 2) and about 1 per cent to be severely malnourished (Gomez 3). Thus overall, approximately 38 per cent showed signs of undernutrition. By 1985, the data show a decline in the nutritional status of children compared with 1978. The overall percentage of children aged 0–4 showing signs of under-nutrition increased from 38 per cent to 41 per cent, with increases in each of the categories on the scale.

TABLE 5.11   *National nutrition status of children 0–4 years, 1978 and 1985*

Gomez grade	1978	1985
Normal	61.7	59.2
Malnourished		
Degree 1	30.5	32.8
Degree 2	6.8	6.9
Degree 3	1.0	1.1

Source: Ministry of Health, Nutrition and Dietics Division.

The decline in nutrition levels characterized both urban and rural areas. The prevalence of undernutrition in urban areas increased from 35 per cent in 1978 to 36.3 per cent in 1985, and in rural areas from 39.8 per cent to 40.3

per cent. These increases are slight but nonetheless represent a significant number of children, given the size of the 0–4 population.

This undesirable trend is confirmed by admission statistics of the island's major children hospital. Table 5.12 shows that the percentages of children suffering from malnutrition and malnutrition/gastroenteritis grew significantly between 1978 and 1985.

TABLE 5.12   *Admission of children 0–59 months with malnutrition and malnutrition/gastroenteritis at the Bustamente Children's Hospital, 1978–1985*

	Malnutrition		Malnutrition/gastroenteritis	
	No.	%	No.	%
1978	68	1.9	55	1.6
1979	91	2.2	69	1.7
1980	98	1.7	58	1.0
1981	110	2.8	90	2.3
1982	86	2.2	75	1.9
1983	98	2.1	95	2.0
1984	110	2.4	122	2.7
1985	124	3.7	160	4.7

Source: Ministry of Health, Nutrition and Dietetics Division.

Both the number and relative frequency of cases of malnutrition and malnutrition/gastroenteritis have increased considerably since the application of the severe stabilization programme. In 1984 nearly 4 per cent of the children admitted to the Bustamente Children's Hospital were diagnosed as suffering from malnutrition compared with nearly 2 per cent in 1978, and nearly 5 per cent as suffering from malnutrition-related gastroenteritis compared with 1.6 per cent in 1978.

III   Impact on social programmes and service delivery

1   Decline in central government expenditure

The five-year period 1981/82–1985/86 saw total expenditure of central government reduced in real terms as increasingly vigorous deflationary policies were applied. Budgeted gross expenditure in 1985/86 was 71 per cent of the 1981/82 level (Table 5.13), and further reductions are expected. Whilst nominal expenditure has rapidly increased, real expenditure has declined due to accelerating inflation. In 1985/86, real expenditure was at its lowest for 11 years (Table 5.13).

The decline in aggregate central government expenditure has been at the expense of social services and economic services. Social services expenditure,

TABLE 5.13   *Real total government expenditure, 1975/76–1985/86 (million Jamaican dollars, 1979/80 prices)*

	Total	Government services	Social services	Economic services
1975/76	1,915	568	630	524
1976/77	2,666	741	638	592
1977/78	1,856	618	591	491
1978/79	2,155	745	676	580
1979/80	1,828	683	641	419
1980/81	2,076	749	595	577
1981/82	2,156	788	662	585
1982/83	2,120	830	664	502
1983/84	2,044	962	618	383
1984/85	1,689	901	448	268
1985/86	1,540	894	372	252

Source: Planning Institute of Jamaica, *Economic and Social Survey of Jamaica:* Ministry of Finance and Planning, *Financial Statements and Revenue Estimates for 1985–86.*

of which the main categories are education, health, and social security, have fallen from a real expenditure in 1981/82 of J$662 million to J$372 million in 1985/86, a reduction of 44 per cent over the last five years. The real level of expenditure in 1985/86 was less than 60 per cent of that 11 years before.

Economic services, which include expenditure relating to the economic infrastructure, such as transport and communications, roads, agricultural and industrial services, have also experienced a sharp fall. In 1985/86 budgeted expenditure for this category was 57 per cent lower than in 1981/82 in real terms. The 1985/6 level was 48 per cent of the 1975/86 level.

The decline in these two categories of expenditure has occurred largely over the last two years, 1984/85 and 1985/86, as adverse movements in both internal and external macro-economic indicators have elicited greater deflationary responses on the fiscal, monetary, and exchange rate fronts. In 1984/85 alone, expenditure on social and economic services fell by approximately 30 per cent in real terms over the previous year. This was followed in the next year (1985/86) by a 16 per cent fall in social services expenditure. These large decreases in social and economic services have significantly and directly affected social welfare as well as general economic performance, as agricultural extension and other economic services have been drastically reduced.

As expenditure on social and economic services has fallen, the expenditure on the public debt and fiscal services has risen. With no capital repayment budgeted for public debt for 1985/86, all budgeted expenditures go towards interest and service payments. This item accounts for the greater part of government expenditure. Recurrent expenditure on this item took up 41 per cent of total budgeted recurrent expenditure in the last budget, 1985/86.

Furthermore, the proportion of recurrent expenditure going to debt service increased consecutively in each year from 1979/80 (see Table 5.14). These increases have far-reaching adverse implications not only for social services but for general economic performance as well, which feeds back adverse effects on social welfare.

TABLE 5.14 *Proportion of recurrent expenditure for debt and fiscal services, 1979/80–1985/86 (percentages)*

'79/80	'80/81	'81/82	'82/83	'83/84	'84/85	'85/86
23.6	25.5	26.3	28.4	33.2	39.7	41.0

Sources: Planning Institute of Jamaica, *Economic and Social Survey of Jamaica:* Ministry of Finance and Planning, *Financial Statements and Revenue Estimates for 1985/86.*

(a) Capital expenditures The decline in aggregate expenditure is accentuated when capital expenditures are examined. Total gross capital expenditure declined from J$780 million in 1981/82 to J$467 million in 1985/86, a decline of 40 per cent in real terms (Table 5.15). Over the last two years, 1984/85 and 1985/86, social services capital expenditure has declined by 28 per cent and 25 per cent, respectively. These levels of real expenditure are well below those of the later 1970s.

TABLE 5.15 *Central government capital expenditure, 1975/76–1985/86 (J$m, 1979/80 prices)*

	Total	Government services	Social services	Economic services
1975/76	765	204	177	348
1976/77	900	311	159	399
1977/78	641	170	136	321
1978/79	784	208	150	409
1979/80	604	159	136	300
1980/81	719	165	102	451
1981/82	780	178	145	456
1982/83	738	184	158	381
1983/84	605	238	94	273
1984/85	461	194	67	187
1985/86	467	235	50	182

Source: Planning Institute of Jamaica, *Economic and Social Survey of Jamaica;* Ministry of Finance and Planning, *Financial Statements and Revenue Estimates for 1985/86.*

In order to effect these reductions the government has had to close down certain schools and downgrade the services offered by some hospitals and health centres, notably those in the rural areas. Capital expenditure on maintenance for equipment and buildings, as well as expenditure on replacement or new machinery and equipment, has had to be severely curtailed.

(b) Recurrent expenditure Recurrent expenditure has also declined (Table 5.16), and expenditure on social services and economic services has declined more than proportionately. Recurrent expenditure on social services has fallen consecutively in 1984/85 and 1985/86, by 27 per cent and 16 per cent respectively in real terms. Social services recurrent expenditure in 1985/86 was the lowest it has been in seven years, with the proportion of total recurrent expenditure going to social services falling from 37 per cent in 1981/82 to 30 per cent in 1985/86.

This rapid rate of decline has generated significant dislocations for both the suppliers of social services (those employed in education and health, for example), and the users of the services. In 1986 many schools throughout the country were closed by both teachers and parents in a prolonged dispute in support of teachers' pay demands.

(c) Expenditure on social services Government expenditure on social services can be disaggregated into its main components of education, health, and social security. Table 5.17 shows a rapid decline in all areas of social services expenditure since the start of vigorous adjustment policies in 1984/85.

2   The impact on education

In constant per capita terms for the 0–14 age group, total expenditure on educational services by the government has fallen by 40 per cent from 1981/82 to 1985/86. Most of that fall has occurred since 1983/84. Recurrent educational expenditure declined by an average of 21 per cent in real terms in each of the years since 1983/84. Recurrent educational expenditure has declined significantly as a proportion of total recurrent expenditure—from 20.2 per cent in 1980/81 to 15.8 per cent in 1985/86.

Reductions of this magnitude effected over a short period of time when the 0–14 age group is expanding absolutely and as a proportion of the population cannot but adversely affect the educational opportunities of those unable to afford private education, and this represents the vast majority of the Jamaican population. Between 1970 and 1982 the proportion of the population aged 0–14 increased from 35.8 per cent to 38.3 per cent, and this expansion is likely to continue.

The impact of the cuts in the educational budget is exacerbated by the characteristics of the Jamaican educational establishment. From the 1960s the general quality of education has declined.

There has been considerable competition for places in primary schools, and even more so secondary schools, which were always in short supply. In 1973, the government took over the financing of secondary schools, providing free secondary education. This move coincided with the large exogenous shocks to the economy initiated by the oil price increases. The rapid deterioration of the economy which followed placed constraints on the government's budget

TABLE 5.16   *Central government recurrent expenditure, 1975/76–1985/86 (J$m, 1979/80 prices)*

	Total	Government services	Social services	Economic services
1975/76	1,150	364	453	176
1976/77	1,266	430	479	193
1977/78	1,215	449	455	171
1978/79	1,371	537	525	171
1979/80	1,264	524	505	119
1980/81	1,357	584	493	125
1981/82	1,376	610	518	129
1982/83	1,382	646	506	120
1983/84	1,439	724	525	110
1984/85	1,228	707	381	81
1985/86	1,072	659	322	70

Sources: Planning Institute of Jamaica, *Economic and Social Survey of Jamaica;* Ministry of Finance and Planning, *Financial Statements and Revenue Estimates for 1985/86.*

TABLE 5.17   *Total social services expenditure breakdown, 1975/76–1985/86 (J$m, 1979/80 prices)*

	Total	Education	Health	Social security
1975/76	630	330	143	23
1976/77	638	333	140	21
1977/78	591	293	139	19
1978/79	676	295	138	22
1979/80	641	276	145	22
1980/81	595	285	139	18
1981/82	662	305	154	22
1982/83	664	313	162	22
1983/84	618	299	144	21
1984/85	448	238	114	19
1985/86	369	193	106	27

Source: Planning Institute of Jamaica, *Economic and Social Survey of Jamaica;* Ministry of Finance and Planning, *Financial Statements and Revenue Estimates for 1985/86.*

expansion. In 1975, due to a chronic shortage of secondary school places, a two-shift school system was introduced. This virtual doubling of the secondary school capacity, however, was immediately entirely absorbed. In 1985, 46,887 children sat the common entrance examination for a total of 10,066 places. In spite of the competition for secondary places, the standard of secondary education has fallen considerably over the last decades, due in great part to constantly falling real incomes of teachers, and poor equipment and capital stock.

One recently published study of a high school in the metropolitan area shows that the proportion of teachers resigning in any year during the 1980s has been in excess of 30 per cent, with approximately 45 per cent resigning during 1984.

The rate of GCE 'O' level/CXC (Caribbean Examination Council) fell from 62 per cent in 1980 to 34 per cent in 1985 (Table 5.18). The rate of passes in the 1980s in both absolute and relative terms is significantly lower in the 1980s than in the late 1970s.

TABLE 5.18   *Number and rate of exam passes, 1976–1985*

	No. passes	Pass rate (%)
1976	617	58
1977	591	57
1978	703	62
1979	755	65
1980	748	62
1981	643	43
1982	566	43
1983	613	40
1984	817	42
1985	636	34

Source: Terry (1986).

Both poor and middle-class children are affected by the educational cutbacks. The already poor educational opportunities provided by government schools have been reduced. At the start of each academic year, families find it increasingly difficult to find places for children, irrespective of whether seeking a free or a fee-paying place. Government primary schools generally operate considerably above capacity, with 50–70 children in a class not unknown. In spite of this, there is still a chronic shortage of places.

The sharp reductions in recurrent expenditure have resulted in delays in disbursements to schools, and this in some cases has led to temporary closures as well as delayed openings.

Children's homes (orphanages) and approved schools faced with budget cuts and delays in receiving finance are often acutely affected as their already low standards are further reduced. These schools are generally unable to raise funds by charity drives and concerts as is increasingly done by most schools.

3   *The impact on health services*

In constant terms, total expenditure on health services by the government has fallen from J$70 per person in 1981 to J$47 per person in 1985, a fall of 33 per cent. Recurrent and capital expenditures have fallen significantly (Table 5.19). The levels of real expenditures in recent years are significantly below those of the late 1970s.

TABLE 5.19   *Government expenditure on health services, 1975/76–1985/86 (J$m, 1979/80 prices)*

	Total	Recurrent	Capital
1975/76	142.5	133.0	9.5
1976/77	139.8	132.5	7.3
1977/78	138.9	130.7	8.2
1978/79	138.2	130.8	7.4
1979/80	144.6	136.7	7.9
1980/81	139.2	129.4	9.8
1981/82	154.0	134.5	19.5
1982/83	161.8	144.0	17.9
1983/84	143.5	134.1	9.4
1984/85	113.7	105.1	8.6
1985/86	105.7	99.1	6.6

Source: Planning Institute of Jamaica, *Economic and Social Survey of Jamaica;* Ministry of Finance and Planning, *Financial Statements and Revenue Estimates for 1985/86.*

Over the years 1983–85, capital expenditure fell by 47 per cent, 9 per cent, and 23 per cent, respectively. This has led to observable deterioration in the health capital stock and equipment. For example, in 1985 the government assumed financial responsibility for the main teaching hospital in the English-speaking Caribbean, at the University of the West Indies Hospital on the campus in Jamaica, as a part of a restructuring of the University of the West Indies. This was immediately followed by closures of certain of its departments as the Ministry of Health was forced to effect budget cutbacks.

Reductions in the recurrent budget have involved falling real incomes for doctors, nurses, and other hospital staff. Despite protests, a programme of rationalizing the health services has not only reduced services in some area but has introduced a wide-based system of charges for health services offered in public hospitals and health centres which were previously free. Although those receiving certain forms of public assistance are exempted, the charges are nevertheless applied to the low paid and the unemployed, and contribute to the economic pressure of the disadvantaged in the society. The increased costs have coincided with significantly poorer personal service as patients frequently have to take their own linen and in some cases food, as hospital supplies become increasingly unreliable and poor. This is quite apart from the increasing difficulty of obtaining treatment.

Exchange rate devaluations, the removal of subsidies, and indirect taxation have served to increase the cost of drugs considerably.

The standard of the Jamaica public health service has been considerably reduced as budgets cutbacks are implemented and more reliance has to be placed on either private resources or charity. The poor have very limited access to these and are thus forced to bear a considerable part of the adjustment burden in respect of health services.

4   Expenditure on water and housing

Expenditure on housing and water have all fallen drastically in real terms as ministries are forced to effect budget cuts.

Official statistics show that while 70 per cent of the population receive treated water, about 20 per cent receive untreated water, and 10 per cent are not served with water, including a good number of households in the metropolitan area. A considerable number of those served obtain their water through standpipes, and this also includes a significant number of people in the Kingston metropolitan area who have to fetch their water.

Accompanying the drastic reduction in expenditure on water, the government increased water rates by 55 per cent at the time of the January 1984 deflationary policy package.

Capital expenditure on housing in the 1985/86 budget was only 11 per cent of the 1982/83 real level. The economic impact of the decline in housing is reflected in the overall decline of the construction industry and the lay-off of much of its large labour force, and the reduction in production of its material inputs.

The virtual collapse of the supply of new low-income houses, for which there is a considerable need, if not demand, is a particularly hard blow to many low-income households faced with living in ghettoes, shanty towns, and over-crowded conditions.

TABLE 5.20   *Percentage change in housing price index, various years* (*1975 = 100*)

	Jan. 1977– Dec. 1980 (4 yrs.)	Jan. 1981– June 1985 (4.5 yrs.)	Jan. 1983– June 1985 (2.5 yrs.)
ALL JAMAICA	60	99	67
Kingston Met. area	57	95	66
Other towns	61	107	70
Rural areas	51	115	71

Source: Bank of Jamaica, *Statistical Digest*, Aug. 1985, Nov. 1981.

The pressure in the housing market has resulted in large increases in the price of housing, in both the urban and rural areas. The price of housing in the rural areas over the four-and-a-half-year period January 1981 to June 1985 increased by 115 per cent. This is significantly higher than the rate of increase over the four-year period January 1977 to December 1980 which saw an increase of 51 per cent (Table 5.20). For the Kingston metropolitan area, the increases over the respective periods were 95 per cent and 60 per cent.

The rate of increase of the price of housing has been more rapid in the 1980s than in the late 1970s. The two-and-a-half-year period January 1983 to June 1985 has seen the rural housing price jump by 71 per cent, and the weighted All Jamaica housing index increase by 67 per cent. Over the 1981–85 period, the rural index increased by 115 per cent and the All Jamaica index virtually doubled.

5 Social security

Legislation introducing a social security scheme was passed in 1965. The Jamaican social security is made up of two schemes. The major component is a contributory National Insurance Scheme (NIS), and the other is the Public Assistance Scheme.

The NIS is obligatory to the labour force as a whole, but is generally avoided by informal sector workers and the self-employed. The primary benefit entitlements under the NIS relate to old age and invalidity pensions. All beneficiaries under the NIS have to be contributors. There is no unemployment or sickness component.

Both the payments and the contribution to the NIS pension scheme are low as neither is inflation indexed, and so have fallen drastically in real terms. In order to protect against financial hardship in old age, people are thus required to make private pension arrangements.

When the NIS was introduced the contributions from employees and employers financed the benefit payments, and the central government contributed to the system by financing the administration of the scheme. Because of budget cutbacks the government stopped its contribution to the scheme from 1983, and now all NIS operations are financed through the contributions made by employees and employers. Nevertheless, the government borrows all the funds of the NIS, using it as a cheap source of credit.

On the whole the NIS can be seen as doing 'something' for those fortunate enough to qualify for a pension, but the vast majority of the very poor do not qualify. Also, not all of those who qualify receive a pension, for one reason or another, and the take-up rate of allowances is a cause for concern. As noted earlier, in 1982 only about 19 per cent of the over-65s were receiving a pension under this scheme.

The Public Assistance Scheme (PAS) is a non-contributory scheme whereby social assistance is provided to people in need. The main elements of the PAS

TABLE 5.21 *Public assistance: social and economic allowance, 1983–1984*

	Jan.–Dec. 1983		Jan.–Dec. 1984	
	No.	Amount (J$000)	No.	Amount (J$000)
Rehabilitation, compassionate and family allowances	4,400	591	855	136
Old age and incapacity allowances	35,788	8,432	33,990	8,110
TOTAL	40,228	9,023	34,845	8,246

Sources: Planning Institute of Jamaica, *Economic and Social Survey of Jamaica*, 1984.

are social and economic disability allowances; a food aid programme, and emergency relief services.

There were 13 per cent less beneficiaries during 1984 than in the previous year (Table 5.21) under the PAS as a whole, and total payments were significantly reduced. In nominal terms, the total amount fell from J$9.0 million to J$8.2 million. This represents a fall of 33 per cent in real terms.

The Emergency Relief Services administers aid in cases of disasters such as fires, floods, and the effects of civil disturbances. Its operations were curtailed during 1984 owing to budgetary cuts. The total amount fell in nominal terms from J$247,616 in 1983 to J$148,862, which represents less than half of the real expenditure in 1983.

IV Conclusions

There is considerable evidence that economic policies in the 1970s and 1980s have served to worsen the condition of the poor in Jamaica. Indeed, the situation appears to be one of continual decline from 1972, but especially from 1975.

The economic decline of the 1970s cannot be regarded as the macro-economic cost to be borne for household gain, as is often argued by those responsible for the policies. There is no evidence to support that view. The evidence instead indicates that the macro-economic decline was accompanied by decline at the level of the household and the individual. This led in structural change in the labour force as people increasingly entered the informal sector, 'higglering' and 'hustling' in order to make a living.

There is ample evidence that real incomes decreased significantly over the 1970s. Real wages at the end of the decade were significantly below those at the beginning of the decade.

The economic adjustment policies of the 1980s, based on deflating the economy, massive devaluations, tax increases, and government expenditure cuts, have had considerable stagflationary effects. The impact on the poor has also been considerable, with decline in quantity and quality of public services on every front—health, education, housing, and water—and increasing costs for what exists.

The government has sought to mitigate these effects by its welfare programme, primarily its Food Aid Programme. This food intervention programme has been weak and fraught with administrative and financial problems. It has not been sufficient to offset the adverse developments on nutrition arising from falling real incomes and rising relative food prices. There has been a marked increase in malnutrition among children in the 1980s.

Prime Minister Edward Seaga acknowledges that under his government the Jamaican economy has been subjected to extreme shocks, designed in conjunction with the IMF, primarily aimed at correcting the balance of payments disequilibrium. He acknowledges that these shocks have resulted in severe pressure on all classes, but especially on the poor who comprise the majority of the population. The removal of subsidies, increasing redundancies and unemployment, and the reduction in social and economic services, *inter alia*, have all had direct adverse effects of significant magnitude.

Despite the shocks which have been administered over the last three-and-a-half years, the economy does not show significant signs of recovery: internal and external imbalances and declining per capita incomes persist. Meanwhile the welfare of households continues to decline.

In all, the situation of the vulnerable groups in Jamaica has undergone long-run deterioration, and the deterioration continues. Changes in the short-run economic policy of the government and an improvement in the administration of social security and other welfare schemes are urgently required.

References

Ahiram, E. (1964), 'Income Distribution in Jamaica, 1958', *Social and Economic Studies,* 13/3, 333–69.

Bank of Jamaica, *Monthly Review.*

—— *Statistical Digest.*

Boyd, D. A. C. (1986a), 'Macro-economic Stabilisation in Jamaica: The Lesson of Recent Experience', Working Paper No. 19, London: Overseas Development Institute.

—— (1986b), 'Stabilization Policies and Income Distribution in Jamaica'. Mimeographed. London: Overseas Development Institute.

Brown, A. (1981), 'Economic Policy and the IMF in Jamaica', *Social and Economic Studies*, 30/4, 1–51.

Girvan, N., R. Bernal, and W. Hughes (1980), 'The IMF and the Third World: The Case of Jamaica, 1974–80', *Development Dialogue*, no. 2.

Jefferson, D. (1972), *The Post-War Economic Development of Jamaica.* Institute of Social and Economic Research, University of the West Indies, Mona, Jamaica.

Kincaid, G. R. (1977), 'Conditionality and the Use of Fund Resources', *Finance and Development*, June.

Lovejoy, R. M. (1963), 'The Burden of Jamaican Taxation 1958', Social and Economic Studies, 12/4.

McLure, J. C. E. (1977), 'The Incidence of Jamaican Taxes, 1971–72,' Institute of Social and Economic Research Working Paper no. 16, University of the West Indies, Mona, Jamaica.

Sharpley, J. (1984), 'Jamaica, 1972–80', in Killick, Tony, ed., *The IMF and Stabilization: Developing Country Experiences.* London: Heinemann.

Statistical Institute of Jamaica, *Census of Agriculture Preliminary Report 1978–79.*

—— *Consumer Price Index.*

—— *National Income and Product.*

Terry, M. B. (1986) 'Teacher Resignations and Examination Results' *Sunday Gleaner,* 2 Feb. 1986.

6

Economic Adjustment and Development in Peru: Towards an Alternative Policy

*Leonel Figueroa**

I Introduction

During the past decade, a set of orthodox policies for economic adjustment was implemented in Peru, as in the majority of the countries in the region. The policies assigned to the market a dominant role in resource allocation, and promoted a greater opening of the economy. This study analyses the results of these policies, particularly in terms of their effects on the living conditions of women, children, and other vulnerable population groups. The main aspects of a new adjustment strategy, adopted in July 1985, are also presented. This recent approach has assigned priority to growth and redistribution of income within a development model that explicitly favours the protection of the most vulnerable groups.

The period under examination is 1977–85. During this time the Peruvian economy and society underwent a gradual but substantial modification in style of development, which from 1969 had been based on import substitution and on a prominent role for the state in economic affairs.

The 1977–85 adjustment process resulted in high social costs, including a substantial decline in per capita GDP to a level equivalent to that of the 1960s, an increase in underemployment and unemployment, acceleration of the inflation process, deterioration in the living conditions of the majority of the population, and increasing social tensions.

Part II of this study briefly analyses the nature and course of the economic policy implemented between 1977 and 1985, linking it to the characteristics of Peruvian underdevelopment during the mid-1970s. Part III considers the effects of economic adjustment policies on the most vulnerable sectors of the population, including an assessment on the behaviour of some socio-economic variables such as income, employment, public expenditures, health, and education. It also describes the principal survival strategies adopted by the lower-income groups in order to attempt to satisfy their basic needs. Part IV discusses the new economic policy implemented by the APRA government since August

* This survey was prepared with the participation of Jose Luis Ramirez Llosa, Dehera Bruce, and Midori de Habich.

1985, as well as the major steps taken in the social and economic sphere. These policies represent a great departure from the traditional adjustment approach, especially considering their expansionary nature and the protection of less-favoured social groups. The initial results of the new economic policy are examined, together with the problems that the policy is now facing.

II Structural problems and economic development, 1977–1985

1 Peruvian underdevelopment

This study does not aim at an exhaustive explanation of the historic process that has led the country to its present state of development, although reference is made to some of the main causes and the structural problems which have emerged during this process.

A crucial element is the means by which Peru entered into the world economy from colonial times. There was a pattern of development based on exports of primary goods, and therefore dependence on the cyclical per-formance of the international economy. Within this pattern, phases of export expansion attracted resources geared towards the foreign sector and dis-couraged the development of production oriented to the domestic market. Particularly since export-related agriculture generated considerable surplus, agricultural production for domestic consumption was badly neglected and resulting food scarcities were compensated for through imports. At the same time, the foreign currency derived from profitable exports led to capital flight and to the consumption of luxury goods which absorbed a large share of the economic surplus that was generated, thus limiting the expansion of domestic industry.

In this context, the influx of foreign capital into commercial and financial activities as well as into primary exports formed a favourable setting for implementing a profit-based economic strategy rather than one that would have met the needs of more balanced national development. This process was facilitated by continuing political alliances between national groups in power and foreign capital. No social group emerged to lead a strategy of national autonomy that would have provided a common national identity uniting the aspirations of different segments of society.

The country's industrialization process was initially a result of the growth and diversification of global demand. Along with growth in primary exports, it was based on progressive substitution of domestic production of final con-sumption goods. During its second stage, industrialization expanded through a deepening of the substitution process adopted earlier. However, local pro-duction of intermediate, capital, and more elaborate consumption goods was not achieved due to the small size of the market, and this intensified the dependence on foreign imports and technology. A series of structural problems appeared and spread across the Peruvian economy. The following have been the most significant:

1. *A low level of per capita income and an unequal distribution of income in personal, functional, and regional terms.* In 1985, real GDP per capita (in 1985 dollar prices) was equivalent to $855, one of the lowest levels in Latin America. The asymmetry of the personal distribution of income revealed the great gaps separating social groups in the country. Estimates from the World Bank for 1983 (Table 6.1) shows that 10 per cent of the population, composed chiefly of groups representing transnational corporations, financial sectors, and the upper middle classes, earned 62 per cent of the national income. Lower-income groups, making up 50 per cent of the total population and including Indian peasants, marginal urban groups, and workers earning minimum wages, received only 7 per cent of the national income. During the 12 years between 1971 and 1983, a regressive distributional process increased the accumulation of the 10 per cent of the population with higher incomes.

TABLE 6.1   *Estimates of income distribution, 1971 and 1983*

% of families		% of national income	
		1971	1983
Bottom	25	1.8	1.6
	25	6.4	5.7
	25	15.3	13.7
	15	18.2	16.9
Top	10	58.3	62.1

Source: World Bank (1985).

2. *Insufficient food supply*, due to low agricultural productivity and weak technical capacity in the majority of food crops that led to continuous food imports. This in turn was a result of an uneven relative price structure.

3. *A low level of industrialization*, with a productive structure that has weak linkages among and within sectors and does not correspond to the basic needs of the population. This is closely related to the lack of a domestic market capable of sustaining major growth in the industrial sector and to dependence on imported technology, inputs, and machinery.

4. *Specialization in the production of primary goods.* 75 per cent of the country's exports are minerals, and the remaining 25 per cent, considered non-traditional exports, contain very little value added.

5. *A concentrated production structure.* Geographically, production is focused in Lima and to a lesser extent the coastal areas. Ownership is also concentrated, given the significance of oligopolistic firms in modern economic activities. In the industrial sector 200 firms account for 60 per cent of production, of which

the 10 largest represent 20 per cent of the income and 21 per cent of total assets. 65 per cent of the volume of physical production is located in Lima (Banco Central de Reserva de Peru 1986*c*).

6. *High levels of underemployment and unemployment.* According to recent official reports, only 35 per cent of the economically active population, which totals six million people, are adequately employed. Employment is one of the most serious economic problems in the country and a source of permanent social tension.

7. *Deficient social and economic infrastructure:*

(*a*) A housing deficit estimated to be one million units at the national level, with approximately 70 per cent of the population inhabiting dwellings lacking basic services.

(*b*) Health services incomplete in coverage and inadequately staffed and equipped.

(*c*) Energy supply which covers only part of the country and is unable to satisfy the demands of many economic activities, especially in the most depressed regions.

(*d*) Insufficient air and land transportation, increasing the difficulties of providing adequate public services and of integrating the different regions of the country.

(*e*) Educational inequalities nationwide, with higher rates of illiteracy in the more depressed areas of the country.

8. *A chronic deficit in the balance of payments*, which shows the vulnerability of the economy to fluctuations in the foreign sector. The deficit has been accentuated in recent years by deterioration in the international terms of trade and by the heavy burden represented by foreign debt service.

9. *Insufficient levels of domestic savings*, which have constantly required the use of foreign credit to cover the gaps between savings and investment.

2 *Economic development during the period 1977–1985*

Between 1977 and 1985 the Peruvian economy was characterized by a combination of recession and inflation which by the end of the period had reduced per capita income to a similar level to that reached 20 years earlier. The explanation of this performance lies primarily in the implementation, with varying nuances and intensities, of an orthodox economic policy that emphasized the market as the main allocator of resources, allowed for only limited state participation in economic activity, and encouraged the opening and liberalization of trade and the economy. The measures adopted to control inflation derived from the view that inflation is principally a result of excess aggregate demand. Through a variety of actions domestic demand was abruptly contracted, and with it the purchasing power of the majority of the population. A related objective in this regard was to free hard currency to service the foreign debt. In summary, this set of policies accelerated the inflationary process and introduced a downward trend in economic activity which not only weakened the already precarious productive structure but also worsened the problems of employment, income distribution, and the living conditions of the poor, so contributing to an increase in social tensions.

This orthodox adjustment model was implemented following a long series of reforms implemented between 1969 and 1975. During that period, the state had played a relatively active role in production. Important projects were undertaken, and a policy of import substitution was implemented with a high degree of protection. Sustained economic growth, averaging 5.4 per cent per year, was achieved. Another important activity during the early 1970s was the redistribution of property, particularly in the agricultural sector, and the redistribution of income within the sectors that were incorporated in the market economy. Yet in attempting simultaneously to satisfy the demands of many social groups, the policies of that period imposed a substantial cost on the state. This involved high levels of subsidy and greatly increased foreign debt, which was made larger by an ambitious programme of military purchases. The first signs of an economic crisis appeared in 1974, conditions worsened in 1975, and the crisis extended into 1976 and 1977.

The introduction of a set of recessionary measures in 1978 resulted in a 4.3 per cent decrease in per capita product over the previous year accompanied by an increase in inflation and a devaluation (73.7 and 100 per cent, respectively). Fortunately, due to a sudden increase in export prices and to several large projects becoming operational at that time, the government was able to stabilize inflation as well as the foreign sector during the next two years, although an accelerated reduction in real salaries began to take place.

The liberalization of imports initiated in 1978 was broadened in 1980, with the effect that imports doubled in value between 1979 and 1981. However, exports did not parallel this growth in spite of a liberal exchange rate policy. The increase in international interest rates also contributed to a heavy debt service burden, which by 1981 had reached 54 per cent of exports.

A second recessionary adjustment process was undertaken in 1982. Its negative effects were deepened in 1983 by droughts in the south and floods in the north and a consequent 12 per cent drop in GDP. Inflation was not controlled; on the contrary, rates of price increases reached three digits, while real remuneration levels continued to fall. The cut-back in imports, although necessary for balancing the foreign account, spread a recession throughout the economy that lasted until 1985.

By July 1985 the main economic indicators showed the following:

1. Annual inflation of 250 per cent.

2. A new uncontrolled loss in purchasing power. Domestic savings in national currency dropped, speculation increased, and a significant part of the country's liquidity was held in foreign currency (in July 1985, according to

the BCRP (1986*b*), foreign currency represented 60 per cent of total bank deposits).

3. Unpaid long-term public debt service reached $1,950 million. Total debt payment requirements (including private and short-term unpaid debt) were approximately $4,750 million, or about 1.4 times the probable level of exports of goods and services for one year.

4. A decrease in per capita product to levels of 20 years earlier.

5. Significant reduction in consumption by the lower-income population.

6. Increase in open unemployment and underemployment, extending to approximately 65 per cent of the economically active population.

7. An appreciable increase in idle installed capacity.

8. Deterioration in indicators of the quality of life of the population.

Table 6.2 presents the evolution of the main indicators of the Peruvian economy, showing the effects of the policies that were implemented during the period.

III   Adjustment policies, 1977–July 1985

1   *The adjustment policies*

Orthodox adjustment programmes consist of a set of economic measures intended to reduce aggregate demand and promote international competitiveness. Between 1977 and 1985, Peru signed the following agreements with the IMF:

Year	*Month*	*Type*	*SDR* (*millions*)
1978	September	Stand-by agreement	184.0
		Compensatory financing	64.0
1979	August	Stand-by agreement	285.0
1982	June	Compensatory financing	199.9
		Extended facility agreement	650.0
1984	April	Compensatory financing	74.7
		Stand-by agreement	250.0

A general prerequisite for signing such agreements is the government's obligation to implement measures towards the achievement of quantitative targets (fiscal deficit, public debt, etc.). In addition, agreements spelled out certain 'terms of understanding' on wages, taxes, and other policies although non-fulfilment of these terms did not necessarily result in the suspension of disbursement. The agreement of 1984 carried the commitment of the Peruvian government to change labour legislation in order to adapt it to the requirements of the prevalent economic policy, as well as legislation regarding landholding which in fact implied reversing the agrarian reform of earlier years.

TABLE 6.2 *GDP, inflation, rate of exchange, trade balance, balance of payments, foreign debt, savings, and investment, 1970–1985*

| | GDP | | Inflation[b] (%) | Rate of exchange[c] | Exports ($m) | Imports ($m) | Trade balance ($m) | Balance of payments ($m) | Total foreign debt ($m) | Savings investment coefficient | | |
	Per capita[a] (000)	Change (%)								(S) Domestic savings/ GDP	(I) Investment/ GDP	(S-I) Domestic savings less investment/ GDP
1970	18.24	4.3	5.7	0.043	1,034	700	335	257	3,681	15.9	12.9	3.0
1971	18.65	2.2	7.5	0.043	889	730	159	−76	3,692	14.3	14.8	−0.5
1972	19.19	2.9	4.2	0.043	945	812	133	50	3,832	13.7	14.1	−0.4
1973	19.82	3.3	13.8	0.043	1,112	1,033	79	13	4,132	13.6	15.7	−2.1
1974	20.60	3.9	19.1	0.043	1,503	1,909	−406	281	5,238	11.8	18.8	−7.0
1975	20.52	−0.4	24.0	0.045	1,330	2,427	−1,097	−577	6,257	11.2	22.4	−11.2
1976	20.64	0.6	44.7	0.069	1,341	2,016	−675	−868	7,384	10.3	18.1	−7.8
1977	20.05	−2.9	32.4	0.080	1,726	2,148	−422	349	8,567	8.9	15.1	−6.2
1978	19.19	−4.3	73.7	0.160	1,972	1,668	304	76	9,324	12.9	14.4	−1.5
1979	19.50	1.6	66.7	0.230	3,676	1,954	1,722	1,579	9,334	21.0	14.1	6.9
1980	19.54	0.2	60.8	0.290	3,916	3,090	826	722	9,595	17.1	17.7	−0.6
1981	19.62	0.4	72.7	0.420	3,249	3,802	−553	−504	9,689	13.5	22.1	−8.6
1982	19.28	−1.7	72.9	0.700	3,293	3,721	−428	124	11,548	14.9	22.8	−7.9
1983	16.54	−14.2	125.1	1.630	3,015	2,722	293	−40	12,520	11.6	17.0	−5.4
1984	16.88	2.1	111.5	3.470	3,147	2,140	1,007	247	13,389	14.5	16.0	−1.5
1985	16.71	−1.0	158.3	10.980	2,966	1,869	1,097	318	13,794	14.6	14.1	0.5

Source: BCRP and Instituto Nacional de Estadistica (INE).

[a] In thousand intis at 1970 prices.

[b] Percentage change Dec.–Dec.

[c] Intis per US dollar, period average.

The chief adjustment measures implemented during the period were the following:

1. *An austerity plan for public sector expenditures* which included reduction of real expenditures for wages and salaries, goods and services, and investment; elimination of subsidies to products of mass consumption, and increased prices for goods and services sold through the public sector.

2. *Limitation of wages and salary increases* to levels below the inflation rate.

3. *Redefinition of the entrepreneurial activity of the state,* by transferring public enterprises to the private sector.

4. *A flexible exchange rate policy,* which resulted in a constant process of mini-devaluation, and the establishment of limits on the loss in net foreign reserves.

5. *Greater openness to foreign trade,* via a significant decrease in tariffs, elimination of restrictions on imports of certain products, and the removal of trade and exchange restrictions.

6. *Limits to the increase in the central bank's net domestic assets,* with the objective of stopping the expansion of net domestic credit to the public treasury.

7. *Controls on the money supply* and on interest rates.

8. *Limitations on new foreign public debt.*

2 Main effects

Evaluating the impact of the adjustment policies is a complex task, since the effects of such policies must be distinguished from long-term trends in a country's development. Nevertheless, it may be concluded that worsening of social problems, and in particular deterioration of the living conditions of the population, can be linked to the contractionary policies implemented. Within the limitations of space and available statistical information, the effects of these policies on levels of employment, income, and government expenditures on health, education, and subsidies, will be discussed.

(a) Effects on employment levels Employment followed a declining trend during the period. There was a noticeable decrease in the proportion of the economically active population considered to be adequately employed, from 55.5 per cent in 1976 to 35 per cent in 1984 (Table 6.3).

The main problems here have been with unemployment and under-employment,[1] which have become more acute with the recession.

Additional employment effects have concerned the growth of the urban informal sector—the long-term process in which an increasing fraction of the population is excluded from high-productivity, adequately paid jobs and forced into self-generating employment as a means of obtaining earnings that allow survival. The informal and the modern sectors are not independent, with evidence of strong links between the two sectors, while the effects of recession reach both sectors. There are thus several further negative effects resulting

TABLE 6.3 *Economically active population 15 years and older, by employment levels, 1970–1984 (thousands)*

	Economically active population	Adequate employment		Under- employment		Unemployment	
		No.	(%)	No.	(%)	No.	(%)
1970	4,167	2,059	49.4	1,913	45.9	196	4.7
1971	4,281	2,192	51.2	1,901	44.4	188	4.4
1972	4,402	2,271	51.6	1,946	44.2	185	4.2
1973	4,535	2,471	54.5	1,873	41.3	190	4.2
1974	4,673	2,533	54.2	1,953	41.8	187	4.0
1975	4,818	2,539	52.7	2,043	42.4	236	4.9
1976	4,968	2,509	50.5	2,201	44.3	258	5.2
1977	5,125	2,357	46.0	2,470	48.2	297	5.0
1978	5,283	2,195	41.5	2,745	52.0	343	6.5
1979	5,442	2,257	41.5	2,797	51.4	388	7.1
1980	5,605	2,343	41.8	2,869	51.2	393	7.0
1981	5,779	2,617	45.3	2,770	47.9	392	6.0
1982	5,958	2,567	43.1	2,974	49.9	417	7.0
1983	6,137	2,301	37.5	3,271	53.3	565	9.2
1984	6,321	2,203	34.8	3,427	54.2	691	10.9

Source: Ministerio de Trabajo y Promocion Social, Direccion General de Empleo.
Prepared by BCRP, Departamento de Estudios del Sector Social.

from stagnation or recession in the modern sector. A decline in wages depresses aggregate sales, and a loss of jobs in the modern sector increases open unemployment which tends to be absorbed by the expansion of the labour force that takes on informal occupations. These effects converge, depressing average incomes in the informal sector.

In this context, the most vulnerable groups of the population, that is, women and children, have been forced to join in such activities more intensively than in the past. For those involved, this has not only resulted in a premature socialization of children but also has exacerbated the instability of family organization by forcing mothers, who are often heads of households and the sole source of family income, to abandon their households and younger children and thus expose them to great dangers, or to bring them to their work place. These women, aside from their activities outside home, must still take care of the household chores. This frequently means working up to 18 hours a day under difficult conditions with the high stress that results from excessive work and low earnings.

The situation is worsened by the fact that such households lack almost all types of services, and that they live in a state of complete abandonment from the point of view of assistance. Given the impossibility of leaving a small child at a day care centre or crêche, there are serious problems of lost working time and earnings when either mother or child is ill, since there is no access to social security benefits.

(b) Effects on income levels The direct effect of adjustment policies on workers' income may be seen in terms of the regulation of minimum wages and of earnings in the private and public sectors, especially among the non-unionized. It is clear that there was a continued deterioration between 1977 and 1985 in the level of real wage income, which by the end of 1985 was only 64 per cent of the 1979 level. (Real salaries, taking 1973 levels as 100, dropped to 44 by May 1985.)

However, these figures refer only to the permanent workers who make up approximately one-third of the economically active population, they do not account for the significant proportion of the economically active population who earn below minimum wages.

In analysing the evolution of national income during the past 14 years in relation to the behaviour of the global economy, three different periods may be identified (Table 6.4). The first period was from 1971 to 1974, in which production grew at an average annual rate of 6.3 per cent and real national income (including wages and salaries) grew at a rate of 7.1 per cent. Within this, wages increased an average of 9.2 per cent per year, mainly due to the distributive reforms and the wage and price policies implemented during those years.

TABLE 6.4 *Average yearly change in real national income, 1971–1974, 1975–1979, and 1980–1984 (percentages)*

	1971–74	1975–79	1980–84
Pay	7.2	− 3.2	− 3.0
Wages	9.2	− 1.6	− 4.8
Salaries	5.3	− 4.1	− 1.0
Self-employment	3.7	1.6	0.4
Real estate	5.8	− 9.0	− 2.9
Profits	11.9	13.0	− 3.2
Net interest	4.2	3.6	20.3
Total	7.1	2.5	− 1.9

Source: BCRP (1985).

In the period 1975–79 the rate of growth declined and there was a drop of 3.7 per cent in average real income. Independent workers maintained their income levels, however, as a result of greater protection through prices and the relative importance of subsistence production in the income of agricultural workers. Between 1980 and 1984, as a consequence of the adjustment policies, the growth rate of production fell to an average of 0.3 per cent per year, leading to a decline in average real income of 3.6 per cent that extended to all segments of the labour market. The share of wages and salaries within total income fell substantially, from 48.3 per cent in 1975 to 33.9 per cent in 1984, while the share of business profits increased from 21.5 per cent to 35.9 per cent over this period.

Although quantitive information is not available regarding rural incomes, evidence on migration and decreasing agricultural production suggests that in recent years there has been a severe deterioration in income levels in the rural areas. There is also evidence of an increase in extreme poverty in Lima and other marginal urban areas of the country, although here too there are no reliable data available for measuring its magnitude. The increased cost of the family basket of goods, and the greater number of Peruvians who live in a situation of unemployment or underemployment, nonetheless supports such an assessment especially in view of the fact (discussed later) that specific programmes directed to cover the primary needs of these population groups were not given prominence.

A variety of efforts were undertaken to alleviate this dramatic situation through the spontaneous organization of communities. Growing numbers of mothers' groups and community kitchens evolved as a positive response to meet basic needs through solidarity and local work. In addition, since 1984 the municipality of Lima has carried out a 'glass of milk' programme through which this basic nourishment has been provided to over one million children. In 1985 there was an attempt to extend the programme to the rest of the country, but this has not yet been successfully implemented.

(c) Effects on the government's social expenditures Examining the classification of central government expenditure according to functions for the period 1977–84, expenditures in general services increased almost seven times more than expenditures in social services. The latter represented an average of 26 per cent of total expenditures for the period 1968–76 and only 18 per cent during the period 1977–84 (Table 6.5). Public investment decreased in the health sector (from 3 per cent to 1.5 per cent) and the education sector (from 3 per cent to 2.2 per cent), which indicates that gross capital formation in both sectors has been neglected in these years.

(d) Health There is evidence of a high concentration of hospital beds and of staff (nurses and doctors) in Lima for the services provided by the Health Ministry, with less access in Apurimac, Amazonas, Ayacucho, and Cusco, areas with a high proportion of rural population.

The central government's health expenditures shows a slightly increasing trend, but at a level that is still very low in terms of proportion of total expenditures as well as in relation to GDP (2 per cent of GDP on average for 1977–83). This, along with the unequal distribution of resources, has resulted in the neglect of important segments of the population. Resources have not reached the levels recommended by WHO, even in Lima (with 3.2 beds per

TABLE 6.5 *Central government expenditure structure, 1968–1984 (percentages)*

	General services[a]	Social services[b]	Economic services[c]	Multi-sectoral	Total
1968	52.0	32.8	15.2	—	100.0
1969	52.3	31.1	16.6	—	100.0
1970	52.9	26.4	19.0	1.7	100.0
1971	52.7	24.6	18.6	4.1	100.0
1972	54.1	25.3	14.9	5.7	100.0
1973	55.7	24.2	16.6	3.5	100.0
1974	56.0	23.9	16.0	4.1	100.0
1975	51.2	23.2	22.8	2.8	100.0
1976	53.2	23.5	21.6	1.7	100.0
1977	64.0	19.0	15.6	1.4	100.0
1978	67.0	17.5	13.7	1.8	100.0
1979	64.3	19.1	15.3	1.3	100.0
1980	61.2	20.0	16.3	2.5	100.0
1981	60.0	21.1	17.4	1.4	100.0
1982	65.3	19.2	13.5	2.0	100.0
1983	69.8	16.9	10.4	2.9	100.0
1984[d]	69.4	16.4	11.3	2.9	100.0

Source: BCRP, Sub Gerencia Sector Publico.
[a] Includes general administration, interior, defence and debt service.
[b] Includes education, health, housing and labour.
[c] Includes agriculture, fishing, industry, energy, mines, transportation, and communications.
[d] Preliminary.

1,000 people, while the recommended level is 5 beds per 1,000 people). In addition, only 40 per cent of the economically active population has access to the benefits of social security, with strong regional inequalities—Lima has 86 per cent coverage, whereas Apurimac has only 9 per cent.

During the period 1977–84, the health status of the population was unsatisfactory, with high risks of disease and death, primarily for children. There was a clear increase in diseases such as typhoid, paratyphoid, hepatitis, dysentery, and malaria (Table 6.6). Special attention should be paid to the evolution of morbidity caused by tuberculosis, which during the years 1981–83 reached an average rate of 121 per 1,000 people, while for 1978–80 the average rate had been 93 cases per 1,000. This is evidence of a deterioration of living conditions of some parts of the population (Table 6.7).

Ministry of Health data indicate a high prevalence of energy and protein malnutrition in the country, particularly within the population under 6 years of age. Levels of general mortality and child mortality (below 5 years of age) reflect the severity of the problem. Several studies have indicated that approximately 44 per cent of Peruvian children under 6 years of age are malnourished: the incidence of malnutrition is greatest in the Sierra and Jungle regions (Table 6.8).

TABLE 6.6　*Main causes of morbidity due to transmissible diseases, 1979–1983*

	1979	1980	1981	1982	1983[a]
TOTAL	204,684	233,664	179,749	318,021	345,070
Dysentery, all forms	56,654	68,935	117,765	152,536	195,944
Worm-related diseases	35,834	39,181	43,170	49,728	42,837
Influenza (grippe)	31,054	31,891	22,603	15,642	12,073
Malaria	17,127	14,982	14,812	20,483	21,608
Respiratory tuberculosis	13,687	14,054	19,861	19,599	20,662
Measles	13,345	19,246	10,071	12,708	8,091
Whooping cough	12,720	12,134	11,973	8,238	6,923
Typhoid and paratyphoid	12,228	20,254	23,871	23,868	20,693
Hepatitis	6,049	6,002	7,822	7,191	7,449
Other	5,986	6,985	7,801	8,028	8,790

Source: Ministry of Health (1984)
[a] Preliminary data.

TABLE 6.7　*Mortality and morbidity caused by tuberculosis, 1970–1983 (rates per 100,000)*

	Mortality		Morbidity	
	No. of deaths	Rate	No. of cases	Rate
1970	4,271	31.8	23,843	177.3
1971	3,747	27.1	23,467	169.4
1972	3,585	25.2	23,173	162.9
1973	3,125	21.4	18,972	130.1
1974	3,585	24.0	16,549	110.6
1975	2,799	18.3	16,688	108.8
1976	2,908	18.5	22,257	141.6
1977	2,836	17.6	17,660	109.6
1978	2,776	16.8	15,506	93.9
1979	3,434	20.3	15,616	92.3
1980	4,464	25.8	16,011	92.4
1981	...	...	21,925	123.5
1982	...	...	21,802	120.0
1983	...	...	22,232	118.9

Source: Ministry of Health (1984).

A report on the nutritional status in the South Sierra prepared for USAID (Sigma One Corporation 1983) points to significant changes in nutritional status between the years 1980 and 1983 among children of ages 0–6 (Table 6.9).

Iodine deficiency and its consequences—goitre and endemic cretinism—continue to be the most widespread and among the most severe problems

TABLE 6.8 *Nutritional status of under-6s (percentages)*

	% of total population of under-6s	Normal	Malnourished			
			Total	1st degree	2nd degree	3rd degree
City of Lima	19	81	19	17	2	—[a]
Coast						
North	11	54	46	35	9	2
Centre	8	72	28	24	4	—[a]
South	9	71	29	22	6	1
Total	28	65	35	28	7	—[a]
Sierra						
North	12	35	65	44	17	4
Centre	10	44	56	38	15	6
South	10	55	45	28	13	4
Total	32	44	56	37	15	4
Jungle						
High	10	44	56	38	15	3
Low	11	32	68	45	20	3
Total	21	38	62	41	18	3
ALL PERU	100	56	44	31	11	2

Source: Ministry of Health (1984).
[a] Less than 1%

TABLE 6.9 *South Sierra: changes in nutritional status of under-6s, 1980–1983*

	% of children 1980	% of children 1983
Normal	58.4	32.0
Malnourished	41.6	68.0
Degree I	28.3	45.0
Degree II	12.5	20.0
Degree III	0.8	3.0

Source: Sigma One Corporation (1983).
Note: Based on a sample of children.

219

arising from malnutrition, particularly as they affect the most vulnerable population groups, i.e. infants and pregnant women.

(e) Education The burden of educational services is chiefly borne by the public sector, which accounts for 84 per cent of total registration, 80 per cent of personnel, and 85 per cent of educational centres. The rest of the system is covered by private education, primarily directed to higher-income groups and concentrated in the coastal, urban areas. The evolution of public spending thus determines the educational status of the majority of the school-age population, almost entirely so in the regions of the Sierra and the Jungle and particularly in the rural areas.

The budget of the Ministry of Education represented on average 20 per cent of the central government budget for the period 1965–76. Its share declined considerably in the period 1977–84, however, when it amounted to only 12 per cent of the total (Table 6.10). Current expenditures have consistently accounted for about 95 per cent of the education budget, and within this category wages are the most important element.

TABLE 6.10 *Evolution in the budget of the Ministry of Education, 1960–1984* (*thousands of intis*)

Budget	Budget of the Ministry of Education				% of the central government budget
	Current intis	Constant intis[a]	Current expenditures (%)	Capital expenditures (%)	
1960	1,488	3,692	96.7	3.3	17.4
1961	1,927	4,518	91.3	8.7	—
1962	2,375	5,219	95.5	4.5	—
1963	2,899	6,015	94.9	5.1	21.2
1964	3,599	6,740	94.1	5.9	—
1965	5,731	9,473	93.5	6.5	25.1
1966	7,155	10,632	97.4	2.6	26.5
1967	7,868	10,491	98.2	1.8	24.8
1968	7,297	8,455	99.0	1.0	19.8
1969	8,008	8,592	98.4	1.6	20.9
1970	9,027	9,027	96.7	3.3	18.8
1971	9,700	9,282	96.5	3.5	16.8
1972	12,924	11,696	96.2	3.8	19.7
1973	14,866	11,789	95.9	4.1	17.9
1974	17,963	12,195	93.6	6.4	18.2
1975	21,848	12,850	96.1	3.9	16.6
1976	28,344	12,281	97.1	2.9	16.1
1977	35,727	11,161	97.1	2.9	13.4
1978	48,542	9,505	96.0	4.0	11.3
1979	76,471	8,473	96.2	3.8	10.8
1980	175,916	12,149	94.4	5.6	12.8
1981	326,128	13,453	95.3	4.7	14.3
1982	484,761	12,040	89.7	10.3	13.3
1983	888,229	10,860	98.3	1.7	11.6
1984[b]	1,176,038	6,840	94.5	5.5	6.9

Source: Ministry of Education (1984).
[a] 1970 intis.
[b] Budgeted level.

TABLE 6.11 *Primary education of minors: promotion, drop-out, and repetition rates, by grade, 1974/75–1982/83*

	1st	2nd	3rd	4th	5th	6th
1974/75						
Promotion	71.2	79.3	83.4	83.1	83.1	76.5
Repetition	15.1	12.4	4.4	8.7	7.4	3.9
Drop-out	13.7	8.3	7.2	8.2	9.5	19.7
1975/76						
Promotion	74.8	82.0	85.2	83.6	85.5	80.0
Repetition	12.0	10.7	9.2	8.5	5.5	3.3
Drop-out	13.2	7.3	5.3	7.9	8.0	16.7
1976/77						
Promotion	73.8	80.6	83.8	81.9	85.6	79.0
Repetition	11.9	11.3	9.8	10.2	7.0	3.2
Drop-out	14.3	8.1	6.4	7.9	7.4	17.8
1977/78						
Promotion	84.3	87.3	87.7	84.5	90.5	84.0
Repetition	7.7	8.7	8.8	8.0	5.1	2.5
Drop-out	8.0	4.2	3.5	7.5	4.0	12.8
1978/79						
Promotion	65.1	79.0	79.8	79.8	80.0	81.7
Repetition	25.3	15.9	15.0	13.1	11.5	6.8
Drop-out	9.6	5.1	5.2	7.1	8.5	11.5
1979/80						
Promotion	62.6	80.2	79.1	81.3	75.9	83.2
Repetition	24.4	14.9	14.2	13.4	14.1	6.0
Drop-out	13.0	4.9	6.7	5.3	10.0	10.8
1980/81						
Promotion	63.2	81.4	80.4	81.2	81.4	85.0
Repetition	24.0	15.0	15.1	14.5	14.6	7.6
Drop-out	13.8	3.6	1.5	4.2	4.0	7.4
1981/2[a]						
Promotion	64.1	81.6	80.8	81.5	82.8	85.4
Repetition	24.0	15.0	15.0	14.0	14.2	7.6
Drop-out	11.9	3.4	4.2	4.0	3.0	6.0
1982/3[a]						
Promotion	60.1	78.3	77.9	77.3	73.3	83.8
Repetition	26.6	16.5	15.8	15.9	15.6	8.0
Drop-out	13.3	5.2	6.3	6.8	11.1	8.2

Source: ME/OSE: Internal Efficiency at the Basic Level (cycles I and II B.E.) Lima, June 1979.
ME/OSE: Indicators of Education Demand and Supply, 1975, 1980, 1981.
ME/OSE: INE, IBM tabulations.
[a] Projections.

The Peruvian educational system has four levels: initial, primary, secondary, and higher education. The structure of current expenditures across these levels shows that the proportion going to primary education decreased in all years between 1977 and 1983 except 1980 and 1981. The emphasis placed on secondary and higher education grew over the period, with the share of education expenditures for these two levels increasing from 35 to 43 per cent. Thus, there was a decline in the relative benefits of public education accruing to the majority of the school-age population—that is, in the primary grades (61 per cent of total registration). The distributional consequences were of course even greater, due to the near universality of the system at lower levels (90 per cent of the children between 6 and 14 years of age are registered), while children from poor families are less likely to be enrolled at higher educational levels. Yet it should be noted that the reduction in resources has not been translated into a decrease in educational coverage. There is in fact evidence of increasing schooling rates at all educational levels, owing to a combination of both demographic and social pressures. (Information is not available, however, on enrolment patterns by income groups.)

Indicators published by the Ministry of Education show that the degree of inequality in the country's hinterlands is very pronounced, especially with regard to illiteracy rates. Major cities absorb the greatest percentage of the budget, both in terms of current expenditure and investment, aggravating the situation of neglect in the rural and frontier areas.

Repetition rates in primary education for the period 1977–84 showed a negative trend in all school grades. Drop-out rates did not significantly change during the period, although the average level of 7 per cent represents a significant cost to the system (Table 6.11). On the other hand, correlation of the repetition and drop-out rates indicates that areas with low levels of coverage offer more limited probabilities of remaining in the system, so that inequalities of access to education appear to be parallelled by inequalities in educational survival.

In general, the decline in expenditures in the education sector over the 1977–84 period affected the less-favoured segments of the population to a greater degree, who were also the ones most strongly affected by the reduction in quality and efficiency of the system. Since education is one of the principal determinants of income levels and productivity, such reductions condition income distribution patterns, not only at present but also in the future.

(e) Subsidies An important component of the adjustment policies adopted to reduce budgetary deficits has been the gradual elimination of public subsidies. While during the years 1977–79 subsidies represented an average of 12.6 per cent of current expenditures in the non-financial public sector, during the period 1980–84 they dropped to 3.3 per cent (Table 6.12).

A survey (Grados and Mora 1981) carried out in the poorest households of the city of Lima shows that in 1979 23 per cent of these families' total expenditures went to buy subsidized foods. The living conditions and nutritional status of this group were alarmingly low: just 69 per cent of the families were able to satisfy 90 per cent of the minimum requirements, and only 22 per cent of the families were above this minimum. In addition, it was

TABLE 6.12 *Evolution of subsidies, 1974–1984*

	1974	1975	1976	1977	1978	1979	1980	1981	1982	1983	1984
Amount millions of intis											
Food	2.5	4.2	7.1	20.6	4.7	41.8	59.5	66.1	150.9	229.8	154.9
Fuel	3.1	5.7	10.5	36.7	56.6	98.3	0.0	0.0	0.0	0.0	0.0
Exports	0.9	0.5	1.4	3.8	12.7	34.5	44.0	54.0	79.0	116.0	418.0
TOTAL	6.5	10.4	19.0	61.1	74.0	174.6	103.5	120.1	237.9	345.0	572.9
Total current expenditures[a] (millions intis)	158.0	201.0	281.0	439.0	702.0	1,302.0	2,546.0	4,059.0	7,031.0	14,707.0	27,637.0
Subsidies as % current expenditure	4.1	5.2	6.8	13.9	10.5	13.4	4.1	3.0	3.4	2.3	2.1
As % of GDP											
Food	0.56	0.76	0.93	1.95	0.28	1.34	1.20	0.78	1.12	0.87	0.26
Fuel	0.69	1.04	1.37	3.47	3.37	3.15	0.00	0.00	0.00	0.00	0.00
Exports	0.20	0.09	0.18	0.36	0.76	1.11	0.86	0.63	0.56	0.44	0.71
TOTAL	1.45	1.89	2.48	5.78	4.41	5.60	2.06	1.41	1.68	1.31	0.97
Percentage of total subsidies											
Food	38.4	40.4	37.3	33.7	6.4	23.9	40.9	55.1	6.9	6.4	27.1
Fuel	47.7	55.0	55.3	60.1	76.4	56.3	0.0	0.0	0.0	0.0	0.0
Exports	13.9	4.8	7.4	6.2	17.2	19.8	59.1	44.9	33.1	33.6	72.9
TOTAL	100.0	100.0	100.0	100.0	100.0	100.0	100.0	100.0	100.0	100.0	100.0

Source: BCRP, Sub-gerencia del Sector Publico.
[a] Of non-financial public sector.

recorded that children were suffering from the effects of malnutrition to a greater extent than in other groups. This supports an assessment that the drop in food subsidies must have seriously affected lower-income segments of the population, worsening their already marginal living standards. It should be noted that the data indicate some degree of regressivity in the effects of food subsidies as benefits have tended to accrue more to urban rather than rural populations. However, the reduction of subsidies has affected a large segment of the urban population which had already experienced a deterioration in living standards due to employment loss and inflation. There was a significant decline in subsidies in 1978, with a further fall in their real value from 1980: in 1983 and 1984 basic food subsidies were only 1.3 per cent and 0.25 per cent, respectively, in relation to the levels of 1977 (Table 6.12 and 6.13).

TABLE 6.13   *Real value of subsidies on basic foods, 1977–1984*

	Amount (constant prices) (1977 intis 1000)	Index 1977 = 100
1977	54,505	100.0
1978	4,533	8.3
1979	14,430	26.5
1980	8,009	0.8
1981	2,944	5.4
1982	2,488	4.6
1983	757	1.4
1984	115	0.2

Source: BCRP, Sub-gerencia del Sector Publico.
Deflated using consumer price index.

While subsidies may not have been the most efficient means of transferring purchasing power to the poor, their reduction nonetheless had impacts on the living conditions of marginal groups.

(e) Summary The effects of stabilization policies on income distribution in Peru have been varied. In terms of income and employment, the greatest contractions have occurred in the basically urban, modern sector, while the reductions in social expenditures have had greater incidence in rural areas. Yet since workers in the modern sector tend to feel the impacts upon them more directly, through the immediate decline in their real incomes, the negative effects may be judged to have been more pronounced in the urban sector. This suggests a process of increasing marginalization of the previously better-off working population, which implies rising social tensions, especially in the cities. In view of the overall decline in real public expenditures in social sectors between 1977 and 1985, it may be further concluded that there was at best no expansion of the coverage of social services, and there was probably a deterioration of their quality as well.

In addition, official figures reflect a significant decline in annual per capita food production, which was only partially compensated by increased imports. In 1985, per capita consumption of food was 26 per cent lower than the already low levels of consumption of 10 years earlier.

These factors have converged and resulted in a clear worsening of the living standards of the population, especially for the most vulnerable groups. This is evident in the experience of higher rates of malnutrition, reappearance of diseases that had been previously under control, lower consumption of calories and protein, greater numbers of children prematurely forced into the labour market, significant numbers of children at risk,[2] and a higher rate of school drop-out.

Official statistics for social variables understate the total effects on the real living conditions, since in many cases, especially in the most depressed areas, the population is in practice deprived of many benefits that should be obtained through social services. Records are not kept for these cases, which presents a major limitation to the understanding of their difficulties.

IV   The new economic policy

Since 28 July 1985 a substantial change has taken place in the social and economic policies of Peru. The new policies question the efficiency of previous adjustment programmes. They are based instead on a diagnosis of the historic development of Peruvian society, on the view that in order to overcome the structural deficiencies of the past pattern of development, as well as the negative effects of the present crisis, it is essential to modify the development paradigm and to reactivate the economy.

This orientation entails initiating an income redistribution process to benefit the traditionally marginal sectors of the population. For this it is necessary to exert greater national control over the surplus generated in the country, with the aim of directing it towards priority activities and sectors. It also calls for social policies that serve not only to relieve and aid, but that are also closely linked to prevailing economic policies. In addition, and contrary to the rule in the immediate past, the policy is intended to be autonomous, loosening the links with the world economy.

For the short term, under the assumption that the inflation of recent years resulted basically from increased costs, an expansive adjustment policy was introduced. This was aimed at a progressive recovery in the purchasing power of the population so that greater disposable income would translate, through demand, into increased production: this would be facilitated by the existence of a large idle industrial capacity.

A further expansion of productive capacity, particularly in sectors producing exportables and/or basic need goods—such as agriculture, non-traditional exports, selected industrial activities, and fishing—has been promoted by the selective use of credit, fiscal pricing, and exchange rate policies. Specific provisions have been made to expand employment and productivity among the poor. Public work schemes have been initiated, while improved access to credit and inputs has been provided to efficient producers in the informal sector and to small farmers. Longer-term increases in labour productivity, as well as improvements in the current standard of living, are being pursued through gradual increases in public expenditure and by a reorientation of social services towards low-cost basic services with extensive coverage, such as immunization, food supplementation for target groups, and primary education.

Control of inflation is pursued through manipulation of the three basic prices in the economy—namely, nominal wages, the exchange rate, and the interest rate. Implementation of these controls depends upon sufficient amounts of foreign currency for importing inputs to production. Meeting this need in the present context of reduced availability of foreign financing requires that an adequate level of foreign reserves be maintained. To achieve this, a decision was made that only 10 per cent of the earnings from exports would be allocated to the service of public foreign debt. Related measures were also adopted to promote growth in exports, to develop an efficient and discriminating import substitution policy, and to regulate the outflow of foreign currency. The state plays a fundamental role in this process by leading and directing the economy and by mobilizing its managerial capacity for the implementation of development programmes and projects. The major elements of the new economic policy are briefly outlined below.

1   Economic policies

(a) Wages and prices Action on wages and prices consists of the following:

1. A wage policy directed at increasing the real purchasing power of the population, especially among less-favoured groups.

2. A phased policy of price adjustment. During the first stage (one year), this involved a selective price 'freeze'. In the second stage it has been characterized by a price management system under which price adjustments were authorized when they were considered justified, within the framework of a national harmonization of relative prices. During the freeze period, cost pressures due to increased wages and salaries were compensated for by low interest rates and by a reduction of indirect taxes, and by a decline in the price of certain energy inputs.

3. Guaranteed fixed prices for agricultural products and elimination of a series of intermediaries who were considered to be responsible for excessive price increases.

(b) Employment A temporary income support programme has been established: its initial aim has been to provide resources to urban marginal populations, and this will later be extended to cover rural areas. The programme offers work opportunities to its beneficiaries in tasks that are related to the improvement of their living conditions, such as sanitation and pavements within their own communities. During the first six months of implementation the programme had approximately 40,000 participating workers. Coverage for 1986 is estimated to reach 150,000 including activities in environmental sanitation, city cleaning, pavement, rehabilitation of water supply lines, and reforestation. When extended, the programme is expected to shift into more productive activities in rural areas.

(c) Fiscal policy Within the framework of achieving an integral tax reform in the medium term, certain measures were established with the objective of reordering the tax system in the short run. These have included:

1. Increasing taxes on rent and property in order to improve income distribution and to contribute to simplification of the tax system.

2. Introducing equity considerations into the income tax, through establishment of uniform rates for firms, and a progressive scale for individuals.

3. Reorienting tax incentives towards priority sectors, namely, agriculture, industry, and fishing, and reducing the bias of the tax system against job creation.

Reordering of the tax system has therefore not implied an increase in overall tax burden but rather its redistribution along more equitable lines principally by eliminating exemptions that had made capital income practically non-taxable.

A second fiscal reform has involved a redirection in the allocation of public expenditures towards the education, health, and agricultural sectors. Emphasis has also been placed on expenditures favouring depressed rural areas and marginal urban areas. Priority in investment decisions has shifted to favour low-cost projects with short maturities.

(d) Monetary and credit policy A major financial reform undertaken has been a progressive reduction of effective interest rates, which fell from 280 per cent in July 1985 to 110 per cent in August, 75 per cent in September, 45 per cent in October, and 40 per cent in February 1986. Fixed promotional interest rates, and even zero interest rates, have been instituted in the Trapecio Andino region (covering Apurimac, Ayacucho, Cusco, Huancavelica, Puno, and other provinces in Arequipa Moquequa and Tacna), which has traditionally been a marginal area in access to credit.

Given the importance of credit for reactivizing the economy, the Banco Central de Reserva has implemented a financial policy geared towards productive activities to which priority has been assigned. It has included:

1. Selective lines of credit for agriculture, for development of cattle-raising activities, and for the creation of an Agricultural Fund, a Fund for the Reactivation of Agricultural Machinery, and a Fund for Rural Community Development, all of which are aimed at promoting agrarian development in depressed areas.

2. An obligation for commercial banks to direct 10 per cent of their credit increase into agricultural activities or in deposits at the Agrarian Bank, for use in this sector.

3. Establishment of a fund for the Reactivation of a Fishing Fleet and a Programme for the financial reordering of the business sector.

In addition, a credit support mechanism has been developed for the informal sector. By providing access to credit at commercial interest rates, this avoids the high cost of non-institutionalized credit for small artisans and signals government support for their enterprises.

(e) External sector Several significant policy measures have been introduced concerning the external sector:

1. Limiting payments on public foreign debt to 10 per cent of the value of exports, with the further requirement that the resources leaving the country in debt payment do not exceed those coming in as new credits.

2. Imposing restrictions, for a period of two years from August 1986 on remittances by foreign enterprises for profit, depreciation, or private debt.

3. Protection of domestic industry through a coherent tariff policy which prohibits the import of certain products and uses licences as the chief means of import regulation.

Two new exchange markets have also been created. The Single Exchange Market, with a fixed rate of exchange since August 1985, deals with priority imports, a small part of exports, and public debt payment. The Regulated Financial Market, which maintains a differential rate (equivalent to 24.9 per cent) relative to the Single Exchange Market, is used for transactions on non-priority imports, the majority of exports, and approved remittances. Finally, the Free Market covers tourism as well as activities not included within the other two markets.

2. *Social development policies and programmes*

According to government plans, social development is to be oriented towards recovery of previously attained levels of quality of life of the population, and improvement of the profound social inequalities prevailing. The public investment programme for 1986–90 assigns higher priority to infrastructure support for social development. Average annual growth rates for investment in the health, education, and housing sectors are forecast at 13 per cent, which would represent 20.8 per cent of total public investment in 1990 in contrast to 17.4 per cent in 1986.

(a) Food and nutrition In the context of the national plan for food security, the food and nutrition policy is aimed at improving the nutritional status of the population, especially of the lower-income groups. The following programmes will be implemented: (*a*) operation of local kitchens in urban marginal communities; (*b*) expansion in the coverage of food assistance through community kitchens; (*c*) distribution and sale of Economical Bags and Basic Foods in marginal urban areas; (*d*) food-for-work programmes with the participation of communities to ensure a minimum nutritional supplement; (*e*) a programme to encourage change in food consumption habits; (*f*) increasing the share of regional products in the available basket of foods; and (*g*) extension of infrastructure for the sale of fish (one of the country's important resources) in marginal urban areas.

(b) Health and social security There has been a reorientation of national policies on health, with emphasis now given to low-cost, broad-coverage primary care services. In this context, the hospital is the centre of a health organization in which simpler health centres accomplish a primary and preventive role. It entails the substantive participation of the population, not only in immunization campaigns (as is traditional) but also in the determination of priorities and in the search for ways to accomplish them at the local level, thus constituting an effective process of decentralization. Community involvement is also intended to play an important role in the establishment of integrated family planning, encompassing education, social communication, and service provision.

A related national programme on essential drugs is also being implemented, covering 85 per cent of the most common diseases. The medicines would be sold at one-third to one-half of normal commercial prices. This programme, aimed at lower-income groups, is providing drugs through hospitals, health centres, clinics, and certain non-governmental services.

The coverage of social security has been extended, with a progressive incorporation of the enrolled worker's spouse and children into health care services. It is projected that the number of beneficiaries will increase from 2.8 million to 5.3 million over several years. Supplementary feeding programmes directed to mother–child groups, pre-schoolers, and school age children are also being strengthened by improving the quality of meals and increasing the efficiency of their distribution to lower-income groups, especially in rural and urban marginal areas.

Priority is being given in investments to low-cost outlays, such as refurbishing local infrastructure and providing a minimum of equipment for peripheral health centres. Such investments would be directed mainly to support services to rural peasants and urban marginal populations, and within these groups, to pregnant mothers and children. Investment is being targeted at the most depressed areas, as identified by health indicators prepared under a national emergency plan. Support is also given to investments utilizing regional or local resources with appropriate technology, and which promote the participation of the beneficiary community.

(c) Education The educational policy is primarily oriented towards strengthening, expanding, and improving educational services and resources at the initial and primary level, and for schooling in rural and urban marginal areas. This will be reinforced by a broad programme for support of educational infrastructure. In addition, the policy seeks to promote the participation of the community in extended non-formal programmes of initial education through volunteer work, a permanent supply of 'a glass of milk', supplementary feeding, as well as primary health care and mother and child care.

(d) Housing and sanitation The priority of the housing and sanitation policy is to promote and develop housing programmes and provide plots with basic services to low-income families. It also includes self-help programmes for the construction of dwellings, based on the organization and training of the rural and urban marginal population with a large supply of bank credit.

(e) Protection of the family nucleus This set of policies is directed to provide for children at high risk and orphans, and to rationalize the various supplementary feeding programmes by concentrating them in priority areas such as the rural Andes and marginal urban areas. Literacy and extra-curricular programmes are promoted in order to incorporate women into the production process and thus help to generate a permanent source of income for the family. A focal point will be established for mother–child care, medical services for women, and family planning programmes. Legal and managerial actions are also being undertaken in order to improve the working conditions of women.

3 Main achievements

Although it is too early to assess the overall performance of the new socio-economic policy, it is possible to evaluate the initial results one year after its introduction:

1. There has been a significant reduction in inflation. The annual growth

in the price index has been reduced from 250 per cent in July 1985 to under 70 per cent in July 1986. At the same time, the purchasing power of workers has increased, especially for those earning minimum wages. As one indication of this, while the inflation rate between August 1985 and July 1986 was 68 per cent, the minimum legal income increased by 94 per cent, and salaries and wages of public and private workers by 92 per cent and 78 per cent respectively.

2. The improvement in real wages and salaries has increased the demand for goods and services, and has contributed substantially to the reactivation of production. A critical factor in sustaining this reactivation has been the continued availability of foreign exchange, made possible by the ceiling of 10 per cent of export earnings on servicing the medium and long-term public debt.

3. During the first half of the year, GDP has grown 3.6 per cent compared with the first half of 1985, and it is estimated that GDP growth will reach 6 per cent by the end of 1986.

4. Employment has increased as a consequence of economic expansion. According to periodic surveys carried out by the Ministry of Labour, April 1986 employment levels in the city of Lima were higher than those of July 1985 in industry (by 5.2 per cent), commerce (by 2.7 per cent), and services (by 2.0 per cent). In addition, by the end of 1986 it was expected to provide some 150,000 temporary jobs in the temporary income support programme.

5. National income distribution has been made more equal. There has been a reduction in the percentage of income going to the upper 10 per cent of the population, from 52 per cent to 49 per cent, while the poorest 10 per cent of the population has increased its share from 10 per cent to 13 per cent of total income.

6. The 'domination of the dollar' in the economy is being reversed. During the first months of 1985, 60 per cent of total liquidity was held in foreign currency; that is, the Central Bank's influence could be directed at less than one-half of the liquidity of the economy. By mid-1986, national currency participation in total liquidity had reached 80 per cent.

7. The significant increase in national currency deposits has allowed for a major rise in the financing of productive activity. This has been done within the framework of a credit policy that supports priority activities such as agriculture, fishing, industry, and non-traditional exports.

8. The management of public finance during the first half of 1986 permitted adequate control of fiscal deficits. However, the administration and execution of public investment has been relatively rigid, and investment levels have been lower than those called for by programme goals, especially in the most depressed areas.

9. The wide range of measures undertaken regarding the foreign sector made possible a continuous increase in the country's foreign reserves up to March 1986. Since that time, however, a decline in the international prices of Peruvian export products and increased imports of food have led to a reduction in foreign reserves. In August 1986 the government adopted additional rules

aimed at preserving the level of reserves judged necessary to maintain the process of reactivation.

10. It is premature to measure results of the new policies in the social sectors, but certain developments may be noted. Following recent primary health care priorities, some 35 million oral rehydration packets and 1.5 million doses of antibiotics have been distributed. Three immunization campaign efforts have been conducted, in which approximately 5 million doses of vaccines against polio, measles, whooping cough, tetanus, and diphtheria were administered to 1.6 million children.

11. An increased level of national support has been given for the protection of children, both directly by the state and by numerous other institutions involved in child assistance activities.

4   Some limitations

The new development policies have at the same time met with a series of restrictions, international and domestic, which may place their eventual success in jeopardy.

Internationally, there is persistent deterioration in the terms of trade affecting Peru's chief export products. In 1986 oil price reductions represented a loss of export income to the country to the amount of $300 million dollars. The increasingly protectionist practices of industrialized countries constrain the expansion of export flows, and the severe contraction of international credit along with the ever-growing weight of foreign debt will further continue to limit the external resources available for development. These problems have been compounded by misunderstandings on the part of other countries, private banks, and international organizations concerning Peru's position on foreign debt payments and its decision to adopt an autonomous economic policy.

At the national level, the bureaucratization and low productivity associated with a centralized government apparatus have increased the difficulties of implementing new development programmes. There has also been some hesitancy by various economic agents in participating fully. Effective reorientation of the adjustment process depends upon continued restoration of order and confidence in government, along with the resolution to carry forward the alternative policies that have been undertaken.

Notes

1. The Ministry of Labor and Social Promotion defines underemployment in two ways: by the hours worked (those who work less than 35 hours per week), or by income (those earn an income that is lower than the minimum wage for 1967 using the consumer price index). An individual is considered to be unemployed if (s)he did not work during the given period but was actively searching for employment.
2. According to the National Institute of Family Welfare, there are 3 million children 0–12 years of age at risk in Peru (46 per cent of all children 0–12), of whom 325,000

are at high risk (5 per cent of the total age group). The number of children who have been completely abandoned is estimated at 11,000.

References

BCRP—Banco Central de Reserva del Peru (1985), 'Resumen de los Acuerdos con el FMI: 1982–84', Sub-gerencia de Analisis Global (in-house paper), Lima.

BCRP (1986a), 'Mapa de pobreza del Peru, 1981' Sub-gerencia de Ingreso y Producto, Lima.

——(1986b) 'Radiografia economica', Gerencia de Investigacion Economica (in-house paper), Lima.

——(1986c), Unpublished working papers on the concentration of wealth.

Gredos, R., and N. Mora (1981), 'La Probeza en Lima Metropolitana', *Economia* (Lima), 7.

Ministry of Education (1984), *Plan operativo sectorial 1984–1985*. Lima.

Ministry of Health (1984), *Plan nacional de desarrollo 1984–1985 Plan Operativo Sectorial*. Lima.

Sigma One Corporation (1983), *Nutritional Status in the South Sierra: Report to USAID*. Lima.

World Bank (1985), *Peru: Country Economic Memorandum*. Washington DC: World Bank.

Redirecting Adjustment Programmes towards Growth and the Protection of the Poor: The Philippine Case

*UNICEF, Manila**

I Background

The period 1973–84 was marked by a series of major external shocks: a sharp rise in the price of oil in 1973–74 and in 1979–80; high real interest rates in the early 1980s, and the worst recession in post-war history.

Historically, the Philippines has been very vulnerable to fluctuations in international commodity prices and the economic performance of developed countries because of the large role of foreign trade in its economy. The situation was made more precarious by the existing inequities in the social structure and weaknesses in the economic structure in the pre-oil-shock period.

The social situation was characterized by a high incidence of poverty—36 per cent in 1971, as estimated by the World Bank. Income inequality was considerable, with the lowest 20 per cent and 60 per cent of families receiving only 5.5 per cent and 30.0 per cent of total income, respectively. The problem of underemployment was already acute, particularly in the rural areas. Real wages for all types of workers were falling, particularly in the first half of 1970s, even while per capita GNP rose. On top of all these was the continued pressure of a rapidly growing population, with population growth averaging around 3 per cent.

The economic structure in the early 1970s was predominantly agricultural, with two-thirds of the population living in the countryside, half of the labour force engaged in traditional activities, and more than one-quarter of GDP contributed by agriculture. Agriculture was traditional in orientation with weak linkages with the rest of the economy despite attempts to accelerate industrialization through import substitution in the previous decade. Although annual economic growth in the 1960s averaged 5 per cent, problems were already evident. The foreign exchange crisis in February 1970 illustrated the inherent deficiency of the previous development strategy, which had created

* The authors wish to acknowledge the assistance in preparing this study of Mr Wilfredo Nuqui, Assistant Director-general, National Economic and Development Authority (NEDA); and Dr Kosslinda Tidalgo-Miranda and Dr Alejandro Harrin, professors at the University of the Philippines.

an excessively protected industrial structure, a narrow agricultural base, and an almost total dependence on imported energy.

This study is divided into six parts. Part II analyses the extent of external shocks and policy responses, 1979–85. Part III describes the characteristics of vulnerable groups in the Philippines. Part IV analyses the impact of adjustment policies on the general conditions affecting vulnerable groups. Part V looks at social policies in more detail and reports on the changing human indicators which have resulted from the economic and social developments described earlier in the study. Part VI presents conclusions and some recommendations.

II Analysis of external shocks and observed responses

1 External shocks and policy responses: 1973–1983

This section provides quantitative evidence of the impact of external shocks on the Philippines and the various policy responses to the shocks, following the methodology used by Balassa (1980).

The effects of the external shocks are measured in terms of trade effects and export volume effects. The terms of trade effect is a measure of the overall effect of export and import price movements on the current account balance. The export volume effect is a measure of the impact of changes in foreign demand for the country's exports.

For analytical purposes, the 1973–83 period was divided into two phases: 1973–78, representing the first oil price increase and the years following; and 1979–83, representing the second oil price shock and the subsequent period of recession. The main developments during these years are shown in Table 7.1.

(a) **External shocks** The effect of external shocks may be summarized as follows:

1. *Export price effect.* The export price effect on the Philippine balance of payments was generally favourable during the period 1973–78. Over the six-year period, the ratio of the export price effect to total external shocks, which indicates the degree of the positive effects contributed by export prices to the current account balance, averaged 106 per cent in contrast to the 77 per cent average from 1979 to 1983 (Table 7.2).

2. *Import price effect.* Import price changes contributed to an unfavourable current account position in 1974–83. The effect was more unfavourable during the period 1973–78, as indicated by the ratio of import price effects to total shocks which denotes the extent to which negative import price effects are reflected in the current account balance. For 1974–83 the average was 186 per cent, whereas for 1979–83 it was significantly lower at 159 per cent.

3. *Terms of trade effects.* The results show that the country's terms of trade increasingly burdened the current account and consequently the balance of

TABLE 7.1 *Selected macro-economic indicators, 1970–1985*

	1970	1971	1972	1973	1974	1975	1976	1977	1978	1979	1980	1981	1982	1983	1984	1985
1. GDP (real growth, %)	4.8	5.7	5.2	8.5	5.0	6.6	7.9	6.1	5.5	6.3	5.3	3.9	2.9	0.9	-5.7	-4.0
2. Terms of trade (1972=100)	118.8	110.6	100.0	113.3	114.5	87.8	77.7	71	78.2	81.3	68.6	60.4	58.7	61.3	59.8	55.86
3. Exports (growth, %)	24.2	7.0	-2.6	70.5	44.4	-15.8	12.2	22.4	8.7	34.3	25.8	-1.1	-12.3	-0.3	7.7	-14.1
4. Imports (growth, %)	-3.7	8.8	3.7	29.8	96.9	10.1	5.1	7.7	20.9	29.8	25.8	2.8	-3.5	-2.3	-18.9	-15.8
5. Current account bal (US$m)	-51.1	-3	9	536	-176	-892	-1,050	-752	-1,102	-1,497	-1,904	-2,061	-3,200	-2,750	-1,116	77
Ratio to GNP (%)	-0.75	-0.04	0.11	5.1	-1.2	-5.7	-5.9	-3.6	-4.6	-5.0	-5.4	-5.4	-8.1	-8.1	-3.5	-0.2
6. Outstanding external debt to GNP ratio (%)	33.9	31.0	32.6	27.0	25.5	31.3	37.5	39.0	44.5	45.2	49.0	54.4	62.8	72.8	80.6	82.1
7. Real effective exchange rate[1] index (Dec. 1980=100)	96.4	100.3	93.5	93.3	111.2	102.3	100.3	97.63	88.1	96	101	101.3	105.2	86.9	82.9	89.1
8. Budget deficit (surplus)	—	481	(401)	1,194	3,588	2,160	2,291	2,240	4,843	8,862	10,215	9,543	7,226	12,119	13,988	13,728
Ratio of deficit to GNP	—	—	(0.7)	0.5	-0.7	1.2	1.8	1.9	1.2	0.2	1.3	4.0	4.3	1.7	1.8	1.8
9. Tax effort (% of GNP)	—	10.6	8.9	8.9	10.4	12.04	11.42	11.10	11.51	11.91	11.52	10.37	10.06	10.43	9.31	10.1
10. Domestic liquidity growth rate (%)	—	11.8	13.1	52.2	34.2	19.2	24.3	22.4	18.0	10.7	18.2	21.1	16.1	18.6	7.3	9.6

Source: Central Bank of the Philippines; National Income Accounts–National Economic and Development Authority; Office of the Budget and Management.
[1] Three-month Libor (London inter-bank offer rate) less inflation rate in OECD.

TABLE 7.2   *Balance of payments effects of external shocks and policy responses, 1973–1978, 1979–1983, and 1984–1985 ($ million)*

	$ million per year			As % of total shocks		
	1973–78	1979–83	1984–85	1973–78	1979–83	1984–85
External shocks[a]						
Terms of trade effect	− 732	− 2,630	− 1,083	− 80	− 82	− 59
Export price effect	966	2,449	2,900	106	77	157
Import price effect	− 1,698	− 5,079	− 3,983	− 186	− 159	− 216
Export volume effect	− 181	− 563	− 763	− 20	− 18	− 41
Total	− 913	− 3,193	− 1,846	− 100	− 100	− 100
Policy responses[b]						
Additional net external financing	− 1,019	− 2,627	− 1,075	− 112	− 85	− 63
Export promotion	− 123	− 896	4	− 13	− 27	13
Import substitution	162	255	− 424	18	9	− 27
Import effects of lower GDP growth rates	68	75	− 353	7	3	− 23
Total	− 912	− 3,193	− 1,847	− 100	− 100	− 100

Source: Derived from data from the Central Bank of the Philippines and National Income accounts.
Note: Total response may not exactly equal to total external shock due to rounding.
[a] Negative sign indicates unfavourable effects.
[b] Negative sign indicates positive responses.

payments. The terms of trade effect was relatively more favourable in the period 1973–78 as against 1979–83, due to the faster rise in export prices than import prices during the earlier period. In contrast, import prices rose faster than export prices in the latter period. From a favourable terms of trade effect in 1973 amounting to 1 per cent of GDP, the terms of trade loss amounted to 1 per cent of GDP in 1974 and rose to 23 per cent of GDP in 1982.

4. *Export volume effects.* The export volume effect of changes in foreign demand was more unfavourable in the period 1979–83 than in 1973–78. This may be traced to a slackening in demand in the developed economies affected by world recession.

Policy responses The principal policy responses were the following:

1. *Additional external financing.* The year 1973 saw a huge current account surplus in the Philippines of $536 million as a result of the world commodity boom. However, starting in 1974, the country began experiencing persistent and increasing current account deficits.

The new inflow of direct foreign investment was minimal at this time, and an increasing need for additional net external financing became evident in 1974. During this year, additional net external financing amounted to 7 per cent of GDP. By the end of 1983, this rose to 20 per cent of GDP. Although additional net external financing almost exceeded total external shocks from 1973 to 1979, the ratio declined from 366 per cent in 1974 to only 77 per cent in 1983, implying a relative slow-down in the growth in external debt in relation to total external shocks.

The period 1979–83 saw a higher level of external financing than 1973–78 (Table 7.2). The relatively favourable conditions in the international financial market in 1976–79 made possible the use of external borrowing to cushion the impact of the current account deficit on the overall balance of payments position. However, after the second oil shock, developed countries pursued tight monetary policies which, coupled with the debt crisis starting in Mexico in mid-1982, dried up loanable funds in the international market, jacked up interest rates, and shortened the loan maturity period. The growing share of short-term loans together with the sharp increase in interest rates increased debt service requirements, placing mounting pressure on scarce foreign exchange resources.

2. *Export promotion.* Increases in export market shares resulting from the country's export promotion policies were recorded for most years. The favourable effects were more significant in 1979–83, particularly since export promotion policies instituted earlier in the decade had started to gain ground. During this period, Philippine trade had been diversified to other countries and manufactured export items had grown substantially as a proportion of total exports.

3. *Import substitution.* High levels of trade protection notwithstanding, the Philippines experienced negative import substitution. This may be explained by the high import dependence of domestic industries, the high import content of rising investments, particularly in the public sector, and the increase in imports associated with the appreciation of the real exchange rate.

4. *Import reduction through income adjustment.* On an aggregative basis, the policy was not effectively pursued over the period. The government did not intentionally pursue this policy to cushion the impact of external shocks since its main objective was the achievement of income growth. In fact, economic growth averaged 6.3 per cent per annum during the 1970s as compared to 4.9 per cent during the previous decade.

2   The debt crisis of 1983–1985

Longstanding structural problems, worsened by external shocks, and inadequate adjustment policies resulted in 1984 and 1985 in the most severe foreign exchange crisis to hit the country in post-war years. From the late 1970s, the Philippines had been running persistent current account deficits, rising from $176 million in 1974 to $3.2 billion in 1982 (Table 7.1).

International reserves fell sharply in 1983, with the loss of confidence partly due to the assassination of Senator Benigno Aquino. Faced with a foreign exchange shortage, authorities declared a series of moratoria on payments of principal on its external debt and imposed foreign exchange restrictions. There was a drastic cut-back in imports, which were mostly intermediate and capital goods. Without the much-needed imports, production fell, shortages resulted, massive lay-offs occurred, and inflation soared to unprecedented levels.

The Philippines entered into its 18th stand-by agreement with the IMF in December 1984 covering the period from January 1985 to June 1986. As such, the country had to comply with stringent performance criteria targets not only in the monetary and fiscal sectors, but also for reforms in the areas of tax and tariffs, public investment, and energy as part of the conditions for a loan amounting to SDR 615 million. At the same time, the Philippines negotiated with private creditor banks, governments, and multilateral institutions for new loans, rescheduling of debt, and resumption of a trade facility (together amounting to $12 billion).

A revised programme is being negotiated between the IMF and the new democratic government.

(a) Economic stabilization The performance criteria under the IMF programme covered external, monetary, and fiscal targets which called for improvement of the balance of payments, reduction of the budget deficit, and lowering the inflation rate.

The exchange rate was allowed to float in 1984, after successive depreciations. Temporary foreign exchange controls were introduced in 1983. Government revenues were raised and the growth of expenditures controlled. Additional revenues were generated from taxes and export duties; tax exemptions of business were reduced and indirect taxes raised.

Cash disbursements of the national government were reduced from 15.8 per cent of GNP in 1982 to 12.8 per cent in 1984, due to a drastic reduction in government expenditure. Capital outlays as a proportion of total expenditures declined continuously, from 39 per cent in 1982 to 29 per cent in 1985. Gross domestic investment of the national government declined from 2.7 per cent of GNP in 1983 to 1.4 per cent in 1985, in contrast to a high of 4.2 per cent in 1981. Current operating expenditures comprised the bulk of total expenditures, of which 18 per cent was used for interest payments. The budget deficit went down from a high of 4.3 per cent of GNP in 1982 to under 2.0 per cent in each year from 1983–85.

In contrast to earlier years, monetary and credit policy in 1984 and 1985 was restrictive in order to reduce inflationary pressures and help correct the external imbalance. The reserve money level was reduced and reserve requirements on short-term deposit and deposit liabilities were increased. The Manila Reference Rate of interest rose to over 40 per cent in November 1984.

The deflationary fiscal and monetary policies cut the peak inflation rate of 64 per cent in October 1984 to 6 per cent by the end of 1985.

The various policy measures adapted improved the balance of payment position. The current account deficit was greatly reduced, by 59 per cent in

1984 and by 93 per cent in 1985 (Table 7.1). The ratio of current account deficit to GNP was reduced from 8.1 per cent in 1983 to 3.5 per cent and 0.2 per cent in 1984 and 1985, respectively. The improvement was mainly due to the large cut-back in imports. In 1984, exports receipts increased by 8 per cent as non-traditional manufactured exports such as garments, electronics, and semi-conductors increased by 21 per cent, while traditional exports fell by 10.5 per cent, although coconut products enjoyed favourable market prices. Imports fell by 19 per cent due to the general scarcity of foreign exchange and priority allocation system. The import cut back was reflected in large decreases in the import value of capital goods and crude petroleum and petroleum products. Moreover, foreign investors as well as domestic entrepreneurs were wary of investing as the political and economic prospects of the country became uncertain.

In 1985, export receipts fell by 14 per cent due to weak world demand, depressed world commodity prices, and protectionism. Receipts from traditional and non-traditional exports dropped by 30 per cent and 5 per cent, respectively. Imports fell by 16 per cent as purchases of capital goods, raw materials and intermediate goods, and fuel were cut back due to the slow-down in domestic production.

There were unfavourable effects on output and employment. For the first time since the Second World War, the Philippine economy experienced two consecutive declines in real GNP—6.8 per cent in 1984 and 3.8 per cent in 1985. Real per capita GNP in 1985 fell to its 1975 level, and personal consumption to the 1979 level. The industry sector was the most badly hit, contracting by over 10 per cent in 1984 and 1985 because of the drastic cut-backs in the manufacturing and construction activities.

Agricultural output declined in 1983 due to the combined effect of bad weather conditions, a low international price for sugar, and high prices for inputs such as fertilizer and pesticides. However, in 1984 and 1985, it was the only sector that managed to achieve positive growth.

The general economic slow-down resulted in mass lay-offs which aggravated the unemployment problem. The lack of raw materials due to import controls, the restrictive monetary and fiscal policies, and a slump in demand caused firms to retrench-workers or to shut down. The open unemployment rate increased from 5.4 per cent in 1983 to 7.1 per cent in 1985 (Table 7.3).

III   Vulnerable groups in the Philippines

1   Profile of low-income families

Obtaining a national perspective on socio-economic and demographic aspects of poverty is hampered by lack of readily available published data. There are fairly comprehensive data for 1971 and more piecemeal information for more recent years.

TABLE 7.3   *GNP, population, and labour force status, 1971, 1976, and 1980–1985*

	1971	1976	1976	1980	1981	1982	1983	1984	1985
Annual per capita GNP at 1972 prices (P)	1,402	1,690	1,690	1,917	1,933	1,921	1,897	1,923	1,618
Labour force (000)	12,895	16,245	15,018	17,308	18,423	18,473	20,311	21,180	21,318
Urban (%)				30.3	30.3	31.0	30.0	37.0	37.0
Rural (%)				69.7	69.7	69.0	70.0	63.0	63.0
Employment (000)	12,228	15,427	14,238	16,434	17,452	17,371	19,212	19,632	19,801
Urban (%)				29.3	29.3	29.7	28.6	35.0	35.2
Rural (%)				70.7	70.7	70.3	71.4	65.0	64.8
Unemployment (%)	5.2	5.0	5.2	5.1	5.3	6.0	5.4	7.3	7.1
Urban (%)				8.2	8.3	9.8	9.3	12.2	11.8
Rural (%)				3.7	4.0	4.2	3.8	4.4	4.4
Underemployment (%)	14.7	10.6	25.5	20.9	24.0	25.5	29.8	36.4	22.2
Urban (%)				19.9	19.5	24.0	30.0	34.0	16.8
Rural (%)				21.4	25.8	26.2	29.8	37.7	25.1

Sources: BCS, *Survey of Households* (for 1971 figures); NCSO, *National Sample Survey of Household Bulletin* (for 1976 August figures); NCSO, *Integrated Survey of Households* (for 1976 3rd quarter figures); computer print-outs of the NCSO Integrated Survey of Households (for 1980–85 figures); and *National Income Accounts* for the years indicated.
Note: For 1971 figures are for August. For all other years, figures are for the third quarter.

(a) Size and Location Analyses of evidence for 1971 (World Bank 1980, 1985; NEDA 1985) may be summarized as follows:

1. Of the 6.35 million families in 1971, 39 per cent fell below the poverty line defined in terms of a 500 peso per capita expenditure standard (see Table 7.4). Poverty incidence higher than the national average was found in six regions: Central Visayas (65 per cent), Eastern Visayas (60 per cent), Northern Mindanao (59 per cent), Cagayan Valley (55 per cent), Bicol (48 per cent), and Ilocos (42 per cent). Over half of the total poor families are found in five regions: Central Visayas, Southern Tagalog, Eastern Visayas, Bicol, and Ilocos.

2. The families with the highest incidence of poverty were in the agricultural sector and they belonged to six social groups constituting 49 per cent of the total families (defined by the occupation of the household head). These groups are farmer owners, farmer part-owners, farmer tenants, other farmers, farm labourers, and fishermen. Some 54 per cent of the families in these groups were below the poverty line and they constitute 68 per cent of all the poor families. In contrast, only 24 per cent of all other families were below the poverty line.

3. Farmer-owners were the largest of the six social groups, followed by farmer tenants, fishermen, farmer labourers, and other families. However, farmer tenants and other farmers showed the highest poverty incidence, while farmer-owners the lowest.

4. Within agriculture, poverty incidence also varied by farming activity. Palay and corn farming accounted for most poverty among farm-related

TABLE 7.4   *Poverty groups, by occupation of household head, 1971*

Occupation of household head	Total (000)	Poor families (000)	Poor families (%)	% families below poverty line
Agriculture				
Farmer owners	1,037	504.4	20.5	48.4
Farmer part owners	187	187	3.9	50.4
Farmer tenants	986	584.0	23.8	59.2
Farmers not specified	286	164.8	6.7	57.8
Farmer labourers	287	148.8	6.1	51.9
Fishermen, fishpond labourers	323	173.2	7.1	53.6
Others in agriculture and mining[a]	71	24.9	1.0	35.1
Total	3,177	1,696.4	69.1	53.4
Non-agriculture				
Transport and communication workers	360	103.5	4.2	28.7
Craftsmen, production workers, and labourers	907	287.5	11.7	31.7
Services, sports, and recreation workers	293	81.2	3.3	27.7
Sales workers	469	94.0	3.8	20.0
Occupation not reported, inadequately described	589	169.1	6.9	28.7
Professional, administrative, clerical	552	24.3	1.0	4.4
Total	3,170	759.6	30.9	24.0
Total	6,347	2,456.0	100.0	38.7

Source: World Bank (1980). Data based on the 1971 Family Income and Expenditure Survey, using a poverty line of 500 peso per capita.
[a] Includes hunters, trappers, and related workers; loggers and other forestry workers; farm managers, administrators and overseers; and miners, quarry-men and related workers.

activities, and was, fairly evenly distributed among regions (apart from Metro Manila). Families engaged in coconut farming and sugarcane farming also constituted a large group in poverty, although together they were only 18 per cent of the size of the families engaged in palay and corn farming. They were concentrated in a few regions: sugarcane farmers in Western and Central Visayas, and coconut farmers in Southern Tagalog, Bicol, Eastern Visayas, Northern Mindanao, and Southern Mindanao.

5. Using the same threshold, 336,000 families in the urban areas were poor, representing 18 cent of total urban families in 1971. The incidence of urban poverty was much higher in Ilocos, Cagayan Valley, Central and Eastern Visayas, and Northern Mindanao than in the other regions. In Metro Manila, poor families constituted 9 per cent of the total families, but this was by far the largest concentration of urban poor in any region, constituting 18 per cent of the total urban poor in 1971.

Lack of similar comprehensive data makes it difficult to be confident how the patterns observed in 1971 have changed over time.

A World Bank study (1985) shows that 19 per cent of urban families constituting a third of total families, were below the poverty line, where poverty incidence was defined in terms of a per capita monthly poverty line of 118 pesos for rural and 140 pesos for urban families. In contrast, poverty incidence was 43 per cent among rural families, constituting two-thirds of total families. A high incidence of poverty was found among agriculture-related activities in both urban and rural areas, and manufacturing in rural areas.

Higher poverty incidence (40 per cent or more) was found in Western Visayas, Central Visayas, Cagayan Valley, Bicol, Ilocos, and Western Mindanao than in other regions.

A study of NEDA (1985) shows that families in the bottom 30 per cent of the income distribution totalled 3.1 million, of whom 73 per cent were in agriculture. The data show higher absolute and relative numbers of low-income families in Bicol, the three Visayas regions, and three of the four Mindanao regions compared to the remaining regions.

(6) General profile of low-income families Evidence from the NEDA (1985) study of low-income groups confirms the common perspective that low-income families are characterized by (*a*) lack of productive assets or control over such assets; (*b*) limited use of modern technology in their production activities; (*c*) limited access to basic economic and social services; and (*d*) limited human capital.

1. *Resource base and asset control.* As noted, 73 per cent of those in the bottom 30 per cent of income distribution were in agriculture. The largest source of income for this group was crop farming. In 1985, the average farm size of low-income families was 1.56 hectares. For the Philippines as a whole, the average farm size was 2.63 hectares in 1980 (NCSO 1984). Even among low-income farm families, the distribution by farm site cultivated is highly skewed. Thirty-five per cent cultivated farms smaller than 1.0 hectare, together representing 11 per cent of total farm area cultivated by all low-income farm families, while 28 per cent cultivated farms of 2.0 hectares or over, representing 60 per cent of the farm area of low-income families. Fifty-two per cent of low-income families do not own the land they cultivate. Thirty-eight per cent of low-income farm families produced rice as the main crop, 30 per cent produced corn, and 20 per cent produced coconuts.

2. *Technology.* In crop-farming low-income families are characterized by the use of traditional subsistence methods of agriculture. Only one-fifth have irrigated land, a little more than one-third use pesticides and fertilizers, less than a quarter use high-yielding varieties, and less than a third practice interplanting or double cropping. Part of the reason for the low rate of adoption of modern technology is the cost of such technology. The data reveal, however,

that it could also be partly due to lack of information: only around 5 per cent of these families made use of the government extension service.

3. *Access to economic and social services.* Few families have access to other government services. According to the survey data, only 16 per cent of agricultural low-income families had used credit during the 1975–80 period. Of these, 30 per cent used credit from government-sponsored credit programmes, and the rest obtained credit mainly from traditional sources (relatives, neighbours/friends, landlords, moneylenders, etc.). The average amount of loans ranged from 980 pesos from relatives to 3,730 pesos from government banks. Interest rates on government loans were reported as ranging from a low of 4 per cent to a high of 60 per cent per annum. Those who borrowed from traditional sources reported paying interest rates as high as 300 per cent from moneylenders to 400 per cent from landlords; the latter were mostly paid in kind.

Of those engaged in crop farming only 39 per cent of palay farmers and 28 per cent of corn farmers were aware of official price supports. Only 7 per cent reported selling palay at the support price, while 83 per cent sold at prices significantly lower than the support price. The remainder (10 per cent), however, were able to sell at higher than support price. A similar situation occurred among corn farmers.

The prices at which crop farmers can sell their produce depends on their access to different marketing outlets. Traders and middlemen account for over three-quarters of palay, corn, and copra sold. The National Food Authority which implements the price support programme for palay and corn accounts for only 2.5 per cent of palay sold and 0.6 per cent of corn sold.

4. *Human capital.* Only 77 per cent of low-income family members age 6 years and over can read and write a simple message. The percentage is lower among agricultural families than non-agricultural families (75 *vs.* 83 per cent).

According to the 1983 Integrated Survey of Households, 10 per cent of the population 15 years old and over among low-income families did not go to school, 37 per cent had some elementary schooling, 26 per cent completed elementary schooling, and 13 per cent had attended high school. These data show that the educational levels of low-income family members tend to be lower than the rest of the population. For example, only 26 per cent of low-income family members had at least some high school education, compared to 42 per cent for the national population of the same age range.

Among low-income family members 15 years old and over in 1985, only 3 per cent had completed some vocational/technical course/training, compared to 15 per cent of the same age group for the national population in 1975.

5. *Other aspects.* Two other aspects regarding low-income families are worth noting. The first is their consumption patterns: 67 per cent of total expenditures are for food, of which 49 per cent are for cereals and another 17 per cent for fish and marine products. The vulnerability of low-income groups to changes in basic food prices is evident. Secondly, relatives and friends provide the main

sources of financial help low-income households can count on in time of extreme economic stress: fifty-four per cent of low-income families reported that relatives were their usual source of financial help; neighbours/friends were reported by 43 per cent, employers/landlords by 13 per cent, private moneylenders by 14 per cent, and 'other sources' by 5 per cent. Because relatives, neighbours, and friends are also likely to be poor, the amount of help they can offer is small, while landlords and moneylenders typically lend at very high interest rates.

Profiles of selected low-income group Micro level studies of specific groups provide more indepth information of particular categories of poor (e.g. Castillo 1979, NEDA 1980, World Bank 1980, Carner 1981).

The major social groups that have been studied include upland farmers, lowland farmers, agricultural wage workers, artisanal fishermen, and urban poor.

1. *Upland farmers.* These farmers generally cultivate a variety of crops. A major distinguishing characteristic is their poor resource base (marginal land on rolling hills and steep mountain slopes), which rapidly deteriorates through soil erosion, leaching, etc. as a result of destructive cultivation techniques ('slash and burn') or inappropriate farming practices. These farmers are located in more remote areas than the lowlanders, have even more limited access to markets, and are likewise relatively inaccessible to economic and social services. Because of the highly seasonal nature of production activities and low productivity, a large proportion engage in non-crop farming activities (e.g. rattan gathering, firewood gathering, production of hand-sawn timber, etc.) or seek farm-related work in the lowlands.

2. *Lowland crop farmers.* By far the largest group among the low-income families are the lowland farmers. These farmers are perhaps the most heterogenous encompassing different crops (rice, corn, coconuts), tenure status (owner, tenant, lessee), and type of cultivation (rainfed and irrigated). Farmer owners are better off than non-owners, irrespective of crop.

The large size of the group and the limited land available tend to result in farm fragmentation further limiting their resource base. The group as a whole have better access to markets and basic services than upland farmers.

3. *Agricultural wage workers.* Landless farm workers are perhaps the poorest among the lowland farm groups. They are either rice and corn labourers or sugar plantation workers. These workers have no productive assets except their labour power. With low education and lacking skills, escape from poverty is most difficult. As their numbers increase, competition for farm work becomes keen. Their low income is aggravated by the high seasonality of their receipts making them highly vulnerable to small changes in job prospects and price increases. Due to the same factors, they have less effective access to basic social services, especially health and education. Moreover, since much of the

agricultural programmes are geared towards farmers, e.g. credit, extension services, etc., they often do not benefit directly by such programmes.

4. *Artisanal fishermen.* Artisanal fishermen are those who fish within three miles of the shore using boats of less than 3 tons in weight. This group competes among themselves over the limited resource base. The resource base is gradually declining with increased numbers of fishermen, poor technology, increased competition from commercial fishermen, and inappropriate fishing practices (e.g. dynamite fishing).

Although fishing is a year-round activity, the volume of catch and the types of species caught vary by season, resulting in fluctuations in income within the year. Moreover, fishermen with non-motorized boats and inadequate gear are unable to exploit alternative fishing grounds during lean months. These fishermen also have less access to alternative marketing outlets, and must face a relatively lower price for their catch than larger fishermen.

5. *Urban poor.* The urban poor is made up of various subgroups. The occupation of household heads includes transport services and sales workers, production and construction workers, and hawkers, vendors, and other workers in the informal sector, scavengers, and mendicants. Their incomes vary by occupation, but their overall income is low because of their low levels of education and skills.

In addition to natural increase, the size of this group is enlarged by the migration of the rural poor. Increased numbers tend to depress wages. Because food and fuel are more difficult to secure in an urban setting, the urban poor are more vulnerable to cyclical changes in industrial production and labour demand as well as to rising prices of basic commodities. Although they have greater physical proximity to schools and health services than the rural poor, their access is similarly limited by their low incomes.

IV   The impact of adjustment policies on vulnerable groups

While there are many complex processes underlying the relationship between world economic conditions and human welfare, three linkages dominate: (*a*) the effects on household incomes through changes in employment, prices and wages; (*b*) the consequences on the rural sector through changes in agricultural incomes and consumer prices; and (*c*) the impact of shifts in government expenditures, especially with respect to social services. A fourth significant linkage involves the second-round effects of declining incomes and dwindling employment opportunities on basic social concerns.

1   Effects on household incomes and consumption

Between 1981 and 1985 real per capita GNP fell by 15 per cent to a level equivalent to that in 1975 (Table 7.3). The economic deterioration of the 1980s caused a marked slow-down in employment growth, rising participation

TABLE 7.5   *Annual growth rate of real GDP (1972 prices) and employment, by sector, 1981–1985 (percentages)*

	Gross domestic product				Employment			
	1981–82	1982–83	1983–84	1984–85	1981–82	1982–83	1983–84	1984–85
TOTAL	3.0	0.8	(5.7)	(4.0)	(0.5)	10.6	2.2	0.9
Agriculture, fishery, and forestry	3.1	(2.1)	2.3	2.4	(0.1)	10.8	(1.4)	(0.4)
Industrial sector	2.4	0.4	(10.6)	(10.2)	(2.8)	11.6	5.3	(3.3)
Services sector	3.5	3.2	(6.3)	(2.9)	0.05	9.8	6.4	4.4
By sector								
Mining and quarrying	(7.3)	(2.5)	(10.7)	0.5	(6.2)	32.9	35.6	(6.6)
Manufacturing	2.4	2.3	(7.1)	(7.3)	(3.6)	8.3	2.4	(0.6)
Electricity, gas, and water	8.5	10.0	2.3	2.0	19.7	47.2	3.8	(9.9)
Construction	4.4	(6.0)	(23.7)	(27.6)	2.0	15.2	9.1	(9.1)
Wholesale and retail trade	3.4	(31.6)	1.0	(0.05)	(2.1)	14.7	11.0	7.1
Transportation, storage, and communication	2.5	2.0	(4.4)	(1.6)	3.3	9.5	5.4	6.4
Financing, real estate, and business services	4.0	60.8	(26.8)	(12.43)	18.2	(7.6)	3.1	6.0
Community, social and personal services			2.8	(2.4)	(1.3)	8.9	3.8	3.1

Sources: Revised Estimate of the National Income Accounts as of April 1986 by the National Economic and Development Authority National Accounts Staff (for 1983–5 GDP figures) and the 1984 *NEDA Statistical Yearbook* (for 1981–82); employment figures were culled from computer print-outs of the Integrated Survey of Households.

Note: Parentheses indicate negative changes.

rates, rising unemployment, and sharply declining real incomes among workers and the self-employed, with a deterioration in income distribution and an increasing proportion of households falling below the minimum poverty threshold.

Employment declined in every sector except services in 1984–85. In aggregate, the employment increase slowed down from 10.6 per cent (1982–83) to 2.2 per cent (1983–84) to 0.9 per cent (1984–85) (Table 7.5). Employment was particularly badly hit in the rural areas where it fell by 7.0 per cent in 1983–84 and 0.9 per cent in 1984–85. In the urban areas, wage and salary employment fell in 1984–85, but rose in the informal sector among own-account workers and unpaid family workers (Table 7.6). The urban informal sector expanded by 30 per cent from 1980 to 1985.

TABLE 7.6   *Annual growth rate of employment, by class of worker and urban–rural location, 1982–1985 (percentages)*

	1982–83	1983–84	1984–85
Urban	2.1	25.0	1.1
Wage and salary workers	5.4	20.7	(1.6)
Own-account workers	(0.2)	36.8	7.3
Unpaid family workers	(19.1)	24.8	1.7
Rural	4.0	(7.0)	(0.9)
Wage and salary workers	5.3	4.5	(1.5)
Own-account workers	8.5	(4.9)	1.3
Unpaid family workers	(5.4)	(24.6)	(4.8)
Total	3.4	2.2	(0.2)
Wage and salary workers	5.3	12.1	(1.5)
Own-account workers	6.9	2.8	2.8
Unpaid family workers	(7.1)	(18.8)	(3.6)

Source: Computer print-outs of the Integrated Survey of Households for the respective years.
Note: Parentheses indicate negative changes.

The decline in employment in industry was partly due to import restrictions and partly to the slump in demand. Reports of employers to the Ministry of Labour and Employment exploring economic reasons for retrenchments or shut-down found that in 1984 and 1985 over 60 per cent were due to lack of raw materials or to a slump in demand. While in 1984 raw material shortage was the dominant reason (40 per cent of the cases), in 1985 slump in demand accounted for 43 per cent and lack of raw materials for only 19 per cent of the reasons given.

Labour force participation rates increased sharply over this period from 60 per cent (1982) to 64 per cent (1984), having been stable in the six years preceding 1982. The increase was particularly great in female participation rates, which rose from 43.7 per cent in 1982 to 48.3 per cent in 1984. The increasing participation rates can be attributed to the crisis, with women increasingly forced to work to help meet minimum family needs.

TABLE 7.7 *Index of real average earnings in cash and in kind of employed persons by industry, 3rd quarter, 1982–1985 (1982 = 100)*

	Urban			Rural		
	1983	1984	1985	1983	1984	1985
Wage and Salary Workers	0.86	0.60	0.54	0.90	0.64	0.69
Agriculture, fishery, and forestry	0.92	0.66	0.61	0.92	0.70	0.70
Mining and quarrying	1.21	0.42	0.46	0.91	0.70	0.78
Manufacturing	1.00	0.62	0.70	0.94	0.66	0.66
Electricity, gas, and water	1.04	0.76	0.66	0.86	0.41	0.61
Construction	0.71	0.44	0.42	0.87	0.71	0.61
Whole and retail trade	0.93	0.63	0.52	0.76	0.72	0.52
Transportation, storage, and communications	0.80	0.59	0.50	0.82	0.69	0.66
Financing, insurance, real estate, and business services	0.88	0.64	0.50	0.88	0.63	0.62
Community, social and personal services	0.84	0.63	0.54	0.94	0.69	0.85
Own account workers	0.98	0.55	0.42	0.74	0.62	0.59
Agriculture, fishery, and forestry	0.38	0.67	0.51	0.76	0.65	0.63
Mining and quarrying	0.29	0.03	0.10	0.67	0.54	0.40
Manufacturing	0.64	0.32	0.24	0.34	0.28	0.23
Electricity, gas, and water	0.92	—	0.05	—	—	—
Construction	1.47	0.42	0.37	0.90	0.15	0.14
Wholesale and retail trade	1.01	0.65	0.46	0.86	0.76	0.52
Transportation, storage, and communications	0.93	0.74	0.66	0.82	0.41	0.42
Financing, insurance, real estate, and business services	1.03	0.97	0.62	0.45	0.35	0.20
Community, social and personal services	1.89	0.43	0.34	1.46	0.56	0.48

Source: Computer print-outs of the Integrated Survey on Households for the respective years.

From 1980–85, the labour force increased by 23 per cent, while employment rose by 20 per cent. As a result open unemployment increased from 5 per cent to 7 per cent over this period (Table 7.4)[1].

Real earnings of all groups of workers declined dramatically from 1982 to 1985 (see Table 7.7) with average earnings of urban wage and salaries decreasing by 46 per cent, and earnings of urban own account workers by 49 per cent. The rural declines were 31 per cent (wage and salary workers) and 37 per cent (own account). The rural–urban income differential declined but rural earnings remained substantially below urban (70 per cent for wage and salaries and 52 per cent own account). These declines *understate* the true decline in real incomes of low-income households because prices of food increased fastest, following by clothing, while low-income households spend a greater proportion of their incomes on these items than other households do.

In 1985, wages and salary workers on average earned just one-quarter of the minimum the World Bank had estimated was necessary to meet minimum nutritional needs for a household of six. Rural wages and salaries were 22 per cent of this minimum average own account earnings were 29 per cent (urban) and 19 per cent (rural). Other poverty-lines are lower, but all show average wages and salaries significantly below the poverty minimum (Table 7.8).

TABLE 7.8   *Proportion of selected income indicators of poverty threshold estimates, 3rd quarter, 1985*

	Monthly income (P)	Ratio to poverty threshold (%)		
		Tan–Holazo	Abrera	World Bank
Wage and salary workers				
Urban	1,206.00	66.2	28.8[a]	24.9
			33.4[b]	
Rural	842.00	53.6	26.5	22.0
Own-account workers				
Urban	1,408.00	77.2	33.7[a]	29.1
			39.0[a]	
Rural	734.00	46.7	23.1	19.2
Agricultural workers				
Palay	762.55	48.5	24.0	19.9
Corn	580.75	37.0	18.3	15.2
Sugarcane	675.44	43.0	21.2	17.7
Coconut	711.55	45.3	22.4	18.6

Sources: Compiled from data obtained from de Dios *et al* (1984); National Wage Councils; Ministry of Labour and Employment.
[a] For Manila and suburbs.
[b] Other urban areas.

Overseas employment provided a safety valve for the lower absorptive capacity of the economy in the early 1980s. During this period, a yearly average of 340,000 Filipinos worked overseas. While there were economic benefits, the social implications were not always positive. One result was broken families due to prolonged separation.

There was a trend towards increasing inequality in income distribution. The positive growth rates in the 1970s did not improve the relative income status of the poorer segments of society. In 1975, the lowest 20 per cent of families were receiving only 5.5 per cent of total income, while the lowest 60 per cent received a mere 30 per cent. Although not precisely comparable, the quarterly income data for the period 1980–83 showed that the income share of the lowest 20 and 60 per cent of families were down to 4 and 25 per cent, respectively. Income distribution, as measured by the Gini coefficient, worsened. The Gini coefficients of 0.5294 and 0.4930 in the third and fourth quarters of 1980 deteriorated to 0.5370 and 0.5124 in the third and fourth quarters of 1983, respectively.

Both urban and rural low-income households were thus adversely affected by declining real wages and declining formal sector employment. Rural households also suffered from a relative bias against agriculture in government policy in most of this period.

2 Consequences for rural welfare

The international recession from 1980 to 1982 adversely affected rural welfare to the extent that it negatively influenced the system of price incentives and, eventually, depressed productivity in agriculture and rural incomes.

Impact on the price structure and the incentive system Those in the agricultural sector, particularly small farmers, are vulnerable to low and fluctuating prices of agricultural commodities both for exports and domestic consumption. Distorted public policies further worked against farmers' conditions. A study on urban–rural welfare differentials (NEDA 1984), noted declining terms of trade in agriculture according to each of four measures for the period 1969 to 1982. Extending the analysis to 1985 gives the same results. Agricultural pricing policy favoured urban consumers through price controls on rice, chicken, eggs and other commodities, until the controls were lifted in 1985.

Effective protection rates (EPRs), which measure the net effect of various price interventions in the product and input markets in protecting domestic value added, indicate an incentive structure that significantly favoured industry against agriculture. Coconut, sugar, and logs were the most penalized in terms of having high negative EPRs (David 1983). Bale (1985) confirmed David's findings, concluding that government price intervention policies in the Philippines implied a redistribution of income from rural producers to urban consumers. This finding was reiterated by Lamberte *et al.* (1985), who indicated that the burden of adjustment in response to the economic crisis in 1983–84 was shouldered more by the private sector, particularly the agricultural and export sectors.

The anti-agricultural bias of domestic policies was due to the impact of measures such as regulated pricing, government control of trade, export taxes, export quotas, and special levies which tended to depress farm prices. Farmers responded to producer prices by producing less, thereby lowering farm incomes. The underpricing of agricultural commodities in the domestic market also slowed the rate of adoption of new technology and the use of modern inputs. Positive measures to help the farm sector through price support, irrigation services, and subsidized credit could not entirely offset the negative effects of these policies.

Government control on agricultural trade in some commodities, such as rice, sugar, and coconut oil has tended to shift profit gains from farmer-producers to the government agencies involved in trading these products.

In sugar, it was found that producers have been subsidizing consumers. It should be noted, however, that domestic policies were not the sole reason for the declining and negative protection for the sugar industry during the years 1975 to 1980: the end of preferential access to the US sugar market with the expiration of the Laurel–Langley agreement and the US Sugar Act in 1974 was also responsible (David 1983).

Some commercial policies designed to promote industrialization through the protection of domestic manufacturing have likewise disfavoured the farm sector. Bale (1985) argues that misaligned exchange rates have inhibited better agricultural performance. The protection given to domestic manufacturers of small tractors and small water pumps for farm irrigation had the unintended effect of increasing their price relative to larger imported equipment (Bale 1985). This has fostered the suboptimal use of larger imported tractors and pumps which are more labour-displacing than smaller equipment (Bale 1985). Moreover, year-round irrigation is available only to lowland farmers, and technology and support services for upland farming, on which six million Filipinos depend for survival, are inadequate if they exist at all.

Impact on agricultural incomes and rural welfare The bias against agriculture before reforms were initiated in 1985 had contributed to the increasing gap in incomes. The income per worker in industry was 4.6 times that of an agricultural worker in 1973 and increased further to 5.2 times in 1983. Policies thus contributed to relative worsening of incomes among rural households, where the incidence of poverty was already particularly high.

Another study (NEDA 1984), analysing post-1975 trends, attests to the widening welfare differentials in favour of urban areas. This was true of almost all the broad indicators of welfare, notably incomes, employment and prices as they were affected by government intervention policies and fiscal operations. In aggregate, the ratio of real average household income in the rural areas to that of urban areas declined from 0.75 in 1975 to 0.61 in 1982.

While agricultural products were generally vulnerable to international prices, some products—particularly coconut and sugar—were especially adversely affected. Prices per pound plunged from 51.3 cents in 1984 to

15.0 cents as of early 1986 for coconut oil and from 28.7 cents in 1980 to 4.0 cents in late 1985 for sugar. Moreover, historical dependence on the US quota market for sugar restrained diversification initiatives, while monopolistic trading in these commodities reduced the returns accruing to small farmers.

But despite the adverse impact of external factors and policy biases, agriculture still performed relatively better than the other sectors of the economy. It showed positive growth of 2.3 per cent in 1984 and 2.4 per cent in 1985 while the rest of the economy contracted (Table 7.5). The sector also fared better in the period 1973–83 when its growth averaged 4.1 per cent annually.

3 *Impact on government expenditure*

A significant shift in the distribution of government expenditures among the major sectors first occurred following the 1973 oil crisis. Prior to 1973, the social services sector consistently received the largest budgetary allocation. However, the government's response to the first oil shock was to increase the allocation for economic services to an average of 42 per cent for the period 1974–78, with the bulk of expenditure going to public infrastructures and utilities. The share of social services in total government expenditures averaged 20 per cent over the same period.

Within social services in 1974–78, education garnered, on average, more than half the total allocation (59 per cent), followed by social security and welfare (20 per cent), health (19.5 per cent), and housing and community development (7 per cent). While the allocation for the social services sector was declining, there was an increase in the share of the defence sector over this period, and the allocation for general public services and debt service also steadily increased.

An analysis of government expenditures during the 1978–80 period indicates that, in real terms and on a per family basis, urban regions benefited more than regions which were predominantly rural. However, the difference is significantly lower in the outlays for social service sectors than for the economic sectors. The allocation for education was higher, on average, in rural than in urban regions, which is consistent with population distribution.

There was a marked change in the level and distribution of government expenditures after the second oil shock in 1979. Since 1979, real per capita government expenditure has steadily declined, falling by 17 per cent between 1979 and 1984 (Table 7.9). During this period the share of debt service rose from 27 per cent to 42 per cent, while the share of social services fell from 21 per cent to 18 per cent (having peaked at 30 per cent in 1982) and economic services from 32 per cent to 16 per cent (Table 7.10).

There was a sharp drop in social sector expenditure in 1984. Education expenditure per capita in 1984 was 30 per cent below the 1979 level; per capita expenditure on both health and housing and community amenities had fallen by one-third. While expenditure on social security and other welfare services

TABLE 7.9 *Real per capita actual national government expenditures, by sector, 1978–1984 (1972 pesos)*

	1978	1979	1980	1981	1982	1983	1984
Total	352	360	300	316	286	309	300
Economic services	108	116	126	141	86	114	49
Agriculture, forestry and fishing	—	28	24	37	22	24	13
Industry, Trade, and tourism	—	12	9	20	5	9	2
Utilities and infrastructure, Transportation and Communication, and other economic services	—	76	93	84	59	80	33
Social services	50	74	55	53	86	80	55
Education	—	36	29	34	36	34	25
Health	—	13	12	11	12	14	8
Housing and community amenities	—	22	7	3	27	24	15
Social security and Welfare and other social services	—	4	6	6	10	8	7
National defence	46	39	27	31	33	31	20
General public services	52	35	48	50	32	28	52
Debt services	95	96	45	40	50	56	125

Source: Commission on Audit, *Annual Financial Report*, for years indicated.

TABLE 7.10 *Distribution of actual national government expenditure, by sector, 1980–1984 (percentages)*

	1978	1979	1980	1981	1982	1983	1984
Economic services	30.8	32.2	42.0	44.6	29.9	36.8	16.2
Social services	14.2	20.6	18.1	16.8	29.9	26.0	18.3
Defence	13.1	10.8	9.0	9.8	11.6	9.9	6.5
General public services	14.8	9.8	15.9	15.9	11.3	9.2	17.3
Debt service	27.0	26.6	14.9	12.8	17.4	18.0	41.7
TOTAL	100.0	100.0	100.0	100.0	100.0	100.0	100.0

Source: Commission on Audit, *Annual Financial Report*, for the years indicated.

rose over the period, expenditure per capita in social services as a whole fell by one-quarter. In 1985 there was a rise in the share of government expenditure going to the social sector.

These trends indicate declining capacity of the public sector to provide for basic economic and social services from 1979, with further worsening as a result of the crisis in 1983–84. Moreover, basic economic and social services that have a direct bearing on the income of the poor (credit, price supports, input subsidies, etc.) have not reached the poor extensively. NEDA (1985) showed that low-income families often did not use services even when they had access. Effective access to basic social services such as health, education, and housing has also been low because such access depends partly on real incomes which have greatly deteriorated in the more recent period.

A more detailed description of developments in the social sectors and their effects on human welfare is given in Part V.

V The social impact of the crisis

The social costs of the first oil shock were not as profound as those of the second oil shock. The shock of 1973–74 did not result in any fall in average per capita income and was accompanied by high commodity prices. However, the 1979–80 oil shock was followed by a severe world recession and a domestic economic crisis which reduced average per capita income to the 1975 level. Moreover, the financial capacity of authorities to provide the adjustment assistance necessary in the 1980s was no longer as great as in the 1970s.

As noted above, the poverty situation was already serious in the early 1970s. From 1974, some public programmes were oriented towards poverty alleviation. Public initiatives to improve social conditions were evident in shifts in focus and greater cost-effectiveness of programmes. Given the increasing costs of health care and the persistence of communicable diseases, a shift from a curative to a preventive approach to health care was instituted. The Primary Health Care concept which seeks the improvement and maintenance of the health status of the whole community was initiated in 1980. The nationwide deterioration in nutritional status similarly prompted the launching of the Philippine Nutrition Programme in 1974, principally aimed at the vulnerable groups—namely, infants, pre-schoolers, school children, and pregnant and lactating mothers.

In education, although there has been a marked expansion in enrolment at all levels, the quality and efficiency of education has worsened through the years. This led education authorities to change the focus from equity to the improvement of the quality and efficiency of education. Accordingly, the Programme for Decentralized Educational Development was launched in 1981 to raise the quality and efficiency of elementary education.

Likewise, the population programme was reoriented from simple fertility reduction to the promotion of total family welfare. From a purely clinic-based orientation, the population programme evolved into the National Population and Family Planning Outreach Project in 1976 with stress on responsible parenthood and maternal and child care as well as family planning.

The social services sector also shifted emphasis from the provision of handouts or direct assistance to the disadvantaged to a more developmental approach including supporting self-reliance. This is evident in programmes such as the Self-employment Assistance and Practical Skills Development where individuals are provided with opportunities to increase their productivity and self-reliance.

The formulation of the National Shelter Programme in 1975 integrated the previous piecemeal and diffused activities in housing production, finance, and regulation. This became instrumental in the construction of a number of housing units, to which families secured access through the Pag-IBIG Provident Fund.

The results of these programmes were reflected in improvement of most social indicators in the 1970s, although pockets of more serious social conditions existed, particularly in the least developed regions. By 1979, the population growth rate was estimated to have decelerated to 2.4 per cent from a high 2.8 per cent in 1974. The 1980 census, however, reported a 2.7 per cent growth rate reflecting a slackening in the pace of fertility and mortality reduction.

Life expectancy increased by an additional four years from 58 years in 1974 to 62 years in 1982, due to improvements in crude death rates and infant mortality rates. The prevalence of malnutrition among pre-schoolers fell from 21.9 per cent in 1978 to 17.2 per cent in 1982 although its incidence remained high in certain depressed areas of the country, e.g. Negros.

Total educational enrolment grow from 10.3 million in 1974 to 13.1 million in 1982. There were also improved transition and cohort survival rates. However, low student achievement levels were reported, particularly in depressed areas, necessitating the shift in focus from equity to quality of education. There was an increased training output of non-formal programmes in response to the demand for basic and middle skills by various industries. Not all graduates were, however, absorbed by industries because of the lack of direct tie-ups between training institutions and factories and companies.

The housing programmes from 1974 to 1982 extended to 202,000 households through the construction of new dwelling units, upgrading of marginal settlements, and sites and services development. Most beneficiaries, however, came from middle and upper income levels leaving out many families belonging to low-income groups, who were the original target of the programme.

The outreach of social services programmes for the most disadvantaged groups increased coverage from 3.8 million to 7.6 million during the eight-year period. Social security benefit payments for government and private employees quadrupled from 1972 to 1982. Similarly, Medicare disbursements doubled during the same period. For a time, these benefits served to augment incomes and sustain welfare. But the advent of the second oil crisis changed the situation.

The impact of the second oil crisis on the social sectors was more pronounced than the first oil shock. The severe contraction of economic output brought about by the crisis triggered widespread unemployment, dwindling incomes, and spiralling prices, which in turn halted and even eroded the social gains previously achieved. The drastic cuts in government expenditures curtailed the delivery of social services such as housing and non-formal training.

1 Health

The deteriorating economic conditions of the early 1980s made access to medical services more difficult, particularly for disadvantaged groups. The cost of hospitalization became prohibitive so that fewer patients, including the critically ill, sought admission to the private hospitals. The escalating cost of private medical care increased dependence on government-subsidized health services such that admissions in government hospitals increased by 6 per cent between 1982 and 1984.

These developments led to a deterioration in people's physical well-being as evidenced by the performance of major health indicators. Although the infant mortality rate continued to decline, the rate of decline has decelerated. From 1975 to 1980, it declined by an average of two percentage points annually while during the period 1980–85 the decrease was only about one percentage point annually. Moreover, the general deterioration in health status is manifested in the higher incidence of morbidity particularly of communicable diseases such as diarrhoea, influenza, pneumonia, tuberculosis, malaria, measles and schistosomiasis.

To cushion the effects of the high cost of medical care, Medicare cash benefits were increased. The development and use of herbal medicines and acupuncture in public hospitals were also advocated to serve as substitutes for expensive medicines and services. Emphasis was placed on indigenous health care technology as well as on the preventive aspect of health care. Health information and education, environmental sanitation, and immunization were given priority. Health programmes towards maternal and child health, malaria eradication, and the control of tuberculosis, schistosomiasis, and diarrhoeal diseases were integrated and intensified.

A closer look at the public health budget indicates a serious misallocation of health resources. The government continued to provide subsidies to support specialized health institutions like the Philippine Heart Center for Asia, Kidney Foundation of the Philippines, and the Lung Center of the Philippines which cater to upper income families. Annual subsidies to these institutions averaged more than $100 million, much higher than the resources being allocated to more mass-based programmes like malaria eradication and schistosomiasis control. During the period 1978–85, the government allocation for malaria eradication averaged only about $20 million per year, while schistosomiasis control was allotted only $14 million a year. The total subsidies being extended to these institutions were higher than the annual government appropriation for Primary Health Care (PHC) which is a major and broader-based health programme. The four institutions received a total of $229 million in 1984–85

while government funds for PHC during the two-year period totalled only
$45 million.

2 *Nutrition*

With the onset of the 1983 economic crisis, there has been a deterioration in
the nutritional well-being of the people. The period 1983–85 exhibited a
decline in the proportion of pre-schoolers who are normal and mildly underweight. From 82.8 per cent in 1982, this proportion slightly decreased to 82.4
in 1983, then to 79.5 in 1984, until it reached 78.0 per cent in 1985.

To respond to the situation, some less conventional approaches were
adopted. A special food discount project was piloted in selected municipalities
with identified nutritionally depressed barangays as a direct approach to the
problem of low energy intake among low-income groups. The number of food
discount stores financed by the government was increased. The approach,
however, was not considered cost-effective, due to its high budgetary subsidy.
It was largely urban-based, competed with the private sector, and did not
carry cost-effective food items.

In the meantime, evidence of malnutrition persisted. Results of a Food and
Nutrition Research Institute survey conducted in October 1984 among selected
households in Metro Manila showed that nutrient intakes of respondents
fell short of the recommended allowances both for families with laid-off and
employed household heads. The energy and protein intakes of the employed
group were 82.3 per cent and 88.2 per cent adequate, respectively, high than
those in the laid-off group, who registered adequacy levels of 79.6 per cent for
energy and 87.4 per cent for protein. A marked deterioration in the adequacy
levels of the nutrient intake of the October sample was also noted compared
to the earlier nutrition survey undertaken in February 1984.

The sugar workers of Negros were among the hardest hit by the crisis. With
the higher cost of production coupled with depressed prices for sugar, sugar
production has been drastically reduced, leaving sugar workers with little or
no income. As a result, many families barely ate one meal a day. In 1984,
26.4 per cent of children weighed were found to be moderately or severely
underweight. The regional hospital in Bacolod City has reported 370 child
and infant deaths during the first half of 1985, 67 per cent higher than the
figure recorded during the same period in 1984.

3 *Education*

Close scrutiny of the government education sector reveals a gradual deterioration in the quality and access to educational opportunities (Table 7.11).

At the public elementary level, participation rates, retention rates and
cohort survival rates fell while repetition rates increased from 1981 to 1984.
Only 88 per cent of the 7–12 age group enrolled in public schools in 1984

TABLE 7.11 *Performance indicators of government elementary schools, 1981–1982 to 1984–1985*

	1981–82	1982–83	1983–84	1984–85
Participation rate	91.66	93.08	87.91	n.a.
Retention rate	91.52	91.10	90.65	90.38
Transition rate	92.86	92.41	92.67	62.13
Cohort survival rate	66.56	66.45	65.23	63.0
Pupil–teacher ratio	1:31	1:31	1:30	1:31
Drop-out rate	2.92	2.78	2.72	n.a.
Repetition rate	2.14	2.31	2.32	n.a.

Source: Ministry of Education, Culture, and Sports, Research and Statistics Division, Planning Service.

compared to 92 per cent in 1981. Retention rates fell from 92 per cent to 90 per cent during the 3-year period; repetition rates increased from 2.1 per cent to 2.3 per cent, with more students dropping out of the system. Only 63 students out of every 100 completed elementary education in 1984 compared to 67 in 1981. These trends are rather surprising in the light of the implementation of government programmes specifically aimed at raising the quality and efficiency of elementary education.

In terms of allocation of government expenditures, education consistently constituted the major chunk of social service expenditures though its share declined from 1974 to 1983. The persistent clamour for higher salaries by public school teachers, manifested in long mass leaves and strikes, resulted in higher budgetary allocations for the Ministry of Education, Culture and Sports in 1984 and 1985. Within the sector, priority is given to elementary education in view of the constitutional mandate; 60 per cent of national government expenditure went to elementary education in 1985 compared to 23 per cent allocated to state colleges and universities. However, a review of the allocation of resources within the sector is required in order to channel limited education resources from tertiary to basic education, which is the sector's foremost priority, while private sector investments in tertiary education could be more strongly encouraged. Meanwhile, cut-backs in training expenditures led to a lower training output in 1984 (172,300) compared to 1983 (206,600) and the peak in 1982 (217,300).

4 Housing

Housing production experienced a sharp drop particularly in 1985 when only 17,770 new units were constructed under both government-assisted and government-financed projects. Drastic cuts in the budget necessitated the cancellation of deferment of these and other government housing projects in

TABLE 7.12 *Selected social development indicators, 1974–1985*

	1974	1975	1976	1977	1978	1979	1980	1981	1982	1983	1984	1985
Population												
Growth rate (%)	2.8	2.8	2.5	2.5	2.4	2.4	3.9	2.5	2.5	2.5	2.5	2.5
Crude birth rate (per 1,000 pop.)	37.5	35.2	34.3	33.5	32.7	31.9	33.7	33.4	33.2	32.9	39.5	31.2
Crude death rate (per 1,000 pop.)	9.8	9.2	9.0	8.8	8.6	8.4	8.7	8.5	8.4	8.2	8.1	7.8
Age dependency ratio	89.2	88.8	86.1	83.9	81.7	79.4	83.3	82.1	81.0	79.9	78.8	77.8
Contraceptive prevalence rate (per 100 married couples of reprod. age)	29	31	33	35	37	39	41	43	45	34	36	37
Health and nutrition												
Life expectancy (in yrs.)	58.2	58.8	59.3	59.9	60.4	61.1	61.6	61.9	62.2	62.5	62.8	63.1
Infant mortality rate (per 1,000 live births)	74.6	72.2	70.8	68.9	67.0	65.1	63.2	61.9	60.6	59.3	58.0	56.8
Calorie intake as % of requirements	n.a.	n.a.	n.a.	n.a.	88.6	n.a.	n.a.	n.a.	89.0	n.a.	n.a.	n.a.
Protein intake as % of requirements	n.a.	n.a.	n.a.	n.a.	102.9	n.a.	n.a.	n.a.	99.6	n.a.	n.a.	n.a.
% pre-school children with weights greater than 75% of the filipino standard weight for age	n.a.	n.a.	n.a.	n.a.	78.8	70.0	81.1	82.5	82.8	82.4	79.5	78.0
Social Services												
Service outreach (million persons)	3.8	4.4	5.1	2.9	5.9	5.9	5.7	7.2	7.6	8.0	12.6	10.42
Self-employment assistance	0.17	0.19	0.15	0.14	0.17	0.14	0.15	0.13	0.12	0.11	0.14	0.12

Practical skills development and job placement	n.a.	0.05	n.a.	0.12	0.24	0.27	0.20	0.21	0.18	0.18	0.18	0.20
Day care and supplementary feeding	0.13	0.30	0.39	0.59	0.88	1.09	1.18	1.35	1.58	1.53	1.77	1.8
Emergency assistance	2.96	3.46	3.46	5.90	2.07	1.41	1.18	1.68	2.35	2.42	5.41	2.5
Family planning and counselling	0.17	0.20	0.35	0.37	0.67	0.72	0.6	0.85	0.91	1.14	1.36	1.7
Special social services	0.34	0.24	0.75	1.04	1.92	2.24	2.31	2.42	2.47	2.61	3.72	4.1
Social security												
Coverage (1,000 persons, cumulative)	5,008	5,658	6,363	6,893	7,557	8,335	9,150	9,711	10,295	10,860	11,069	11,251
Benefit payments (million pesos)	586.7	636.9	773.2	804.1	1,135.6	1,230.7	1,402.4	1,660.4	2,030.6	2,379.8	2,680.9	3,165.4
Medicare												
Beneficiaries (1,000 persons)	755.8	838.2	1,021.2	1,034.1	1,182.5	1,209.2	1,213.3	1,227.8	1,384.2	1,443.3	1,406.5	1,428.2
Coverage (million persons, cumulative)	9.9	11.0	12.3	13.4	14.6	15.9	17.4	18.4	19.5	21.1	26.3	30.1
Disbursements (pesos million)	176.5	200.2	243.4	257.6	262.2	310.6	320.8	339.9	382.1	400.4	414.5	437.9
Abandoned children												
Served	n.a.	n.a.	n.a.	n.a.	n.a.	n.a.	5,088	n.a.	n.a.	941	1,520	2,306
Neglected children												
Served	n.a.	n.a.	n.a.	n.a.	n.a.	n.a.	4,030	n.a.	n.a.	1,046	1,291	3,239
Crime rate	207.5	185.5	184.0	213.7	246.6	252.2	275.3	288.4	302.9	319.1	332.0	n.a.

Source: Philippine authorities.

the pipeline. A marked increase, however, was apparent in the development of sites-and-services schemes which rose to 18,700 plots in 1985 from 12,870 plots in 1983 as a result of the move to focus on the housing needs of low-income groups.

The tight money situation trimmed down the regular flow of funds into the secondary mortgage market, subsequently limiting the capability of the banking system to accommodate more borrowers for housing purposes. Interim financing for loans was suspended for 1985 due to scarcity of credit resources. As the number of firms closed down and employees and workers found themselves unemployed with depressed business conditions, increases in Pag-IBIG members and contributions dropped substantially. Certain sectors even agitated for exemption from the mandatory fund contribution, and this was recently granted.

To soften the adverse economic repercussions on housing and expand benefits towards more low-income members, the interest rates of the Pag-IBIG Home Lending Programme were restructured in 1984 thereby encouraging lower loan values to build more low-cost housing units. Furthermore, Pag-IBIG shifted its thrust to provident loans, i.e. home improvement and personal loans to enable more members to use its services.

The urban housing shortage remained critical, particularly in Metro Manila, in view of the unabated migration to the cities in quest of better income opportunities. As of 1985, Metro Manila slum dwellers were estimated to have reached 1.9 million.

5   Demographic impact

The major cut in government contribution to the population programme from $178 million in 1982 to $94 million in 1983 constrained the promotion of family planning, which in turn affected the attainment of targeted contraceptive prevalence rates (CPR). The CPR slid from 41 per cent in 1980 to 34 per cent in 1983. There has, likewise, been a deceleration in the rate of decline in the crude birth rate (CBR). During the period 1975–79, CBR was declining at an average rate of about one percentage point while for 1980–85, only an estimated 0.3 percentage point decline was noted. Moreover the preliminary results of the National Demographic Survey of 1983 indicate that population growth may have been higher than projected earlier on the basis of the 1980 census.

6   Welfare of children and other critical concerns

The economic crisis has taken a heavy toll on children. There has been a significantly higher admission rate for abandoned children in government child institutions. The Reception and Study Center for Children reported admissions of 2,306 abandoned children in 1985 compared to 941 in 1983.

Similarly, the number of neglected children served under the Ministry of Social Services and Development rose from 1,046 in 1983 to 3,239 in 1985. This indicates that there were more children abandoned and neglected during the 'crisis' period than in previous years. It was also observed that there was a tendency to give up children right after birth.

Meagre opportunities for adult employment has driven an increasing number of children and youth to the streets selling newspapers, cigarettes, sampaguita, and other commodities or doing odd jobs such as car watching or car wiping to supplement household incomes. In Metro Manila alone, street children numbered from 50,000 to 75,000 and the incidence of children begging, stealing, scavenging through refuse, and engaging in prostitution has also increased. The exposure of these young people to street life has also made them prime candidates for drug abuse and juvenile delinquency.

The increasing incidence of crime is reflected in the annual crime rate which increased from 320 per 100,000 population in 1980 to 332 in 1984. Index crimes, which include the more serious crimes such as murder, homicide, robbery, theft, rape, and physical injuries, constituted more than one-half of total crimes in 1983 and 1984. Theft accounted for over a third of index crimes, with 95 reported cases daily in 1984 compared to only 75 cases per day in 1983, indicating the fierce struggle for day-to-day survival.

As a stopgap measure, social adjustment assistance was extended to disadvantaged individuals and families. For laid-off workers, unemployment assistance loans, advance payments of vacation and sick leave benefits and grants of separation pay for those who went on forced leave were extended by the Social Security System. A total of $115 million was released in unemployment assistance loans in 1985, but only 4,134 retrenched workers have made use of these loans. This was due to the fact that some retrenched workers were not members or were non-eligible for such benefits. Only around 60 per cent of the total employed labour force were covered by social security in 1984 and 1985. Social security benefits payments amounting to $3 million and Medicare benefits totalling $438 million were also granted in 1985.

A study by Lamberte *et al.* (1985) revealed that although social security decreased the inequality of income distribution in the country, payments lagged behind inflation and vulnerable non-members had to rely on the traditional extended family system for support. Government employees were even less fortunate. The Government Service Insurance System had less capacity to extend assistance during the 1983–85 crisis due to the less prudent management of its resources and investments in low-yielding assets.

Meanwhile, various social services reached a total of 10.4 million disadvantaged individuals in 1985 tapering off from a high of 12.6 million in 1984 when the impact of the crisis was most severely felt.

Social adjustment measures failed to abate the corrosive effects of the crisis on family structures and processes, particularly those of the urban poor. The chronic maladjustment of some families to crisis situations is manifested sociologically through non-support by the household head, wife and child abuse, excessive drinking, desertion, persistent extra-marital relations, serial marital unions, abandonment of children, disregard for neighbourhood rules, and alienation from relatives. For families of overseas workers who have been left behind, the sociological problems were of a different nature. In some instances, the lonely and anxious wife who must take on the stressful role of a dual parent has been found to resort to infidelity and/or overspending on material goods as a coping mechanism (Sevilla 1982).

VI   Conclusions and recommendations

In the 1980s external shocks and economic management policies contributed to the worst economic crisis experienced by the Philippines. While the government response substantially reduced current account and budget deficits and lowered inflation, this was achieved at considerable social cost. GNP per capita fell to its 1975 level and real wages fell by 40 to 50 per cent. Employment fell in every sector except services, and the unemployment rate rose. Government expenditure on the social services was cut back.

There is evidence of rising malnutrition among children from 1982; the fall in the infant mortality rate decelerated. Participation rates and retention rates in public elementary school fell and drop-out rates rose. Contraceptive prevalence rates fell and the decline in the crude birth rate decelerated. The worsening of conditions among children is shown by increasing numbers of street children.

1   Recommendations

The analysis of Philippine development experience in the last one-and-a-half decades shows that despite conscious attempts to redress fundamental problems, adjustment has been inadequate. In particular, the substantial resort to foreign savings and protectionist economic policies contributed to the external debt crises, while the inappropriate social response exerted a down-ward effect on human conditions. These deeper problems necessitate major corrective measures.

The following recommendations outline the perspectives which 'adjustment with a human face' should adopt, if the aim is to protect and improve the lives of the people.

Firstly, the new government must immediately initiate an economic recovery programme which emphasizes structural reforms and improved human con-ditions. Obviously, this requires an expansionary adjustment process in order to create the demand and incentives for growth, productive employment and an equitable development process. Debt service payments should be reduced and subordinated to growth in the development agenda. Secondly, public policy should be directed towards attacking the root causes of poverty. Programmes need to be designed and implemented to focus on target groups. Monitoring and systematic evaluation of impact should be an integral component of programmes towards the low-income. Specifically, the following actions are necessary:

1. *Development strategy.* The development strategy and recovery programme should be redirected towards agricultural modernization and rural-based labour-intensive programmes. In this way, economic recovery can be competitive and effective and the social returns will be shared by the majority of the population and of the vulnerable groups. Reforms are needed to correct the distortions caused by unsound policies towards the agricultural sector.

Past policies have penalized rural agriculture where two-thirds of the population and nearly three-quarters of the poor get their livelihood. Therefore development should be focused on their needs. Structural reforms recommended include: (*a*) removal of all policy disincentives like high costs of farm inputs, export taxes, and others; (*b*) promotion of activities which help small farmers gain access to credit, technology, and alternative product markets; (*c*) expansion of the agrarian reform programme, with a complementary package of inputs, the development of appropriate technology, and upgrading of extension services; (*d*) decentralization of economic and social programmes and strengthening of local government units; (*e*) provision of rural infrastructure both for agricultural production (irrigation, flood control, etc.) and ancillary facilities (rural roads, electricity, etc.) which will contribute directly to short- and long-run employment creation; and (*f*) promotion of food production at the family level, augmented by cost-effective subsidies on food to low-income families.

2. *Overcoming the external debt problem.* The debt overhang will continue to be a drag on development efforts due to high debt service payments unless constructive solutions are implemented. Hence, development objectives should be given top priority in the implementation of debt-management.

Equitable sharing of the debt burden by all parties is called for by the present situation. Multiyear rescheduling relief, extending consolidation and restructuring periods to at least 10 and 25 years, respectively, is needed. Innovative debt burden sharing, conversion of debt to equity, and even outright repudiation or litigation for loans proven to have been obtained in fraudulent or spurious circumstances need to be pursued by both creditors and debtor.

3. *Redesigning stabilization programmes with IMF support.* Future IMF programmes must give priority to the resumption of economic growth and sufficiently provide for essential social services to address basic needs. In this way, exports can be generated faster and internal capacity to pay external obligations be raised without the risks of generating destructive socio-political tensions. The Philippine experience has established that orthodox IMF prin-

ciples need to be modified to explicitly consider the human dimension of economic adjustments.

4. *Mobilizing international support and co-operation.* The international community has responded positively to the needs of countries affected by external economic shocks and natural disasters. This response mechanism should be further enhanced through improved assessment of local needs, in co-operation with donors, to avoid undue duplication of efforts and to increase the relevance and effectiveness of aid.

5. *Enhancing the impact of social services.* In view of the tight budgetary situation, more focused and cost-affective interventions need to be implemented on a wider scale, while the reallocation of resources within sectors should ensure that the bulk of resources goes to avowed sectoral priorities. Therefore, innovative, low-cost, community-based, and people-powered programmes must be promoted and strengthened. Complementary to this should be capacity-building and institutional development measures at the grassroots level to improve access to basic services.

To promote improved health and nutritional status, programmes for immunization, oral rehydration, breast-feeding, and other programmes for poor families and vulnerable members should be strengthened and expanded. Equally important is the reduction of fertility. In education, the thrust on improved quality of instruction and retrieval of drop-outs and out-of-school children, particularly at the primary level, should be emphasized. Government participation in housing construction should be limited to site and services development, slum upgrading and core housing directed to the needs of low-income groups. In co-operation with non-governmental organizations, government should regularly conduct visits to assess and address the special needs of cultural communities.

6. *Enforcing environmental laws.* The deterioration of the resource base due to indiscriminate logging in the uplands has to be arrested through better enforcement of forestry laws and sustained reforestation programmes which would also absorb the large number of unemployed. The government should also take ecological factors into account in its policies towards agriculture. This is necessary to preserve the ecological balance for the benefit of future generations. In addition, a stricter enforcement of fishing laws against dynamite fishing and the destruction of marine life habitats is needed.

7. *Monitoring.* Finally, closer surveillance and monitoring of the impact of the adjustment programme is necessary for timely intervention. More frequent specialized surveys on the status and condition of the bottom 30 per cent of the population and other disadvantaged groups should be conducted, like the Low-Income Group Study Project of NEDA (1985), but surveys should include a system for reporting on and predicting basic nutritional status. Special surveys should be initiated in depressed areas of the country.

Notes

1. Using quarterly estimates. Another series shows much higher unemployment (11.1 per cent October 1985).

References

Balassa, B. (1980), *The New Industrializing Developing Countries After the Oil Crisis.* World Bank Staff Working Paper no. 437, Washington, DC: World Bank.

Bale, M. (1985), *Agricultural Trade and Food Policy: The Experience of Five Developing Countries.* World Bank Staff Working Paper no. 724. Washington, DC: World Bank.

Carner, G. (1981), 'Survival, Interdependence and Competition among the Philippines Rural Poor', *Philippine Sociological Review*, 29 1–4: 45–58.

Castillo, G. T. (1979), *Beyond Manila: Philippine Rural Development Problems in Perspective.* Ottawa: International Development Research Centre.

David, C. (1983), 'Economic Policies and Philippine Agriculture'. Paper presented at the Workshop on the Impact of Economic Policies on Agricultural Development, Tagaytay City, March 25–26.

de Dios, *et al.* (1984), 'An Analysis of the Philippine Economic Crisis'. School of Economics, University of the Philippines, Manila.

Lamberte, M. B. *et al. (1985), A Review and Appraisal of the Government Response to the 1983–1984 Balance of Payments Crisis.* Philippine Institute for Development Studies Monograph Series, no. 8. Manila.

NCSO—National Census and Statistics Office—*National Sample Survey of Household Bulletin.*

—— (various years) *Integrated Survey of Households.*

NEDA—National Economic and Development Authority—(1980), 'An Inventory of Poverty-related Surveys in the Philippines'. Manila.

—— (1984), *Some Aspects of Rural–Urban Welfare Differential.* Manila.

—— (1985), *Socio Economic Survey of Special Group of Families.* Manila.

Sevilla, J. C. C. (1982), *Research on the Filipino Family: Review and Prospects.* Pasig, Metro Manila: Development Academy of the Philippines, Research for Development Department.

World Bank (1980), *Aspects of Poverty in the Philippines: A Review and Assessment.* Washington, DC: World Bank.

—— (1985), *The Philippines: Recent Trends in Poverty.* Washington, DC: World Bank.

8

The Impact of Adjustment and Stabilization Policies on Social Welfare: The South Korean Experiences during 1978–1985

Sang-Mok Suh and David Williamson

1 The South Korean economy in the 1980s

In 1980, South Korea stood at a crossroads in its economic development. Export growth, which had fuelled the rapid expansion of the South Korea economy in the 1960s and 1970s, was stagnating in the face of inflationary pressures and world-wide recession. The second oil crisis raised South Korea's petroleum import bill from $2.2 billion in 1978 to $5.6 billion in 1980, with the price-induced increase equal to nearly 6 per cent of GNP during 1979 and 1980. These problems were compounded by the intense political instability following the assassination in late 1979 of President Park Chung Hee. Finally, unfavourable weather conditions in 1980 caused a 22 per cent decline in agricultural output, equivalent to over 4 per cent of GNP.

As a result of these difficulties, real GNP in South Korea recorded a 5.2 per cent fall in 1980, the first such decline in nearly 20 years. While the economy rebounded somewhat in 1981, the increase in non-agricultural GNP was only 3 per cent, far lower than in the past. Furthermore, between 1979 and 1981, per capita real income declined by around 10 per cent. Thus the new political leadership which assumed power in 1980 had to contend with several severe problems, both internal and external, before it could steer the nation back onto the path of high growth. In particular, four issues arising from South Korea's experience over the previous two decades demanded special attention.

The first of these dealt with the style of economic management. Ever since the launching of the First Five-year Plan in 1962, the government had exerted tremendous influence in all aspects of economic planning. From 1963 to 1978, the South Korean economy grew at the remarkable average rate of 9.9 per cent, with exports and manufactured output increasing annually at 40.6 and 18.8 per cent, respectively. This high performance, however, had the psychological effect of making managers overconfident and thus less wary of potential problems—many of which surfaced in the late 1970s.

By 1981, South Korea's GNP had risen five-fold to over $60 billion, and it was apparent that no longer could the nation's increasingly sophisticated and

TABLE 8.1   *Major economic indicators, 1978–1985*

	Economic growth rate (%)	GNP[b] ($m)	GNP per capita[b] ($)	Change in industrial production (%)	Change in exports[b] (%)
1978	9.7	51,960	1,406	23.8	26.5
1979	6.5	62,374	1,662	12.1	18.4
1980[a]	− 5.2	60,327	1,589	− 1.9	16.3
1981	6.6	66,262	1,719	13.4	21.4
1982	5.4	69,383	1,773	5.3	2.8
1983	11.9	76,037	1,914	16.4	11.9
1984	8.4	82,392	2,044	15.5	19.6
1985	5.1	83,072	2,032	4.1	3.5

Source: Bank of Korea
[a] New series from 1980.
[b] In current prices.

extensive economy be directed from above. Rather than a heavy-handed, top-down system of management, more reliance needed to be placed on decentralized market mechanisms to rationalize and improve the competitiveness of South Korean industry. In this regard, a broad liberalization effort touching on the financial sector, the trading system, and the management of public enterprise was required. Competition throughout the South Korean economy needed to be bolstered; the influence of government in the decision-making of private firms needed to be reduced.

A second issue stemming from South Korea's early development was the need for stabilization of both prices and wages. A tightening labour market during the 1970s caused money wages in the manufacturing sector to increase by 34 per cent per annum. Wholesale price increases, meanwhile, were also on the rise, jumping from 12 per cent in 1978 to 39 per cent in 1980. During these years, however, productivity rose by only about 10 per cent per annum. This internal rate of rapid inflation had been preceded by a long period of moderate to high inflation during 1960s, reinforcing a pervasive psychology of inflation which made wage and price reductions difficult. In addition to these problems, price uncertainties skewed the efficiency of resource allocation, both on the government and firm level. Fiscal austerity on the part of the government was another important priority, as the budget deficit as a percentage of GNP had been rising steadily throughout the 1970s. A policy of fiscal and monetary stabilization, it was felt, would address these issues.

Third, South Korea needed to pursue a wide-ranging programme of structural adjustment. In the early stages of its economic development, South Korea relied on exports of low-scale, labour-intensive products to spur growth. As the world economic system deteriorated in the 1970s, however, protectionism in the advanced countries became more prevalent and competition between the developing countries themselves became very tough, especially in labour-intensive manufactures. Partly in response to this situation, and partly in response to the perceived need to establish a domestic defence industry, in the early and mid-1970s South Korea targeted 'strategic' heavy and chemical industries for development. Building up such industries from scratch required a massive transfer of investment funds away from the traditional light manu-facturing sector; in addition, preferential 'policy' loans—often at negative real interest rates—were granted to firms in the 'strategic' sector. As a result, the heavy and chemical industrial drive was marked by overinvestment in rela-tively inefficient projects while also severely restricting the development of the financial sector.

Today, some of South Korea's most competitive industries—electronics, steel, and engineering—are part of the so-called 'strategic' sector. Nonetheless, while these have prospered, the competitiveness of labour-intensive industries has been eroding, especially with the rise in price and wage inflation. In short, South Korea's pattern of comparative advantage is shifting, and the nation must move up-stream into skill-intensive production of higher technology goods if growth is to be sustained. This will require a significant realignment of both the industrial and employment structure, as well as the cultivation of scientifically trained manpower.

The last issue concerns the desirability of balanced development. During the first 15 years of South Korea's economic expansion, income disparities widened, especially in the 1970s, as skilled workers in the heavy and chemical industries earned far more than their unskilled counterparts. In addition, there was a wide income differential between agricultural and non-agricultural workers.

The disparities between urban and rural household income underscored another troubling problem, that of regional balance. Through South Korea's history, a preponderance of national attention, resources, and investment have been focused on the capital, Seoul, and since the early stages of South Korea's industrialization, the population of Seoul has grown dramatically. From 1975 to 1980 alone, Seoul grew by over 21 per cent, and with a current population of almost 10 million comprises roughly a quarter of the nation's total population. While trends of urban migration are difficult to measure, it is safe to assume that the biggest factor in Seoul's population boom has been an influx of rural residents seeking employment opportunities in the city.

The incredible growth of Seoul has had a number of negative side effects. There has been a disproportionate allocation of resources to the city, for one, primarily at the expense of more remote areas. These resources include not only development finance and industrial investment, but also services such as schools and medical facilities. In addition, the sharp rise in population has exacerbated an already tight housing market in the capital, resulting in the spread of low-income squatter areas. Health, sanitation, and welfare conditions in these areas are often worse than in the rural areas from which the residents originally migrated.

II Adjustment and stabilization policies

Faced with these pressing challenges, the new government launched a comprehensive economic reform package designed to revitalize the economy, bolster the competitiveness of South Korean industry, and address the income distribution problem. At the centre of the reforms were four broad policy thrusts—stabilization to curb wage and price inflation; liberalization to reorient the economy towards market principles; structural adjustment to increase productivity, employment, and competitiveness; and efforts to improve social welfare in line with the other policy objectives.

1 Stabilization

To eliminate the destructive cycle of inflation, the government introduced a series of tight monetary and fiscal measures. Aggregate demand was controlled through a restrictive monetary policy which aimed at limiting the overall rate of expansion of the money supply. More important, however, was the implementation of a programme of government fiscal austerity. Government sector expenditures, which throughout the 1980s had been running in deficit, were cut back sharply; in 1984, the government even froze spending at 1983 levels. The success of this tight fiscal policy is apparent from Table 8.2: the overall government budget deficit as a ratio of GNP dropped from 5.6 per cent in 1981 to just 1.5 per cent in 1985.

TABLE 8.2　*Budget deficit as percentage of GNP, 1978–1985*

	Budget deficit (W billion)	Deficit/GNP (%)
1978	−626.7	2.6
1979	−458.5	1.5
1980	−1,288.4	3.5
1981	−2,536.8	5.6
1982	−2,235.0	4.4
1983	−929.1	1.6
1984	−1,000.5	1.5
1985	−1,123.7	1.5

Source: Ministry of Finance.

Another important component of the stabilization programme involved incomes policy, obviously essential to break the inflationary trend of the economy. By issuing suggested guidelines for wage increases and freezing government employees' salaries, the government has engaged in strenuous efforts to keep nominal wage increases at reasonable levels. Indeed, these actions seemed to have worked, as average nominal wage increases dropped from 23.4 per cent in 1980 to 9.2 per cent in 1985. Real wages, after suffering declines in both 1980 and 1981, rebounded in 1982–85, with an average increase of 7.0 per cent, down from 18 per cent in 1978 (Table 8.3).

TABLE 8.3   *Wage increases, 1978–1984*

	Nominal wages[a]		Real wages	
	Level (won)	Increase (%)	Level[b] (won)	Increase (%)
1978	111,201	35.0	169,256	18.0
1979	142,665	28.3	183,610	8.5
1980	176,058	23.4	176,058	−4.1
1981	212,477	20.7	175,167	−0.5
1982	245,981	15.8	189,071	7.9
1983	273,119	11.0	203,062	7.4
1984	296,907	8.7	215,775	6.3
1985	324,283	9.2	229,988	6.6

Source: Ministry of Labour, *Report on Monthly Labour Survey.*
[a] monthly.
[b] 1980 prices.

A further measure designed to stabilize wage rates has been a steady reduction in the government's procurement price for rice, South Korea's staple crop: there was a 25 per cent increase in 1980, but this figure dropped to zero in 1983, a slight 3 per cent rise in 1984, and 5.5 per cent rise in 1985.

Real estate speculation has also been targeted as an area for stabilization. With the exceptionally rapid expansion of Seoul during the 1960s and 1970s, speculation was rampant, especially on apartments in the newly developed residential districts in the south of the city. As a result, a great deal of domestically generated capital and savings were being siphoned off into non-productive sectors, to the detriment of the economy as a whole. The government has since cracked down on speculators, adjusting the tax structure and subjecting all real estate transactions to tough scrutiny. In addition, a law passed in 1982 and scheduled for implementation in 1986 will require full disclosure of all real estate holdings. While speculation continues, it appears to be less widespread than before; more important, housing prices seem to have stabilized as well.

The most ambitious and unique element of the government's stabilization programme, however, has been a nation-wide economic education campaign. The objective of this campaign has been to break the psychology of inflation through better understanding of the issues. The government perceived that it could not simply mandate an end to inflation, but rather had to convince the South Korean people of why price stability was in their own best interest and why certain painful measures were necessary in the short run to alleviate long-term tensions. This campaign has been promoted through television, newspapers, and other media; in addition, the basic concepts of the stabilization policy are being taught in schools. In this way, it is hoped that a general social awareness of the problems of inflation will arise, and that a consensus to solve these problems will develop.

2   Liberalization

In conjunction with its stabilization programme, the government has also been pursuing a wide-ranging policy of economic liberalization. Through a variety of internal and external reforms, the government is attempting to give more autonomy to the private sector while at the same time allowing market principles to play a larger role in the economy. As mentioned before, the government has long been the main actor in national economic affairs, and an important legacy of the first four Five-year Plans was the centralization of economic leadership. Under the liberalization policy, however, the government is deliberately removing itself from centre stage. Rather than tightly controlling the economy in a top-down fashion, the government is seeking to transform its role into one of a policeman, setting guidelines and intervening in the marketplace only as need demands. In many respects, this is a radical departure from South Korea's previous forms of economic management, but one which reflects the increased size and complexity of the South Korean economy.

A first element of the liberalization policy was the enactment in 1981 of the Anti-Monopoly and Fair Trade Act. This piece of legislation established the Fair Trade Administration as a bureau within the Economic Planning Board, South Korea's economic 'superministry'. Responsible for overseeing the activities of the nation's large business groups and reducing unfair trade practices, the Fair Trade Administration has a very important potential impact. It has the authority to counter monopolistic actions, but as conceived should not be required to exercise that authority very often. Rather, the Fair Trade Administration is meant to have a preventive effect—in other words, the existence of the organization will dissuade business from entering into monopolies.

South Korea's industrial policy has also undergone a very fundamental change as part of the liberalization effort. In the 1960s and 1970s, targeted sectors received preferential financing; under the liberalization programme, all subsidized 'policy' loans have been eliminated, and the government no longer targets certain areas of the economy for preferential financial treatment. Market forces increasingly dictate which sectors will prosper. This is obviously a significant change from South Korea's earlier growth strategy, but it reflects the reality that the subsidized loans policy had resulted in overinvestment in some industries, unbalanced industrial development, and an underdeveloped financial sector.

In this regard, liberalization of the financial sector is another key component of the government's current economic reforms. One of the first actions taken in this area was to denationalize the five commercial banks. Previously, the government was an absolute majority stockholder in all South Korean commercial banks, and while the government still holds a substantial percentage of bank equity, its influence over banking operations has diminished considerably. Furthermore, entry barriers for foreign banks have been lowered, which has increased competition and thus allocative efficiency. Foreign firms also have been given greater access to the South Korean securities market. A last element of financial sector liberalization, interest rate deregulation, has not yet been accomplished, however, as there are fears that this step would lead to a high rate of inflation. In view of this possibility, the move towards deregulation will be gradual.

The government has also been liberalizing the management of public enterprises. In an effort to lessen direct government intervention in such enterprises, boards of directors have been created to supervise operations. Government representatives still sit on the board of directors of public enterprises, but in general, management has become much more open. In addition, a performance evaluation system has been introduced for public enterprises. A bonus system linked to performance has been instituted, with incentives provided for those public enterprises which show signs of exceptional performance.

The most significant—and controversial—aspect of the liberalization programme, however, has been import liberalization. Again, import liberalization is designed to harness the market mechanism to improve the quality of South Korean products. During the 1960s and 1970s imports were tightly restricted, and consequently South Korean manufacturers faced little outside competition. Quality thus lagged behind the levels achieved in other countries, threatening South Korea's export-dependent economy. Import liberalization, by introducing foreign competition at a steadily increasing pace, is expected to pressure domestic producers to enhance both productivity and quality.

To be sure, this policy has encountered great domestic opposition, especially from the business sector. There is a widespread perception as well that import liberalization will have a negative effect on the balance of payments, an area in which South Korea has run steady deficits. Given the deteriorating state of the world trading system, however, the South Korean government felt that the only way to diffuse protectionist sentiment against South Korean products was to open the domestic market. Accordingly, the import liberalization ratio has risen from 68.2 per cent in 1980 to 87.7 per cent in 1985 and by 1986 will reach over 90 per cent—the level of most industrial countries. Tariff rates have been reduced concurrently, and in line with the government's goal of fostering a competitive domestic environment, foreign investment restrictions and regu-

TABLE 8.4 *Average tariff rates and the import liberalization ratio, 1978–1985 (percentages)*

	1978	1979	1980	1981	1982	1983	1984	1985
Import liberalization ratio	53.9	68.2	69.1	69.4	74.7	76.6	80.4	87.7
Tariff rate	38.7	24.9	24.9	24.9	23.7	23.7	21.9	21.3

Sources: Ministry of Commerce and Industry; Ministry of Finance.

lation have also been eased. Both the import liberalization and tariff figures are presented in Table 8.4.

3 Structural adjustment

In keeping with the changing pattern of global comparative advantage, South Korea is in the process of attempting to transform its industrial structure. As noted, in recent years South Korea's competitive edge in labour-intensive industries such as textiles and parts assembly has been eroding as other developing countries have become more advanced. At the same time, the pace of technological development in the industrial countries has been increasing, making it ever more difficult for South Korea to enter the high-growth technology market. These two factors, combined with South Korea's rapidly expanding work force, necessitate a fundamental change in the structure of the South Korean economy.

Science and technology form the basis of South Korea's structural adjustment policy. Indigenous technological innovation as well as adaptation of foreign technical advances are both being stressed, as are programmes to train scientific and technical manpower. In addition, by offering incentives and new opportunities to talented South Korean scientists educated in the developed countries, the South Korean government is attempting to reverse the brain drain that has plagued so many developing countries. Finally, scientific research institutions, such as the Korea Advanced Institute of Science and Technology (KAIST), have been upgraded and expanded. The combined effect of all these steps, it is hoped, will result in both higher quantity and quality of scientific manpower.

Other government efforts have been directed towards increasing public recognition of the importance of science and technology. A notable step to further this goal was the creation of the Science and Technology Promotion Council. Other measures to bolster the strength of domestic technology include tax and credit incentives granted to firms involved in scientific and technological research. Government research and development expenditures have been increasing as well, and the percentage of R & D to total GNP has risen dramatically in recent years. In 1978 only 0.63 per cent of GNP was directed towards domestic research and development, but in 1984 the figure reached 1.28 per cent and will continue to increase. Nonetheless, South Korea still lags far behind the developed countries in this respect—in the United States over 3 per cent of GNP is spent annually on R & D—and must allocate a greater proportion of its resources to research and development.

The focus on science and technology is designed to create a better environment in which smooth structural adjustment can take place. The liberalizing policies are in themselves conducive to structural adjustment, but will take time to have a real impact. The problem, however, is of the moment, and South Korea cannot wait for the liberalization programme to effect the necessary changes. Government packages of tax and credit incentives to assist companies in the early stages of adjustment to make a smooth transition have started, but much more needs to be done. Structural adjustment is a very urgent issue—both in South Korea and elsewhere—and deserves prompt and effective attention.

4 Social welfare

In the course of South Korea's industrialization drive of the 1960s and 1970s, improving the nation's social welfare system received relatively low government priority. Welfare functions were basically the responsibility of the people themselves; with GNP per capita rising rapidly and with South Korea's traditional extended family system, it was possible to direct attention towards other areas. Even so, considerable progress was made, both in health and education. The infant mortality rate fell from 80 in 1960 to 37 per 1,000 live births in 1980, while the death rate for children aged 1–4 declined even faster, i.e. from 9 per 1,000 in 1960 to 2 per 1,000 in 1980. School enrolment ratios also rose impressively: by 1980 they were over 100 per cent for primary schools and between 80 and 100 for secondary schools.

By 1980, however, social welfare was becoming an increasingly important issue as the nation became more urbanized and its people required more education. Motivated by these social pressures, the new government in 1980 emphasized as one of its primary goals the development of a welfare state. However, following a reassessment of national priorities, the government adopted a strategy to pursue social welfare policies in harmony with the other policy thrusts of stabilization, liberalization, and structural adjustment, which were deemed of greater short-term significance for the nation's economic health. To date, therefore, the government has not been very aggressive in fostering the 'welfare state', although it does recognize the long-term complementarity between economic growth and improved social welfare.

A number of programmes have been implemented, however, especially in the health and medical fields. In 1979, a medical assistance programme was organized so that members of the lowest income groups could receive medical care which they otherwise would have been unable to afford. At present, over

3 million people, or some 8 per cent of the population, are covered by this programme, which provides all medical services free to those below the poverty line who are unable to work. For those low-income persons able to work, the programme pays for 50 per cent of hospital costs and all out-patient expenses. Government expenditures for the medical assistance programme have grown rapidly, from 8.1 billion won in 1980 to 30.5 billion in 1984 (Table 8.5).

TABLE 8.5   *Medical insurance and aid, 1978–1985*

	Medical insurance		Medical aid		
	Eligible persons (000)	% of population	Expenditure (Wm)	Eligible persons (000)	% of population
1978	3,878	10.5	5,661	2,095	5.7
1979	7,791	20.7	6,718	2,134	5.7
1980	9,113	24.0	8,171	2,142	5.6
1981	11,406	29.5	16,952	3,728	9.6
1982	13,513	34.4	24,530	3,728	9.5
1983	15,577	39.0	30,516	3,728	9.4
1984	17,050	42.0	30,516	3,259	8.0
1985	17,580	43.4	—	3,259	8.0

Source: Ministry of Health and Social Affairs.

Furthermore, health insurance coverage has been extended significantly. Only 10.5 per cent of the population had health insurance in 1978, a year after the programme began, but by 1985 over 43.4 per cent were covered. This dramatic increase was brought about partially by government legislation which in 1979 made insurance compulsory for all government officials and school teachers. In 1980, further legislation extended coverage to all military dependents and in 1981 to pensioners and their dependents. Those in the poverty group have been covered under the medical assistance programme since its inception in 1977.

General assistance to the poverty group has also been expanded considerably. Those who are capable of working are given better chances at obtaining employment through expanded job opportunities and training, although direct transfer programmes are made available only to those who cannot work due to infirmity or age. In addition, the children of those in the low-income bracket are granted tuition exemptions for middle school and for vocational training institutes. A national pension scheme is also under review, with the timing and extent of such a scheme being considered.

Total government expenditures on welfare have shown a steadily increasing trend, especially during the 1970s. As a percentage of overall government outlays, welfare expenditures rose from 21.4 per cent in 1974 to almost 30 per cent during 1982–85. The largest component in this figure was education,

TABLE 8.6 *Trends in government social welfare expenditures, 1974 and 1978–1985*

	1974	1978	1979	1980	1981	1982	1983	1984	1985	Growth 1978–85 (%)
Social welfare expenditures (billion won)										
TOTAL	257.0	954.5	1,347.2	1,885.6	2,866.1	3,573.9	3,630.5	4,273.2	4,383.7	24.3
Education	154.7	605.0	863.0	124.4	1,465.6	1,980.5	2,188.6	2,258.1	2,479.3	22.3
Health	13.1	68.3	56.8	78.3	103.4	140.6	180.4	172.9	210.9	17.5
Social security	61.8	189.2	283.0	437.9	496.5	991.5	568.9	670.0	776.5	22.3
Housing	16.2	55.0	105.5	191.1	763.8	383.4	589.1	1,061.5	766.6	45.7
Others	11.2	37.0	38.9	53.0	56.8	77.9	103.5	110.7	150.4	22.2
As percentage of government expenditures										
TOTAL	21.4	21.7	22.5	24.5	28.1	30.7	29.8	31.8	29.9	
Education	12.9	13.7	14.4	14.6	14.4	17.0	17.9	16.8	16.9	
Health	1.1	1.5	0.9	1.0	1.0	1.2	1.5	1.3	1.4	
Social security	5.1	4.3	4.7	5.7	4.9	8.5	4.7	5.0	5.3	
Housing	1.3	1.2	1.8	2.45	7.5	3.3	4.8	7.9	5.2	
Others	0.9	0.4	0.6	0.7	0.6	0.7	0.8	0.8	1.0	

Source: Economic Planning Board.

which went from 13.7 per cent of total government expenditures in 1978 to about 17 per cent during 1982–85. Although this indicates an emphasis on indirect assistance, expenditures in other areas, notably housing, have also registered an increase. Table 8.6 contains a detailed breakdown of public welfare expenditures.

Two other social welfare policies are noteworthy. The Livelihood Protection Programme, based on the Livelihood Protection Act of 1961, provides basic assistance for those deemed absolutely poor. In-kind grants in the form of cereals are given to those unable to work, and cash assistance for fuel and tuition expenses is available. In 1982, about two million people, or some 5.4 per cent of the population, received benefits from the Livelihood Protection Programme. The other policy is the Community Primary Health Demonstration Project, initiated in 1975 designed to improve health and sanitation awareness and education, especially in rural areas. This project has helped extend the health care system into many regions where such services previously were scarce.

A more ambitious area of endeavour has been the government's efforts to address the problem of regional disparity. Rural household income has long lagged behind urban income, and the agricultural sector is widely recognized as one of the major constraints on the growth of the South Korean economy. In a move to raise the standard of living in remote rural areas, therefore, more off-farm employment opportunities are being created. Rural industrial complexes have been established in a number of regions, and several rural areas have been targeted for gradual industrial expansion.

A primary objective of this programme is to increase rural income without incurring the kind of urban migration that bloated the population of South Korea's urban centres during the early period of industrialization. In this regard, the government has also been studying ways to reduce the concentration of population in Seoul by stressing the development of other cities. The entire problem of regional development, however, remains a thorny issue. Many of these problems have not yet been adequately addressed, and the government harbours few illusions that they will be solved in the 1980s.

III Evaluation of current reforms and the impact on social welfare

1 Overall evaluation

In retrospect, the stabilization aspect of the government's reform programme has been fairly successful in achieving its goals. As seen in Table 8.7, the rate of increase in consumer prices declined rapidly, from 28.7 per cent in 1980 to only 2.5 per cent in 1985. Furthermore, current forecasts project that increases will remain at about this level in coming years, perhaps reflecting a break from the inflationary expectations of the past. Price stability has been accompanied

TABLE 8.7   *Price trends, 1978–1985*
(percentage rate of change 1980 = 100)

	1978	1979	1980	1981	1982	1983	1984	1985
Consumer prices	14.5	18.3	28.7	21.3	7.3	3.4	2.3	2.5
Wholesale prices	11.6	18.8	38.9	20.4	4.7	0.2	0.7	0.9

Source: Bank of Korea.

by a satisfactory recovery in the GNP growth rate, which recorded rises of 9.5 per cent and 7.5 per cent in 1983 and 1984, respectively. The balance of payments deficit has improved gradually as well, as shown by Table 8.8. From a high of $5.3 billion in deficit, the current balance dropped to just $0.9 billion, reflecting reduced energy prices and consumption as well as better export performance.

TABLE 8.8   *Balance of payments, 1978–1985 ($ million)*

	1978	1979	1980	1981	1982	1983	1984	1985
Trade balance	−1,781	−4,396	−4,384	−3,628	−2,594	−1,764	−1,036	−30
Current balance	−1,085	−4,151	−5,321	−4,646	−2,650	−1,606	−1,371	−882

Source: Bank of Korea.

In terms of social welfare, price stability seems to have had the most beneficial impact on urban workers. While the trend in nominal wages has been declining, real wages have risen (Table 8.3). In addition, price stability had bridged some of the income distribution gap by limiting opportunities for windfall profits in real estate and other speculative ventures. Indeed, the stabilization programme has come under attack from certain quarters precisely because such opportunities are no longer as profitable as they were during the period of high inflation. Price stability, and the concurrent fiscal and monetary belt-tightening, have rationalized the interest rate structure somewhat. Nonetheless, this issue has yet to be fully resolved, and accordingly a complete assessment of the stabilization policy will not be possible for some time.

It is also early to assess the success of the liberalization policy, although there has been steady progress on import liberalization (Table 8.4). The liberalization of the financial sector has yet to achieve substantial results, primarily because the government still controls the interest rate. However, deregulation of the interest rate will have to be a gradual process to avert the expected initial shock such an action would have. The current interest is high in real terms but due to the residual inflationary expectations in the economy, deregulation could bring about temporarily higher interest rates and thus hamper economic performance. As the stabilization programme has taken firm hold, though, movement on deregulation has begun in earnest, albeit at a slow pace.

In terms of foreign investment, liberalization seems to have had a very positive effect. After several years of relatively stagnant growth, including a 24 per cent drop in 1980, foreign investment expanded rapidly in 1984, making a 68.3 per cent increase over 1983 to reach $170.7 million. Figures for 1985 indicate a continuation of this trend (Table 8.9).

TABLE 8.9   *Foreign investment, 1978–1985*

	1978	1979	1980	1981	1982	1983	1984	1985
$m	100,457	126,977	96,635	105,448	100,598	101,434	170,708	250,325
% change	−1.8	26.4	−23.9	9.1	4.6	0.8	68.3	46.4

Source: Ministry of Commerce and Industry.

Nonetheless, the liberalization policy continues to receive criticism from those vested interests affected by import liberalization and the greater autonomy of the financial sector. The government thus needs to strengthen its efforts to educate the public and overcome domestic opposition. At the same time, this opposition has been a major factor in preventing the government from implementing liberalization as quickly or extensively as it would have wished.

Structural adjustment, however, remains the major issue facing the South Korean economy, and at present it is too early to evaluate the effectiveness of the government's programme in this area. A number of factors are complicating a smooth transformation of the industrial structure, not the least of which is the hesitancy of domestic producers to carry out adjustment measures. Much of this opposition has resulted from the low rate of inflation, which has driven up real interest rates to around 10 per cent in real terms. With high inflation and high growth in the past, businesses were able to borrow at negative real interest rates, and much of the expansion of South Korean industry in the sixties and seventies was funded in this manner. In addition, businesses invested a great deal of this borrowed money in the lucrative real estate speculation market rather than in upgrading their export products or efficiency.

Low inflation therefore, is a problem for South Korean business management, and the current period of adjustment and belt-tightening has elicited cries of protest from those most directly affected. Given the critical importance to South Korea of moving out of less competitive industries, however, it is clear that rather than complaining, the affected industries should buckle down to the task of adjustment. By waiting they are only hurting themselves—and the South Korean economy as a whole—in the long run. Again, at this stage, assessing the adjustment policy is difficult, but one can conclude that the somewhat lower growth figures of recent years are partially the result of business intransigence in following the government's lead.

2 Impact on social welfare

In assessing the impact of economic policy on social welfare, perhaps the most aggregate index is per capita GNP. As per capita income and real wages rise, there is a corresponding rise in the average quality of welfare, and the opposite holds true as well. In South Korea, per capita GNP in 1980 fell for the first time in 20 years, as seen in Table 8.1; in addition, real wages declined in both 1980 and 1981. The negative implications of these macro trends on welfare are clear. Since 1981, however, both per capita income and real wages have grown steadily, with the attendant positive effects on average welfare, as borne out by the micro indicators of welfare like height and weight of children, nutrition, and infant mortality (see below).

TABLE 8.10 *Income distribution, selected years*

	1965	1970	1976	1980	1984
All households	0.3439	0.3322	0.3908	0.3891	0.3567
Gini coefficient	19.34/	19.63/	16.85/	16.06/	18.86/
Decimal distribution ratio	41.81	41.62	45.34	45.39	42.28
Non-farm households	0.4167	0.3455	0.4118	0.4053	0.3655
Gina coefficient	14.05/	18.87/	15.36/	15.29/	18.40/
Decimal distribution ratio	46.95	43.09	48.70	46.89	43.53
Farm households	0.2852	0.2945	0.3273	0.3555	0.2992
Gina coefficient	22.57/	21.24/	19.45/	17.48/	21.36/
Decimal distribution ratio	38.03	38.64	40.62	42.19	37.92

Source: Korea Development Institute.

Overall income distribution is another means of determining the effect of the national economy on welfare. As seen in Table 8.10, South Korea's income distribution pattern showed a negative trend during the 1970s, caused both by the increasing wage disparities between skilled and unskilled workers and by the economic recession following the second oil crisis. The Gini coefficient for all households, for example, rose from 0.3322 in 1970 to 0.3908 in 1976 and 0.3891 in 1980. Furthermore, the ration of earnings by the bottom 40 per cent of the population to the top 20 per cent dropped during the same period. With economic recovery, however, the income distribution figures have improved somewhat, with the Gini coefficient dropping to 0.3567 in 1984. The improvement has been significant in both farm and non-farm households. Again, the correlation between overall economic performance and social welfare as measured by distribution of income appears obvious.

The improvement in income distribution since 1980 can be attributed mainly to the price stability in recent years. This trend towards stable prices has not only reduced opportunities for windfall profits in real estate and other speculative ventures, it has also ensured a steady rise of real incomes for wages and salary earners.

Looking at the lower end of the spectrum where social welfare needs are greatest, the incidence of absolute and relative poverty in South Korea conforms closely with the trend of per capita income and the pattern of income distribution. In the 1960s, both absolute and relative poverty declined to the point that in 1970, only 4.8 per cent of the total population were defined as relatively poor. During the 1970s, though, these figures rose dramatically, with 12.4 per cent and 13.3 per cent of the population being relatively poor in 1976 and 1980, respectively. With the economic recovery of the early 1980s and a favourable trend in income distribution, relative poverty again seems to be on the decline, with the 1984 figures indicating that relative poverty has fallen to 7.7 per cent (Table 8.11). Absolute poverty, on the other hand, has seen a steady decline, even in 1980. This is most likely attributable to the nation-wide increase in per capita GNP and other effects of sustained economic growth.

TABLE 8.11   *Trends in the incidence of poverty, selected years (percentages)*

	1965	1970	1976	1980	1982	1984
Absolute poverty[a]	40.9	23.4	14.8	9.8	7.7	4.5
Urban	54.9	16.2	18.1	10.4	8.2	4.6
Rural	35.8	27.9	11.7	9.0	7.0	4.4
Relative poverty[b]	12.2	4.8	12.5	13.3	11.8	7.7
Urban	17.9	7.0	16.0	15.1	12.7	7.8
Rural	10.0	3.4	9.2	11.2	10.5	7.5

Source: Korea Development Institute.
[a] Absolute poverty line defined as 121,000 won in 1981 prices per month for a five-member family.
[b] Relative poverty line defined as one-third of the average household income in a given year.

A detailed micro analysis of the social welfare implications of macro-economic performance is difficult for the South Korean case because of the lack of adequate statistics. This holds especially true for indicators of children's welfare. Within the constraints of the data, though, certain trends appear. In general, during the recessionary period of 1979–81, overall welfare deteriorated, while over the past three years of economic recovery, conditions have improved.

Health statistics are among the more reliable indicators of this trend. As a broad measure, average household expenditures on health have been increasing, both in absolute terms and as a percentage of total household expenditures. As late as 1974, for example, only 2.6 per cent of urban household expenditure was spent on health services, while in 1984 this figure was 5.9 per cent. It is noteworthy, however, that during the recession of 1979–80, the percentage increases were very small, rising from 5.2 per cent in 1979 to 5.3 per cent in 1980 (Table 8.12). Another broad measure of health services, the ratio of doctors and nurses to total population, is somewhat less conclusive, rising during the early 1970s to a peak in 1974 at 1,879 persons per physician, but declining steadily since then to 1,284 in 1984. Persons per nurse, on the contrary, declined steadily from 1,309 in 1971 to 277 in 1984 (*Yearbook of Public Health and Social Statistics*). A factor influencing the temporary dislocation in doctors per person may have been the increase in South Korea's population during the period, which has been offset in recent years by the continued effort to train medical personnel.

TABLE 8.12   *Household health expenditure, 1976–1984*

	Urban households		Farm households	
	Annual Health Expenditure (won)	% of household expenditure	Annual Health Expenditure (won)	% of total household expenditure
1976	46,692	4.5	26,841	3.6
1977	49,188	4.3	41,383	4.2
1978	70,260	4.6	60,615	4.6
1979	108,636	5.2	75,170	4.5
1980	173,016	5.3	95,895	4.4
1981	174,912	5.7	117,341	4.4
1982	210,852	5.9	166,335	5.1
1983	235,296	5.9	213,027	5.3
1984	255,996	5.9	219,271	5.1

Sources: Economic Planning Board, *The Family Income and Expenditure Survey;* Ministry of Agriculture and Fisheries, *The Farm Household Economy Survey.*

TABLE 8.13   *Per capita daily calorie and protein intake, 1977–1984*

	Average daily calories	Protein (grams)	Beef (grams)
1977	2,427	73.9	6.0
1978	2,533	73.8	8.5
1979	2,599	76.2	8.2
1980	2.485	73.6	7.1
1981	2,531	76.9	6.6
1982	2,588	78.3	7.4
1983	2,595	79.5	7.9
1984	2,610	79.8	7.2

Source: Korea Rural Economics Institute, *Food Balance Sheet;* National Livestock Co-operative Federation.

In terms of nutrition, the impact of the 1980 economic downturn is very evident. Average daily calorie intake fell from 2,599 in 1979 to 2,458 in 1980.

Indeed, even as late as 1983, calorie intake had not recovered its pre-recession levels. As for protein consumption, intake dropped from 76.2 grams daily in 1979 to 73.6 grams in 1980. Daily beef consumption witnessed a sharp plunge from 1979 to 1980, falling from 8.2 grams in 1979 to 7.1 grams in 1980 and even further to 6.6 grams in 1981 (Table 8.13). All of these declines were far steeper than any previous negative changes in these indices over the past 15 years, reflecting the seriousness of the recession and the direct correlation between economic conditions and as basic an area as food consumption.

A measure of dietary sufficiency may also be found in the data on the average height and weight of school children. While these figures have been rising gradually throughout the period of rapid development, the rate of increase from 1979 to 1980 was very slow. In the cases of male children aged 9 and 12 there was even a slight decrease in average weight. In terms of height, the average increase for 12-year olds from 1979 to 1980 was 0.3 centimetres for boys and 0.4 centimetres for girls. By contrast, from 1980 to 1981, the average increase was 1.1 centimetres for boys and 0.9 centimetres for girls (Tables 8.14 and 8.15). The interpretation of such data, however, is far from simple, and it is not evident that the variations observed can unambiguously be attributed to the economic changes of these years rather than to cohort effects and/or other factors. To arrive at such conclusions, a much more sophisticated analysis would be required.

Other important indicators of social welfare are the infant and maternal mortality rates. From 1976 to 1979, infant mortality per 1,000 births fell from 40.4 to 37.6, while in 1980 the figure was 36.8—a slower rate of decline than either before or since. More revealing are the maternal mortality rates, which dropped from 5.0 per 1,000 births in 1976 to 4.2 in 1979. In 1980, this figure remained constant, before falling slightly in 1981 and 1982. In 1984, the maternal mortality rate was down to 3.6 (Table 8.16).

IV Conclusions

From the South Korean experience during the 1980 recession, it is clear that social welfare is directly affected by general economic conditions. In particular, per capita income and income distribution patterns—both dependent on the national economy—determine all major trends in welfare conditions. In South Korea, per capita GNP had made tremendous advances, yet in the one year of negative growth—1980—a distinct drop in most social welfare indicators is discernable. In this regard, the so-called 'linkage effect' definitely applies to the South Korean case. While a lack of statistical data makes an exact evaluation of the linkage effect difficult, there can be no doubt of the linkage between the macro-economic situation and welfare.

This linkage notwithstanding, poverty, health, and nutrition of the population, and of children in particular, continued to improve (if at reduced rates) even during 1980 and 1981, when real wages fell considerably and employment

TABLE 8.14   *Average weight of students, 1977–1984 (kilograms)*

	Age 6		Age 9		Age 12	
	Male	Female	Male	Female	Male	Female
1977	19.4	18.7	25.9	25.8	35.1	37.0
1978	19.7	19.7	25.9	25.8	35.1	37.4
1979	19.8	19.2	26.6	25.9	35.7	37.8
1980	20.1	19.2	26.8	26.3	36.4	38.1
1981	20.3	19.4	27.2	26.4	36.4	38.3
1982	20.1	19.5	27.4	26.7	36.7	38.7
1983	20.3	19.5	27.5	26.8	37.3	38.7
1984	20.4	19.7	27.5	27.1	37.8	39.5

Source: Ministry of Education.

TABLE 8.15   *Average height of students, 1977–1984 (centimetres)*

	Age 6		Age 9		Age 12	
	Male	Female	Male	Female	Male	Female
1977	114.2	112.9	128.8	129.7	143.8	145.1
1978	114.2	113.1	129.1	129.4	143.8	144.6
1979	114.6	113.8	129.4	128.6	143.9	146.1
1980	115.0	113.7	129.9	129.4	144.2	146.5
1981	115.4	114.5	130.8	130.1	145.3	147.4
1982	115.5	114.6	131.2	130.4	145.5	147.7
1983	116.0	114.8	131.2	130.4	146.4	147.9
1984	116.4	115.4	131.4	130.4	146.8	148.4

Source: Ministry of Education.

TABLE 8.16   *Infant and maternal mortality rates, 1976–1984*

	1976	1977	1978	1979	1980	1981	1982	1983	1984
Infant mortality rate (per 1,000 live births)	40.4	39.5	38.5	37.6	36.8	35.8	35.0	34.2	33.3
Maternal mortality rate per 10,000 persons)	5.0	4.6	4.3	4.2	4.2	4.1	4.0	3.8	3.6

Source: Ministry of Health and Social Affairs, *Yearbook of Public Health and Social Statistics.*

opportunities declined. During this period, social policy was deliberately used for buffering the poor from the adversities of economic recession. While previous programmes such as Medical Insurance, Medical Aid and Livelihood Protection, among others, were substantially expanded, new schemes were introduced with the specific purpose of sustaining the incomes, health, and nutrition of the lower segment of the population. Among such schemes, the Public Work Programme and the Community Primary Health Demonstration Project were of a particularly innovative nature.

With its outward-oriented economy, South Korea would seem very susceptible to the 'multiplier effect'—the concept that a small downturn in the advanced economies causes a big decline in less advanced industrial countries and an even bigger one in developing nations. To be sure, recession in the advanced industrial countries has a negative impact on the South Korean economy, and if left to market mechanisms, doubtless this impact could be potentially disastrous. However, there is also a policy variable in dealing with the multiplier effect: during the initial phases of a recession, the government has the option to increase public expenditure to sustain aggregate demand and, in this way, to stimulate the economy. In 1981, for example, South Korea raised spending on the poor, especially in rural areas, and thus used both macro-economic and welfare policies to offset the anticipated adverse effects of the recession. While such an expansionary policy is of course sustainable for only a short period, from the South Korean example, one can see that the multiplier effect need not be devastating if the government intervenes with appropriate policies at a correct time.

Finally, with respect to the time lag between recession in advanced countries and the negative impact on developing countries, South Korea seems to be an exception to the rule. This may be explained in part by the openness of the South Korean economy. Because South Korea is heavily dependent on international trade, when the world economy recovers, the South Korean economy recovers as well. Furthermore, South Korea responded to the global recession of the early 1980s with an aggressive macro-economic policy. While somewhat constrained by the balance of payments situation, in 1982 in particular, the government expanded employment possibilities with low import requirements. Thus, the government was able to create enough domestic demand to give the economy the impetus needed to pull out of the recession, and indeed the South Korean economy recovered more quickly than did the industrialized countries. While this solution may be unique to South Korea, the nation's experience in coping with the multiplier effect and the time-lag problem suggests that sound management policies can do much to mitigate the effects of world recession.

9

Sri Lanka: The Social Impact of Economic Policies during the Last Decade

UNICEF, Colombo

I Economic reforms and adjustment policies

From independence and even before, Sri Lanka was committed to maintaining a welfare state with three major social policies: a food subsidy, an entirely free education system, and a free health care service on a universal basis. In the 1970s Sri Lanka emerged as an outstanding example of a developing country whose level of social progress was high in relation to the per capita income of the country.

Sri Lanka's impressive achievements on the social front, however, were accompanied by a relatively low rate of growth of the country's national income. The universal nature of the welfare services involved increasing the budget as the population grew and inflation rose. Low per capita income and the inability to generate budget surpluses restricted savings capacity, resulting in a low rate of investment. Thus, while the social policies of Sri Lanka contributed to human capital development there was not the corresponding growth in physical capital formation which was vital to enhance both pro-ductive and labour absorptive capacities of the country.

From the late 1950s Sri Lanka faced continuous and chronic balance of payments problems. In response to these difficulties successive governments introduced exchange and import controls and measures to direct invest-ments towards import substitution. Two decades of these measures failed to resolve the balance of payments problems and led to economic stagnation and very high rates of unemployment. Adjustment policies were required to restore the viability of the economy and improve the efficiency of resource utilization.

The government of Sri Lanka introduced a new set of economic policies from November 1977. This package of fundamental policy changes aimed at transforming the Sri Lankan economy from an inward-looking, closed, and controlled economy to an outward-looking economy with a heavy market orientation.

Exchange rate reform was one of the main elements of the new policy package. A more realistic exchange rate and a rationalized tariff structure replaced the system of quotas, licences, and controls. The policies also aimed at ending public sector monopolies in a large range of items. Price controls were abolished and subsidies were phased out. The policy was in line with the government's attempt to shift resources from consumption to investment through budgetary savings resulting from the curtailment of subsidies.

The need to encourage exports and diversify the export structure was emphasized. The government recognized the need to expand and improve infrastructure facilities, to promote export-oriented activities, industrialization, and private investment. Accordingly, economic overheads—transport, tele-communication, and energy—occupied an important place in the investment programmes.

Efforts were also directed to ensuring adequate producer incentives for domestic agricultural production. Agricultural pricing policy and input sub-sidies were geared to maintaining adequate producer margins. The govern-ment decided to maintain a modified form of the food subsidy programme and an income support scheme to assist the needy segment of the population in the short run until such time as production and income effects of the new policies became widespread and percolated to the masses in general.

The investment strategy of the government was to embark on capital-intensive, capacity-expanding projects with a long gestation period. Tax ben-efits, liberalized trading and other investment incentives were granted to the private sector, which was expected to play a more important role.

II Macro-economic performance

Sri Lanka's macro-economic performance during the period 1978–84 reflects the impact of the economic policy reforms. The rate of growth of GDP doubled in real terms, averaging over 6 per cent per year during 1978–84 as against an annual average of 2.9 per cent in 1970–77. After allowing for population growth, per capita GDP registered an annual average growth rate of 4.3 per cent per year. However, due to unfavourable trends in the country's net factor income from abroad, GNP grew more slowly than GDP, at 4.7 per cent per year in real terms. Despite a cumulative growth of GNP of 27 per cent over the period 1978–84, per capita income in Sri Lanka in 1984, at $340, was still rather low by international standards. Hence, even if such a growth rate were sustained, it would not be sufficient to make a significant impact on poor income groups in the medium term. Therefore, the current emphasis on rapid and sustained economic growth needs to be supplemented with appropriate social programmes targeted to benefit the vulnerable.

The acceleration of the economy following the policy reform of 1977 was assisted by a substantial increase in investment activity (Table 9.1). Invest-ment, which stagnated at an annual average of 16 per cent of GDP prior to 1978, reached a peak of 34 per cent in 1980 and averaged 28 per cent during the period 1978–84. However, the domestic savings ratio, which was below 13 per cent during the period 1970–77, made a modest improvement in 1978 and

TABLE 9.1   *Trends in selected economic variables, 1970–1977 and 1978–1984*

	1970–77 (Annual average)	1978	1984	1978–84 (Annual average)
1. Population growth rate (%)	1.6	1.8	1.2	1.8
2. Economic growth rate (real GDP, %)	2.9	8.2	5.1	6.1
3. Per capita growth rate (%)	1.3	6.4	3.9	4.3
4. Investment as % of GDP	16.0	20.0	26.1	27.7
5. Savings as % of GDP	12.7	15.5	23.2	16.9
6. Current account budget deficit/surplus as % of GDP	+2.4	+2.4	+3.9	+3.9
7. Overall budget deficit/surplus as % of GDP	−13.7	−13.7	−10.0	−10.5
8. Increase in money supply narrow (%)	34.0[a]	10.6	14.0	17.9
broad (%)	35.5[a]	24.9	16.6	25.9
9. Exchange rate (Rupees per SDR)	10.42[b]	19.47	26.08	—
10. Change in wholesale price index (% per annum)	—	15.8	26.0	—
11. Change in consumer price index	—	12.1	16.3	18.0
12. Export volume index (1978 = 100)	—	100.0	127.0	—
13. Import volume index (1978 = 100)	—	100.0	185.0	—
14. Terms of trade change (%)	—	−7.1	18.7	−3.3
15. Current account balance in balance of payments as % of GDP	+3.0	+3.0	−0.1	−0.7
16. Debt service ratio (as % of exports of goods and services)	—	15.5	17.2	—
17. Unemployment rate (%)	24.0[c]	—	—	11.7[d]

Source: Central Bank of Ceylon.
[a] 1974–77.
[b] Nov. 1977.
[c] 1973.
[d] 1982.

then stabilized at an average of 17 per cent over 1978–84. A sizeable share of investment activity therefore had to be financed by external sources, and the country's dependence on foreign assistance since 1978 has been rather heavy (Table 9.2). The ability to sustain the high momentum of growth in the years to come will depend on the ability to enhance domestic savings. National savings were greatly assisted by a considerable inflow of foreign exchange remittances from Sri Lankan workers in the Middle East, enabling the overall savings ratio to rise to 23.2 per cent in 1984. The lack of growth of domestic savings coupled with the ambitious public investment programme pursued since 1978 entailed both budgetary and balance of payment deficits, which in turn contributed to inflationary pressures in the economy.

The positive performance of the economy between 1978 and 1984 was due to growth in a number of sectors including domestic agriculture, construction, trade and transport (Table 9.3). Domestic agriculture grew at about 5 per cent per annum, mainly due to significant improvements in paddy production, which has enabled the country to come close to self-sufficiency in rice. Trade and transport activities, in particular, accelerated, and the services sector as a whole registered a growth rate of more than 7 per cent per annum.

Despite the satisfactory growth rate achieved in domestic agriculture, there were several problems in the input delivery system. This was particularly so for credit for small farmers—in all, there was a drastic reduction in institutional credit to the rural sector. The interest rate reform which formed a main element of the adjustment policies exerted a further burden on the rural sector through the increased cost of borrowing. Hence the enhanced prices for agricultural products may not have percolated through the farm gate uniformly among farmers. Small size of land holding and increased cost of cultivation due to higher input prices were among the major constraints to improving conditions of the subsistence farmers. In this context it is important to devise innovative approaches to rural credit if the benefits of irrigation facilities, land development, newer technology, and better agricultural prices are to accrue to the majority of the rural poor.

Despite the fact that adjustment policies have been in effect for over seven years, the structure of Sri Lanka's economy has not undergone significant changes (Table 9.3). The economy remains predominantly agricultural and service oriented, with a thin and heavily import-dependent manufacturing sector. The share of the industrial sector still remains around 14 per cent of GDP. The small, labour-intensive industrial sector faded away due to the pressure of competition from imports and has not been replaced by a sound industrial structure based on the principle of comparative advantage. Similarly, there has not been an appreciable growth in export-oriented manufacturing activities, while even in the case of industries which have shown some progress local value-added has been rather low. It is vital to strengthen and diversify the production sectors of the economy to ensure rapid and sustained growth in the long run.

Much of the investment activity during the period 1978–1984 was the result of a vigorous public investment programme which was responsible for almost 60 per cent of investment outlay. The private sector has not contributed adequately, particularly in the field of manufacturing and industrial activities. Given the recent ethnic disturbances, prospective investors, both foreign and domestic, have adopted a rather cautious attitude towards committing resources for medium- and long-term projects.

The sustenance and success of an open economy depends on the performance of exports and behaviour of the balance of payments (Table 9.4). The marginal

TABLE 9.2   *Capital formation and investment financing, 1970–1977 and 1978–1984*

	1970–1977 (averages)	1978	1984	1978–1984 (averages)
Gross domestic investment (Rs. million)	3,523	8,554	39,850	24,954
National savings (Rs. million)	2,799	6,622	34,337	15,182
Investment savings gap (Rs. million)	724	1,932	5,513	9,772
Investment as % of GDP	16.0	20.0	26.3	27.7
Savings as % of GDP	12.7	15.5	22.7	16.9
Foreign financing as % of gross domestic investment	20.5	22.6	13.7	39.0
Private investment as % of gross domestic investment	51.9	40.5	39.9	40.1
Public investment as % of gross domestic investment	48.1	59.5	60.1	59.9

Source: Central Bank of Ceylon and the Ministry of Finance and Planning.

TABLE 9.3   *Sectoral growth rates of the economy, 1971–1977 and 1978–1984 (percentages, constant 1970 prices)*

	1971–1977 (annual)	1978–1984 (annual)	Value added as % of GDP	
			1977	1984
Agriculture	2.1	3.9	26.7	23.2
Plantation crops	−1.7	0.3	6.5	4.4
Domestic agriculture	3.5	5.1	20.2	18.8
Mining and quarrying	27.1	6.7	3.2	3.3
Manufacturing	1.0	5.1	14.6	13.7
Construction	−2.6	7.4	3.8	4.2
Services	3.7	7.3	51.5	55.7
Gross domestic product	2.9	6.1	100.0	100.0

Source: Annual Reports of the Central Bank and Ministry of Finance and Planning.

growth rate in exports compared with the rapid rise in imports since 1978 resulted in strains in the balance of payments. In real terms the level of export earnings doubled during the 1978–84 period, while import payments trebled. This rapid growth of imports was accompanied by a change in the composition of imports, with a greater concentration on intermediate and investment goods. The share of consumption goods diminished from 43 per cent in 1977 to 19 per cent in 1984.

The high degree of vulnerability of the economy to changes in the inter-

TABLE 9.4 *Balance of payments performance, selected years (SDR millions)*

		1978	1980	1982	1984
1.	Exports	675	818	918	1,439
2.	Imports	819	1,576	1,808	1,864
3.	Trade balance	− 144	− 752	− 890	− 425
4.	Services	6	40	− 16	− 60
	Receipts	99	214	303	330
	Payments	93	174	319	390
5.	Goods and services (net) (i.e. 3+4)	− 138	− 718	− 906	− 485
6.	Private transfers	17	105	240	270
7.	Current account balance (i.e. 5+6)	121	− 613	− 666	− 215
8.	Financing				
	Grants	46	106	147	150
	Direct investment	1	33	58	35
	Other private long term (net)	7	33	182	− 29
	Central government (net)	125	125	231	321
	Short term (net)	0	115	0	—
	SDR allocation	0	12	0	—
9.	Overall balance	65	− 166	− 24	297
10.	Debt service ratio (as % of exports of goods and services)	15.5	13.3	18.6	17.2

Source: Central Bank of Ceylon and the Ministry of Finance and Planning.

national economic scene, such as fluctuations in commodity prices, deterioration in terms of trade, and the protectionist trade policies of the industrial countries, is another major area of concern. Therefore, the prospects for a high growth scenario for the second half of this decade need to be carefully reviewed.

There were unprecedented rates of inflation in 1978–84 due mainly to large budget deficits and depreciation of the exchange rate. The removal of price controls, phasing out of consumer subsidies, and resort to market pricing reinforced the upward trend in prices.

The migration of approximately 200,000 (as at end 1984) of mainly semi-skilled and unskilled labourers to the Middle East not only relieved the pressure for job creation but also enabled the country to obtain a sizeable amount of foreign exchange as inward remittances (approximately $280 million or more than 7,000 million rupees in 1984). This source of employment and foreign exchange is likely to weaken with the fall of the world oil price.

The reliance on market forces tends to lend itself to income inequalities. The trend towards greater equality in income distribution which was evident during the 1953–73 period was reversed in 1978/79 and 1981/82. The Gini coefficient has risen from 0.35 in 1973 to 0.44 in 1978/79 and further to 0.45 in 1981/82 for spending units. Similarly, the share of the income of the bottom 40 per cent has declined from 19.3 in 1973 to 16.1 in 1978/79 and further to 15.3 by 1981/82 (see pp. 251–4). The fruits of rapid growth appear to have been distributed rather unequally. This should not cause too much concern if the mean income of poorer groups increased in real terms after allowing for inflation. The evidence, however, suggests that there has been a deterioration in the real income of the poorest deciles, even causing reductions in their food consumption.

III   The effects of policies on real income and employment

This part assesses the impact of recent economic policies on prices, wages, employment, and unemployment, real incomes, and income distribution.

1   An analysis of price changes

Price increases were moderate prior to 1977 as inflationary pressures were somewhat suppressed by price controls and rationing. In contrast, after 1977 inflation accelerated.

Prices were affected by several policies. The first of these is the change in the exchange rate of November 1977, followed by a progressive depreciation of the rupee (Table 9.1). Secondly, prices were affected by changes in policies with respect to subsidies and particularly the prices of basic commodities, termed 'administered prices'. The change in subsidies for basic items like rice, wheat flour, bread, and sugar coupled with the depreciation of the rupee and a pricing policy based on the full cost of the commodity resulted in higher prices of all these commodities. Thirdly, the influx of considerable foreign funds for development work generated increased money incomes for those who provided services for these projects, without a commensurate increase in production of goods and services in the short term. Consequently, there was upward pressure on prices. There was also a rapid increase in money supply in the post-1978 period (Table 9.1).

Since commodity prices rose at different rates, the rate of inflation varies according to the price index adopted.

(a) The Colombo Consumer Price Index (CCPI) Price increases on the Colombo index 1977–84 varied from 30 per cent (chillies) to 733 per cent (kerosene). The price of open market rice increased by 158 per cent, wheat flour by 386 per cent, bread by 339 per cent, and milk powder by 345 per cent. The fact that import and export commodity prices increased much more than domestically produced commodities implies that the depreciation of the rupee had a significant effect on the post-1977 inflation.

The CCPI (which uses on the 1953 consumers' expenditure pattern as weights) indicates a very low rate of inflation from 1975 to 1977. The index increased at over 10 per cent per year in 1978 and 1979. The lower rate of inflation prior to 1977 is mainly due to price controls and rationing which would have resulted in a degree of suppressed inflation. The price increases reached a peak of 26 per cent in 1980. There was an increasing trend in prices again in 1983 (14 per cent) and 1984 (17 per cent).

TABLE 9.5 *Colombo consumer price index (CCPI), 1975–1983 (1977 = 100)*

	All items	Food	Clothing	Fuel and light	Rent	Miscel- laneous	Average annual rate of increase
1975	97.6	100.5	93.0	92.1	100	92.1	7
1976	98.8	99.4	103.0	103.0	100	97.8	1
1977	100.0	100.0	100.0	100.0	100	100.0	1
1978	112.1	116.8	101.1	101.8	100	107.9	12
1979	124.2	129.5	103.3	127.6	100	121.0	11
1980	156.6	167.1	107.2	219.0	100	141.0	26
1981	184.7	196.6	115.2	298.2	100	165.9	18
1982	204.8	221.5	122.3	317.0	100	181.0	11
1983	272.2	294.1	137.4	498.1	100	238.4	17
% change 1977–84	172	194	37	398	0	138	—

Source: Department of Census and Statistics.

The breakdown of the index by commodity groups given in Table 9.5 indicates that food items increased faster than the total with an increase of nearly 200 per cent, and fuel and light by nearly 400 per cent. The increase of clothing prices was modest, at 37 per cent.

(b) The Special Consumer Price Index (SPCI) The SCPI shown in Table 9.6 uses the 1973 expenditure pattern[1] of spending units in Colombo City whose incomes were below 500 rupees per month (79 per cent of the spending units in Colombo). This index eliminates some of the biases in the CCPI, which uses a 1953 consumption pattern, and the SCPI is also more relevant to low-income households. The prices used in the index were obtained from Colombo markets. This index discloses a 226 per cent increase in prices between 1977–84. The highest increase was in 1980, when prices rose by as much as 46 per cent. The increases in recent years (1982–84) have been similar to those in the CCPI.

A comparison of the two indices is given in Table 9.6 and Fig. 9.1. While the CCPI indicates price increases of around 180 per cent, the SCPI indicates increases of over 300 per cent in the last decade.

TABLE 9.6   *Comparison of price trends according to different indices, 1975–1984 (1975 = 100)*

	CCPI	Annual change (%)	Special consumer index (SCPI)	Annual change (%)
1975	100.0	7	100.0	6
1976	101.2	1	106.6	7
1977	102.4	1	123.9	16
1978	114.8	12	135.5	9
1979	127.2	11	154.1	14
1980	160.4	26	224.4	26
1981	189.1	18	278.4	24
1982	209.7	11	309.6	11
1983	239.0	14	345.2	11
1984	278.7	17	403.9	17

2 Analysis of wages

The behaviour of wages is an important indicator of the welfare of the working population because it mainly affects the less affluent sections of the population. About two-thirds of the employed are in the unorganized sector, which includes small-scale agriculture, self-employed, casual labour, and other employment outside the government service, public corporations, and institutionalized private-sector businesses. This analysis concentrates on the lower and middle-wage income groups, analysing wages in both the organized and unorganized sectors.

The minimum wage rate indices used here have many deficiencies, as they cover only trades which have Wages Boards (about 40 per cent of employment in the organized private sector) and include only the minimum wage rate, while actual payments would tend to be higher because of overtime payments, service charges, and bonuses. Since they are the only systematic data available, however, they are used for this analysis.

(a) Organized sector The organized sector can be divided into three sub-sectors—the government, school teachers, and those trades in the private sector and corporations which are governed by Wages Boards.

When real wages are calculated by deflating nominal wages by the CCPI, which does not reflect price increases adequately, real wages in the private sector and for school teachers declined and government sector real wages improved slightly in 1984 compared to 1978. However, when the wage indices are deflated by the SCPI, a sharp deterioration is seen in real wages of workers in Wages Board trades, all central government employees, and government

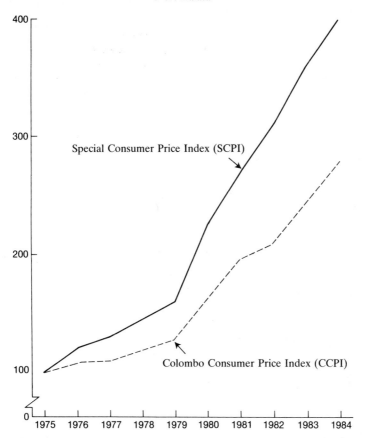

Source: UNICEF—Sri Lanka (1985)

Fig. 9.1　Sri Lanka: prices indices, 1975–1984

teachers (Fig. 9.2). Even the real wages of all workers in agriculture declined in 1984 compared to 1978.

(b) Unorganized sector In the unorganized sector, where wages are more flexible and data on other aspects of employment are scanty, the trend in wage rates is a good indicator of the level of economic activity, income levels, employment, and the viability of enterprises. But data (from the country-wide data collection system of the Central Bank) on wage rates for the unorganized sector are only available since the latter part of 1978; this includes small-holding cultivations of tea, rubber, coconut, and paddy, and building construction activities.

On the basis of price increases in the CCPI, real wage rates improved in all sectors, except female wages in rubber cultivation and male wages in tea

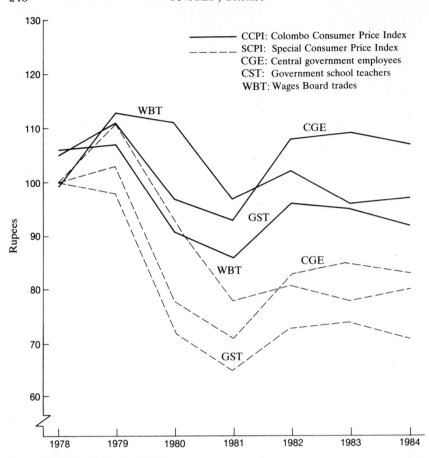

Source: UNICEF—Sri Lanka (1985)

Fig. 9.2   Sri Lanka: real wage rate indices, 1978–1984

cultivation. When the nominal wages are deflated by the SCPI there is a deterioration in the real wages among all categories of workers in all sectors in most years. The biggest deterioration in real wages was in tea and rubber cultivation and the least in paddy cultivation and construction (Figs 9.3 and 9.4). In fact, it may be argued that if a more appropriate index based on relevant consumption patterns and prices is used real incomes may not have deteriorated in these activities.

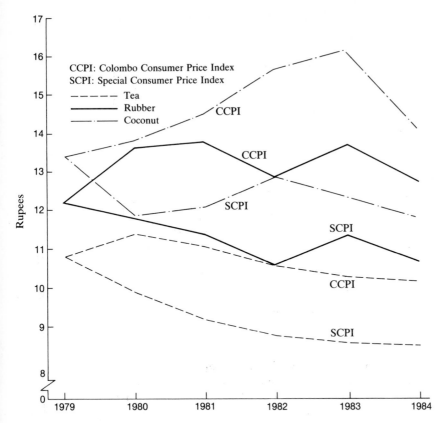

CCPI: Colombo Consumer Price Index
SCPI: Special Consumer Price Index
------- Tea
———— Rubber
—·—— Coconut

Source: UNICEF—Sri Lanka (1985)

Fig. 9.3 Sri Lanka: real daily wages (male) in tea, rubber, and coconut, 1979–1984

3 Employment and unemployment

One of the important strategies of the new economic policies was to increase employment. Job-related income was to compensate for the removal of the subsidies. The Mahaweli Accelerated Project, the Urban Renewal Programme, the investments in the Free Trade Zone and under the Foreign Investment Advisory Committee were among the projects expected to generate new employment opportunities.

There is strong evidence that the very high rate of unemployment in the early 1970s has been abated by the measures taken. All-island unemployment, which had reached 24 per cent in 1973, was reduced to 11.7 per cent in 1981/82. In all sectors, the rate of unemployment was cut by at least half during this period. The most conspicuous drop in unemployment was in the estate sector, where unemployment fell from a high of 12 per cent in 1973 to 5 per cent in 1981/82 (Table 9.7).

TABLE 9.7 *Unemployment as a percentage of work force, 1973, 1978/79, and 1981/82*

	1973	1978/1979	1981/1982
Sector			
Urban	32.1	20.7	14.2
Rural	24.5	14.6	12.0
Estate	12.0	5.6	5.0
All island	24.0	14.7	11.7
Age			
14–18	65.8	30.7	30.8
19–25	47.5	31.1	28.8
26–35	15.2	13.1	8.8
36–45	3.9	2.7	1.7
46–55	1.2	0.8	0.5
Over 55	0.8	0.2	0.4
All ages	24.0	14.8	11.2

Source: Consumer Finance Surveys, Central Bank of Ceylon.

The information on rates of unemployment is supported by data on employment: employment in the formal sector increased by around 315,000, or 24 per cent, during the period 1977 to 1983. A substantial portion of employment generation is likely to be in the unorganized sector. The new economic opportunities generated new employment in the rural sector as well as in large numbers of small private sector enterprises. A clear example is the employment generated in private transport and wholesale and retail trades, which by and large is not reflected in official statistics. Such business enterprises, for the most part, do not contribute to the Employment Provident Fund, often have a high turnover, and employ a large amount of casual labour. The economic growth rate of 6 per cent per annum on average during the period 1977–84 and the fact that several sectors in which growth occurred were in the unorganized sector support the view that employment generated during the period has been much higher than that indicated in formal sector statistics.

Despite these improvements in the overall employment situation, unemployment continues to be a major problem in the economy. Three features should be considered. Given a youthful population, the number entering the labour force every year is estimated at about 125,000. Therefore, while the rate of unemployment is being reduced, the number unemployed continues to be very high. In 1984 the number unemployed in the country, at the same rate of unemployment as in 1981/82, may be estimated at around 650,000.

Secondly, it is very clear that unemployment among youth is serious. In fact, unemployment decreased in all age-groups except the 14–18-year age group where it has remained more or less static at 31 per cent. In the 19–25-year age-group the rate of unemployment was as high as 28 per cent. Unemployment rates for the age groups above 36 years were relatively insignificant (Table 9.7).

Thirdly, the problem of unemployment continues to be one of finding jobs for those with secondary education and above. Nearly 10 per cent of those who were unemployed had an education of secondary level and above. Nearly 25 per cent of those with GCE O level and nearly 35 per cent of those with GCE A level are unemployed (Table 9.8). This high rate of educated unemployed is particularly significant for social and political stability.

Some factors have ameliorated the unemployment situation. First the large exodus of persons in the work force for employment in West Asia (around 200,000); secondly, there has been the out-migration of about 337,000 persons of Indian origin from the estate sector under the Indo-Sri Lankan Agreement; thirdly, there has been a slight ageing of the population.

TABLE 9.8   *Unemployed population, by education, as a percentage of work force, 1973, 1978/79, and 1981/82*

	1973	1978/79	1981/82
No schooling, illiterate	8.4	3.5	2.4
No schooling, literate	6.8	2.8	1.9
Primary	14.1	6.6	4.8
Secondary	37.1	21.3	14.6
GCE, 'O' level	47.4	27.6	24.5
GCE, 'A' level	44.4	36.4	34.8
Undergraduates	—	50.0	41.2
Graduates	16.2	5.3	9.7
Other	—	0.1	—
All persons	24	14.8	11.7

Source: Consumer Finance Surveys, Central Bank of Ceylon.

4   Real incomes

This section analyses the behaviour of real incomes with an emphasis on how the poorer sections of the community have fared. The analysis is restricted to the three periods covered by the Consumer Finance Surveys—1973, 1978/79, and 1981/82.

Macro-economic data indicate that 1973 was a year of recession and the resource availability in the economy was particularly low. The international

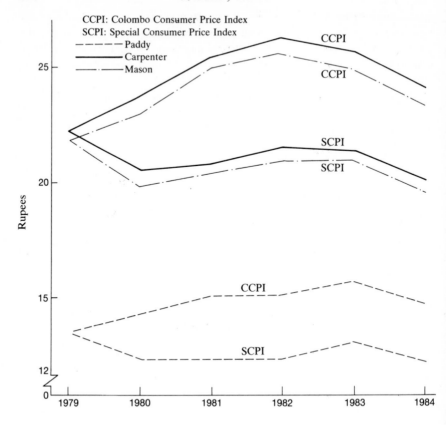

Source: UNICEF—Sri Lanka (1985)

Fig. 9.4   Sri Lanka: real daily wages (male) in paddy and construction, 1979–1984

recession, the oil price hike, the dislocation caused by the Land Reform of 1972, the shock of the April 1971 insurgency, and crop failures due to poor weather conditions contributed to the poor economic performance of that year. There was a modest up-turn in the economy from 1975 onwards, and by 1977 living standards are likely to have improved from the low level in 1973.

Therefore, the comparison of 1978/79 with 1973 may exaggerate the magnitude of the improvements since 1977. Further, the 1978/79 survey period was only one year after the economic adjustment and reflects only the initial impact of the change. The data of the 1981/82 survey is more representative of the period after the economic adjustment.

The analysis which follows is based on income receivers and income per spending units. A spending unit consists of all members of a household who act as a unit in decision making for spending.

Table 9.9 gives the monthly mean and median incomes of income receivers and spending units for three years. There was a significant improvement in real incomes between 1973 and 1978/79, which was more marked for spending units than income receivers. There was a deterioration in real incomes between 1978/79 and 1981/82 but the deterioration was much less significant for spending units than income receivers. This analysis is based on the SCPI. On the basis of a CCPI deflation, real incomes increased significantly.

TABLE 9.9   *Average monthly income per income receiver and per spending unit, 1973, 1978/79, and 1981/82, rupees*

	Nominal income			Real income at 1973 prices[a]		
	1973	1978/1979	1981/1982	1973	1978/1979	1981/1982
Per income receiver						
Mean income	228	616	1,111	228	337	302
Median income	180	408	612	180	223	167
Per spending unit						
Mean income	311	921	1,635	311	503	445
Median income	250	658	1,159	250	360	315

Source: Consumer Finance Surveys, Central Bank of Ceylon.
[a] Using SCPI to deflate.

The behaviour of incomes in the three sectors—rural, urban, and estate—provide useful insights as to whether significant differences occurred between the sectors. Between 1973 and 1978/79, nominal incomes more than doubled in all three sectors. Between 1978/79 and 1981/82, rural and urban incomes increased by about 82 per cent but estate incomes increased by only 49 per cent. Since prices doubled between 1978/79 and 1981/82, all sectors were worse off in comparison to 1978/79 levels, but the substantial wage increases in the estate sector in 1984 are likely to have changed this.

When the income deciles of spending units are analysed, we find an improvement in real incomes between 1973 and 1978/79 for all deciles but a considerably greater improvement for the higher deciles. Between 1978/79 and 1981/82 all deciles of spending units suffered a loss in real income. When 1981/82 real incomes are compared to 1973 incomes, real incomes increased by 15 per cent or less for the lowest 40 per cent of spending units and for the 6th decile, but the other deciles had a significantly greater increase in real incomes (Table 9.10).

It was shown above that prices of food commodities increased at a higher

TABLE 9.10   *Mean monthly income per income receiver, by decile, 1973, 1978/79, and 1981/82, rupees*

Decile	Mean income			Real mean value at 1973 prices		
	1973	1978/1979	1981/1982	1973	1978/1979	1981/1982
Lowest	40.92	74.38	134.42	40.92	40.66	36.58
2nd	72.08	158.13	276.61	72.08	86.44	75.27
3rd	99.54	222.56	325.47	99.54	121.66	88.56
4th	129.60	294.81	512.11	129.60	161.15	139.35
5th	161.44	366.68	618.76	161.44	200.44	168.37
6th	198.96	450.83	769.83	198.96	246.44	209.48
7th	240.12	563.51	950.91	240.12	308.03	258.75
8th	287.64	695.41	1,181.97	287.64	380.13	321.62
9th	361.71	943.60	1,646.31	361.71	515.80	447.98
Highest	681.70	2,413.70	4,632.34	681.70	1,319.39	1,260.52

Source: UNICEF-Colombo (1985).
Note: Real incomes have been obtained by deflating by the SCPI.

rate than other commodities. This fact implies that the real incomes of the higher income deciles may have improved even more than indicated here.

5   Income distribution

Income data from successive Consumer Finance Surveys of the Central Bank from 1953 to 1981/82 indicate that income inequality as measured by the Gini coefficient was lowest in 1973. Compared to 1973, income distribution was more uneven in 1978/79, and deteriorated further in 1981/82 (Table 9.11).

The sectoral income distribution data elicit interesting differences from this overall trend. In the rural sector, which comprises about 70 per cent of total households, income distribution deteriorated significantly between 1973 and 1978/79, while the estate sector, income distribution improved between 1973 and 1978/79. In both these sectors income distribution did not change between 1978/79 and 1981/82. The urban sector provides a contrasting picture of a continuing deterioration in income distribution; a sharp decline from 1973 to 1978/79 and a continuation of this trend to 1981/82.

Analysis of income distribution by geographical region indicates a deterioration in the Gini coefficient for all regions in 1978/79 compared to 1973. But between 1978/79 and 1981/82, the experience is mixed with a trend of greater equality in predominantly agricultural areas and a deterioration in the more urbanized regions, and the up-country region. This analysis implies that the areas of agricultural expansion 'would have opened up new sources of income both in agriculture as well as other dependent activities (which) may have helped to check deterioration of income distribution' (Central Bank of Ceylon 1982, p. 193). Inequality was highest in Colombo city in 1981/82.

Analysis of the income shares of the lowest four deciles of spending units

TABLE 9.11   *Income distribution, 1973, 1978/79, and 1981/82 (Gini coefficient of income receivers)*

	1973	1978/1979	1981/1982
All island	0.41	0.49	0.52
Rural	0.37	0.49	0.49
Estate	0.37	0.32	0.32
Urban	0.40	0.51	0.54

Source: Consumer Finance Surveys, Central Bank of Ceylon.

TABLE 9.12   *Percentage of total income received by the lowest 40 per cent of spending units, 1973, 1978/79, and 1981/82*

	1973	1978/1979	1981/1982
Lowest 10%	2.79	2.12	2.18
Next 10%	4.38	3.61	3.55
Lowest 20%	7.17	5.73	5.73
Next 10%	5.60	4.65	4.35
Next 10%	6.52	5.68	5.24
Lowest 40%	19.29	16.06	15.32

Source: Consumer Finance Surveys, Central Bank of Ceylon.

(Table 9.12) discloses a progressive decline in the share of incomes of the lowest 40 per cent from 1973 to 1978/79 and to 1981/82. The share of the lowest decile increased in 1981/82 compared to 1978/79 but was lower than in 1973. There is, however, a significant distinction between the 1973–78/79 comparison and that between 1978/79–81/82, in that the former deterioration occurred with a real income increase, while in the latter period real incomes too decreased.

IV   Impact on social programmes and service delivery

1   Overview

Expenditure on social services as a whole (Table 9.13) fell as a percentage of the government budget from 33 per cent in 1977 to 22 per cent in 1983, and as a percentage of GNP from 9 per cent to 8 per cent over this period. Real per capita expenditure hardly increased for the social sector as a whole, despite large capital investments, since recurrent expenditures declined by 4 per cent per annum.

TABLE 9.13   *Per capita expenditure on social services, 1970–1983*

| | Actual expenditure (rupees) | | | | | | | | | Rate of change per annum (%)[a] | | | | | |
| | 1970 | | | 1977 | | | 1983 | | | 1970–77 | | | 1977–83 | | |
	R	C	T	R	C	T	R	C	T	R	C	T	R	C	T
Education	34.65	1.86	36.51	62.94	7.20	70.14	150.58	17.50	168.08	−1	10	—	−1	−1	−1
Higher education	4.88	1.02	5.90	2.12	0.87	2.99	11.13	16.00	27.13	−22	−33	−20	13	39	24
Health	17.32	1.23	18.50	33.12	3.15	36.27	88.61	50.11	138.72	—	4	1	1	36	7
Youth affairs	—	—	—	—	—	—	6.96	1.05	8.01						
Social services	2.58	0.06	2.64	4.03	6.25	10.30	9.97	0.10	10.07	−4	75	11	−4	*	−15
Housing	0.14	—	0.14	0.36	1.74	2.10	0.70	42.12	42.82	−4	—	34	89	46	42
Water supply	0.51	1.23	1.74	0.11	0.22	0.33	12.95	67.04	79.99	−37	−41	−40	2	222	214
Cultural affairs	0.44	—	0.44	0.64	0.34	0.98	1.68	1.75	3.43	−4	10	2	2	13	6
Labour	1.00	0.06	1.06	1.17	0.23	1.40	3.26	0.50	3.76	−8	—	−6	−13	−2	1
Food subsidy	26.13	—	26.13	101.93	—	101.93	111.06	—	111.06	11	—	11	—	—	−13
TOTAL[b]	87.64	5.46	93.10	206.44	20.00	226.44	396.91	196.16	593.07	3	10	3	−4	25	1
As % of government budget		31.9			32.6			22.3							
As % of GNP		9.0			9.1			8.4							

Source: Budget estimates.

Note:

* More than 50% decrease p.a.

R: Recurrent costs.

C: Capital costs.

T: R + C.

[a] At constant prices obtained by using GDP deflater adjusted to exclude exports.

[b] Includes expenditure under Buildings Department, Decentralised Budget and Integrated Development Programmes.

(a) Infrastructure rehabilitation In 1978 and 1979 funds were readily made available for new projects to improve infrastructure. The Ministries of Health, Higher (tertiary) Education, and Housing and Construction were able to initiate several new large-scale infrastructure projects as well as obtain large amounts of equipment for ongoing programmes.

General and technical education, however, were subjected to several reviews, and little attempt was made to obtain more budgetary resources for the school system since the direction in which it should develop was still unclear. It was not until 1985 that projects were formulated to implement proposals put forward in 1981. Rehabilitation of technical education started in 1984.

Capital expenditure grew very fast in all other sectors (except the Social Services Ministry where food aid has distorted the picture). In the health sector capital expenditure grew from 9 per cent of the health budget in 1977 to 19 per cent in the period 1978–82, increasing sharply to 36 per cent in 1983. Equipment purchases quadrupled, with a focus on high technology items. Building activities shifted from provincial and base hospitals in the mid-1970s to teaching hospitals at the end of the decade.

(b) Considerable foreign aid inflow The impact of foreign aid on the health sector and water supply was considerable. Two new hospitals and a large amount of equipment and vehicles were obtained by the health sector as grants. Items such as contraceptives and malathion were also made available on aid. The dependence of the community health services on foreign aid increased from 7 per cent of its total budget in 1976 to 53 per cent in 1979. In 1982, foreign aid came to about one-fifth of total health expenditure. Assistance from foreign voluntary organizations to health and health-related activities came to 42 million rupees in 1982.

(c) Restriction of recurrent expenditure In January 1978, the food ration programme was restricted to households with annual incomes of less than 3,600 rupees, thereby containing the effect on the government budget of the rupee devaluation at the end of 1977. In September 1979 the ration programme was ended and food stamps introduced for the same target group, providing the same purchasing power as under the ration programme. However, in January 1980 the prices of essential food commodities sold in the co-operatives were allowed to rise—flour by 85 per cent, sugar by 64 per cent and rice by 34 per cent—and the impact of this subsidy on the budget was more than halved: from 14 per cent of total government expenditure or 6 per cent of GNP in 1979 to 7 per cent and 3 per cent respectively in 1980. The value of the net food subsidy fell from 2,326 million rupees in 1979 to 305 million rupees in 1980 and has continued around this level, being mainly confined to milk food. The value of food and kerosene stamps started off at 1,777 million rupees in 1980 and has been maintained at around 1,685 million rupees since 1981.

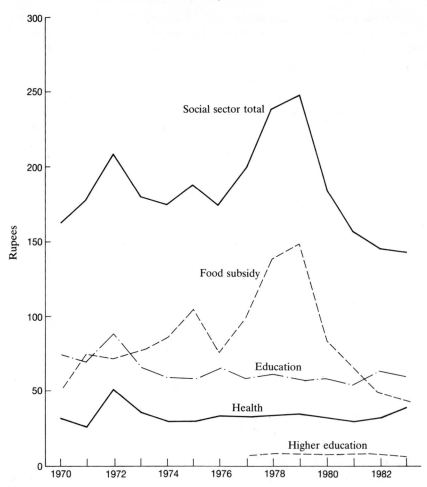

Source: UNICEF—Sri Lanka (1985)

Fig. 9.5　Sri Lanka: per capita real recurrent government expenditure, 1970–1983

The real value of recurrent expenditure was barely maintained in other ministries (see Fig. 9.5). This had a very serious effect on general education in particular, as this sector had already been experiencing a decline in recurrent expenditures per capita during the period 1970–77. Real per capita recurrent health expenditure had been virtually constant since 1970. In both sectors, repairs and maintenance of existing infrastructure (buildings and equipment) were badly neglected and consumables required for providing these services reduced.

(d) Change of emphasis in funding There were very substantial increases in expenditure on water supply and housing during the period 1977–83; on capital account in 1983, these totalled 109 rupees per capita compared to a provision of 73 rupees per capita for education and health. The food subsidy only accounted for 19 per cent of social sector expenditures in 1983, compared to 45 per cent in 1977.

There was also a change of emphasis within the sectors. Higher education increased its share of the education budget from 7 per cent in 1977 to 16 per cent in 1983. Within the health budget, expenditure on patient care services increased from 62 per cent of the total budget in 1977 to 74 per cent in 1983.

(e) Distribution of benefits There has been a marked change in the structure of benefits accruing to different income groups (Table 9.14). In 1973, the middle-income groups benefited most, while in 1980 there was a definite decline in per capita benefits as income rises. This is mainly due to a change

TABLE 9.14 *Benefits accruing from major social expenditures, by income groups, 1973 and 1980*

Household annual income[a]	Population (%)	Benefits per capita (1980 rupees)			
		Education	Health	Food subsidy	Total
1973					
Under 1,200	2.8	93	70	50	213
1,201–2,400	21.7	108	59	104	271
2,401–4,800	49.7	134	49	147	330
4,801–9,600	21.5	166	38	148	352
9,601–12,000	2.1	177	27	64	267
Over 12,000	2.6	190	18	−3	206
Average		132	50	130	312
1980					
Under 3,000	0.4	184	86	167	437
3,001–6,000	4.6	135	88	198	421
6,001–12,000	35.0	109	61	181	351
12,001–24,000	44.7	106	48	131	285
24,001–30,000	6.7	99	31	78	209
Over 30,000	8.5	96	29	42	167
Average		108	58	141	300

Source: Alailima (1984).
[a] Estimated price increases between 1973 and 1980 derived from the GDP deflator come to 250.8 per cent. Hence, there is a fortuitous correspondence between the income ranges given for 1973 and 1980.

in the distribution of benefits from education. A marked improvement took place in the participation of low-income children in primary school in this period, so that a greater share of the expenditure on primary schooling accrued to these groups. The restriction of the food stamps to the low-income groups also improved the proportion of benefits accruing to the poor even though targeting is weak. The bottom 40 per cent of the population derived more benefit from government expenditure in 1980 than in 1973 relative to other income groups as well as in absolute terms.

(f) Encouragement of the private sector This was done by extending direct support as well as relaxing restrictions affecting its activities. In education, for private non-fee-levying schools government took over the payment of teachers' salaries from 1980 onwards. A private medical college (affiliated to Colombo University) was set up in 1982. Enabling legislation was passed in 1985 for the establishment of tertiary level independent degree- and diploma-granting institutions to provide further training for the large number of school leavers.

In the health sector, restrictions on the movement of health personnel were removed and the right of private practice granted to government doctors. The import of drugs was liberalized, with only drugs to the government sector being compulsorily channelled through the State Pharmaceuticals Corporation.

2 Education

(a) Present status Census data indicate that between 1971 and 81 there was a marked improvement in the proportion of the school-going age-group attending school, in part due to the reduction of the age of admission from 6 to 5 years in 1978. Literacy also improved over this period. However, the Central Bank Consumer Finance Surveys suggest that these improvements took place prior to 1978/79. Between 1978/79 and 1981/82 school avoidance rates increased slightly and there was a slight deterioration in literacy rates.

There was also a significant increase in the participation rates of the poorest 40 per cent of the population in the school system between 1969/70 and 1980/81 (Table 9.15). This group improved the participation of their 5–9 and 10–14 year olds at a faster rate than the average for the whole population, thereby narrowing the disparity between the rich and the poor considerably. Participation rates for the 15–19-year-olds in low income households, though still very much below average, doubled over this period.

(b) Major constraints in the delivery of general education services The sudden increase in enrolment between 1977 and 1978 put an already weakened school system under further strain. Subsequent increases in capital expenditure were almost entirely devoted to providing accommodation for these children. Increases in the recurrent budget were not commensurate with the additional numbers, and per student real expenditure fell from 336 rupees in 1977 to 260 rupees in 1983. The percentage of recurrent expenditure

TABLE 9.15 *Participation rates in education, by age and household income group, 1969/70 and 1980/81 (percentages)*

	5–9	10–14	15–19	20–24
1969/70				
Rs. 100	61.9	64.7	29.1	6.3
Rs. 100–199	68.9	73.9	28.9	2.2
Average (all income				
groups)	73.8	79.3	38.8	6.8
1980/81				
Rs. 350	68.0	77.8	33.8	3.3
Rs. 350–450	67.9	79.0	43.5	4.5
Rs. 450–525	71.5	80.3	38.0	4.5
Rs. 525–626	75.1	62.0	41.3	6.2
Average (all income				
groups)	74.3	83.0	46.4	8.4

Source: Department of Census and Statistics, *Socio-Economic Surveys 1969/1970 and 1980/1981,* special tabulations.
Note: Participation rates were calculated by taking the number classified as students as a proportion of the total population in that age group and household income level.

going to teacher salaries was 90 per cent in 1977, 95 per cent in 1980, and 91 per cent in 1983, with less than 10 per cent available for provision of school books and teaching aids. Today there are some schools where children do not even have mats to sit on (UNESCO 1982). Many schools do not have water supplies or toilet facilities.

Large intakes of untrained teachers between 1979–80, the neglect of in-service training during this period, and a decline in teachers' morale due to falling real wages probably also contributed to a decline in the quality of schooling. The real wage rate index for government school teachers fell by 11 per cent from 1977 to 1983, while the rate for all central government employees went up by 6 per cent in the same period. The practice of private tuition became widespread as a means of supplementing teachers' income.

By 1982, it was evident that the quality of education provided by the school system was inadequate, with 'a marked disparity among schools, between urban and rural schools and between the two sexes. ... The performance of the average, below average and small school is shockingly poor as to warrant immediate remedial action' (Kariyawasam and Wanasinghe 1982).

In the urban slums and estate areas, children often do not attend because they are supplementing the family income or looking after siblings so that their parents can work. In 1979, it was estimated that a quarter of a million children aged 8–14 did not attend at all, and about a third of a million of this age group had left school before completing Grade 8. Around 10 per cent of those aged

10–19 declared themselves illiterate at the 1981 census, and the true size of this group may be even greater.

3 Health

(a) **Present status** Mortality and morbidity patterns are changing in Sri Lanka. Mortality has fallen for all age groups (Table 9.16); cardio-vascular diseases, road accidents, and suicides are increasing; and infectious diseases, anaemia, and infant perinatal disorders are falling. At the same time there are areas, for example the estates, where infant mortality is still high but declining, and where the dominant problems are infectious diseases and respiratory diseases. While relatively low crude death rates and infant mortality rates are reported for the country as a whole, geographic variations are substantial.

TABLE 9.16   *Trends in vital statistics, 1977–1983*

	Crude death rate		Infant mortality rate	
	Estates	Sri Lanka	Estates	Sri Lanka
1977	12.7	7.4	85	42
1978	13.0	6.6	83	37
1979	14.4	6.5	80	38
1980	12.4	6.2	n.a	34
1981	n.a.	6.0	n.a.	n.a.
1982	n.a.	6.1	n.a.	n.a.
1983	n.a.	6.1	n.a.	n.a.

Source: Department of Census and Statistics, *Bulletin of Vital Statistics and Socio-economic Indicators for Sri Lanka.*

A significant decrease in disease-specific mortality in hospitals without parallel decrease in morbidity suggests that although curative intervention is available, the preventive aspects of health care have not been given due emphasis.

(b) **Major constraints in the delivery of health services** The increase in capital expenditure with a tendency towards purchasing higher-cost sophisticated health technology, combined with restriction of recurrent expenditure has contributed to difficulties in maintaining buildings and equipment,[2] supervision, and falling service standards.

The liberalization of imports in 1977 ended the State Pharmaceuticals Corporation's monopoly to import drugs. A very high level of drug consumption subsequently built up. In 1979 it was estimated that the private sector was spending 285 million rupees and the public sector 117 million rupees. Periodic shortages of drugs have however occurred at the primary health care level of the public health service. This has been partly due to a doubling of the cost of the package of basic drugs between 1979 and 1981 without a commensurate increase in budgetary provision; partly to leakages and maldistribution within the system; and partly to the tendency to prescribe more expensive drugs.

The declining purchasing power of doctors' salaries has contributed to an exodus of doctors from the country—at present there are about 1,000 vacancies in the cadre. To counteract this brain drain and as part of its general policy to encourage the private sector, doctors were permitted to engage in private practice from 1977 onwards. No controls were instituted to ensure that doctors attended to their duties in their substantive posts. The privilege of private practice was widely abused throughout the health service, leading to a deterioration of morale, discipline, and the quality of service provided by supporting staff. However, private practice has helped attract doctors to peripheral units and district hospitals in remote areas.

Permitting two systems to function simultaneously within the health service—one with a profit motive and the other with a service objective—has led to preferential access and utilization of government facilities by the former. An unofficial system of 'fee-levying' developed, whereby patients had to pay individual hospital staff to obtain services which the state was providing free. Pilfering of drugs and consumables also became widespread, leading to recurrent shortages of essential items.

The morale and motivation of health staff outside the curative services has also been affected. Administrative positions and public health positions, where private practice is not allowed, remain vacant—8 out of 19 Superintendent of Health Service posts and 42 out of 144 Medical Officer of Health posts. During the last five years, only eight doctors have joined the Medical Officer of Health cadre.

More recently, paramedical cadres have also been affected by the lure of more lucrative jobs abroad and 10–15 per cent of the cadres of laboratory technicians, radiographers, pharmacists, and midwives are currently vacant.

Weaknesses in management and supervision within the health services, aggravated by the exodus of medical and paramedical manpower and the introduction of private practice within the context of restricted recurrent expenditure, has led to a deterioration in the quality of the health services. The preventive services have been particularly affected.

4 Welfare

(a) Nutrition Anthropometric measurements as well as consumption data indicate that undernutrition or protein-calorie malnutrition is widespread and serious in Sri Lanka. At present about 35 per cent of pre-school children are stunted and 13 per cent are wasted. Measurements made of estate and rural pre-school children in 1974/75 (USAID 1976) and 1980/82[3] (Table 9.17),

TABLE 9.17 *Comparison of undernutrition, 1980/82 and 1975/76*

Age-group (months)		Stunting[a]		Wasting[b]	
		Rural	Estate	Rural	Estate
6–11	1980/82	6.6	21.8	8.9	10.4
	1975/76	9.3	27.4	4.8	6.7
12–23	1980/82	15.6	40.0	13.1	14.8
	1975/76	21.5	47.2	10.5	13.5
24–35	1980/82	17.6	43.6	8.6	7.5
	1975–76	29.4	62.6	6.6	9.2
36–47	1980/82	26.5	46.3	7.7	5.5
	1975/76	36.5	71.5	4.2	9.1
48–60	1980/82	31.2	52.3	8.7	6.2
	1975/76	37.4	73.1	4.6	7.1

Age-group (months)		*Gomez classification*[c]			
		Normal	First degree	Second degree	Third degree
6–11	1980/82	27.3	51.2	19.5	2.0
	1975/76	22.0	51.8	22.0	3.4
12–23	1980/82	14.0	53.7	30.7	1.8
	1975/76	10.8	50.0	35.0	4.2
24–35	1980/82	12.6	54.6	30.9	1.7
	1975/76	9.9	53.8	33.8	2.5
36–47	1980/82	9.7	53.2	35.2	1.8
	1975/76	9.0	47.5	36.9	3.3
48–60	1980/82	7.2	49.8	40.8	2.2
	1975/76	5.8	39.3	43.2	3.5

Source: Sahn (1984).

Notes: Comparisons are limited to rural and estate sectors since the 1975/76 survey covered only these areas.

[a] Percentage of children with height-for-age less than 90% of standard.

[b] Percentage of children with weight-for-height less than 80% of standard.

[c] 'First degree' is percentage of children with weight-for-age 75–89.9% of standard; 'second degree' is 60–74.9%; 'third degree' is less than 60%.

however, indicate that stunting has decreased in both rural and urban sectors and for all age groups. However, wasting has increased for all age groups in the rural sector, but only for 6–23-month-olds in the estate sector[4].

Consumption surveys indicate that food intake appears to be generally adequate to meet recommended minimum calorie requirements (Table 9.18).[5] This conclusion is supported by Food Balance Sheet data on food availability (Table 9.19). Calorie consumption was similar in 1981/82 to that in 1969/70, but in the interim period registered a fall in 1973 and recovered thereafter.

However, disaggregated data show serious calorie deficiencies in the lower income groups (Table 9.18). The bottom 30 per cent of the population has had an uninterrupted decline in calorie consumption since 1969/70. By 1981/82, the middle 20 per cent achieved consumption levels close to those they had in 1969/70 after experiencing a decline in the interim period. The top 50 per cent after an initial set-back in 1973 improved their intakes rapidly between 1978/79 and 1981/82 to levels far higher than they had in 1969/70.

TABLE 9.18   *Per capita daily calorie consumption, by decile, 1970, 1978/79, 1980/81, and 1981/82*

Decile	1969/ 1970[a]	1978/ 1979[b]	1980/ 1981[b]	1981/ 1982[a]
Lowest	2,013	1,335	1,221	1,181
2nd	2,065	1,663	1,590	1,558
3rd	2,123	1,848	1,788	1,794
4th	2,170	1,994	1,964	2,008
5th	2,227	2,157	2,113	2,168
6th	2,284	2,377	2,303	2,373
7th	2,346	2,528	2,519	2,553
8th	2,409	2,738	2,666	2,838
9th	2,486	3,054	2,971	3,120
Highest	2,565	3,296	3,261	3,216
Average	2,269	2,283	2,240	2,271
Food balance sheet (2-year average)	2,287	2,321	2,184	2,194

Source: UNICEF-Sri Lanka (1985).
[a] Income deciles used.
[b] Expenditure deciles are used.

Anthropometric and consumption surveys, supported by Food Balance Sheet data, suggest that nutritional status improved between 1977–79. In January 1979, the ration programme was restricted to the low-income groups. This continued to ensure minimum consumption levels for some of these groups. The introduction of the food stamps scheme in September 1979, with a fixed value in stamps, resulted in a reduction in the quantity of food obtainable owing to the sharp increase in the prices of basic foods after the removal of the subsidies in early 1980. The improvement in incomes of the upper income groups enabled them to cope with the restriction of the ration in 1979 and the price increases in 1980. In contrast, the incomes of the lower deciles did not permit them to acquire the same quantities of food as before (Table 9.20), even though they shifted from flour and bread to cheaper calories from rice.

The districts where dietary inadequacies and stunting and wasting are most obvious are Kandy, Nuwara Eliya, Matale, Badulla, Trincomalee, Batticaloa, and Amparai, where 24 per cent of the population reside. Other districts where

TABLE 9.19　*Per capita daily calorie availability, 1970–1983*

	1970	1971	1972	1973	1974	1975	1976	1977	1978	1979	1980	1981	1982	1983
Rice	1,080	984	876	854	944	788	897	1,042	929	878	966	983	944	1,003
Wheat	294	223	316	327	311	368	386	410	429	362	204	240	265	254
Other cereals	21	17	16	24	28	33	31	37	26	21	22	19	21	23
Total cereal	1,395	1,224	1,208	1,205	1,283	1,189	1,314	1,489	1,384	1,261	1,192	1,242	1,230	1,280
Yam and potatoes	73	105	88	160	190	262	199	145	150	140	130	138	146	170
Nuts oils and fats[a]	443	476	476	448	438	451	429	448	444	527	457	452	454	441
Sugar	243	226	190	173	70	52	61	96	147	173	167	156	138	183
Other sources	217	200	196	183	155	173	169	165	200	216	223	212	221	287
TOTAL	2,371	2,231	2,158	2,169	2,136	2,127	2,172	2,343	2,325	2,317	2,169	2,200	2,189	2,361

Source: Department of Census and Statistics, *Food Balance Sheets.*
Notes: (a) Including coconuts (shelled), coconut oil, butter, desiccated coconut, margarine, cheese.

TABLE 9.20　*Per capita weekly consumption of selected items, by each twenty per cent of spending units, 1978/79 and 1981/82*

	Rice (grams)		Wheat flour (grams)		Bread (grams)		Sugar (grams)		Coconut (nuts)	
	'78/79	'81/82	'78/79	'81/82	'78/79	'81/82	'78/79	'81/82	'78/79	'81/82
Lowest	6,927	6,868	1,518	902	2,004	1,154	623	590	7.52	7.04
2nd	7,055	7,558	1,538	988	1,863	1,283	611	633	7.10	7.02
3rd	7,345	8,418	1,487	935	1,883	1,414	657	771	7.22	7.36
4th	7,891	8,940	1,451	935	1,977	1,563	742	897	7.83	7.81
Highest	8,645	9,570	1,071	707	2,213	1,963	934	1,144	8.48	8.75

Source: Central Bank of Ceylon, *Report on Consumer Finances and Socio-economic Survey 1981/82.*

inadequacies are high are Kegalle, Ratnapura, Galle, Matara, Hambantota, and Moneragala,[6] with 25 per cent of the population.

Nutritional standards are lowest among households where the main income earner is an agricultural or animal husbandry worker, a labourer, a cultivator, or a farmer (Sahn 1984). These occupational groups cover 48 per cent of all households. Households where the main income earner is in these groups make up 61 per cent of those in the lowest expenditure quartile. Attempts to identify most vulnerable indicate that 60 per cent of the 'ultra poor' are from these occupational groups.

'Ultra poor' are defined as those households where calorie intake is less than 80 per cent of requirement and more than 80 per cent of their total expenditure is going on food.

Agricultural and animal husbandry workers, comprised almost equally of rural farm workers and estate workers and casual labour, derive 72 per cent of their total income from wages. Among households where the primary income earner is a farmer or cultivator only 33 per cent of income is from the sale of home-produced products; 20 per cent is represented by home consumption; wages account for 15 per cent; pensions, etc., 10 per cent, and profits 12 per cent (Sahn 1984). Even among paddy producers, half are net purchasers of paddy from the market.

The purchasing power of these vulnerable groups is therefore to a large extent dependent on wages. The relationship between sources of income (by way of wages or sale of produce) and food prices is a crucial one. As an indicator of the welfare of these groups, their purchasing power can be estimated by relating their wages to the main foods they consume, using a ratio estimating price per calorie in terms of wage units. Table 9.21 shows how wages of labourers in the small-holding tea, rubber, and coconut sectors, in paddy cultivation and the building trades (a proxy for urban labour) between 1977 and 1984 were related to the prices of six food commodities which constitute 85–95 per cent of the calorie consumption of the poor.

The price per calorie in terms of wage units differs considerably between the foods examined, coconuts being the most expensive and manioc the cheapest. Since 1977, wage rates of agricultural labour increased rapidly, exceeding the price increases of rice, manioc, coconuts, flour, and sugar up 1979. In terms of wage units, these goods were cheaper in 1979 than in 1977. From 1979–81, prices escalated and the purchasing power of wage labour deteriorated.

The picture that emerges from this analysis supports the conclusions derived from calorie consumption data, i.e. deterioration between 1978/79 and 1980/81 and a slight improvement (except for the lowest two deciles) in 1982. Consumption data, however, stops there, while the data on price per calorie in terms of wage units indicates a continuing improvement in 1983 and 1984. Unless the number of days worked fell, the welfare level of the poor also probably improved to a level commensurate with what they had in 1977.

TABLE 9.21 *Calorie price in terms of wage units, 1977, 1980, 1982, and 1984 (unorganized sector labour)*

Item	Price per kg (Rs.)	Calories per kg	Tea	Rubber	Coconut	Paddy	Building
1977 Average wage rate (Rs)			6.95	8.93	6.65	9.60	11.45
Calorie equivalent [c]							
Rice (ration)	1.46[a]	3,450	0.061	0.047	0.064	0.044	0.037
Rice (off-ration)	3.21	3,490	0.132	0.103	0.138	0.096	0.080
Flour	1.58	3,480	0.065	0.051	0.068	0.047	0.040
Manioc	1.19	1,570	0.109	0.085	0.114	0.079	0.066
Sugar	10.87	3,980	0.393	0.306	0.410	0.284	0.239
Coconut[b]	3.26	1,302	0.360	0.280	0.377	0.261	0.219
1980 Average wage rate (males) (Rs)			17.89	21.30	18.47	22.35	18.99
Calorie equivalent [c]							
Rice	4.22	3,450	0.069	0.057	0.066	0.054	0.064
Flour	4.90	3,480	0.078	0.066	0.076	0.062	0.074
Manioc	2.02	1,570	0.071	0.060	0.069	0.057	0.067
Sugar	12.16	3,980	0.170	0.143	0.165	0.136	0.160
Coconut[b]	4.49	1,302	0.192	0.162	0.186	0.154	0.181
Bread	4.31	2,450	0.098	0.083	0.095	0.079	0.093
1982 Average wage rate			21.81	26.32	27.12	30.80	25.94
Calorie equivalent[c]							
Rice	5.73	3,450	0.076	0.063	0.061	0.054	0.064
Flour	6.52	3,480	0.086	0.071	0.069	0.061	0.072
Manioc	2.40	1,570	0.070	0.058	0.056	0.050	0.059
Sugar	13.52	3,980	0.156	0.129	0.125	0.110	0.131
Coconut[b]	4.43	1,302	0.156	0.129	0.125	0.110	0.131
Bread	5.91	2,450	0.111	0.092	0.098	0.078	0.093
1984 Average wage rate			28.02	32.82	33.63	38.10	33.21
Calorie equivalent[c]							
Rice	6.10	3,450	0.063	0.054	0.053	0.046	0.053
Flour	7.69	3,480	0.079	0.067	0.066	0.058	0.067
Manioc	3.16	1,570	0.072	0.061	0.060	0.053	0.061
Sugar	12.21	3,980	0.109	0.093	0.091	0.081	0.092
Coconut[c]	11.59	1,302	0.318	0.271	0.265	0.234	0.268
Bread	6.73	2,450	0.098	0.084	0.082	0.072	0.083

Sources: Alailima and Sanderatne (1982). Data sources cited there are as follows: Department of Labour, *Sample Survey of Earnings for 1977 wages in the Public Sector*; Central Bank, *Wage and Price Statistics for 1979, 1980* for agricultural small holdings and unskilled helper in building trade; Department of Census and Statistics prices for 1977.

[a] 4 lb. provided free and 8 lb. at Rs 1.00/lb. per capita per month. Average price per kg for 12 lb.

[b] Medium-size coconut contains 12 oz. kernel and provides 444 calories and calorie content calculated for 1 kg kernel.

[c] Calculated as the price per calorie (K cal) in wage units, i.e. $\dfrac{\text{price per kg} \times 1{,}000}{\text{daily wage rate} \times \text{calories per kg}}$

(b) The Food Stamps Programme The Food Stamps Programme transfers income to marginal groups but, unlike the ration programme does not have a specific nutritional objective. In 1984, there were 5,591,730 persons over 12 years receiving stamps of 15 rupees each month; 729,712 children aged 8–12 receiving stamps of 20 rupees each month, and 679,593 children under 8 receiving stamps of 25 rupees each month. Altogether, 44 per cent of the population were receiving food and kerosene stamps.

Eligibility for food stamps was based on household income, the number of stamps given being determined according to a sliding scale which discriminated against larger poor families. A household of six persons, with a monthly income of 300 rupees or less would all qualify for food stamps, whereas a household of similar size with a monthly income of 301–360 rupees would have only one member receiving food stamps. Due to this, many large families earning a little over 300 rupees per month get very little relief.

In March 1980 it was decided that no additions should be made to the numbers already receiving food stamps. This disqualified all new-borns (about 1.9 million) and families which subsequently suffered serious income losses.

Due to large-scale underdeclaration of incomes and the difficulty of verifying them, 50 per cent of the population was included in the scheme originally. It is estimated (Alailima 1984) that 20 per cent of the benefits from the scheme accrued to households with income of less than 400 rupees per month, i.e. 14 per cent of the population; 30 per cent to those with 400–600 rupees per month, i.e. 21 per cent of the population; 36 per cent to those with 600–1,000 rupees per month, i.e. 34 per cent of the population, and 14 per cent to those with incomes over 1,000 rupees per month, i.e. 31 per cent of the population. Most of the beneficiaries (80 per cent) were in the rural sector where accurate income estimation was difficult. Only 3 per cent of benefits accrued to the estate sector where incomes were easily verifiable.

The real value of the stamps declined drastically from 1979 onwards due to food price increases. In 1984, to buy the same basket of goods as in 1979, a 15-rupee stamp would have had to be increased to 38 rupees (148 per cent); a 20-rupee stamp to 49 rupees (130 per cent) and a 25-rupee stamp to 67 rupees (168 per cent).

The recent decision to transfer the programme to the Ministry of Social Services with social service officers to target the programme effectively will deal with some of these problems. But the discrimination against larger poor families remains in the new scheme proposed, and no determination regarding the value of the stamps or how their real value will be maintained has been made.

V Summary

The economic policies followed since 1977 have led to accelerated economic growth, expanding employment, and reduced unemployment. But they have also had some adverse effects on the welfare of vulnerable groups. The policies have resulted in very high price increases, particularly for food items and kerosene. Consequently, real wages appear to have declined in the organized sector. The deterioration in real wages in the informal sector has been much less and real wages may not have declined in the paddy and construction sectors. There has been a deterioration in income distribution, particularly between 1973 and 1978/79. Since 1978/79 the overall deterioration in income has been entirely due to a deterioration in income distribution in the urban sector.

The post-1977 period was characterized by a decline in the prominence of the social sectors as a whole despite substantial increases in investments in higher education, water supply, housing and health, financed to a large extent by foreign aid.

Restraints of recurrent expenditures in the major social sectors aggravated manpower shortages and resulted in a deterioration in the quality of service provided which may have serious consequences for the quality of future generations. In the general education and health sectors the post-1977 policy prolonged a period of neglect which started in the early 1970s. However, in the nutrition sector, the change to food stamps of declining real value at a time when the purchasing power of the poor was falling removed the security of the guaranteed minimum consumption level provided by the free rice ration; the consumption level of the lowest decile fell as low as 1,181 calories per person per day in 1981/82—lower than in 1973 for this group. There was evidence of rising malnutrition among children in the rural areas.

The economic growth experienced since 1977 may not be sustainable, since it is highly dependent on foreign finance. There is little or no evidence of restructuring in the economy towards more self-reliant growth, which would require a higher proportion of domestic finance of investment, and faster growing and more diversified exports.

Notes

1. Since no data are available for gauging rental changes, the 8 per cent of expenditure on housing was distributed among all other times.
2. 'Only about 0.6 per cent of the replacement cost of equipment was budgeted for maintenance and repairs, in contrast to a requirement of at least 4 per cent'. 'Taking past capital expenditure into account, the "under funding" of the health services may now be in the region of 20 per cent of existing budget approvals'. (World Bank 1983). 'Building maintenance is also severely constrained due to lack of funds. A reasonable allowance for annual building maintenance is 1.5 per cent the total value (of the stock) and this would have been equivalent to about Rs 27 million in 1982. In that year, however, only Rs 20 million was allocated for building maintenance.' 'Funds provided for the use of vehicles were also inadequate' (World Bank 1984).
3. Surveys designed and carried out by the Food and Nutrition Policy Planning Division, Ministry of Plan Implementation. Since all these surveys were done on children below 5 years, stunting (measured by height for age) will reflect changes in the nutrition status of this group during the five years immediately preceding the survey, while wasting (measured by weight for height) will reflect recent and acute dietary inadequacy occurring at the time the survey was conducted. A composite indicator (the Gomez Index) also measures whether children are underweight for

their age, which combines the effect of stunting and wasting. A standard reference population is used against which the percentage of the Sri Lanka population malnourished is gauged. The reference population used in both surveys is that of the National Centre for Health Statistics, USA.

4. These results have to be interpreted with caution. If the Gomez classification is taken, there is a slight but definite improvement between the surveys for all age groups—there are less children with second- and third-degree protein-calorie malnutrition and more who are normal or with first-degree malnutrition in 1980/82. However, since this measure picks up the substantial improvement in stunting, it is probably more indicative of nutritional status prior to the 1980–82 period.

5. Estimated by the Medical Research Institute as the minimum average calorie requirement for the current Sri Lanka population by adding the calories required by each age and sex group (assuming moderate activity levels) and dividing by the total population. Average minimum per capita calorie requirements work out at 2,200 per day.

6. Extracted from Ministry of Plan Implementation (1984). Region 10 has been split up and the districts re-ranked.

References

Alailima, P. (1984), *Fiscal Incidence in Sri Lanka, 1973 and 1980*. WFP 2–32/WP 56. Geneva: I L O.

Alailima, P., and N. Sanderatne (1982), 'Trends and Future Prospects for Food Consumption and Supply Implications for Food Policy in Sri Lanka'. Unpublished mimeographs.

Central Bank of Ceylon (1982), *Report on the Country's Finances and Socio-Economic Survey 1981/82*. Colombo.

Edirisinghe, N. (1985), *Preliminary Food Stamp Scheme in Sri Lanka: Distribution of benefits and Impact on Nutrition*. Washington, D C: I F P R I.

Kariyawasam, T. and J. Wanasinghe (1982), *Achievement of Primary Level Students of Sri Lanka in Reading and Mathematics, Grades 2–5*. Colombo: Ministry of Education.

Ministry of Plan Implementation (1984). *Nutrition Strategy*. Colombo.

Sahn, D. E. (1984), *Food Consumption Patterns and Parameters in Sri Lanka: The Causes and Control of Malnutrition*. Washington, D C: I F P R I.

United Nations Children's Fund—Sri Lanka (1985), *Sri Lanka: The Social Impact of Economic Policies during the Last Decade*. Colombo: U N I C E F.

U N E S C O (1982), *Improving the Physical Environment of Sri Lanka Primary Schools*, Bangkok: Regional Office for Education in Asia and Pacific.

USAID (1976), *Sri Lanka Nutrition Status Survey: September 1975–March 1976*. Washington, D C.

World Bank (1983), *Population and Health Sector Mission Aide Memoire*. Washington, D C: World Bank.

—— (1984) *Sri Lanka Population and Health Sector Report*. Washington, D C: World Bank.

10

Adjustment Policies and the Welfare of Children: Zimbabwe, 1980–1985

Rob Davies and David Sanders*

I Introduction

The aim of this study is to assess the likely impact of adjustment and stabilization policies on the welfare of children in Zimbabwe over the 1980–85 period against the broad backdrop of health, education, and welfare programmes developed by the Zimbabwean authorities, despite difficult circumstances since independence. The study, however, is not intended to be an assessment of either health and welfare policies in Zimbabwe since independence, or of the efficacy of adjustment and stabilization policies.

Zimbabwe, which became independent in April 1980, inherited a typical underdeveloped economy further distorted by racial inequalities. Land ownership was extremely skewed. The Land Apportionment and Land Tenure Acts assigned ownership of a large part of good quality farming land to the white minority. At independence, 4,800 large-scale farms occupied about 15 million hectares of land while the communal land sector included some 700,000 families on 16.3 million hectares of mostly poor land. Educational opportunities were also unequally distributed, with primary enrolment rates of close to 100 per cent for the European population and ranging between 30 and 40 per cent for the African inhabitants. This combination of underdevelopment and racial inequalities was further reflected in the disease pattern of the black majority. The predominant health problems were, and are, nutritional deficiencies, communicable diseases, and conditions related to pregnancy, childbirth, and the new-born. These problems particularly affect two vulnerable groups of the population: young children and women in the child-bearing period. Malnutrition, a major problem in Zimbabwe as in other developing countries, underlies much of the morbidity and mortality. In pregnancy it is a major cause of low birth weight with its attendant morbidity and mortality in the early months of life. In young children, it is an important cause of mortality and forms the basis for the frequency and severity of many infections: the most

* The authors wish to thank Renaud Decoster, Korkut Boratav, Lynda Loxton, Charles Todd and Geoff Foster for their comments and assistance.

significant are diarrhoea, acute respiratory infections, and the immunizable diseases of measles and tuberculosis.

Since independence, substantial changes have occurred in several of these areas. Indeed, over the 1980–84 period, government policy has consistently aimed at rectifying the distortions inherited from the previous regime and at dealing with the most glaring problems of underdevelopment still affecting the country. However, two factors, both beyond the control of the national authorities, inflicted a serious blow to these government efforts. They were the international recession, which began in 1981 and which was immediately transmitted to the national economy, and an extremely severe drought lasting from 1982 to 1984. Facing growing losses of output, household incomes, budgetary resources, and foreign exchange, the government introduced a series of policies aiming at reducing external and internal imbalances while trying to tackle the most urgent domestic issues.

When assessing the effects of these policies in terms of child welfare, it is particularly difficult to separate the impact of stabilization policies from that of other influences on the economy, or from the effects of drought which clearly affected health and nutrition levels.

This study is organized as follows. Part II illustrates macro-economic developments over the period 1980–85 with particular attention to the nature of the stabilization policies introduced between 1982 and 1984. Part III examines the impact of these policies on the general economic environment (prices, incomes, etc.), on government expenditure, and on the provision of social services, health sector programmes in particular. Part IV establishes how these internal and external changes have affected the welfare of children, while brief general conclusions follow in Part V.

II Adjustment and stabilization experience

1 *Macro-economic background*

Three distinct phases can be identified in Zimbabwe's post-independence macro-economic experience: the boom of 1980/81, the recession of 1982/83, and the recovery which started in 1985. In 1980 the removal of sanctions, which had been in existence 15 years, stimulated the economy by allowing cheaper imports and better export prices, as the premiums paid on imports and the discount on exports were removed. This was compounded by wage increases which fuelled a consumer-led boom, by an extremely good agricultural season in 1980/81, and by a generally more optimistic mood in the country. GDP per capita in constant prices—which had been negative through the late 1970s—increased by 8.0 and 9.8 percent in 1980 and 1981 (Table 10.1). But the drought, which started in 1981/82 and lasted until the end of 1984, coupled with the impact of international recession on export demand, then led to a domestic recession. It has also been suggested that the redistributional policies followed by the government during the first phase may have contributed to the subsequent downturn, but this has not been well established. Growth of GDP per capita became negative in 1982 and, particularly in 1983 (-6.1 per cent). The economy bottomed out in 1984 and preliminary data indicate that a 2 per cent increase in GDP per capita was recorded in 1985.

Several other macro-economic variables show less variation during the 1980–85 period, suggesting that some of the economic problems were structural rather than cyclical (Table 10.1). Inflation rates, for instance, moved into double figures from 1981 onwards. Although wage employment picked up marginally at independence, there appears to be a long-term structural problem of chronically stagnant employment. Similarly, although the balance of trade moved into deficit in 1981 and 1982, slightly preceding the recession, its deterioration had in fact started from 1978, again suggesting that a structural rather than contingent process was at work. The same is true of the current account balance (Table 10.1).

The central government budget shows a similar trend. Expenditure in nominal terms between 1980 and 1984 grew at an average rate of 24 per cent per year, but it had grown at an average annual rate of 17 per cent in the five years prior to independence. There was thus an acceleration of an already existing trend, rather than the establishment of a new one. However, the reasons for the expansion differed: prior to independence it was the increasing cost of defending the regime; post-independence it was largely due to the expansion of social expenditures. These government expenditures expanded rapidly in 1981 and 1982. Initially revenues also increased rapidly, as the government tried to finance its expanded social expenditure programme through taxation, so that the deficit was reduced, both in constant price terms and relative to GDP. However, the increase in tax revenues was not sustained and the deficit grew in 1982 in the aftermath of the recession. The government attempted to curtail expenditure, so that there was actually a small fall in real terms as well as a slight reduction in the deficit relative to GDP in 1983. Although the government continued to restrict the expenditure side of the budget in 1984, the impact of the domestic recession on tax revenues meant that the deficit increased, both absolutely and relatively, in 1984 (Table 10.1). Despite the introduction of stabilization policies, the government budget remained expansionary.

The phases identified above are useful in discussing official attitudes towards stabilization and adjustment issues. In the boom, government spending on social services rose, minimum wages increased, and there was a generally optimistic view in government as to how fast it could go in redressing the inherited inequalities. By late 1982, however, this mood had changed and the government, under the stimulus of an IMF stand-by credit, introduced a fairly standard stabilization package, the main components of which included

TABLE 10.1 *Main macro-economic indicators, 1975–1984*

	Unit	1975	1976	1977	1978	1979	1980	1981	1982	1983	1984
Population	m	6.28	6.49	6.70	6.92	6.99	7.20	7.41	7.63	7.85	8.08
Gross domestic product											
Current prices	Z$m	1,902	2,064	2,069	2,257	2,651	3,226	4,049	4,609	5,081	5,699
Real annual growth[a]	%	-0.2	-0.8	-7.4	-0.9	1.5	10.7	12.2	0.0	-3.5	1.0
GDP per capita											
Current prices	Z$	308	318	309	326	379	448	546	604	647	705
Constant[a]	Z$	498	478	430	413	415	448	492	478	449	440
Real annual growth[a]	%	-3.5	-4.0	-10.0	-4.0	0.5	8.0	9.8	-2.8	-6.1	-2.0
Inflation											
Change in GDP deflator	%	6.2	9.0	7.6	9.6	14.6	8.9	10.5	12.9	13.2	10.4
Change in low-income CPI	%	10.1	11.0	10.3	9.7	13.8	5.4	13.1	10.7	23.1	20.2
Employment	'000	1,050	1,033	1,012	986	985	1,010	1,038	1,046	1,033	1,039
Balance of payments											
Balance of trade	Z$m	-23.6	84.3	52.3	82.3	-5.4	-103.2	-324.9	-309.0	-205.5	-18.4
Current account	Z$m	-87.9	6.3	-8.8	25.0	-73.9	-156.7	-439.3	-532.8	-457.0	-148.1
Capital account	Z$m	70.1	-3.8	-4.2	23.1	173.7	75.8	310.2	518.4	292.7	266.2
Gross public debt of central government											
External	Z$m	94	78	89	224	353	415	514	841	987	1,436
Total	Z$m	696	789	868	115	1,482	1,843	2,099	2,481	2,853	3,747
External/total	%	13.5	9.9	10.2	19.5	23.8	22.5	24.5	33.9	34.5	38.3
Net borrowing	Z$m	5.5	92.9	79.4	281.9	332.5	361.0	255.3	382.7	371.7	893.7
Net borrowing/GDP	%	0.3	4.5	3.8	12.5	12.5	11.2	6.3	8.3	7.3	15.7
Central government budget[b]											
Total expenditure including maturing debt	Z$m	518	577	754	848	995	1,162	1,623	2,274	2,624	3,054
Current receipts	Z$m	423	482	553	628	593	687	1,139	1,542	1,894	2,117
Deficit	Z$m	95	95	202	220	352	475	484	732	730	937
Deficit/GDP	%	5.2	4.8	9.8	10.2	14.3	16.2	12.0	15.9	14.4	16.4
Expenditure[a]	Z$m	802	819	978	1,030	1,086	1,162	1,416	1,676	1,661	1,725
Receipts[a]	Z$m	654	684	717	763	647	687	994	1,136	1,199	1,195
Deficit[a]	Z$m	148	135	261	267	239	475	422	540	462	530

Sources: CSO, *National Income and Expenditure Report*, Harare, Oct. 1985.
CSO *Quarterly Digest of Statistics*, Harare, Sept. 1985.
Reserve Bank of Zimbabwe, *Quarterly Economic and Statistical Review*, Harare, June 1982 (1975–1980), Dec. 1983 (1981/82), and Dec. 1985 (1983/85).

[a] At 1980 prices.
[b] Until 1980, figures refer to year ending June 30; from 1981 they refer to calendar year. For row 26, figures for 1975 through 1980 are based on average

devaluation of the Zimbabwe dollar, restrictions on government credit expansion, and a wage freeze.

It can be argued that policies adopted in response to the domestic recession had a negative impact on children. However, this has to be viewed against a background of substantial gains in redressing inequalities inherited from the past. Immediately after independence, the government introduced a number of significant redistributional measures. These included raising the incomes of low-paid workers through minimum wage legislation, and of poor peasants particularly by improving credit and marketing facilities; a dramatic expansion of the educational system, and greatly improved access to health care, particularly by providing a free health service for low-income groups. The government, acting on a presidential directive to accelerate promotion of blacks, also substantially redressed the racial imbalance in the civil service.

2   Stabilization and adjustment policies

Although the terms 'stabilization' and 'adjustment' are widely used, there is little consistency in their use. In general, stabilization policies refer to a fairly standard set of policies designed to manage either one, some or all of the following: the balance of payments, inflation, and the government budget deficit. Because of the strong association of the IMF with such policies in underdeveloped countries in recent years, there has been an increasing tendency for stabilization policies to be identified solely with balance of payments disequilibria, with the control of inflation and the budget deficit being regarded implicitly as instruments to be used in the achievement of balance of payments stability.

'Adjustment policies' and stabilization policies are often regarded as complementary in that stabilization policies tackle the short-term problems to provide the breathing space within which adjustment policies can be used to tackle the long-term structural causes of the problems. However, it is debatable whether they are not contradictory in practice. Thus, for example, a stabilization package which restricts government spending is likely to curtail its ability to finance structural adjustment.

There seems to be a trend not only to interpret adjustment policies in an increasingly narrow way—essentially involving the removal of restrictions on, and interferences with, the market—but also to see them as synonymous with stabilization policies. In part this is because of the practical difficulties of distinguishing between the two. Almost any policy has structural consequences; some adjustment policies have stabilization consequences even though not introduced with stabilization in mind. Nevertheless, blurring the distinction between the two is not useful. Stabilization policy should be interpreted in the traditional narrow way as the use of standard macro-economic instruments aimed at traditional macro-economic targets. Adjustment policies should be interpreted in a broader sense. In this study attention in predominantly concentrated on the stabilization policies adopted since independence, the main instruments of which are summarized in Table 10.2. The most significant instruments were the removal of subsidies, the wage freeze, and attempts to restrict the growth of government expenditure. These policies will be examined in greater detail when discussing their effects on the health and nutrition of children.

No attempt is made to examine the efficacy of these measures. There appears to have been a recovery in the economy in 1984 and, particularly in 1985, so that there is prima facie evidence that the policies may have worked, although a much more detailed analysis would be needed to establish the actual causes of the recovery. It is interesting to note that the balance of payments measures listed under A3 in Table 10.2 were introduced much against the will of the IMF and were partly responsible for the suspension of the agreement. However, they do appear to have worked in improving the invisible account, and many of the controls have since been relaxed.

TABLE 10.2   *Chronicle of main macro-economic policy instruments used by government since 1980*

Instrument	Date	Comment
A *Balance of payments and exchange rate policies*		
A1 Devaluation	8 Dec. 1982	Explicit devaluation of 20% against basket of currencies
	Jan. 1983	Zimbabwe dollar allowed to depreciate a further 5%
	1983–84	Agreement that Zimbabwe dollar would not be allowed to rise against major trading currencies
A2 Restrictions on new non-concessional foreign borrowing	From 23 Mar. 1983	Part of IMF agreement
A3 Balance of payments controls	27 Mar. 1984	(*a*) Temporary suspension of remittances of dividends, branch and partnership profits; (*b*) temporary reduction of emigrants' settling-in allowances; (*c*) acquisition of the blocked external securities pool; (*d*) release of blocked funds of companies and individuals; (*e*) temporary suspension of all income remittances; (*f*) control of government external expenditures

continued

Instrument	Date	Comment	
continued from p. 277			
B Price and wage controls			
B1 Cuts in subsidies and increases in administered prices	May 1982	Beef	30%
	July 1982	Fertilizer	12%
		Steel	25%
	Oct. 1982	Electricity	22–49%
	Dec. 1982	Maize meal	50%
	May 1983	Railway tariffs	10–25%
	Sept. 1983	Beef	30–55%
		Maize meal	40–45%
		Bread	25–30%
		Milk	50%
		Vegetable oils	25%
B2 Wage freeze	Jan. 1982	Wage increases not allowed to exceed half the annual rise in the Consumer Price Index as part of IMF agreement	
C Government budget policies			
C1 Restriction on government credit expansion	From 23 Mar. 1983	Part of IMF agreement	
C2 Restriction on new recruitment by government	1983/84		
D Monetary policies			
D1 Interest rates	Feb. 1981	Bank rate up from 4% to 6%	
	Sept. 1981	Bank rate up from 6% to 9%	
	Apr. 1984	Post office savings bank rates raised	
D2 Restriction on domestic credit expansion	From 23 Mar. 1983	Part of IMF agreement	
D3 Minimum liquidity ratios	28 Mar. 1984	Raised for building societies	
	1 May 1984	Raised for commercial banks and accepting houses	

III   The impact on general economic environment and health inputs

In the 1982 census, Zimbabwe's total population was estimated to be 7.55 million, with 4.28 million (56.7 per cent) in communal lands, 1.57 million (20.8 per cent) in commercial farms, and 1.67 million (22.2 per cent) in urban areas. Stabilization policies cannot be expected to affect each of these groups equally or uniformly. Initially the analysis focuses therefore on the urban sector (wage earners and informal sector producers), while the impact on rural population which comprises those living on communal lands and on commercial farms is examined thereafter.

From the point of view of this study, two of the most significant components of stabilization policies in Zimbabwe have been the freeze on wages and the removal of food subsidies. Both have seriously affected the movement of real earnings, and would be expected to have had serious direct consequences for nutrition. The section begins by examining the relation between stabilization policies, incomes, prices, and nutrition.

Stabilization policies have also affected the government's ability to provide welfare services, an important part of the social wage. These effects are examined separately.

1 Effects on wages, incomes, prices, and subsidies

Zimbabwe inherited an extensive system of price controls and subsidies, which it continued to operate after independence, placing more emphasis on its use to keep the cost of basic food items low. Two forms of subsidy were used. Firstly, the government met the deficits of the various agricultural marketing boards, which arose because prices to producers were higher than those to consumers. Both sets of prices were under direct government control. Secondly, the government paid a direct subsidy to certain private producers of basic foodstuffs.

In nominal terms, subsidies rose rapidly from 1980/81 until 1983/84, since when they have remained relatively constant. However, in constant price terms, although there was a sharp rise between 1980/81 and 1981/82, there have been reductions in each subsequent year, highlighting the attempts by government to control subsidies. This is also demonstrated by the fall in the share of subsidies in government current expenditure since 1981/82 (Table 10.3).

Because of the growing burden placed on the budget, the government already wanted to reduce subsidies before the IMF agreement. However, it was only under that agreement that this happened.

In 1982/83 some subsidies were removed while others to processors of basic foods were reduced. There was some attempt to minimize the impact this had on prices by delaying permission to increase retail prices. Nevertheless, there were price increases over the 1982/83 period—some 100 per cent for maize meal, 25–30 per cent for bread, and 25 per cent for edible oils (Table 10.2).

Apart from the direct effects of the removal of food subsidies, raising controlled prices of electricity, railway tariffs, and fertilizer also influenced the general price level, albeit with some lag (Table 10.2).

The combined effect of these price increases can be gauged from the movement of the consumer price index. Between August and September, 1983, which was when the most significant removal of subsidies took place, the CPI for low income urban families rose by 15.6 per cent, while the index of food

TABLE 10.3   *Level of subsidies and their pattern over time, 1980/81–1985/86 (Z$ thousand)*

	1980/81	1981/82	1982/83	1983/84	1984/85	1985/86
To marketing boards						
Beef	9,619	25,730	33,289	36,518	41,630	39,283
Dairy	4,110	10,354	18,329	—	31,682	39,329
Maize	9,662	5,110	22,910	86,000	36,719	43,731
Soya	1,919	956	—	—	4,608	1,608
Wheat	—	—	—	—	11,638	9,173
Sorghum	—	—	—	—	1,400	581
SUBTOTAL	25,310	42,150	74,528	122,518	127,676	133,715
To private firms						
Bakers flour	6,663	8,500	1,939	—	—	—
Edible oils	5,700	6,200	—	—	—	—
Maize meal	20,156	64,800	49,186	28,000	22,000	15,000
Opaque beer	1,048	400	—	—	—	—
SUBTOTAL	33,567	79,900	51,125	28,000	22,000	15,000
TOTAL	58,877	112,050	125,653	150,518	149,676	148,715
As % of current government expenditure	5.2	7.7	6.9	6.7	6.1	5.3
Value of subsidies in constant 1980 prices	55,258	94,041	89,977	88,723	77,532	70,884

Source: Zimbabwe, *Estimates of Expenditure*, Harare 1981/82 to 1985/86.

prices for this group rose by 27 per cent. Clearly, attempts to reduce and remove subsidies contributed significantly to the rise in the cost of living (Table 10.1).

This inflationary impact was reinforced by the 1982 devaluation and subsequent depreciation of the Zimbabwe dollar. Although it is difficult to quantify, the fact that Zimbabwean production is highly import-dependent means that a fall in the value of the dollar is fairly rapidly translated into higher domestic prices.

(a)   Effects on wage earners How were the earnings of urban wage earners affected by stabilization policies? Since independence the government has adopted a policy of administered wages, particularly for the low paid. There were minimum wages for particular sectors before independence, but the government introduced national minimum wages in July 1980. Table 10.4 shows how these minima have moved. Obviously the number of workers on the minimum varies from sector to sector; the only wage distribution data available use too wide a grouping to be able to tell how many workers are on the minimum, but the minimum wage for each sector tends to fall in the modal group. This suggests that for most workers the minima are significant.

TABLE 10.4 *Chronicle of minimum wage changes, legislated monthly minima (Z dollars), 1980–1985*

Date	Domestic workers		Agricultural workers		Industrial workers	Mining workers		Low Income Urban CPI	Construction and Domestic	1980 Prices Industrial	
	(a)	(b)	(a)	(b)		(a)	(b)	(a)	(a)	(a)	(b)
Jul. 1 1980	30	(c)	30	(c)	70	43	70	99.2	30	(c)	71
Dec. 30 1980	30	(c)	30	(c)	85	58	85	102.4	29	(c)	83
May 1 1981	—	62 (e)	—	—	—	(d)	85				
Jan. 1 1982	50	67			105		105	117.1	43	53	90
Sep. 1 1983	55	77	55	65	115		110	169.5	32	40	68
Jul. 1 1984	65	93			125		120	184.2	35	42	68
Jul. 1 1985	75		75	93	143		143	196.9	38	47	73

Notes:— *Source:* CSO *Quarterly Digest of Statistics*, Harare, various dates.

(a) For those workers who also receive payments in kind.
(b) For those who do not receive payments in kind.
(c) Benefits to be added to cash wage but value of benefits not specified.
(d) From this date mineworkers not paid in kind.
(e) From this date three grades of domestic workers were recognized with the minimum rising by $2.00 for each grade; $50.00 was the lowest grade.

While minimum wages substantially increased in real terms over the 1980–82 period, between January 1982 and September 1983, minimum money wages were not raised. This was a direct consequence of stabilization policies. Prime Minister Mugabe acknowledged this in January 1984 when he said, 'We were given up to January last year not to increase wages, but we have gone beyond that because we realize that our economy can't handle that burden' (*Zimbabwe Herald*, 4 Jan. 1984). The increase in September 1983 was said to be compensation for the increases in basic food prices. But, as can be seen from the movement of the real wage, it did not fully compensate for previous inflation. In other words, the fairly substantial gains made between independence and January 1982, were not subsequently maintained. By July 1984, real minimum industrial wages were slightly below the 1980 level. In 1985, however, the 1980 level was exceeded again by about 7 per cent.

Table 10.5 shows the movement of average earnings. They follow the same pattern as minimum wages, although lagging slightly behind, so that the downturn in real average earnings was in the third quarter of 1982. The disaggregation of movements in real earnings into movements in nominal earnings and the price level demonstrates quite clearly the forces lying behind it. The operation of the wage freeze can be seen clearly from the lower rate of increase of average earnings after 1982; in the same period, the price level rose, largely because of the removal of subsidies.

Thus there is a fairly clear picture of the position of wage earners improving considerably after independence up to 1982 but being eroded thereafter, caught between the wage freeze and subsidy removal, both introduced explicitly as

TABLE 10.5   *Movements in average earnings for all sectors excluding agriculture, 1979–1984 (Z$ per annum)*

Quarter	Nominal average earnings (Z$)	CPI (1980 = 100)	Real earnings index 1980(1) 1980$ = 100		Instantaneous rate		
					Nominal earnings (%)	CPI (%)	Real earnings (%)
1979 (1)	1,955	90.4	2,163	94.4	—	—	—
1979 (3)	2,057	96.8	2,125	92.7	5.1	6.8	−1.8
1980 (1)	2,297	100.2	2,292	100.0	11.0	3.5	7.6
1980 (3)	2,510	98.3	2,554	111.4	8.9	−1.9	10.8
1981 (1)	2,668	110.3	2,419	105.5	6.1	11.5	−5.4
1981 (3)	2,847	114.0	2,498	109.0	6.5	3.3	3.2
1982 (1)	3,210	122.5	2,620	114.3	12.0	7.2	4.8
1982 (3)	3,388	127.3	2,661	116.1	5.4	3.8	1.6
1983 (1)	3,564	146.4	2,434	106.2	5.1	14.0	−8.9
1983 (3)	3,709	169.5	2,188	95.8	3.9	14.7	−10.7
1984 (1)	3,886	178.4	2,178	95.0	4.7	5.1	−0.5

Source: CSO, *Quarterly Digest of Statistics*, Harare, various dates.
Note: Only first and third quarters are shown as fourth-quarter figures are distorted by annual bonuses.

part of a stabilization package. By 1985, real minimum wages were 5–10 per cent higher than at independence.

Changes in the low-income consumer price index are used as a measure of inflation. This index assumes that families spend 55 per cent of their income on food, based on expenditure surveys carried out almost 10 years ago. It seems likely that poorer households spend more than this, and that subsidized foods form a more important part of their consumption, so that for them the fall in real earnings has been even greater.

(b) Effects on informal sector producers Estimates of the size of the urban informal sector in Zimbabwe are very crude, but it is estimated that there are about 0.5 million people in the sector. They are affected by stabilization policies both as consumers and as producers. As consumers, it is clear that the impact is much the same as that on wage earners; they find their real income declining as food subsidies are removed. Many informal operators are at the lower end of the income scale, so are likely to spend more of their earnings on food and are more severely affected by food price increases.

As producers, informal sector operators depend mainly on low-income earners for their market. Falling real earnings in the formal sector will therefore reduce their market. There is, however, the possibility that the informal sector can increase its market share *vis-à-vis* the formal sector in times of economic stagnation. If formal producers are adversely affected by, for example, more stringent credit policies, it is possible that the informal sector is able to benefit. However, a priori this seems likely to be a marginal effect compared to the shrinkage of the overall market.

Since it appears likely that the informal sector is adversely affected by stabilization policies both as consumers and as producers, it is plausible that the overall effect on informal sector incomes is similar to that observed in its formal counterpart.

(c) Effects on communal farmers The problems of separating the effects of the drought on communal areas from those of stabilization policies are enormous. These problems are not only methodological but also arise out of the complete absence of any systematic and comprehensive data on communal household incomes and their distribution. Therefore, the following analysis is more qualitative than quantitative.

The main effect of stabilization policies on the income of communal land dwellers was through the increase in food producer prices. The producer price for maize, for instance, consistently kept ahead of inflation during the period examined. Whether or not this benefits a household depends on whether it is a net producer or a net consumer of food. For net producers, rising food prices lead to a rise in real income; for net consumers, they lead to a fall. Assessing the overall impact therefore requires some idea of the degree of stratification in the communal lands as well as of the amount of the food surplus marketed by the communal farmers.

Some indication of the extent of rural stratification is given by the results of the National Household Capability Survey 1983/84, which showed, *inter alia*, that about 6 per cent of households have no access to land; that 50 per cent of the land is controlled by about 20 per cent of households; that approximately 50 per cent of households have no cattle; and that about 10 per cent of households own half the cattle. Similarly, figures concerning communal area sales of all agricultural products to marketing boards show great differences between the various provinces. Such large differences between provinces are probably also to be found amongst households within provinces.

Since independence there has been a remarkable rise in the contribution of communal producers to marketed output, particularly of maize and cotton. By 1985 sales of crops by communal farmers accounted for 20 per cent of all sales; they never reached 10 per cent before independence. This rise can partly be attributed to the large expansion in, and thus greater accessibility of marketing depots as well as improved access to credit. The Agricultural Finance Corporation (AFC), which had previously been solely concerned with large-scale farming, introduced a Small-farm Credit Scheme after Inde-pendence. By 31 May 1982 there were 24,957 communal farmers receiving 32,713 short-term loans, valued at Z$7.7 million. By December 31, 1985 there were 95,176 farmers, or 15 per cent of all communal households, receiving 155,344 loans valued at Z$20.2 million. Although commercial farmers continue to dominate the medium- and long-term loans from the AFC, their share fell from 98.8 per cent in 1982 to 89.1 per cent in 1985. The expansion of marketed output from communal areas implies that communal households are becoming more productive. While it is possible that some households and/or regions benefited more than others, the rise in the marketable surplus seems to be indicative of the success of the Small-farm Credit Scheme and of the increase in producer prices.

Those households in rural areas who are net buyers of food have been harmed by the removal of subsidies. While precise data are lacking, the census data quoted above show that the landless population (negatively affected both by the price increases and the removal of the subsidies) accounts for 6 per cent of the total, a relatively modest proportion. However, the removal of subsidies is also not likely to have affected rural consumers in a major way, as their access to subsidized food is generally limited.

It thus appears that while communal farmers may have been negatively affected indirectly by a decline in the income of their family members in urban areas, which would in turn have affected the level of urban–rural remittances, the adjustment policy of increasing communal farmers' access to credit, mar-keting, and improved seeds, as well as the increases in real producer prices for farm products, seem to have had positive medium-term effects. However, between 1982 and 1984 a severe drought affecting most of the country posed a serious threat to the nutritional status of the population, and of children in particular. As will appear clear later, however, considerable protection against this threat was provided by the Drought Relief Programme and the Children's Supplementary Feeding Programme.

(d)   Effects on commercial farm labourers   The 1982 census showed that there were about 1.5 million people living on commercial farms. In June 1982, there were 265,780 wage employees, some 70,000 of whom were either casual or contract workers. Casual or contract workers—who form an increasing proportion of the work-force, particularly in plantation areas where work is seasonal—generally receive less than the minimum wage for permanent workers. The minimum wage for agriculture then was Z\$50 per month; the available wage distribution data show that 84 per cent of the permanent work-force earned incomes between Z\$50 and Z\$75 per month (CSO 1983). This suggests that the wages of farm workers are determined primarily by legislation and that, in the short term, stabilization policies that affect the profitability of commercial farms will not affect nominal wages. (In the longer term, of course, such policies may affect the level of employment in agriculture). Thus, unlike communal farmers, commercial farm workers were not directly affected by increases in agricultural producer prices.

These families were therefore primarily affected as consumers. Loewenson (1986, pp. 48–57) has demonstrated that food prices for farmworkers are considerably higher than for urban consumers. While the effect of the removal of food subsidies might have negatively affected this group, it is likely that they have very limited subsidized food, as indicated by the evidence that they pay higher food prices than urban consumers.

The wage freeze between January 1982 and September 1983 also applied to agricultural workers. This restriction of nominal wages, coupled with the price increases, undoubtedly led to a fall in the real earnings of this group.

2   Expenditure on land, resettlement, education, water and drought relief

Stabilization policies also affected the ability of the government to provide inputs into the social wage. Four of these—resettlement, education, water development, and drought relief—are discussed below. It should be emphasized that the discussion concentrates essentially on the funding of these services. It does not show how far the changes in funding was reflected in the provision of real services. More important, no attention is given to how use of the services was affected by the stabilization policies.

(a)   Resettlement programme   The land question was central to the liberation struggle. The government introduced a resettlement programme after independence to try to deal with some of the starker aspects of rural underdevelopment and inequality. This required government funding both to buy land for resettlement and to provide infrastructure and support for resettled households. Securing adequate funding has always been difficult, with the result that resettlement has in practice been double edged. On the one hand, a number of effectively landless people have been resettled, albeit mostly onto marginal land. On the other hand, because of poor technical support and preparation, compounded by the drought and the lack of adequate infrastructure (e.g. stores, transport, and health care facilities), settlers are in some areas acknowledged to be the worst off in terms of health and nutrition status.

In the 1983 budget, in the middle of the IMF period when government was attempting to curtail expenditure, the severest cuts fell on resettlement programmes. Expenditure on land acquisition was cut from Z$28 million in 1982/83 to Z$6 million in 1983/84. It has been suggested that the slowing down of the resettlement programme allowed for a rethink of the whole approach. This may well have been the case, and it was undoubtedly true that some changes were required. While there were several other reasons for the slow progress of resettlement, the primary reason for the cutback was the fiscal stabilization issue.

(b) Education The government's abolition of fees for primary education at independence undoubtedly accounted for a substantial rise in the real incomes of households with school-age children, even though parents still had to pay for uniforms, transport to school, and, in effect, the lost input of their children. Subsequently, however, the pressures of funding the rapidly expanding system have forced the government to raise the cost of schooling to parents. In some cases (mainly in the rural areas) this has been done by requiring parents to provide labour inputs such as, for example, helping to build new classrooms. In other cases, schools have been allowed to charge levies. This puts pressure on parents to reduce family expenditure on other items, including food. There is no systematic evidence on the extent to which this has occurred. It has been suggested that the Children's Supplementary Feeding Programme (see Part III), which provides a meal at some schools, has substituted for rather than complemented home meals. This is an indication of the fine balance which poor households have to make between alternative calls on their resources.

(c) Water development Since independence, there has been a government programme under the impetus of the UN International Drinking Water Supply and Sanitation Decade to improve water supplies and sanitation in the communal lands. In 1984 about one-third of the communal area population had access to improved water sources; this proportion appears to have risen slowly in recent years and is continuing to do so.

Table 10.6 shows expenditure on rural water development programmes between 1982 and 1985. It can be seen that there was a rise between 1982/83 and 1983/84 followed by a reduction. This was mainly due to the completion

TABLE 10.6   *Expenditure on water supply in communal areas, 1982–1985*

	1982/1983		1983/1984		1984/1985	
	(Z$m)	(%)	(Z$m)	(%)	(Z$m)	(%)
Government funding	8.3	68	9.0	48	6.0	42
Donor funding	5.0	32	12.0	52	12.7	58
TOTAL	13.3	100	20.1	100	18.7	100
In constant 1985 prices	18.9	—	24.0	—	18.7	—

Source: Zimbabwe, *Rural Water Supply Programme*, volume 3, Harare, 1986.

of the programme to reconstruct facilities destroyed during the war, and cannot therefore be attributed to stabilization policies. The share of expenditure funded by donors has risen dramatically over the period, so that the amount of government resources going to rural water development has fallen sharply. It is arguable that this is an example of how aid donors have cushioned the effects of stabilization policies in particular areas.

(d)   Drought relief The drought relief programme, which operates through the Ministry of Labour, Manpower Planning, and Social Welfare, was introduced in 1982. It was allocated Z$19.1 million in the 1982/83 budget, or about 1 per cent of total expenditure. In 1983/84 it was allocated Z$55.7 million, or slightly over 2.3 per cent. It then fell to Z$26.9 million in 1984/85 and Z$4 million in 1985/6. The government therefore chose to expend expenditure in this crucial programme despite the overall budgetary restraint of 1982–84. It is also relevant to note that the government initially underestimated the amount that it had to allocate to the programme and had to make supplementary allocations of some Z$25 million in 1984, which was one of the reasons behind the suspension of the IMF agreement.

3   Health sector expenditure and services

(a)   Post-Independence health sector programmes Zimbabwe inherited a health care system which highlighted all the features typical of an inappropriate, inequitably distributed, developing country service, compounded by inequalities based on racial discrimination. For example, in 1980/81 the average annual expenditure per capita for private sector medical aid society members was Z$144 compared with Z$31 for the urban population using public services and Z$4 for the rural population. The latter concealed further disparities, for only the rural population surrounding urban areas were relatively well served (MOH 1984*a*, p. 30). There were also disparities in the distribution of health care personnel and access to facilities. In 1980/81, 44 per cent of publicly funded services went to the urban-based, sophisticated central hospitals serving about 15 per cent of the population while only 24 per cent went to primary and secondary level rural health services for the majority of the population (MOH 1984c, p. 1).

Given this, the health sector is one of the areas in which there has been a major government thrust since independence, with both a qualitatively new approach and a number of specific programmes being introduced. The thrust of these programmes is stated in documents such as *Planning for Equity in Health* which 'advocates the adoption of the Primary Health Care (PHC) approach whose key components are appropriateness, accessibility, affordability and acceptability of the care provided' (MOH 1984a p. i).

In line with this new approach, the changes and programmes introduced since independence include:

1. *Free health care.* Health care has been provided free of charge to those earning less than Z$150 per month, or the vast majority of the population.

2. *Hospital and rural health centre building programme.* A vigorous construction and upgrading programme for health care facilities has been undertaken. By January 1985, 163 rural health centres had been completed and a further 23 were under construction (ZANU (PF) 1985, p. 219). In addition a number of provincial and district hospitals as well as many rural clinics have been upgraded.

3. *Zimbabwe Expanded Programme on Immunization.* An expanded programme on immunization against the six major childhood infectious diseases and tetanus immunization of pregnant women was initiated in 1981. Studies on coverage show that since 1982 the percentage of children between 12 and 23 months who are fully immunized had risen in rural Zimbabwe from 25 per cent of 42 per cent in 1984 and in Harare City from 48 per cent to 56 per cent in 1983 (MOH 1984b, p. 88), and to approximately 80 per cent in 1986 (City Medical Officer of Health, personal communication). Recent data for Manicaland and Mashonaland East provinces, where coverage is probably better than the country average, show that 63 per cent and 69 per cent respectively of this age group are fully immunized (S. Ramji, Provincial Epidemiologist, personal communication).

4. *Diarrhoeal Disease Control Programme.* In February 1982 diarrhoeal disease control was declared a priority. Emphasis has been placed on improved case management—mainly by oral rehydration therapy (ORT), epidemic control, improved nutrition, prolonged breast-feeding, and improved environmental hygiene through water supply and sanitation (see above). Although hard data are not available, questionnaire responses and interviews conducted in October/November 1984 suggest that the number of attendances for diarrhoea at health care facilities has decreased (Cutts 1984). Although the evidence is sometimes conflicting, on balance there appears to have been a significant increase in the percentage of rural mothers who can prepare a correct solution for ORT (De Zoysa *et al.* 1984; Mtero *et al.* 1985; MOH 1984b; S. Ramji, personal communication; D. Sanders, personal observation).

5. *National nutrition programme.* A Department of National Nutrition was established, whose activities include nutrition and health education with particular regard to breast-feeding and weaning practices, growth-monitoring and nutrition surveillance using child health cards, and supervision of the Children's Supplementary Feeding Programme and food production plots. By June 1984, 80 per cent of children aged 1 possessed a growth card (as against 71 per cent in 1982), and 83 per cent had been weighed at least twice in the first year of life (58 per cent in 1981) (MOH 1984*b*, p. 14) although only 35 per cent of Harare mothers could consistently and correctly interpret the growth curves (MOH 1985). The Children's Supplementary Feeding Programme was initiated in November 1980 by a number of non-government organizations and taken over by the Ministry of Health a year later. A daily energy-rich supplementary meal was supplied predominantly to undernourished young children in communal areas. The programme operated between 1981 and 1985 during the height of the drought. At its peak, over a quarter of a million children in over 8,000 communal area feeding points received food (Working Group 1982, MOH 1984*c*).

6. *National village health worker programme.* The National Village Health Worker Programme was launched in November 1981 to train village-selected and village-based multipurpose basic health workers. Of a projected eventual 15,000 Village Health Workers, about 4,000 had been trained by June 1985. Related to this programme was the Traditional Midwives Programme, designed to upgrade the skills of household-level women operatives in identifying at-risk pregnancies, basic midwifery, elementary hygiene, and basic child care.

7. *Child spacing.* The Zimbabwe National Family Planning Council, a parastatal established in 1981, superseded the voluntary, government-assisted Family Planning Association. Largely as a result of its activities, Zimbabwe has the highest rate of contraceptive use in Sub-Saharan Africa.

TABLE 10.7 *Central government budget allocation to the Ministry of Health, 1978/79–1985/86*

Fiscal year	Vote allocation			Actual expenditure			Actual growth rate	
	Current prices (Z$m)	1980 prices (Z$m)	Budget share (%)	Current prices (Z$m)	1980 prices (Z$m)	Budget share (%)	Current prices (%)	1980 prices (%)
1978/79	46.2	58.2	4.6	45.6	57.4	4.8,	—	—
1979/80	54.2	61.5	4.4	53.5	60.7	4.6	17.3	5.7
1980/81	83.7	83.7	5.1	77.4	77.4	5.3	44.7	27.5
1981/82	108.9	116.8	5.1	106.1	113.8	5.6	37.1	47.0
1982/83	131.6	110.5	4.5	123.1	103.4	4.8	16.0	−9.1
1983/84	139.0	117.3	4.6	139.0	117.3	4.8	10.5	13.4
1984/85	159.4	118.2	4.5	156.6	116.2	4.9	12.7	−0.9
1985/86	183.7							

Source: For 1978/79–83/84: Zimbabwe, *Annual Report of the Comptroller and Auditor General*, Harare. For 1984/85–85/86: Zimbabwe, *Estimates of Expenditure*, Harare.

(b) **Expenditure on health, 1980–1985** All these and other programmes required an expansion in government expenditure. Table 10.7 shows how the vote allocations and the actual expenditure of the Ministry of Health changed over the period. In current price terms, there was an immediate expansion of 44.7 per cent; in real terms 27.5 per cent. The ministry's share of the budget rose to 5.1 per cent, showing the relative shift in emphasis. This growth continued into the next budget year. Thus by fiscal year 1981/82, the ministry's actual expenditure had almost doubled in real terms. Because of the general restraint on government expenditure, however, there was a 9 per cent real decrease in expenditure in the 1982/83, the year in which the IMF stand-by credit came into operation. It is significant that in this year there was a discrepancy between the allocation made before the agreement and actual expenditure. This restraint continued at least into FY 1984/85, so that the ministry's expenditure has only marginally increased in real terms since 1981/82.

It is important to recognize that changes in the *level* of spending may imply changes in the *pattern* of spending. Table 10.8 looks at the pattern of the government health expenditure according to two criteria. Firstly, according to the service: here it can be seen that there has been a rise in the share of preventive services and a fall in that of medical care services. This positive change does not follow any pattern which ties in with the stabilization period in any obvious way, and probably reflects the impact of the changed philosophy of the ministry after independence.

The second criterion reflects use. It can be seen that there has been a steady rise in the share of the ministry's budget for salaries and allowances. This mainly reflects increasing personnel but also rising wages. Again, there seems to be a steady trend, rather than a pattern which correlates clearly with stabilization policies. However, it should be noted that, because of the politics of government budget cuts and the unwillingness of governments to fire salaried employees, one would expect the share of salaries in the budget to rise in a period of reduced expenditure.

There has also been a steady decline in the share of the ministry budget allocated to grants. There are two significant recipients of these grants. Firstly, the Parirenyatwa Hospital Board of Governors, which is responsible for the administration of the main hospitals in Harare. Their share of grants fell from 47.9 per cent in 1980/81 to 30.3 per cent in 1982/83, primarily as a result of the removal of the Harare Central Hospital from their portfolio, and increased to 34.4. per cent since 1982/83. In constant 1980 prices their grant has moved from Z$21.5 million in 1980/81 to Z$23.3 million in 1981/82, Z$21.8 million in 1982/83, Z$14.8 million in 1983/84 and Z$15.8 million in 1984/85.

The second, and more important, recipients of MOH grants are the local authorities, missions, and voluntary organizations. These bodies provide health care services at the local level, particularly, in the area of child survival, in outreach programmes. Their share of grants rose from 49.3 per cent in 1980/81

TABLE 10.8 *Ministry of Health: internal allocation of expenditure 1979/80–1985/86 (percentages)*

	Allocation by service				Allocation by use			
	Administrative and general	Medical care	Preventive services	Research	Salaries and allowances	Grants	Supplies/ services	Other
1979/80	4.0	87.1	7.9	1.0	—	—	—	—
1980/81	3.5	88.0	7.6	0.8	26.8	53.8	10.2	9.2
1981/82	4.1	85.7	9.4	0.8	28.2	52.0	11.0	8.8
1982/83	5.1	82.9	11.2	0.8	34.9	38.9	16.1	10.1
1983/84	3.7	81.5	13.7	0.8	37.8	35.0	14.9	12.3
1984/85	3.2	82.1	14.0	0.6	40.3	36.5	11.0	12.2
1985/86	7.5	77.9	14.0	0.6	44.7	33.3	11.1	10.9

Sources: For 1979/80: Zimbabwe, *Annual Reports of the Comptroller and Auditor General*, Harare, For 1983/84–85/86: Zimbabwe, *Estimates of Expenditure*, Harare.

to 62.9 per cent in 1982/83, but has subsequently fallen back to 58.5 per cent in 1985/86. In real terms their grant has moved from Z$22.2 million in 1980/81 to Z$35.9 million (1981/82), Z$26.5 million (1982/83), Z$23.3 million (1983/84), and Z$24.4 million in 1984/85. This fall in real resources has somewhat constrained these organizations' ability to continue their contribution to health care, particularly their outreach work (Zimbabwe Association of Church Related Hospitals, personal communication).

One of the more obvious effects of the ministry's attempts to restrict its expenditure was severely limiting the operation of the free health care system. When this was introduced in September 1980, the maximum income for users was set at Z$150 per month. This ceiling has not subsequently been raised. At the same time, however, nominal wages have risen, so that people have been excluded from the service even though their real incomes have not risen. Thus, in September 1982, when the minimum wage for industrial workers was Z$105 per month, about 42 per cent of industrial workers earned less than the Z$150 ceiling. In July 1986 the minimum for industrial workers was raised to Z$158, so that none qualify for free health care.

Those who do not qualify for the free service have been affected by rising charges for some services. There are early indications that this may have affected perinatal mortality rates in Greater Harare.

Foreign aid has played an important role in mitigating some of the effects of the reduced resources allocated by government to the health sector. Although the total amount of aid going to the sector has not been large in comparison with the overall budget of the Ministry of Health, it has been significant in relation to the funding allocated to specific projects. In the Expanded Programme on Immunization in 1983, 18 per cent of the budget came from aid sources. While this percentage may appear to be small in relation to the government's contribution, it offsets any self-imposed reductions because of the stabilization package.

In the first year (1981) the funding for the Child Supplementary Feeding Programme came from various national and external voluntary agencies. Since 1982, the Swedish International Development Agency has assumed the dominant funding role in this programme and the food production plots which it spawned. Later, a substantial proportion of the food came from the World Food Programme as part of the drought relief assistance, while UNICEF contributed personnel training and evaluation (Working Group 1982, MOH 1984c). Although no figures are available, these programmes, introduced initially during the reconstruction period following the liberation war and subsequently continued as part of the drought relief exercise, were costly. They were largely externally funded through the Ministry of Health with small contributions from non-governmental organizations. Here then is an example of foreign aid initiated before stabilization policies, but nevertheless crucial and timely in allowing the government to mount a massive relief programme while attempting to restrict its own expenditures.

IV   Effects on the health, nutrition, and education of children

1   Mortality and morbidity

Pre-independence estimates of infant mortality rates vary, but it is agreed that for the African population as a whole the IMR was of the order of 100 to 150, with the consensus average being about 120. Sanders (1983) gives estimates of 120 to 150, with wide disparities between urban and remote rural areas.

Since independence the IMR derived from a nationwide survey is 83, a figure calculated from the 1982 census (Zimbabwe 1986*a*). There are no other nation-wide data, but it is agreed by most workers in the field, on the basis of small studies and casual observation, that the IMR has declined significantly since 1980. Data on child mortality (1–4 years) is even more scanty. The census calculations, however, suggest that here too there has been a fall since independence. The most important causes of death for under-5s were, and are, diarrhoea, respiratory tract infections, measles, prematurity, and neonatal tetanus. Malnutrition is hardly ever cited as a cause of death but is acknowledged to be an important associated cause, especially in the cases of diarrhoea and measles. Morbidity patterns closely parallels the pattern of mortality.

It is difficult to be anything but speculative about the precise impact of the health sector interventions described in Part III on child mortality and morbidity, given the paucity of data. However, the aggregate declines in mortality noted above can be attributed with some certainty to these interventions. Even if disease-specific data were available it would be impossible to disaggregate the impacts so as to apportion it to individual programmes separately, in part because of time-lag between intervention and impact, which vary with the specific interventions. Finally, even the actual or expected benefits of these interventions—individual and aggregated—might have been offset by the 1982–1984 drought.

Nevertheless, it is likely that certain programmes have had a rapid positive impact on child survival and morbidity, the most important being the immunization, diarrhoea control, and child feeding programmes, particularly in the context of the drought. Some reduction in deaths from diarrhoea would be expected to have resulted from increased usage of oral rehydration therapy as well as from protection against measles by immunization. Measles deaths would also have been reduced by improvement in immunization coverage, and neonatal tetanus deaths might have been reduced slightly by immunization of pregnant women and more hygienic child birth practices resulting from increased training of traditional midwives. Some reduction in deaths from pneumonia and other respiratory infections as well as meningitis has probably resulted from greater accessibility to health care. Also some positive impact on perinatal and neonatal deaths may have accrued from the Traditional Midwives Programme. Malaria deaths may have been reduced by better access to health care, especially through treatment administered by voluntary health workers.

However, any significant impact on death rates from pneumonia and other respiratory infections, prematurity and other neonatal causes, and meningitis, as well as deaths resulting either directly or indirectly from malnutrition, would require improvements in nutritional status of both children and mothers as well as lower levels of crowding and further improvement in access to health care. Indeed even a sustained reduction in deaths from diarrhoea and measles would also require these more general improvements as well as improved environmental and personal hygiene in the case of diarrhoea.

Those programmes which incorporate preventive or promotive components (e.g. the Zimbabwe Expanded Programme of Immunization, Child Spacing, Voluntary Health Workers, and Traditional Midwives programmes) will, if sustained, have a positive long-term effect. The Voluntary Health Workers Programme, and even such programmes as the rural health centre building programme, will also lay the infrastructural basis for sustained health sector interventions in the future.

Part III showed that the main effect of stabilization policies was to slow down the growth of health sector interventions and particularly the ability of the Ministry of Health to fund such interventions. Thus, while it is true that there has been a reduction in mortality and morbidity from the expansion of certain health care programmes, these improvements would probably have been greater had their expansion not been constrained by the imposition of stabilization policies. It was indicated, for instance, how the expansion of immunization was adversely affected in 1984–85 in the mission sector by the stagnation or slow growth in funds allocated for travel for outreach. Similar examples can be offered for the case of diarrhoea control or other programmes.

Thus, while the government managed to maintain real levels of health expenditure during a severe crisis and to expand highly efficient programmes, it can be argued that stabilization policies have slowed the rate of reduction of child mortality (and some areas of morbidity) through their effect on health sector interventions. However, it is likely that their indirect impact on health through the general economic environment, and in particular real incomes, was more significant.

2   *Nutritional status*

In 1983 a World Bank Report summarized available data on nutrition, gathered from 18 nutrition surveys undertaken at various times and seasons between 1980 and 1982, using different methodologies and anthropometric standards. Allowing for these differences, it concluded as follows:

Overall, using weighted averages to reflect sample sizes, we see a picture of 21 per cent of the under-five population with second or third degree malnutrition based on weight for age. Using a weighted Bindura figure which probably reflects a better cross sample of the population, 23 per cent fall in this category. Stunting is seen in 28 per cent of Zimbabwean children (30 per cent in the cross community Bindura sample). Wasting is found in 9 per cent of Zimbabwean children (12 per cent in Bindura). (World Bank 1983, p. 73.)

The surveys summarized were all carried out before the prolonged drought had affected Zimbabwe.

In 1982 the Ministry of Health carried out a survey of 1,776 children. This showed the proportion of underweight children aged 0–3 to be 18–22 per cent in non-urban areas and 10–11 per cent in urban. Wasting was found in 9 per cent of non-urban and 13.5 per cent of urban children. Thirty-six per cent of the under-4s were stunted in non-urban areas, and 16 per cent in urban areas (UNICEF 1985, p. 35). A ministry survey conducted in July 1984 showed 16.4 per cent of rural children between 12 and 59 months of age to be below 80 per cent of the fiftieth centile of the Gomez nutrition (Harvard reference group) standard (UNICEF 1985).

These two surveys provide the only nation-wide time-series data on children's nutrition. The 1982 survey distinguished between urban and rural children, while the 1984 study surveyed clusters drawn from rural and urban areas, excluding Harare, Bulawayo, and Chitungwiza. Because of this lack of comparability the only conclusion that can be drawn is that there has probably been no significant change in the prevalence of undernutrition amongst rural children. The results of the 1985 National Nutrition Survey are still awaited.

The Harare City Health Department conducts regular examinations of school pupils' nutritional status. These have shown that the proportion of Grade I pupils below the third centile was 29 per cent in 1981, 30 per cent in 1982, 27 per cent in 1983, and 25 per cent in 1984 (City of Harare, 1984). Unfortunately the Report does not state on which anthropometric measures these percentages are based, although the high percentages suggest that they refer to height for age rather than weight for age. If weight for age was used, it suggests a deterioration in nutritional status between 1981 and 1982 and a rapid improvement in the following year. If, however, height for age was used the figures probably reflect the lagged effects of a process a few years previously.

Some mini-surveys carried out by University of Zimbabwe medical students provide some crude time-series data for specific localities (Table 10.9). Since these surveys were conducted at under-5s' and immunization clinics it is probable that the children measured form a sample that is biased in the direction of better nutrition.

The mini-surveys in Table 10.9 do not reveal any consistent trend in nutritional status, apart from what appear to be expected seasonal changes: harvest time is between March and October. There is, however, a striking reduction in undernutrition in the Musame area of Murewa district, which is fairly close to Harare and was less affected by the drought than most areas. This marked improvement could be related to the success of the food production plots arising out of the Child Supplementary Feeding Programme.

TABLE 10.9   *Nutrition status of children in selected localities*

Locality	Date	Sample site	Underweight (%)	Stunted (%)	Researcher
Nyadiri	Mar. '82	50	44	71	Miller-Cranko
	Oct. '83	100	28	42	Wakefield
	Mar. '85	36	42	39	Deary
Bonda	Oct. '82	33	15	48	Wilson
	Oct. '84	44	16	9	Wulff
	Mar. '85	97	29	32	Chaita
Musiso	Mar. '82	62	31	54	Ternouth
	Mar. '84	200	31	33	Gwinji
	Oct. '84	25	24	28	Kumalo
Musame	Mar. '82	50	52	73	Mushambi
	Oct. '84	75	12	20	Libersidge

Source: University of Zimbabwe Medical School, Fifth-year Field Projects.

Loewenson (1986) has shown that there appears to have been a reduction in measured levels of both chronic (as evidenced by prevalence of stunting) and acute (as evidenced by underweight and wasting) forms of undernutrition between 1981/82 and 1983. These were observed in commercial farming areas, communal areas, and mining areas. Additionally, since equivalent reductions were observed on commercial farms which had initiated health projects as well as those which had not, it seems likely that these reductions in undernutrition were due not to health sector interventions but rather to a general improvement in living conditions. Loewenson's surveys covered the period of economic boom and thus coincide with rising real earnings. Unfortunately, there is no equivalent data for the later period when stabilization policies reduced real earnings for wage workers.

Thus there is little evidence that changes in the nutritional status of young children in rural and urban Zimbabwe have followed any discernible or consistent pattern since independence. This is somewhat surprising, given the fall in real incomes resulting from the drought and stabilization policies. The most plausible explanation of this is the impact of the Drought Relief Programme (which involved food distribution) and the Children's Supplementary Feeding Programme, and of a relatively good and rapidly improving immunization coverage, spread of knowledge about ORT, and better access than in many African countries to curative health care.

3   Education

Educational attainment improved throughout the 1980–85 period in Zimbabwe, and there is clear evidence that the government policy of rapid expansion of free primary education has been broadly unaffected by the stabilization policies. Indeed, Zimbabwe's phenomenal post-independence expansion in primary school enrolment can be seen as having had positive effects not only on education as such but also, indirectly, on health and nutrition. Total numbers at school grew steadily from 892,000 in 1979 to 2,727,000 in 1985, with an annual average increase of over 20 per cent. Primary school enrolment absorbed most of the increase (Table 10.10).

TABLE 10.10   *Primary school enrolment, by grade, 1979–1984*

	1	2	3	4	5	6	7	Total
1979	170.1	140.0	130.1	109.6	98.6	88.3	82.2	818.9
1980	376.4	207.9	170.4	144.7	126.0	112.9	97.1	1,235.4
1981	471.4	375.2	229.9	185.6	162.5	148.8	140.7	1,714.3
1982	408.8	421.5	351.8	226.4	184.0	164.1	148.9	1,905.4
1983	368.3	374.9	397.7	331.0	219.8	183.5	168.8	2,044.0
1984	359.6	341.5	360.8	372.6	314.0	214.9	182.7	2,146.2

Source: 'Women and Children in Zimbabwe: A Situation Analysis', UNICEF and government of Zimbabwe, Harare, July 1985.

The slow-down in the rate of expansion observed in 1983 and 1984 was largely due to the tensions generated by such a phenomenal rate of expansion in terms of additional teachers, training, and provision of physical facilities. Despite the observed slow-down, primary enrolment expanded in 1983 and 1984 by 100–150,000.

VI   Conclusion

This study has reviewed child welfare and the economy of Zimbabwe from the immediate pre-independence period through the periods of post-independence economic growth, recession, and drought, imposition of stabilization policies, and the recent beginnings of economic recovery. It has attempted to show how stabilization has affected the general economic environment, and how this in turn may have influenced child health, nutrition, and education. Analysis of stabilization has been carried out against the broad backdrop of the adjustment and development policies followed by the country since independence. Although data is inadequate and patchy, some general conclusions may be drawn.

First is the obvious point that in order to assess the impact of stabilization policies on health it is necessary to improve the collection of relevant data. This must be collected at regular time intervals, using comparable standards, and in a disaggregated fashion.

Second, there is evidence of a sharp improvement in infant and young child mortality despite drought, recession, and stabilization policies. It is recognized that these improvements have resulted mainly from an energetic expansion and reorientation of health care provision. The adverse effects of drought and stabilization policies have been offset by aid-supported relief feeding programmes and particularly health care programmes. On the other hand, economic recession and stabilization policies have reduced the post-independence gains in real incomes for large numbers of urban households and some rural households. While these income drops were unavoidable to a large extent, real wages in most sectors were only marginally higher in 1985 than 1980. The relatively high levels of childhood undernutrition seem to have remained static or improved only very slightly, despite the health care drive. While the problem of nutrition will require considerable efforts in the years to come, it is important to underscore that nutrition levels did not appear to deteriorate during a most severe drought which claimed thousands of lives in other countries, including some neighbouring ones. There is also evidence of continued improvements in education as well as in areas such as access to water, contraceptive use, immunization coverage, and other health facilities.

With the timid recovery of 1984 growing stronger in 1985, there are preliminary indications that the adjustment and stabilization policies adopted during the 1980–85 period have managed to contain the economic decline to only two to three years.

All in all, while stabilization policies did erode, and in certain cases completely offset the post-independence gains in real incomes of important segments of the population, the Zimbabwean experience illustrates how government policies, supported by aid donors, allowed for continued improvements in the survival of children—if at slower rates—during a very difficult period.

References

City of Harare (1984), *Annual Report of the City Health Department*. Harare.

CSO—Central Statistical Office (1983), 'Wage Distribution of Employees in Agriculture (June 1982), and Other Industries (September 1982)' Mimeographed. Harare.

Cutts, F. (1984), 'The Use of Oral Rehydration Therapy in Health Facilities in Zimbabwe'. London: Save the Children Fund–London School of Hygiene and Tropical Medicine.

de Zoysa, I. *et al.* (1984), 'Home-based Oral Rehydration Therapy in Rural Zimbabwe', *Transactions of the Royal Society of Tropical Medicine and Hygiene*, 78, pp. 102–5.

Loewenson, R. (1986), 'Farm Labour in Zimbabwe: A Comparative Study in Health Status', *Health Policy and Planning* 1/1.

MOH—Ministry of Health (1984a), *Planning for Equity in Health*.

——(1984b), *Report on a Joint Mission to Evaluate Primary Health Care in Zimbabwe*. Harare.

——(1984c), *The Evaluation of the Child Supplementary Feeding Programme*. Harare.

——(1985), 'A Study to Determine the Knowledge of the Child Health Card and

Maternal and Childhood Immunisation of Mothers attending Children's Clinics'. Mimeographed. Harare.

Mtero *et al.* (1985), 'Assessment of Knowledge, Attitudes and Practices in the Management and Prevention of Diarrhoea in Zimbabwe'. Draft. Ministry of Health, Harare.

Sanders, D. (1980), 'A Study of Health Services in Zimbabwe', in *Zimbabwe: Towards a New Order—an Economic and Social Survey*, Working Papers, vol. ii. New York: United Nations.

——(1983), 'Major MCH Problems in Zimbabwe', in MOH, *Maternal and Child Health Workshop*, Juliasdale.

UNICEF–Zimbabwe (1985), *Children and Women in Zimbabwe: A Situation Analysis* Harare: UNICEF.

Working Group (1982), *The Children's Supplementary Feeding Programme in Zimbabwe*', Harare.

World Bank (n.d.), *Zimbabwe: Local Processing, Storage and Input Supply Project Preparation Report*. Washington, DC: World Bank.

——(1983), *Zimbabwe: Population, Health and Nutrition Sector Review*', vol. ii. Washington, DC: World Bank.

ZANU (PF) (1985), *Zimbabwe at Five Years of Independence*, Harare.

Zimbabwe (1986*a*), *Statistical Yearbook 1985*, Harare.

Zimbabwe (1986*b*), *Rural Water Supply Programme*, vol. iii, Harare.

Index